THE RECORDER

THE YALE MUSICAL INSTRUMENT SERIES

Books in this series trace the history and development of a particular instrument or family of instruments from its origins to the present day, with an explicit emphasis on performance practice. Authors are at once leading scholars and acknowledged performers.

Jeremy Montagu TIMPANI AND PERCUSSION
Ardal Powell THE FLUTE
Geoffrey Burgess and Bruce Haynes THE OBOE
Trevor Herbert THE TROMBONE
Eric Hoeprich THE CLARINET
John Wallace and Alexander McGrattan THE TRUMPET
James B. Kopp THE BASSOON
Stephen Cottrell THE SAXOPHONE
David Lasocki and Robert Ehrlich THE RECORDER

THE YALE MUSICAL INSTRUMENT SERIES

THE RECORDER

DAVID LASOCKI AND ROBERT EHRLICH
WITH A CONTRIBUTION BY NIKOLAJ TARASOV
AND AN EPILOGUE BY MICHALA PETRI

YALE UNIVERSITY PRESS
NEW HAVEN AND LONDON

For information about this and other Yale University Press publications, please contact:
U.S. Office: sales.press@yale.edu   yalebooks.com
Europe Office: sales@yaleup.co.uk   yalebooks.co.uk

Set in Fournier MT by IDSUK (DataConnection) Ltd
Printed in Great Britain by TJ Books, Padstow, Cornwall

Library of Congress Control Number: 2022946380

ISBN 978-0-300-11870-4

A catalogue record for this book is available from the British Library.

10 9 8 7 6 5 4 3 2 1

CONTENTS

ILLUSTRATIONS

ACKNOWLEDGEMENTS

The authors would like to thank the following people for their invaluable help in preparing this volume.

David Lasocki appreciates Lilin Chen and our son Lucien Lasocki, who accompanied him on a challenging research trip to Spain and supported his passion for research over the course of writing this book in countless ways. At the eleventh hour, Giulia Tettamanti stepped up to read drafts with alacrity and offer both indispensable suggestions and the inspiration to finish the book.

Robert Ehrlich thanks his husband Martin Eberhardt for sharing everything he cares about for more than twenty years, including the material summarized in his chapter.

Nikolaj Tarasov thanks his parents and his wife Dorothée for their unshakeable confidence in him.

Mr A. A. Levit†, a research colleague of David Lasocki's grandfather at Imperial Chemical Industries in Manchester, first suggested that David learn the recorder. His childhood friend Helena Koczur and the Manchester branch of the Society of Recorder Players provided early assistance. His recorder teacher Edgar Hunt†, Walter Bergmann†, and J. M. (John Mansfield) Thomson† all spurred and encouraged his interest in research.

David also thanks Frederick B. Crane†, Sven H. Hansell†, Edward L. Kottick, Albert T. Luper†, Betty Bang Mather, and Himie Voxman† (The University of Iowa), and Thomas Binkley†, Mary Wallace Davidson†, David Fenske, R. Michael Fling, Bernard Gordillo, Eva Legêne, David Pickett, and Philip Ponella (Indiana University) for their guidance and support over many decades.

Numerous other musicians, scholars, and instrument makers around the world have generously provided David with valuable insights and out-of-the-way research materials as well as intellectual and moral support. They include: Andrew Ashbee, János Bali, Ture Bergstrøm, Brian Blood, Pierre Boragno, Jan Bouterse, Inês d'Avena Braga, Adrian Brown, Lucia Carpena, David Peter Coppen, Mark Davenport, Maricarmen Gómez Muntané, Richard Griscom, Bruce Haynes†, Peter Holman, Eugene Iliaronov, Beryl Kenyon de Pascual, Maggie Kilbey, Martin Kirnbauer, James Kopp, Nicholas Lander, Ana López Suero, Douglas MacMillan, Marianne Mezger, Patricia Michelini Aguilar, Herbert W. Myers, Fernando Duarte de Oliveira, Giulio Ongaro, Vicente Parrilla López, Keith Polk, Ardal Powell, Michel Quagliozzi, Patricia M. Ranum, Benito Rivera†, Andrew Robinson, Anthony Rowland-Jones†, Juan Ruiz Jiménez, Alejandra Fernández Sanz, Pedro Sousa Silva, Pedro Couto Soares, Michael Talbot, Peter Thalheimer, Dina Titan, Taavi-Mats Utt, Peter Van Heyghen, Nichola Voice, William Waterhouse†, and Thiemo Wind.

The staff of the Interlibrary Loan Department and the Digital Library Program of the Indiana University Libraries, as well as the interlibrary loan departments of the Cedar Mill Community Library and Multnomah County Public Library, assisted with endless interlibrary loans and scans; Paula Hickner, Misti Shaw, and Carla Williams provided more scans.

The staff of the London branch of Yale University Press have been gracious, persistent, and forbearing over the long course of researching and writing this book.

The authors have published articles containing preliminary versions of the research for the book in *American Recorder*, *Galpin Society Journal*, *Journal of the American Musical Instrument Society*, *Tibia*, and *Windkanal*, whose editors past and present are hereby acknowledged. David Lasocki also appreciates the path-breaking symposiums organized by STIMU, Utrecht, which set a high standard for collective scholarly writing about the recorder.

Robert Ehrlich thanks the Hochschule für Musik und Theater 'Felix Mendelssohn Bartholdy' (HMT) Leipzig for granting him a sabbatical term in the Winter semester 2004/05 for preliminary research, and the staff of the Cook Music Library at Indiana University, the British Library, the Deutsche Nationalbibliothek Leipzig, the Bundesarchiv Berlin, the Musikinstrumenten-Museum Markneukirchen, and the library of the HMT Leipzig for their assistance. Stefan Altner, Hans-Maria Kneihs, Gerd Lünenbürger†, Kailan Rubinoff, and Albrecht Winter read drafts of his chapter attentively; Louise Rummel lent him a copy of her Diplomarbeit, and his students at the HMT Leipzig and the Guildhall School of Music and Drama in London helped him sort the wheat from the chaff by debating key points of recorder history in seminars.

INTRODUCTION
DAVID LASOCKI

Today the recorder is probably most familiar to people around the world for its educational role, helping to introduce young children to both music and playing an instrument. Yet it is also played by countless amateurs and professionals, supported by a diverse array of teachers, instrument makers, and even scholars such as myself.

The history of any instrument is a complex 'system', populated by its various physical forms over the years as well as its players (professional, amateur, child), repertoire, instructional materials, makers, listeners, and critics. The book seeks to answer the following broad questions: Who has played the recorder at various times in its history? How has the instrument's construction developed from the Middle Ages to the present? Which pieces of music involving the recorder are of lasting significance? What do we know about the recorder's technique and performance practice in different ages? What have the symbolism, associations, and social status of the recorder been? The recorder's history is long and space in this volume is limited, so priority has been given to times and places when the instrument was of special significance.

Before we go any further, let us take a look at the instrument's scholarly classification. In the group of instruments that organologists call *aerophones* (4 in the Hornbostel–Sachs classification scheme), the sound is produced directly by vibrations in air.[1] The most familiar of these instruments are *wind instruments*, in which the vibrations are confined within the instrument itself (4.2). In the first subgroup, called *edge instruments or flutes*, the vibrations stem from directing the airstream against a dividing edge (421). Skipping over end-blown flutes (421.11) and side-blown flutes (421.12), we come to a sub-subgroup called *duct flutes* (421.2), in which the head of the tube of the instrument is partially blocked to allow the airstream to go through a *duct*, or *windway*, leading to a sharp edge (*lip* or *labium*) at the base of a mouth (*window*).[2] This type of instrument also belongs to the looser category of flutes called 'vertical' – that is, pointing in front of the player. The most common types of duct flute in the world are *flutes with internal duct*, in which an internal block of wood or some other material creates a windway between itself and the inner wall of the instrument (421.22), or what is colloquially called a whistle mouthpiece. Such flutes are further classified into ones in which the end of the tube is open, partially stopped, or stopped. Finally, at the end of our classification journey for the purposes of this book, we arrive at *open flutes with internal duct . . . with finger-holes* (421.221.12).

We know from numerous surviving examples and depictions that such duct flutes were prevalent in western Europe in the period 1100–1500, and their form was far from standardized.[3] At first, they were diminutive and possessed from two to seven finger-holes, in various layouts. A particular version known nowadays as a 'tabor pipe' – a narrow-bore 'pipe' played one-handed by a performer who used the other hand to beat a small drum ('tabor') slung around the neck – tended to have a thumb-hole and two finger-holes.[4] In the fourteenth century, at some point impossible to determine with certainty from the evidence that has turned up so far, people in several parts of Europe began to use a form of duct flute with a thumb-hole and (basically) seven finger-holes that would become widespread and play a significant role in art music after 1500 – the *recorder*.

Another type of duct flute with two thumb-holes and four finger-holes, the flageolet, became standardized by the early seventeenth century, had a parallel existence to the recorder through the eighteenth century, and became more prominent in the nineteenth century, when it underwent a great deal of development. Although this book focuses on the recorder, it takes occasional glances at the flageolet.

The name *recorder* has become ambiguous since the invention of magnetic tape recorders in the twentieth century, but it has the advantage in the world of organology of referring to the specific instrument defined above. The names in various languages before the twentieth century are traced in the individual chapters, as terminological questions loom large in the recorder's history, especially in distinguishing it from its transverse cousin, the flute. Languages have differed in which aspect of the recorder to single out: the vertical orientation, the sweet sound, the block, the beak, the ostensible English or Italian origins and associations, or the number of finger-holes.

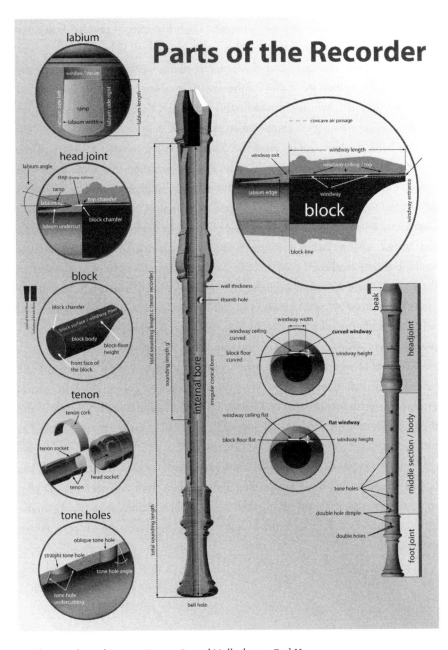

1. The recorder and its parts. Poster, Conrad Mollenhauer, GmbH.

In this book, fingerings are notated using numbers from 0 to 7. 0 represents the closed thumb hole and 1 to 7 the closed front holes from top to bottom. Open holes are indicated by the omission of a number. Each fingering is divided into three parts: thumb hole, left hand, and right hand. For example, 0 123 4 67.

For medieval, Baroque, and modern recorders, we have opted to use the international terminology of alto for the size in f^1 and soprano for the sizes in c^2 or d^2, rather than the British equivalents of treble and descant, respectively. Our Renaissance terminology is explained on pp. 53–54.

Our book has had a long gestation. When we set out to write a history of the recorder in 2003, we independently came to the conclusion that some important aspects of that history had never been researched adequately – or at all.[5] We then set out to research these aspects ourselves: in particular, Robert Ehrlich on Nazi Germany;[6] Nikolaj Tarasov on duct flutes in the Classical and Romantic periods; and myself on: medieval writings; Renaissance recorder players and makers; Spain, Portugal, and their colonies; the works of Charpentier and Lully; sizes in the Baroque and Classical periods; and colonial North America.[7] The newly available databases of newspapers in England and colonial North America yielded delightful, hitherto unknown information, as did my compilation of the recorder's presence in inventories, purchases, and sales from 1378 to 1800.[8]

Given its focus on the significant, this book can represent only the tip of the recorder research iceberg. So, if your favourite subject comes up short, please explore the countless articles and books on aspects of the history listed in the Bibliography and the recorder bibliography by Richard Griscom and myself,[9] as well as the essays published by Instant Harmony.[10]

Beyond contributing the chapter on the twentieth century, Robert Ehrlich has helped to shape this book by reading innumerable drafts of sections, making copious suggestions for improving their accuracy and clarity, and advising on the focus of the book and the selection of material. For this reason, he has been named as co-author.

Portland, Oregon, USA, October 2021

THE ERA OF MEDIEVAL RECORDERS, 1300–1500

DAVID LASOCKI

This opening chapter seeks to answer fundamental questions about the early history of the recorder: its origins, physical characteristics, sizes, makers, performers, music, and symbolism or associations in works of art. Despite intense research into evidence from surviving instruments, archival records, literature, and artistic depictions over the last twenty years, however, we still have few certain conclusions. Moreover, we must always keep in mind that 'Lack of evidence is not necessarily evidence of lack', and almost any new piece of evidence helps to refine previous speculations. Some researchers' attempts to create good stories have already fallen by the wayside. Rather than have those stories impede our own, they have been relegated to the endnotes.

ORIENTATION

Several members of the flute family were prevalent in the fourteenth and fifteenth centuries. First, the subfamily of duct flutes, which included tabor pipes, other duct flutes played with one or two hands and having a varied number of finger-holes, and the recorder, which we have defined as a specialized type of duct flute having holes for seven fingers and the thumb. Second, the subfamily of transverse flutes, which included the flute as well as a narrower-bored military type called the *fife*, although the two instruments are not always well differentiated. Third, panpipes, made from a series of end-blown pipes of different lengths joined together.

The first certain information about some aspects of recorder history stems from the end of the fifteenth century and later. The first description of the recorder linked to a name is found in a Latin treatise by Johannes Tinctoris, *De inventione et usu musice* (Naples, ca. 1481–83).[1] Tinctoris mentions the *fistula* (literally, pipe or tube), a particular type of woodwind instrument (*tibia*) with 'seven holes in front and one behind'. The terms *fistula* and *tibia* go back to ancient times. In Greece, *aulos* usually denoted a wind instrument consisting of two pipes and two (probably double) reeds, but could also refer to any instrument consisting of a single pipe with or without a reed.[2] For essentially the same double-reed pipe, the Romans employed the term *tibia*, or occasionally *fistula*, a word that poets used for the shepherd's panpipes.[3] Tinctoris is also familiar with the practice of doubling the seventh finger-hole on some unnamed types of *tibia*, so that players could play the instrument with either hand uppermost. Such an arrangement was common on pre-Baroque recorders.

The first securely dated vernacular description of the recorder linked to a name, the first description linked to a picture, and the first fingering chart all stem from Sebastian Virdung's *Musica getutscht* (1511). He calls the instrument *Flöte*. The main term used for the recorder in Philibert Jambe de Fer's *Epitome musical* (1556), which also depicts the instrument and provides fingerings for it, is *fleute à neuf trous* (flute with nine holes – including the doubled seventh finger-hole). This term indirectly furnishes the earliest corroboration of the meaning of *recorder* in English – first documented in 1388 – because Jean Palsgrave's English–French dictionary, *Lesclarcissement de la langue francoyse* (London, 1530), includes the unpunctuated definition: 'Recorder a pype *fleute a. ix. neuf trous* . . .'[4]

All the sixteenth-century treatises deal with a recorder on which uncovering the lowest hole produces a whole tone. Let us call this instrument *recorder-T*. The instrument is fully chromatic from cross-fingering – putting one or more fingers down below an open hole; half-holing is required only for the lowest accidentals.

SURVIVING EXAMPLES OF RECORDER-S

The most certain evidence about the earliest recorders ought to be the surviving examples, but their dating is less than certain and their state sometimes incomplete. Ten such instruments, – two only fragmentary, and one of these only speculatively identified – have been discovered in archaeological digs in Copenhagen (Denmark), Dordrecht (the Netherlands), Elbląg (Poland), Esslingen (south-western Germany), Göttingen (north-central Germany), Nysa, Płock, and Puck (Poland), Tartu (Estonia), and Würzburg (south-central Germany).[5] The lowest interval is a semitone (Dordrecht, Elbląg, Göttingen, Nysa, Tartu), a whole tone (Copenhagen), or else unknown or unknowable (Esslingen, Płock, Puck, Würzburg). Let us call a recorder on which uncovering the lowest hole produces a semitone *recorder-S*. (The Copenhagen recorder is discussed later in the Recorder-T section.)

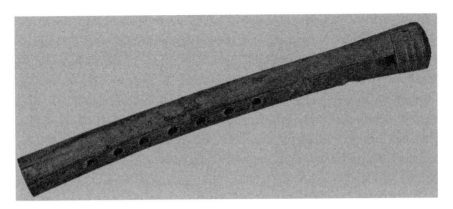

2. Tartu recorder.

The instrument in the best state of preservation was found by the archaeologist Andres Tvauri in 2005 during a dig in a latrine in Tartu, then studied by the recorder player Taavi-Mats Utt.[6] It is now held in the Tartu Linnamuuseum (Tartu City Museum).[7] The house where the 'Tartu recorder' was excavated seems to have belonged to a wealthy German merchant. Other artifacts such as pottery found with the instrument stem from Germany, north-west Russia, and the Baltic; they generally date from the second half of the fourteenth century. The logs from which the latrine was made were cut down in 1335. Radiocarbon dating of the recorder's maple wood, representing the age of the tree rings of the wood sample, gives 95.4 per cent certainty for each of 'two possible time intervals' of 1260–1315 and 1355–90. Still, given that the tree rings could have been decades older than the cutting down of the tree, the wood had to be dried, and the instrument could have been used for a number of years, the recorder was almost certainly made in the fourteenth century, and perhaps even towards the beginning of it. During this period Tartu, then known as Dorpat, was an important city in the Hanseatic League, dominated by German culture, and obtaining its main income from transit-commerce between western and northern European Hanseatic towns on the one hand and Novgorod and Pskov in Russia on the other.

The instrument is turned, with ornamental rings at the mouthpiece end. The body is made from maple, the block from birch. The total length is 246.7 mm (just less than 10 inches) and the sounding length 225.4 mm, so the instrument is similar in size to a modern sopranino in f^2 at A 440. The bore *contracts* (obconical) from about 13.7 mm at the top to 12 mm just past the block line (the contraction would help to keep the block in place), then is more or less *cylindrical* (apart from one perhaps unintentional expanding 'blip'), and finally, from about halfway between the seventh finger-hole and the end, *contracts* again to 11.5 mm. The ramp is roughly made, with a bow in the middle, and the window is wide for the size of the instrument. The windway is evenly concave and of high quality. The finger-holes are similar in diameter, regularly placed, cylindrical, and all in a line. The front of the recorder has a flat area, perhaps to make it easier to cover the finger-holes or to stop the instrument rolling off a table. Utt reports that the instrument is playable and has the surprisingly large compass of two octaves and a second.[8] The high notes sound easily – curiously, with Baroque fingerings – but the low range is weak and the octaves III–X and V–XII are narrow. Uncovering the bottom finger-hole produces an interval of a semitone.

The best-known medieval recorder was found in 1940 when the former moat of a fortified mansion, the Huis te Merwede, near Dordrecht, was excavated. The instrument is now held in the collection of the Gemeentemuseum, The Hague.[9] Because there is no archaeological evidence of an earlier settlement on the site, the 'Dordrecht recorder' presumably dates from the time of occupation of the mansion (1335–1421) and mostly likely the late fourteenth century.[10] The instrument is 270 mm long with a narrow cylindrical bore (about 11 mm in diameter), corresponding to a modern soprano in d^2. It is made of close-grained fruitwood, possibly plumwood. There are double holes for the bottom finger to allow for playing with either the left or right hand uppermost. Both ends of the instrument are turned to form tenons; the one at the upper end has two incised grooves, the lower one of which is slightly tapered. The ramp is damaged, so the instrument cannot be played.

Only the bottom of another possible recorder – perhaps actually part of a reed pipe – was discovered in a fourteenth-century well in the Salhof (manor house) of Würzburg and first described in 1953. It is now preserved in the Mainfränkisches Museum there.[11] The instrument is reportedly made of cherrywood and similar in bore and finger-holes to the Dordrecht recorder.[12] There is a lateral hole towards the foot of the Würzburg fragment, together with a small groove around its base and a crack running exactly through the lateral hole, which Rainer Weber takes to indicate end-stopping by means of a plug inserted in the bore. The groove may have carried a wire to counteract the tendency of this plug to split the wood. In fact, Weber interprets both the Dordrecht instrument and the Würzburg fragment as end-stopped or partially end-stopped recorders reminiscent of certain internal-duct flutes of the Middle East.[13] Other scholars consider it more likely that the lower tenon was fitted with a lower mount, either prolonging or restricting the bore.[14]

An instrument now held in the Städtisches Museum, Göttingen, was discovered in 1987 in the lowest layer of a latrine of a medieval house in that city.[15] The first scholar to write about it, Dietrich Hakelberg, concluded: 'We can probably assume that the instrument was deposited during the fourteenth century', although his own arguments imply a dating anywhere from 1246 to the mid-fifteenth century – a wide margin of error.[16] As Hans Reiners describes, the instrument is 256 mm long and made of fruitwood (cherry or plum).[17] One side of the top end is broken off, and the ramp is chipped. The bore has a diameter of 13.6 mm at 110 mm of length, *contracts* to 13.2 mm between finger-holes 1 and 2, *contracts again* to about 12.7 mm between 2 and 3 (showing circumferential reamer's marks in each case), *contracts sharply* to 11.5 mm behind the doubled seventh hole, then *expands* to a bulbous foot of 14.5 mm. The finger-holes are bored obliquely, widening towards the outside. Reiners aptly observes: 'Comparing the Göttingen [recorder] with the "Dordrecht" find, I can hardly imagine anything more dissimilar than these, without actually being different kinds of instrument.'[18] Again, the bottom interval is a semitone. 'The widest surface areas of the bulbous bottom end of the [recorder] show signs of having been subjected to a good deal of percussive strain, as one might expect if it had been used not only as a [recorder], but at least occasionally as a drumstick.'[19] A reconstruction by Reiners had a timbre that he described as strident and penetrating, and the range was two octaves, extending into a third octave with fingerings rather like those given in Silvestro Ganassi's *Fontegara* (1535). Julia Doht, however, reports another reconstruction with a range of only an octave and a minor sixth.[20]

Another fragmentary recorder, reportedly from the fourteenth century, was excavated from the sediment of the mill channel of the Karmelitenkloster (Carmelite Monastery) in Esslingen, near Stuttgart.[21] It is now kept in the Landesdenkmalamt Baden-Württemberg, Stuttgart. One broken light-coloured fragment is made of boxwood; a better-preserved fragment about 255 mm long is made of fruitwood and has a thumb-hole and five finger-holes. Hakelberg states that it has the same profile (external shape) as the Göttingen recorder.

In 1962, a recorder was found in a latrine dating from 1350–1420 in the city of Nysa, Poland, and is now housed in the Muzeum Powiatowe w Nysie (Nysa County Museum).[22] Nysa, one of the oldest towns in Silesia, near what is now the Czech border, was the capital of the duchy of Nysa in the Middle Ages, then, from 1342, became part of the Bohemian Crown. The instrument is made from elder (*Sambucus nigra*) and is 317 mm long. Although the block is missing, details of the window and ramp are unmistakable. The holes, all single, are lined up, and the lowest interval is again a semitone. The bore is slightly obconic, ranging from 22/16 mm (outer/inner diameter) at the top to 16/14 mm at the bottom.[23]

A recorder in good condition made of spruce was discovered in Puck, Poland, in 2011 in a latrine next to the market square built in the 1360s–70s, although all the objects in it have been dated from the end of the fourteenth century to the mid-fifteenth.[24] The instrument is 259 mm long, with an internal diameter of 14 mm at the window and 10.1 mm at the end. The lowest finger-hole is offset to the right (and not doubled). Below the windway is a shallow carved circle, perhaps a maker's mark.

Another intact instrument was found in 1998 in the latrine of a rich merchant's house in the former Hanseatic city of Elbląg (Elbing), near Gdańsk (Danzig), Poland, and is housed in the Muzeum w Elblągu (Elbląg Museum).[25] Although Dorota Popławska claims that 'the archaeological context permits a dating of the instrument in the 14th–15th century' and Popławska and Hubert Lachowicz place it in the late fifteenth to early sixteenth century, Martin Kirnbauer reports that Grażyna Nawrolska, the person responsible for the archaeological work, told him that the objects in the latrine date from the fifteenth century.[26] The seventh hole is doubled and the lowest interval is a semitone. Kirnbauer believes that the wood might be maple, although that cannot be determined now because it was treated with polyethylene glycol. The instrument is 299 mm long, with a sounding length of 270 mm, and a cylindrical profile. The bore also cannot be determined because of the instrument's current state. The front of the instrument has a flat area. In making a reconstruction, Eugene Ilarionov found that for the octaves to be in tune, the bore had to be slightly obconical, then a small flare below hole 7.[27] His reconstruction has a range of two octaves and a semitone, and requires something like the Baroque buttress or supporting fingering, with fingers 5 and 6 being held down for half the notes in the first octave. He observes that the instrument has a large, high window, which creates a lot of 'chiff' (the noisy attack at the beginning of the tone).[28]

Whoever the maker was, he literally left his mark – a circle with a hole in the middle 'like the impression of a drawing pin'. He displayed fine workmanship in the undercut finger-holes, precisely cut window and ramp, and a unique feature: 'In the inner bore sits a wooden block; on both visible sides are inserted thin pieces of wood, working like a wedge, which help to fix the block in the inner bore as well as to lift the two sides of the wind channel, resulting in a more sophisticated guidance of the air stream.' No woodwind makers are known from the archival records in Elbląg, but a *proconsul cum fistulatorum*, apparently some kind of wind player, was mentioned in 1348.

Finally, a recorder from the end of the fifteenth century (confirmed by dendrological tests) was found on the grounds of a house in Płock, Poland, in 1997, and is now in the Muzeum Mazowieckim w Płocku (Mazovian Museum).[29] The cylindrical instrument, made of elder, is 355 mm long.

In sum, the nine certain surviving recorders just discussed were excavated in northern Europe (Germany, the Netherlands) or eastern Europe (Estonia, Poland with Hanseatic or Teutonic connections, Bohemia/Poland), so all or most were probably made in the region of Germany. This preponderance may simply reflect that archaeological exploration and methods have been less developed in countries where Romance languages are spoken.[30] All these recorders apparently date from the fourteenth or fifteenth centuries. They stem from houses (Elbląg?, Göttingen, Nysa?, Płock, Tartu, Würzburg?), the town square (Puck), a fortified mansion (Dordrecht), and a monastery (Esslingen), suggesting that they were all played by amateurs for their own entertainment. The instruments are soprano- or sopranino-sized. The bores of the instruments are of four main types: cylindrical (Dordrecht, Płock); cylindrical then contracting (Tartu); slightly contracting (Nysa); and contracting then expanding (Esslingen, Göttingen). The seventh finger-hole is doubled in four instances (Dordrecht, Elbląg, Göttingen, Würzburg), single in four other instances (Nysa, Płock offset, Puck, Tartu). As already mentioned, the lowest interval is a semitone (Dordrecht, Elbląg, Göttingen, Nysa, Tartu) or else unknown or unknowable (Esslingen, Płock, Puck, Würzburg). All the instruments are made from wood (fruit such as cherry or plum, as well as birch, box, elder, maple, and spruce). Such recorders were not whittled by a shepherd from a twig or a bone using a knife. They all imply the use of a lathe with augers and spoon reamers – tools that presumably only a professional turner would have possessed.

THE SIGNIFICANCE OF RECORDER-S

On *recorder-S*, the semitone below the six-fingered note creates a leading tone (*subsemitonium modi*) to the final of the six-fingered mode. The *subsemitonium modi* occurred naturally if the final was C or F; otherwise, the pitch needed to be raised. Such a semitone was 'characteristic of much of the secular monody of the Middle

Ages'[31] and would have been familiar to duct-flute makers from the bagpipe. Moreover, since at least the tenth century, shawms had been designed with a seven-finger system in which the lowest hole produced a semitone,[32] and recorders may well have been made by the same craftsmen.

Reconstructions of recorders-S suggest that a fully chromatic scale can be obtained, but only by half-holing most of the accidentals, thereby making them challenging to play, especially fast.[33] Because of the semitone's relationship to the final of the six-fingered mode, researchers have conjectured that recorder-S was developed in two stages from a six-holed duct flute, which naturally plays diatonically and obtains the second octave by overblowing.[34] But did a six-holed duct flute actually exist in the Middle Ages and, if so, how likely is it that the recorder was derived from it?

In the 1970s, Frederick Crane and Christine Brade catalogued about 200 surviving medieval duct flutes, predominantly made from bone.[35] Bone has the advantage that it can be fashioned into various kinds of flutes using only knives (and the disadvantage that it cannot be fashioned easily by more sophisticated tools). Only six of the instruments have as many as six holes; of these instruments, four also have thumb-holes. These instruments would constitute valuable evidence, if only we could be sure about their dating. The only one dated by the museum that holds it (in Randers, Denmark) is estimated unhelpfully as 'fifteenth to eighteenth century'.[36] The rest have no such estimates, and the fact that three of them are made from turned wood rather than bone suggests a later date. Catherine Homo-Lechner reported an eleventh-century duct flute with six finger-holes and a thumb-hole from a dig near Charavines (Isère) in south-eastern France; but three years earlier she had claimed it as some kind of reed instrument.[37] The only strong piece of evidence is the carved capital of a stone pillar from the Eglise de St Georges in Bourbon-l'Archambault (Burgundy), dating from the eleventh century, which depicts a musician playing a duct flute with six finger-holes and a thumb position suggestive of recorder playing.

The other conjectural stage of evolution of recorder-S, before or after the seventh hole, was adding a thumb-hole. That may sound like a radical invention, but a surviving shawm from the tenth century or earlier has one.[38] And a surviving Moorish duct flute from Sicily with four finger-holes and a thumb-hole dates back to at least the middle of the eleventh century.[39] According to Brade's research, about one-quarter of the surviving medieval duct flutes from Belgium, Denmark,

Germany, the Netherlands, Norway, and Sweden have thumb-holes (along with two or more finger-holes).[40]

Pinching the thumb-hole acts as what would later be called a 'speaker hole', enabling notes in the second octave to be produced more easily and with lower breath pressure. It is the most widespread example in recorder technique of partially covering or uncovering holes to facilitate changes of register or timbre as well as correct intonation.[41] Another advantage of the thumb-hole is that, as the maker Adrian Brown points out, 'you can use a large bore, which will generally give you a stronger low register, but still get the instrument to overblow' to the next harmonic.[42]

So in theory, having a duct flute with seven holes and a thumb-hole could have been viewed as a logical extension of existing instruments any time from the tenth century onwards. That we do not have even hints of this development before the early fourteenth century may just be an accident of how instruments and artworks have survived.

Once recorder-S existed, as Anthony Rowland-Jones suggests: 'from here, surely, it must have been found that, by moderating the breath input, high notes could be played more softly than lower notes, thereby imitating the way vocalists were taught to sing'.[43] In support of this last point, he cites a treatise by Conrad von Zabern, *De modo ben cantandi* (Mainz, 1474), to the effect that 'middle notes should be sung with a moderate voice and high notes with a soft voice, with a gradual change according to the movement of the melody; low notes are full in tone and high notes thinner and more delicate'.[44] Although this reference is from the late fifteenth century, 'it seems more likely that von Zabern was describing a long-standing mode of singing rather than a newfangled one, especially as his advice regarding affect and expressivity . . . concurs with remarks by several much earlier writers'.

DUCT FLUTES: NAMES AND CONTEXTS[45]

Between about 1100 and 1500, although terms for duct flutes and their spellings were far from standardized, some general tendencies can be noted. See Table 1.

The tabor pipe begins to appear in iconographical sources in the second half of the thirteenth century, in two basic forms: first, the long kind depicted by Virdung having the holes towards the end; and, second, a short and fat instrument, with the finger-holes in the middle.[46] Nine languages had terms that usually signified the tabor pipe: Catalan, Occitan, and Spanish (*flauta*), Dutch (*fleute/floyte*), English

Table 1. Names for members of the flute family, thirteenth–fifteenth century

Language	Date	Name	Probable instrument
Catalan	14th century	flauta, flaute	tabor pipe, duct flute
	1378–15th century	flahute, flauta	recorder
Cornish	15th century	recordys (plural)	recorder
Dutch	14th century	fleute, fleuyt, floyt, floyte, flute	tabor pipe, duct flute
	15th century	vloyte	recorder
English	13th–15th century	flagel, flegel, floute, flowte, floyte, flute, fristel	tabor pipe, panpipes
	1388–15th century	recordour, recorder	recorder
	15th century	flout, flowte, floyte, whistle	duct flute, tabor pipe
	1492	flote, flout	recorder
Anglo-French	12th–14th century	frestel	panpipes, duct flute, tabor pipe
	12th–14th century	flaüte, fleute, floute	tabor pipe, duct flute
French	12th–14th century	frestel	panpipes, duct flute, tabor pipe
	12th–14th century	flaüste, flaüte, fleute, flaütele	tabor pipe, duct flute, panpipes
	13th–15th century	flajol, flegel, flute, flageolet	duct flute, tabor pipe, panpipes
	late 14th–15th century	fleuste, fleute, fleutre, fluste, flute, gran fleuste, grosse fleute pleniere	recorder
	15th century	flajol, flajolet	tabor pipe
	15th century	flute	panpipes

German	12th–13th century	floite, floüte	tabor pipe, duct flute
	late 14th–15th century	floyte	recorder
Italian	14th century	zufolo	tabor pipe
	14th century	flaùto	duct flute
	15th century	fiauto, fiuto, flauto, zufolo	recorder
Latin	12th–14th century	fistula	duct flute, tabor pipe
	13th century	tibia	duct flute
	15th century	fleut	duct flute, recorder
	15th century	fistula	recorder, duct flute
Occitan	12th–13th century	flauta, flauteu, flaïtz, frestel, flestella	tabor pipe
	13th century	flaustel, flaütella	panpipes
	13th century	flaujol	duct flute
Spanish	14th–15th century	flauta	tabor pipe, duct flute

(*flagel, flute*), French (*flaüte*), Anglo-French, formerly known as Anglo-Norman – the dialect of French spoken in England after the Norman Conquest in 1066 until about 1475 (*fleute/floute*), German (*floite*), and Italian (*zufolo*). In French poetry, the *flaüte* is almost exclusively associated with minstrels and tower watchers, occurring slightly more in loud contexts (such as with brass and percussion) than in soft contexts (such as with bowed and plucked strings).

In 1320, a new spelling turns up in France: Plumion, a minstrel of Louis I de Clermont, Duc de Bourbon, was given money by King Philippe V 'le Long' to buy 'a *flute* of ivory'.[47] An ivory instrument for practical use rather than a precious object suggests something other than a tabor pipe – certainly some other kind of duct flute.

The earliest account of members of the flute family is found in the Latin *Yconomica* (1348–52) of Konrad of Megenberg, a German who studied and taught at the University of Paris.[48] The book contains study material for the young sons of princes. One section addresses the servants of a household, including its musicians, who are among the servants providing entertainment. Konrad views such musician-servants as distinct from professional jongleurs, and vastly superior to them. Wind players are divided into two types: *macrofistulus* and *microfistulus*. The latter 'is the one who makes music on a smaller pipe [*fistula*]; and I call those pipes "smaller" – named *flatillas* in the vernacular – because they give sound with a little blowing of the breath of the mouth, but the sound is weak and feeble. Whence they sometimes play together with fiddles.'[49] The term *flatilla* is similar to the *flaütele*, or small *flaüte*, mentioned in five French sources of the thirteenth century but clearly linked to the tabor in two of them.[50]

Later Konrad writes that *flatillas* 'arouse or exasperate amorous spirits, and to an extent move them to the sweetness of [religious] devotion. Organs, therefore, on account of their variety and multitude [of flute pipes], are fittingly allotted a place in churches where divine services are celebrated.'[51] It seems that, despite their name, his *flatillas* were soft duct flutes suitable for chamber music, and they anticipated the dual sexual/spiritual associations the recorder developed in the fifteenth century. Without further evidence, however, we cannot say that *flatillas* were definitely recorders.

Only French (*flajol*), Occitan (*flaujol*), and Italian (*flauto*) had special terms for a kind of duct flute that was differentiated from the tabor pipe. Citations of the *flajol* in French poetry are evenly split between minstrels and shepherds, with one notable (and noble) exception. A poem by Eugène Deschamps (1378), purporting to have been written by the ailing young Pierre de Navarre (1366–1412), includes the lines: 'I have not been so sick in the eye [or finger] that I have been prevented from learning to play the *eschequier* and the *flaiol*.'[52] Pierre, who also bore the title Comte de Mortain, was the son of Charles II 'le Mauvais' of Navarre (pretender to the French throne and patron to Guillaume de Machaut) and of Jeanne de France (daughter of the French king, Jean II 'le Bon').[53] Machaut is not documented as having any dealings with Charles of Navarre after 1361, so it is unlikely that Pierre received any musical instruction from the great composer. Pierre and King Charles VI jointly commissioned the 'royal' stained-glass windows in the choir of Évreux Cathedral in the period 1390–98. The windows in the cathedral's Rosary Chapel (completed around 1397), 'doubtless from the same studio',[54] include an angel playing a duct flute with at least six finger-holes, although the representation is too sketchy to determine whether it was intended to be a recorder.[55]

A French poem by Adenès Li Rois from around 1285 refers to the variety of *flajols* available: 'There are enough tabors and bagpipes and *flajols*, thin and thick [or high and low].'[56] Several poems describe the *flajol* or its music as *douce*, which can mean both soft and sweet, although the context in which the instrument is found is sometimes suggestive. In the thirteenth-century *Bestiaire d'amour*, Mercury lulls Argus before decapitating him, 'With the sweet [*dou*] melody of the *flagol*'.[57] Yet Machaut's epic poem *La Prise d'Alexandrie*, written towards the end of his life (ca. 1370–72), mentions 'more than ten pairs of *flajols*, that is to say, of twenty kinds, both loud and soft'.[58] In his earlier *Le remède de Fortune* (1340s?), Machaut had already singled out *Flajos de saus*, *flajols* made of willow.[59] Deschamps in the late fourteenth century mentions 'The sweetly/softly resounding *flajole*, which we make from wood of the forest.'[60] They were presumably small *flajols*.

In Italian, a poem by Immànuel Romano (ca. 1292–ca. 1352) provides some clues about duct flutes: 'There Germans, Italians and French, Flemings and English talk together; and make a trumpeting, which seems to resound like trumpets that want to sound softly. Guitars and lutes, vielles and *flaùti*, loud and high voices one hears singing here. *Stututù ifiù*, *stututù ifiù*, *stututù ifiù*: play the tabor and pipe.'[61] Thus *suffolare* means to play the tabor pipe, and its sound is rendered onomatopoeically as *ifiù*. Moreover, the instrument is clearly differentiated from *flaùti*, which are playing alongside soft instruments and loud singers.

During the fourth quarter of the fourteenth century, the newly developed recorder began to take over the terms that had meant tabor pipe in Catalan, Dutch, French, German, Spanish, and Italian (in the last case, also the *flaùto* that had meant duct flute).

MINSTREL SCHOOLS

Between about 1313 and 1447, a highly effective communication mechanism existed among minstrels internationally: the so-called minstrel 'schools'.[62] Rob Wegman observes: 'These were not schools in the modern sense but international assemblies, the counterpart of conferences or trade fairs in our time.'[63] They were held roughly annually during Lent – when secular music stopped being performed everywhere[64] – in cities in France, the Low Countries, and occasionally England and Germany, apparently organized by urban minstrel guilds and confraternities. At least in France, the hosting cities provided board and lodging for the minstrels.[65] Attendees came from cities and courts as far away as Greece and Spain, returning home by Easter. Maricarmen Gómez Muntané has suggested that permanent music schools may have been located in Flanders, too;[66] and perhaps woodwind makers were also resident in Flanders at this time.

The purposes of minstrel schools are documented as keeping the craft up to date, purchasing instruments, recruiting, and learning by oral transmission 'new songs', presumably including the sense of 'pieces'.[67] The Limburg Chronicle, written by the town clerk Tilemann Elhen von Wolfhagen from 1378 to 1398, records many instances of 'new songs' played on shawms and trumpets and sung by the people.[68]

Wegman writes: 'if minstrels were prepared to travel hundreds of miles each year to learn new songs, then musical novelty must have been at a very high premium in their profession, much more so, one assumes, than among singers and composers. Since the minstrel school was attended by musicians from nearly all countries, it allowed new songs to become instant hits, and new styles of playing and singing to break through almost overnight.'[69] The same would have been true of new instruments.

WRITINGS FROM ARAGÓN[70]

The earliest account of what were almost certainly recorders comes from Aragón. From 1387 to 1396, King Juan I (b. 1350) ruled the Crown of Aragón – a confederation formed from the Kingdom of Aragón, the County of Barcelona (Catalonia), and the Kingdom of Valencia, in north-east Spain. On 23 July 1378, when he was still the Crown Prince, Juan wrote the following letter from his political capital of Zaragoza to his chamberlain, Petro d'Artes: 'I certify to you that Matheu, our conjuror, is going under our licence to the city of Valencia, and as he is very good at making harps, we want him to ask Ponç, who makes lutes, that with the counsel and assistance of the said Matheu he will make us a double harp, and provided that he works every day until the said harp is finished, and I anticipate that it will be necessary for him to do that, and the said Matheu bring it to us, and send us the lutes and the *flahutes* as quickly as possible.'[71]

Doubtless Ponç had made the lutes, which, like the *flahutes*, seem to have been ordered earlier. But it is not spelt out in this letter or the ensuing receipt whether the *flahutes* had also been made by him or someone else in his workshop, or perhaps had even been obtained elsewhere. In any case, when the instruments arrived, Juan wrote to d'Artes again and declared that he had received them 'to my complete satisfaction'.[72]

3. Exterior view of the Aljafería, Zaragoza, Spain, the palace where Juan I of Aragón (1350–96) lived. A letter of Juan's from 1378 concerning his purchase of *flahutes* is probably the earliest documentation of the recorder.

4. Interior view of the Aljafería, looking out.

What were these *flahutes*? Terms for members of the flute family go back to the early fourteenth century in Aragonese sources: three instances of *juglar de flauta* (1312, 1327–36, and 1345); *flautes* that played with drums and cymbals (1328); and *flautes de bahanya* (made of animal horn, 1349).[73] The *flauta* is mentioned in a Spanish literary source, *Libro de buen amor* by Juan Ruiz, Archpriest of Hita (revised 1343), which links the instrument with the tabor played by *joglares*.[74] Furthermore, the poem distinguishes the *flauta* from the *axabeba*, a term derived from the Arabic *shabbāba*, which scholars have generally taken to be the transverse flute, introduced to Spain by the Moors in the eighth century, although the word is used today for an obliquely held rim-blown flute made out of cane.[75]

Thus in Aragón *juglars* (cognate with what the French called *jongleurs*) tended to play the *flauta*, which in a manuscript from nearby Guadalajara is identified with the tabor pipe. But the term *flahute* or *flaute* was also employed, so, as in all linguistic matters, the terminology was not clear-cut. Because Prince Juan's sister-in-law pronounced him 'completely French',[76] it may be significant that the French language used *flaüte/flahüte* to mean tabor pipe. Then, as we will see, probably by the late fourteenth century and certainly by the early fifteenth, *flaüte* in French began to shift its spelling to *fleute* and its meaning to recorder. Therefore, it may again be significant that Juan chose the term *flahutes* rather than *flautas* for the instruments he had ordered. More significance may be attached to him ordering more than one *flahute* and at the same time as lutes. Finally, as we will see, clear depictions of the recorder begin to show up in art from Aragón around the 1380s. In research on the Middle Ages, little is certain; but all things considered, Juan had almost certainly bought a set of recorders.[77]

In 1367, twenty years before he ascended to the throne, Juan was given his own pair of musicians, who played *cornamusa* and trumpet. After he got married for the first time, to the French infanta Juana de Valois, at the age of 21 in 1371, Juan hired for his personal service four musicians – now for the first time at court called 'minstrels': Thomasi (Tomasinus de Xaumont, probably Chaumont in France), Tibaut (Tibaldus de Barrenes), Jacomi (Jacobinus de Bar, in France), and Lupi (Luppus tibalerius, piper?), 'from France and other countries'.[78] Their contract introduced to the court the term *coblas de ministriles* (associations of minstrels, apparently in the sense of ensembles). This particular *cobla* was based on the duo of Thomasi, shawm, and Jacomi, *cornamusa*, with the other two minstrels presumably adding an accompaniment of other instruments, not necessarily all winds, although their eventual replacements both played the shawm.

Pere Tomich in his history of Aragón (1438) wrote about Juan: 'he had at his court many *coblas* of all kinds of minstrels dancing and singing to amuse himself.'[79] Reporting more than a century after the fact (1495–1513), another chronicler of Aragón, Pere Miquel Carbonell, noted of Juan: 'His biggest concern was to order the search around the world for the best minstrels to be found, strings as well as winds and singers, so that they would play and sing in his presence three times a day – that is, one in the morning, another at noon, and another in the afternoon; and he wanted this rule to be observed every day of the week.'[80] Did Juan play instruments himself, like some monarchs of England? The only surviving evidence of his own musical ability is that, 'helped by my singers', who had been newly recruited from the Papal court in Avignon, he composed a three-voice rondeau in 1380.[81] It is worth noting that he was helped by singers, not minstrels.[82]

Juan regularly sent his minstrels to the schools in Flanders and elsewhere, where among other things they learned new pieces. When they returned, they taught the pieces to other local minstrels.[83] Juan wrote to his cousin, Alfonso I, duke of Gandia, on 1 March 1378, 'Our minstrels have taught yours six new songs, and when our said minstrels have returned from the schools, send yours again and ours will show them our instruments. This way, we will deliver to them two shawms, two *cornamusas*, one large and one small *museta*, a small shawm, and a bombard.'[84] Not only was Juan obtaining instruments from the schools, he was passing them on to a neighbouring monarch's minstrels.

By late 1377, Juan acquired his best-ever shawm player, Johani Estrumant, previously in the service of the Count of Flanders. Thus it was that in the spring of 1378, the year that Juan bought *flahutes*, he sent six men to the minstrel schools in Bruges: the *cobla* consisting of Estrumant, shawm, Johani Coecre, *cornamusa*, Johani de Sent Luch, shawm, and Jaquet de Noyo, psaltery and fiddle; plus Matheu (the harp maker, who was also a performer). These minstrels returned tardily in August, to Juan's despair. As early as 22 May he had already written to his brother Martin: 'Because the instruments of the Duchess's minstrels that are now here torment us when they are played, I beg you that your man bring us the *musetes* of yours that Tibaut, your minstrel, brought to you from Flanders this year.'[85] Note that these instruments were brought from Flanders, presumably in connection with the minstrel schools. It was also to Flanders that Juan dispatched another minstrel named Everli to buy instruments 'of [a] new type' in 1388.[86]

By the time Juan's minstrels returned to Aragón in August 1378, the *flahutes* had been transported to the court. Who else but these minstrels could have played the *flahutes*? Juan tells us himself that some singers also played instruments. His father kept a steady number of six *chantres* – the French name for the singers suggesting they came from Avignon and sang French Ars Nova Masses. But Juan did not start organizing his own chapel until his second marriage, to the French noblewoman Yolanda de Bar, in August 1379. At that time he hired eight singers, mostly French and mostly from Avignon, writing to his ambassador there: 'and we want them to bring all the Mass chants notated in a book containing also motets, rondeaux, ballads, and virelais. . . . And let us know if they can play instruments too, and which ones, since we have all kinds of them. . . .'[87] We know the names of no fewer than twenty-six of Juan's singers over the period 1379–96, mostly French, but there is no surviving record of any instruments they might have played or any compositions they wrote;[88] moreover, none of the fourteenth-century secular vocal repertoire has survived in Aragón.[89] Some Ars Subtilior music – the modern name for Ars Nova music of particular rhythmic and notational complexity – in the Chantilly Codex, compiled around 1375–95, was associated with Juan and Martin, who may have commissioned it for performance at court.[90]

On 30 July 1378, a week after Juan referred to an order for *flahutes*, and shortly before his own minstrels came back from the minstrel schools, he wrote again to Martin:

> we know that your minstrels, who have just returned from the schools, have brought with them many instruments, big and small [in the sense of *haut* and *bas*, or loud and soft categories],[91] and we would be very grateful if, in case you think that listening to the big instruments would not be agreeable or fruitful, then, dear brother, we would kindly ask you to send us your minstrels, especially with the small instruments, although we would prefer that they bring all of them.[92]

This document confirms that Juan was concerned to stay abreast of the latest developments.

Yet it seems clear that the *flahutes* mentioned in Juan's two letters to d'Artes had nothing to do with the attendance of court musicians from Aragón at the minstrel schools in 1378, not least because he had ordered the instruments before July that year. *Flahutes* may have arrived in Aragón previously from the minstrel schools, perhaps accompanying one of the many minstrels visiting the Court or a newly hired minstrel, Estrumant being an obvious candidate. It is unlikely that a maker in Valencia, within Juan's own territory, would have invented or acquired a novel instrument unbeknownst to the prince. More probably, Juan acquired at least one *flahute* through a minstrel in 1377 or early 1378, subsequently asking Ponç to make copies. If Ponç, a maker of stringed instruments, had been new to recorder making, it would certainly have taken him a while to master the appropriate use of the lathe and reamers, especially in order to make more than one size. Perhaps he simply subcontracted the work. In any case, Juan's hurry to obtain the *flahutes* from Valencia may well have been to guarantee that they would be available when his minstrels finally returned.[93]

If Juan's haste also suggests that he 'seemed to like' the recorder, as one researcher put it,[94] we have no further evidence of such affection; and indeed it was the shawm that he found 'the most agreeable sound' of all instruments,[95] especially when it was accompanied by the *cornamusa*. He went to considerable lengths to obtain the best lead shawm player he could, before and throughout his reign. If his shawm players also played the recorder, as shawm players generally did in the following century, that would have been a bonus, and the string players who were sometimes members of *coblas* could have accompanied the recorders.

How many *flahutes* did Juan purchase in 1378 and what sizes were they? The only pertinent evidence we have is from 1410, on the death of Martin, who had ruled the Crown of Aragón as his successor since 1396. Martin's possessions were given to his widow, including 'three *flautes*: two large and one small black one . . . two *flautes*: one small black one and another transverse one'.[96] Were the 'black' instruments made of a dark hardwood, a sign of their great value? The instruments listed first apparently constitute a set of three in two different sizes – the first clear reference to more than one size of recorder. Martin strongly supported the royal chapel, but seems to have had less interest in minstrel music than Juan, so the *flautes* could easily have been passed down from his brother.

When minstrels wanted to learn new repertoire, they travelled to the minstrel schools, where they acquired the repertoire orally, later passing it on orally to other minstrels. When singers wanted to learn new repertoire, they read the music, or composed some themselves. So when the *flahutes* arrived in Zaragoza in August 1378, they were presumably handed to Juan's minstrels, who were used to oral transmission of pieces and perhaps did not even read musical notation. Then the minstrels would probably have simply played their usual memorized repertoire on these new instruments.

Researchers have conjectured that Juan's recorders, perhaps in conjunction with his lutes, were used to play the latest French chansons, that the recorder was developed for this very purpose, and that the practice of playing chansons on recorders might have spread from Aragón around Europe.[97] How plausible are these theories? Certainly, instruments of the type recorder-T, much easier to play chromatically, would have been helpful for playing polyphonic music – if such instruments already existed. Herbert W. Myers has observed, 'Two sizes of recorder built a fifth apart would suffice for most written [three-part] polyphony of the [late fourteenth and] early fifteenth century; three sizes become necessary later with the general adoption of the *contratenor bassus*, whose range is typically a fifth below that of the tenor.'[98] Singers from Avignon, who could read musical notation, might have learned an instrument like the recorder, which needs no special embouchure, and used it to play chansons, with or alternating with voices, in Aragón. And it has been proposed that, doubling at least the tenor, the recorder would have been able to help singers with their challenge noted by one writer in 1434: 'it becomes most difficult to keep the notes at the right pitch for a long time, even for one song'.[99] The singers might have even taught the minstrels to play chansons by rote – a familiar practice for minstrels used to oral transmission – or from the notation – which would have been something new for them. We even have a beautiful quotation from the court of Savoy – but one hundred years later! – showing that such things happened: in 1479 a singer was paid 'for having shown *chansons* to the minstrels of the said Lord'.[100] It is worth noting that Juan of Aragón obtained chansons as well as motets for his singers. Although no other researcher has suggested the possibility that his singers played motets on recorders, that would have been as plausible as singers playing chansons.

No less a figure than Guillaume de Machaut provides some relevant evidence about the instrumental performance of chansons. In a poetic letter written in 1363–65, he observes about his ballade *Nes qu'on porroit*, 'I beg you to be willing to hear and learn the piece exactly as it has been written without adding to or taking away any part . . . and whoever could arrange [it] for the organ, bagpipes, or other instruments, that is its very nature.'[101] Lawrence Earp suggests that 'this does not mean an ensemble of instruments literally playing the written music, but some kind of creative rearrangement, and thus not "exactly as it has been written", because that segment of the musical practice [i.e. instrumental performance] was carried on in a largely unwritten tradition'.[102] One suggestive piece of evidence in favour of recorders playing at least some vocal music is that as early as 1385, in a nuptial Mass in Cambrai for the future John II of Burgundy, both singers and *flusteurs musicals* performed – whether at the same time or alternately, is not mentioned. Otherwise, we have no further evidence of vocal music being played on recorders until 1468. Neither do we have evidence either for or against instruments taking part in French secular chansons at the same time as the voices.[103]

As for the idea that playing chansons on recorders might have spread from Aragón: if such a practice existed in 1378, or developed soon afterwards, probably it originated in Burgundy or Avignon. In sum, unless more evidence is discovered, although recorders may have been used to play arrangements of chansons (and motets), the idea that the recorder was developed in Aragón for this very purpose, and that the practice of playing chansons on recorders might have spread out from there, is doubtful.

In the fifteenth century, recorders can be traced further in Aragón. In 1417, Martin's successor's successor, Alfonso V the Magnanimous (1416–58), hired the celebrated shawm player Jehan Boisard, alias Verdelet, for an unknown period, but less than ten years. Verdelet was also celebrated as a player of the *flaiolet*, which term could easily have embraced the recorder at some point in his career. Guillelmus d'Ager, 'turner or *flahute* maker, citizen of Barcelona', was noted in a legal document in 1420.[104] Sometime in the fifteenth century, records of the numerous musical instruments moving from Aragón to Castile through the customs office in the city of Calatayud list *flautas* as by far the most predominant instrument, followed by the vihuela.[105] In Valencia in 1430, a city record mentions 'payments to players of stringed instruments, of recorder (*flauta*) and cornamuses and others'.[106] The probate inventory of Antón Ancóriz, a citizen of Zaragoza, in 1472 included five *flautas*, probably a set. Tess Knighton writes of the inventory of another citizen of Zaragoza, Martín Zayda, in 1475, that he 'had "a vihuela, a recorder and a songbook" among his possessions when he died . . . which raises all kinds of interesting questions regarding his ethnicity and position in society, and whether he was a professional or amateur musician'.[107] Finally, the *bas* band for the Corpus Christi procession in Girona in 1481 consisted of harp, lute, two guitars, vihuela, and recorder (*flahutam*).[108]

RECORDER-T

The development of recorder-T, which has a whole tone for the lowest interval, changed the instrument in two main ways. The instrument became fully chromatic by means of cross-fingering and half-holing the lowest notes. Less positively, it removed the semitone as the lowest interval, so that a leading tone to the mode of the six-fingered note now had to be made by half-holing the seven-fingered note, inevitably with a weaker tone.

The new need for chromatic instruments in the fourteenth century is well illustrated by Timothy McGee's book on medieval instrumental dances, which includes all the surviving dance music.[109] The seventeen monophonic dances from England and France in the thirteenth century have either no accidentals or B♭ (sometimes in the key signature), with only two instances of E♭ and one instance of F♯, regardless of whether the final of the mode is C, D, F, G, or A. Ten of the nineteen dances from Italy around 1400, on the other hand, have from two to four accidentals – C♯, E♭, F♯, G♯, and B♭ – for exactly the same selection of finals. These accidentals are in monophonic music: no need to posit playing polyphonic chansons to justify them.[110] The sets of recorders discussed in the following sections strongly suggest, but do not in themselves prove, the existence of recorder-T throughout the fifteenth century.

One surviving instrument of type-T has recently been described for the first time, although it was discovered in 1919.[111] It belongs to the Nationalmuseet in Copenhagen, Denmark.[112] Ture Bergstrøm writes that 'the recorder cannot be dated precisely, but according to the accessions register of the museum it was found "among predominantly late medieval things", which suggests a date in the second half of the fifteenth century. Several of its features confirm that here we have a recorder from the late Middle Ages, shortly before the ensemble instruments of the Renaissance made their entry.'[113] The instrument, made of boxwood, is fairly well preserved but extremely warped, and the block is missing. The finger-holes are in a straight line, apart from the lowest, which is doubled. The instrument is 283 mm long, with an external diameter of 20.5 mm at the top, contracting to 16.7 mm at finger-hole 4, then expanding to 23.5 mm at the bottom end. But the inner bore has two cylindrical sections: upper 12.7 mm and lower 10.3 mm in diameter, with a distinct step just below the window. The finger-holes are slightly conical: the opposite of undercut (cf. the Göttingen recorder). Two holes on the side in line with the middle of the block suggest the latter was kept in position by a transverse peg, and a strip was filed flat on the front of the instrument (cf. the Tartu and Elbląg recorders). The turning and workmanship are crudely executed.

WRITINGS FROM GERMANY AND FRANCE

An intriguing record from Frankfurt-am-Main in 1387 describes how 'the fiddlers of the Duke of Bavaria and the *floyter* of the Bishop of Mainz played together'.[114]

The term *floite* had meant tabor pipe, sometimes duct flute, but here the impromptu *bas* ensemble strongly suggests recorders. In Prussia in 1410, a payment was made to 'minstrels with *floyten*'.[115]

In France, the term *flaüte*, which had primarily referred to the tabor pipe, shifted its principal spellings by the early fifteenth century. In 1416, the accounts of Isabeau of Bavaria, wife of Charles VI of France, include a payment to Haquin Regnault, instrument maker, 'for the purchase of 8 *grans fleustes*' and another payment to a *gainnier* (case maker) for a large case 'to put and carry 5 *grans fleustes* on which they [two *écuyers* of the queen] play in front of the said lady'.[116] Regnault is the earliest confirmed recorder maker in Europe that we know by name.[117] The regular performance before the queen suggests an intimate setting, unsuited to tabor pipes, and five or eight tabor pipes would be redundant. Rather, the case of five, larger than usual, strongly suggests a matched set of more than one size. All in all, *grans fleustes*, literally 'large flutes', seems to be a new term to identify recorders. Does the size imply altos and tenors rather than sopranos?

As corroborating evidence, in one of the few pastoral sources for the *fleute*, Arnoul Gréban's mystery play (by 1452), the character Pellion asserts wittily that the shepherd 'is a little king' when he is well-equipped with a luxurious bread basket, wicker garland, awl and case, hook and crook, box of pitch, a fine long-sleeved tunic, leather shoes with tassels, 'and, for amusement, his *grosse fleute pleniere*' (large fat *fleute*) – perhaps also phallic symbolism?[118] Immediately afterwards Pellion mentions 'two or three *flajolets*, choice tabors and *fleutes*', clearly distinguishing the *grosse fleute pleniere* from both *fleute* as tabor pipe and the little *flajol*.[119] Moreover, Octavien de Saint Gelais's *Le séjour d'honneur* (1490) describes the 'soft harmonies and melodious sounds' of the paired *fleuste* and lute, differentiating the former from the *flajol* of a shepherd.[120]

WRITINGS FROM BURGUNDY AND THE LOW COUNTRIES

Before the end of the fourteenth century, *fleutes* had already begun to turn up at the court of Burgundy in situations that suggest recorders. In 1383, 'a bagpipe and some *fleutes*' were bought for the future John II 'the Fearless', then only 11 years old.[121] That same year Duke Philip II 'the Bold' gave to the French king 'a *flajolet* decorated with copper/brass inlay and painted'.[122] Thus the *fleutes* were given to a youth and distinguished in name from the *flajolet*, so presumably they differed from both that and the tabor pipe. As we have seen, when John married Margaret of Bavaria in Cambrai in 1385 at the tender age of 14, the nuptial Mass was performed by 'many fine singers and *flusteurs* who sang very well'; the setting would have been far more suitable for recorders than tabor pipes or flutes.[123] Myers writes: 'While we may be jumping to an unwarranted conclusion to assume . . . that instrumental doubling of vocal lines is implied here – *alternatim* practice seems more likely for this period – the context at least suggests the involvement of the instruments in the performance of sophisticated polyphony.'[124] And not only polyphony but sacred polyphony, which is remarkable considering that even the organ, generally the only instrument permitted in sacred music during the Middle Ages, was not universally accepted.[125] A choir-stall made by the Dijon carpenter Jean de Liège in 1388 and installed in the abbey church of Chartreuse de Champmol, near Dijon, the mausoleum of the dukes of Burgundy, bears John's arms. The carved oak seat-back of the choir-stall depicts four angel musicians playing a vielle, hurdy-gurdy, *tambourin de Béarn* with two beaters, and what seems to be a duct flute, perhaps even a recorder, 'an association of instruments which might actually have been played for dancing at the ducal court'.[126]

In 1402, the records of Deventer, a trade city belonging to the Hanseatic League, mention a payment to 'three journeymen with pipes (*pipen*) and lutes', the pipes being at least duct flutes in this *bas* context.[127] In Ypres, a major manufacturing centre in Flanders, payments for the annual procession included 'two fiddles and a *vloyte*' in 1410–11.[128]

In 1426, Duke Philip III 'the Good' of Burgundy bought the following from Loys Willay in Bruges to send to the Marquis of Ferrara, Niccolò II d'Este: 'four large minstrel instruments [probably a set of shawms], four *douçaines* [apparently soft double-reed instruments], and four *fleutes*, all furnished with leather cases and chests'.[129] Note the presence of a woodwind maker in Flanders, from where new instruments tended to come in the fourteenth century.

Although the set of four *fleutes* implies that recorders of different sizes were played, it still does not necessarily indicate their use for four-part polyphony. The earliest surviving chanson from the Burgundy court that seems to have been written in four parts is 'Filles à marier / Se tu t'en marias' by one of the major composers of the day, Binchois (Gilles de Bins; ca. 1400–60), dating from the 1430s.[130] Binchois had joined the court sometime in the 1420s and spent the bulk of his career there.

Nevertheless, references to sets of four recorders persist. In 1443, the court paid the *luthier* Jean Chapuis for '4 ivory *flutes*, one decorated with gold and jewels, and the others not decorated'.[131] Three members of this set seem to be referred to in an inventory of Philip's (undated but at the latest 1467, the year of his death): 'three leather cases, covered with gold, in all of them ivory *flutes*, both large and small; one of the large *flutes* is ornamented with gold on the mouthpiece, and lower down decorated with two gold rings and strewn with little emeralds, garnets, and rubies, and nothing is lacking'.[132] The sets of four, the different sizes, and the view of the instrument as valuable enough to be so expensively decorated strongly suggest the establishment of a new artistic member of the duct-flute family, the recorder.

Jeanne Marix remarks that 'At the court no minstrel was paid as a recorder player, but no doubt the virtuosi of the shawm and bombard knew also how to use it on occasion – for example, Verdelet, the so-called "minstrel of the king of minstrels," who had a great reputation [see also earlier under Aragón, p. 21]. According to Martin le Franc (*Le Champion des dames*, ca. 1440), "never have we encountered on *doucaine* or *flaiolet* anyone who played it like the late Verdelet used to do." '[133] Even if Le Franc knew enough about duct flutes to tell a flageolet from a recorder, the pressure on minstrels to keep up with the latest instruments makes it probable that Verdelet would have (also) known and played the recorder. Marix provides biographical details of two players, father and son, with this nickname: Jehan Boisard dit Verdelet, 'former king of minstrels', and his son, 'minstrel of the king of minstrels'.[134] She suggests that the son received his title because he was 'entrusted' (presumably apprenticed) to Jehan Facien, the king of minstrels at that time. 'Facien's authority evidently held sway in all regions which recognized the king of France as overlord.'[135] Both Verdelets were among the five minstrels that King Charles VII of France offered in payment of his debts to Alfonso of Aragón in 1426. By 1436, the younger Verdelet seems to have been in the service of the duke of Bourbon, when he fell ill at the Peace of Arras, then died soon afterwards. This pattern of players being sent around to different masters no doubt spread recorder playing around Europe further, at a time when the minstrel schools were petering out. To return to the ivory recorders supplied by Chapuis in 1443, the Burgundian court had five wind players at that time: Jehan Van Artinghem, Jehan Caresme, Pierre Claisonne le Brun, and Thibaut de Strasbourg, *ménestrels*;[136] and Hennequin Janson, *trompette des ménestrels*.[137] The simplest inference is that the four minstrels played the recorder, although we cannot rule out that the slide-trumpet player did so, too.

The *fleutres* mentioned in court performances starting in the next decade were almost certainly sets of recorders. At the Banquet du Vœu (Feast of the Pheasant), held in Lille by Philip on 17 February 1454: 'four minstrels with *fleutres* played most melodiously'.[138] Victor Coelho and Keith Polk, arguing that 'it was almost certainly the court shawmists who performed on recorders', wonder about the report of four, although as we have seen, four-part chansons originated in the 1430s. 'One possibility is that the players simply memorized one of the exceptional contemporary four-part pieces. Three players could also have played a three-part piece from memory while the fourth improvised a free counterpoint.'[139]

On 3 July 1468, in the city of Bruges where we have already encountered the recorder maker Willay, Duke Charles 'the Bold' of Burgundy was married to Margaret of York, sister of two kings of England, Edward IV and Richard III. Reinhard Strohm has written of this occasion that 'The minstrels and court singers of the town worked side by side with the court minstrels and those of the English delegation.'[140] Yet we know from the researches of Marix and Barbara Haggh that the number of minstrels at the Burgundian court had dwindled towards the end of the reign of Philip 'the Good' (d. 1467), to the point that in 1468 only one was left, a man named Jacques de Rectre, player of the slide trumpet, and even he had previously been listed as a field trumpeter. This suggests that the bulk of the instrumental music at the opulent wedding celebrations was played by the city minstrels of Bruges, whom we discuss later.[141] A series of suppers was held every day for ten days, at which music was performed by musicians disguised as animals. At one supper there appeared 'four wolves having *flustes* in their paws, and the said wolves began to play a chanson'.[142] Later in the wedding, a minstrel dressed as a monkey played 'a small *tabor* and a *flajol*'.[143] Using for the tabor pipe the term *flajol*, which had meant duct flutes that were not tabor pipes, confirms that the meaning of *fluste* had shifted from tabor pipe to recorder.

WRITINGS FROM ITALY

In 1408, a *pifaro* (shawm player) named Bartolomio da Urbino, who worked for the count of Urbino in east-central Italy, was paid for 'four new *flauti*' he had sent to the court in Brescia, in the Lombardy region of northern Italy, presumably having bought them locally, or even made them himself.[144] Especially in light of the Burgundian references from the fifteenth century, the number of instruments suggests recorders of more than one size.

In 1414, Niccolò d'Este of Ferrara visited France, where he dined with the Dauphin and nobles, and 'harp, fiddle, recorders (*flauti*), and lute were played excellently'.[145] A poem by Simone Prodenzani, *Il Saporetto*, written around 1415 in Orvieto, describes festivities at a fictional court.[146] Although the veracity of the instrumental combinations has been questioned,[147] the *fiauto* (presumably recorder) is placed with two other *bas* instruments: monochord and psaltery.

In Florence, three inventories employ the term *ʒufoli*, which had previously meant tabor pipe. The inventory of Piero di Cosimo de' Medici's possessions (1463) contrasts 'four Flemish *ʒufoli*' and 'three of our *ʒufoli*', and also mentions 'three *ʒufoli* decorated with silver'.[148] The inventory of his son Lorenzo 'il Magnifico' de' Medici (1492) clarifies the grouping of these instruments as well as the relationship of silver to wood: 'A set of large *ʒufoli* in a wrapping. . . . A set of *ʒufoli* for the use of the *pifferi* with black and white ferrules, five in all. . . . Three *ʒufoli* with silver ferrules in a wrapping garnished with silver. . . .'[149] A ferrule is a metal ring that strengthens a joint or an end of the instrument. *Zufoli* seems to have been the standard Italian term for fifes from about 1509: two *tamburini* were appointed consisting of *ʒufolo et tamburino*.[150] But before that date there is little evidence for fifes, or even flutes, played by Italians in Italy, and we have some Flemish references that almost certainly point to recorders. Some recorders in the sixteenth century are described as being in a 'wrapping', perhaps containing pockets: for example, 'In a case five recorders with their case in which there is a small ivory one with its pieces of green cloth.'[151] Finally, the inventory of the possessions of the Florentine painter Filippino Lippi, clearly an amateur musician who would not have played the fife or flute, included 'five good *ʒufoli* in a small bag'.[152] So *ʒufoli* seems to have been a Florentine term for recorders.

In Milan, the recorder may have been signified by the term *fiauto*. The dance treatise of Antonio Cornazano (published 1465) observes: 'Piva . . . is a rustic dance; its melody, the model for all other [dances], was invented by shepherds on blades of oat. From blades of oat it was transferred to reed cane, and as taste became more refined, from thence to *fiautti* and other instruments made and used by us today. . . .'[153] At the Burgundian court in 1468, a payment was made to 'certain Venetian companions who played the recorder (*fleute*) in front of my Lord' during a meeting of the Order of the Golden Fleece.[154] When a group of three *sonatori* visited Siena that same year, they played in the *bas* combination of lute, rebec, and recorder, the scribe apparently using a local Sienese term for the recorder (*fiuto*).[155]

In Pesaro, at the festivities accompanying the marriage of Costanzo Sforza and Camilla of Aragón in 1475, a theatrical entertainment was performed, together with music played by 'lutes, bells, harps, triangles, recorders (*flauti*), and various instruments that made a very sweet harmony'.[156] *Fiauto* as recorder seems to have been established by 1484 in Verona when the group of four city musicians who petitioned the council said that their '*musica*' consisted of 'shawms, sackbuts, recorders (*fiauti*), harps, lutes, organ, and singing'.[157]

In 1498, Francesco Gonzaga in Mantua was offered an apprentice of the Ferrara player Piero (Piedro) Trombono who 'plays with sensitivity the sackbut and also the recorder (*fiauto*) and the cornetto'.[158] William Prizer, who discovered this document, proposes that Piero had a kind of school for young sackbut players, because the same letter refers to him as teacher of Jacomo Trombonzino of Mantua, and in 1490 Duke Ercole I d'Este wrote to the duke of Mantua that 'Piedro, our sackbut player, is prepared to teach Bartholomeo, your trumpeter, the manner and art of playing the sackbut'.[159] These documents could mean simply that Piedro had apprentices or was willing to take them on. In any case, 'the manner and art of playing the sackbut' could include the manner and art of playing the recorder.

WRITINGS FROM ENGLAND AND SCOTLAND[160]

By the fourteenth century, although their meanings were not standardized, English had no fewer than five possible names for duct flutes: *flagel, floute, fristel, pipe*, and *whistle*. Nevertheless, towards the end of that century, a new name was coined: *recorder*. The earliest authenticated occurrence dates from 1388, in the household accounts of Henry, Earl of Derby, the future Henry IV of England: '*1. fistula nomine Recordour*' (one pipe named Recorder).[161] The instrument was bought in London and charged to Henry's 'necessaries', apparently for his domestic music-making, at the high cost of 3 shillings 4 pence (about 100 hours' pay for a labourer).[162] As other entries in the household accounts include strings and pegs 'pro domina', presumably for the *canticum* (gittern?) of the Countess of Derby, we can imagine noble domestic chamber music played on recorder and gittern. Similarly, a carved misericord in Chichester Cathedral, dating from around 1330, depicts a duct-flute player and a harpist.

Was Henry's *Recordour* a recorder in our sense? One hundred and fifty years later there would have been no room for doubt, as we saw from Palsgrave's dictionary. It seems plausible, but of course not certain, that the name 'recorder' was indeed applied to this specific duct flute going back to 1388. Why a new name was coined in English, when the Romance and Germanic languages of the Continent managed with existing terminology, is less clear, but it may be because

English had no special name for a duct flute distinguished from tabor pipe: *flegel* had changed its meaning from the French *flajol*.

Modern authorities all derive 'recorder' from the verb 'to record', stemming from the Old French *recorder*, and ultimately from the Latin *recordari*, to remember (*re-*, back, plus *cord*, from *cor*, heart or mind; thus to bring back to mind).[163] The comprehensive *Middle English Dictionary* sets out no fewer than seven families of meanings for 'to record' in the fourteenth century, deriving the instrument from meaning (6), 'repeat, reiterate, recite, rehearse (a song)', and also comparing it to the Old French *recordëor*, a word which the Tobler–Lommatzsch dictionary of Old French indeed defines as a 'reciter'.[164] Eric Partridge's etymological dictionary spells out his theory about this connection: the Middle English noun *recorder* 'has agent *recordeor*, a rememberer, a relater, a minstrel (whence the musical instrument)'.[165] But these authorities left out an important intermediate step in the derivation of the verb: Anglo-French. Curiously, the equally comprehensive *Anglo-Norman Dictionary* does not cite any use of *recordëor* in Anglo-French, only *recordour* in the legal sense of 'person officially appointed to make a record'. Nevertheless, the dictionary shows that the language did transmit meanings of the verb *recorder* that made their way into Middle English, including remember, repeat, recite, and learn by heart.

The *Oxford English Dictionary* sees the origin of 'recorder' in two senses of 'record': 'To practise (a song, tune, etc.). In later use only of birds', and 'Of birds (rarely of persons): To practise or sing a tune in an undertone; to go over it quietly or silently.' The first sense agrees with (6) from the *Middle English Dictionary*. But the second sense is unlikely, as the earliest example cited stems from 1518: 'Therfore first recorde thou, as birde within a cage, / . . . thy tunes tempring longe, / And then . . . forth with thy pleasaunt songe.'[166] The definition even seems erroneous, as the examples imply instead the well-known later usage of a bird's first essays at singing, as in Palsgrave (1530): 'Recorde as yonge byrdes do. . . . This byrde recordeth all redy, she wyll synge within a whyle.'[167] Later, by extension, 'recorder' could refer to the sound-producing mechanisms of birds: 'From which the byrds the purple berries pruned / And to theyr loves their small recorders tuned' (1595)[168] – and even to birds themselves, 'List to that sweete Recorder; / How daintily this BYRD his notes doth vary' (1613).[169] 'Byrd' is a punning reference to the composer William Byrd, whose works are contained in the collection.

What did 'flute' mean in England? In the second half of the fourteenth century, the great poet Geoffrey Chaucer left some ambiguous references. A section marked 'The Dream' in the early, unfinished love-vision *The House of Fame* (1369–70?)

describes an enormous group of minstrels: 'Many thousand tymes twelve, / That maden lowde mynstralcies / In cornemuse and shalemyes, / And many other maner pipe, / That craftely begunne to pipe, / Bothe in *doucet* and in rede, / That ben at festes with the brede; / And many *flowte* and liltyng horn, / And pipes made of grene corn.'[170] The mixed context suggests panpipes or tabor pipes.[171]

The accomplished 'gay young Squire' in the Prologue of Chaucer's *Canterbury Tales* (1380s–90s) is described as 'syngynge . . . or *floytynge* all the day. . . . He coude songes make, and wel endite [write them down].'[172] Although the *Middle English Dictionary* suggests 'to whistle' (with the lips) as a possible sense of *floytinge*, the variant 'pipyng' in one manuscript suggests otherwise. The presumed mixture of indoor and outdoor locales in the squire's day does not help us to determine the nature of the instrument in question.

Curiously, although Chaucer 'brought Anglo-Norman words into the mainstream of English literature and language',[173] he did not use the word 'recorder'. Let us therefore explore the possibility that by the beginning of the fifteenth century, as in French-speaking countries, *flowte* or *floyte*, the equivalent of 'flute', not only referred to the tabor pipe but was now also employed as a synonym for recorder.

In literature the first dateable occurrence of 'recorder' comes in the poem *The Fall of Princes* (1431–38) by John Lydgate: 'Pan, god off Kynde [Nature], with his pipes sevene / Off recorderis fond first the melodies.'[174] In other words, Lydgate saw panpipes as the original type of duct flute, a corruption of Virgil's assertion that 'Pan first taught to unite many reeds with wax.'[175]

In two of his earlier poems, Lydgate used *flowte*/*floyte* in ambiguous situations. In *Reason and Sensuality* (1407), he writes of the god Mercury: 'In his lifte honde A flowte he held, / When so him list the longe day, / Ther with to pipe and make play, / Oonly him self for to disporte, / And his hert to comforte / Wyth the sugred armonye, / Which gaf so soote a melodye / That no man koude him selfe so kepe, / But hyt wold make him slepe.' Although left-hand playing might suggest a tabor pipe, the instrument puts people to sleep, as confirmed a few lines later in an initial reference to a Siren: 'But al her syngyng was in weyn / To be compared, in sothness, / Unto the excellent swetnesse / Of this Floyte melodious, / By force of which Mercurius / Made Argus slepe.'[176] Elsewhere in the poem, the accomplishments of Venus's first son, Pleasure, include the ability to: 'Pipe and floyte lustely. / And also eke ful konyngly / In al the crafte and melody / Of musyke and of Armony. . . .'[177] 'Lustily' could mean both 'with vigour or energy' and also 'with pleasure or delight'.

Guillaume de Deguileville's *Le pèlerinage de la vie humaine* (1331) contains a passage about the bellows blast of Pride, which 'makes pipes and *fleutes* and shawms emit sound'.[178] A translation probably made by Lydgate, *The Pilgrimage of the Life of Man* (1426), renders the passage loosely: 'Bombardys and cornemusys, / Thys ffloutys ek, with sotyl musys, / And thys shallys loudë crye.'[179] The *Floutys* with their 'subtle music' sound more like recorders than tabor pipes, even though Pride's blast forces them to 'loud cry'. A little later, the French text refers to another member of the flute family: 'for I deceive them all with my *flajol*'.[180] But the English version uses the same term as before: 'So swetly with my *ffloute* I pype.'[181] Thus the translator saw *fleute* and *flajol* as interchangeable terms for soft duct flutes, rendered as *floute*.

Yet the implication from Lydgate's work that 'recorder' may have not been widely known until the 1430s is countered by a literary reference at least ten years earlier in Middle Cornish, the Celtic language spoken in Cornwall – at least if the dating is correct. According to the latest scholarship, the miracle play known by its Latin title page as *Ordinale de origine mundi* (or *Ordinalia*) was probably 'written between 1395 and 1419 by an ecclesiastic living in or near Bodmin in central Cornwall'.[182] King David has been told by the Angel Gabriel in a dream to bring 'the rods of grace from Mount Tabor' that Moses planted.[183] Before he sets out, he orders his musicians: 'Blow minstrels and tabors; Three hundred harps and trumpets; Dulcimer, fiddle, viol, and psaltery; Shawms, gitterns and nakers; Organs, also cymbals, Recorders (*recordys*) and symphony.'[184] So on balance, it looks as though in English *flowte*/*floyte* overlapped with the new word *recorder* (first documented in 1388) until the 1430s.

A *Complaint* that begins 'Alas for thought' is found in two surviving manuscripts, dating from around 1430 and 1450, of Lydgate's *Temple of Glass* (written ca. 1403). It contains the revealing lines: 'Wher as these lytylle herdegromys / Floutyn al the longe day, Bothe in aprylle & in may, / In here smale recorderys, / In floutys & in rede sperys [stems], / Aboute this flour, til it be nyght.'[185] Recorders and flutes are clearly distinguished now, although both can 'flute'.

The Savoy ambassadors sent to Scotland for marriage negotiations in 1444 reported that they made a payment to three people 'from the city of Glasgow who played with *fleutis* and a cithara'.[186] Given the chamber setting, the *fleutis* were almost certainly duct flutes and probably recorders.

Could 'pipe' have been another synonym for recorder? The coat of arms of the Pype family has survived in a number of places, notably a brass on the tomb of Sir William Vernon (d. 1467), who married Margaret Swynfen, heiress of the

Pype family.[187] The arms include a pair of crossed duct flutes, serving as 'pipes'. Hilda Hunter described them as recorders although admitting they have 'only six finger-holes, the lowest of which is divided [i.e. there are paired holes]' – perhaps a botched attempt to render a recorder.[188] The arms are also found at All Saints, Bakewell, Derbyshire, and at Haddon Hall, near Bakewell. One version of the instruments has incised rings in the window area reminiscent of the Dordrecht recorder. We have already observed in Palsgrave (1530) that the recorder was equated with 'pipe' in the next century.

Recorders are found in the hands of both *bas* and *haut* minstrels. At court at the end of the fifteenth century, the Treasurer of the Chamber made payments to 'the childe that pleyeth on the records' (4 March 1492), then a month later on 6 April to the Flemish sackbut player 'Guillim [van den Burgh] for flotes with a case'.[189] The year 1492 is a few decades earlier than any secure knowledge of the family of (transverse) flutes in England, so the Fleming was probably using a cognate of 'flutes' to describe his consort of recorders.[190] Nine years later, in 1501, Guillim was paid 'for new recorders' he had provided for court use.[191] We cannot expect consistency in Treasury record(er)s. . . . Van den Burgh remained at the court until 1513. In 1498, one 'Arnold, player at recorders', was given a payment; he was presumably the same as the 'Arnold Jeffrey, organ player' paid a quarter's wages two months later and the 'Arnold, my Lord Prince'[s] minstrel' paid the previous year.[192]

CHILDREN AND THE RECORDER

We have already seen three instances of children playing the recorder or a similar duct flute: the poem about the 12-year-old Pierre de Navarre (1378), the instrument bought for the 11-year-old John II 'the Fearless' (1383), and a child who performed at the English court (1492). A couple of other documents suggest an educational use for the recorder. Around 1492, the Venetian embassy reported that in the city of Ulm, 'in the evening came the Stadtpfeifer and played excellently, also recorder (*Flöte*). The host has a very beautiful daughter, who then began to play recorders with the pipers, and afterwards sang with other singers that were added. She is virtuous and pretty, plays the recorder and lute, dances well, and is very playful.'[193] In 1500, the Holy Roman Emperor Maximilian I visited Augsburg, where the court accounts include a payment among the visiting musicians to 'four boys, who piped on recorders (*fleyten*) before His Majesty'.[194] But perhaps the boys were actually apprentices of minstrels.

Juan, Prince of Asturias, son and heir of the Catholic monarchs Ferdinand and Isabella of Aragón and Castile (1478–97), was taught composition by the royal chapel master Juan d'Anchieta, and enjoyed singing. Moreover, 'In his chamber there was a claviorgano, which was the first one to be seen in Spain . . . and he had organs, clavichords, vihuelas and violins, and *flautas*, and all these instruments he knew how to play and put his hands on them.'[195]

CONRAD PAUMANN

Keith Polk proposes for the recorder 'a distinct and unique position among the instruments of the fifteenth century', because, as already mentioned, it was common to both *haut* and *bas* minstrels. 'We may fairly claim, then, that the instrument had a universality attained by no other instrument before 1500.'[196]

5. Conrad Paumann's epitaph, Frauenkirche, Munich.

The most famous example of a *bas* player who sometimes played *haut* instruments was the blind German composer, organist, and lutenist Conrad Paumann (ca. 1410–73), who worked briefly in Nuremberg and then, after 1450, at the Bavarian court in Munich, also amazing distinguished listeners on his many travels by his powers of improvisation.[197] Paumann was buried outside the Frauenkirche in Munich, where an epitaph, now inside the church, shows him with what are presumably the main instruments he played: portative organ, lute, fiddle, harp, and recorder.[198] Yet two accounts of him indicate that he also played some loud instruments: one chronicler described him as being able to play 'on organ, lute, [other] plucked strings, fiddle, recorder, pipe, and sackbut, and on all musical instruments'; and in 1470 an observer in Mantua, where he was dubbed the 'miraculous blind man', marvelled that 'if he heard a verse or a song, he knew how to play it [by ear] either on the organ, or the bagpipe, or on plucked string instruments, or on the harp, or on the shawm'.[199]

The records are silent about how Paumann used the recorder. Solo, like the blind seventeenth-century musician Jacob van Eyck? In an ensemble with some combination of fiddle, lute, and harp, as depicted in some fifteenth-century paintings? Or in a recorder consort with his *bas* colleagues, as in Burgundy?

THE BRUGES CITY MINSTRELS

In 1470, Adriaen Willemaert sold some *fleutes* to Gerolamo Strozzi, a Florentine banker and merchant occasionally resident in Bruges.[200] Willemaert belonged to the city's band of four *scalmeyers* – literally 'shawm players', who probably constituted a standard *haut* band of two treble shawms, tenor shawm (bombard), and sackbut. In 1482–83, the band expanded to five players, probably by adding a second sackbut player, their names being recorded as Anthuenis Pavillon, Jan van der Schuere, Anthuenis van der Beke, Jan Fauset, and Willemaert himself. That same year, Pavillon was sent to Antwerp 'to find a trumpet', the city bought five trumpets for the band, and Willemaert was paid for teaching a boy 'to master the art of the trumpet'. Doubling was a cheap way for the city to have a shawm/ sackbut band and a trumpet band. That at least four of these minstrels also played the recorder had already been confirmed the year before, 1481–82, when the city bought 'a case with recorders (*fleuten*)' for their use.[201] But as we have seen, one member was already dealing in recorders, so presumably he and probably others had previously used their own instruments with the band, or else the city's were being replaced.

In 1485–86, on the city's behalf, Pavillon and Willemaert began teaching the recorder in their own homes to four 'youngsters'.[202] When Willemaert died about a year later, Pavillon continued teaching two of the boys for at least two more years. This arrangement is puzzling, since only recorders are mentioned. A normal apprenticeship would have also included shawms and sackbuts, perhaps also trumpets. Since the boys were housed in the minstrels' homes, the most likely explanation is that they had full apprenticeships and 'recorders' was shorthand for 'wind instruments'. The only recorder maker we know of from that city after Willay (1426) and perhaps Chapuis (1443) is Jean van Pilchem, *fleutmaker*, mentioned in a document from 1541.[203]

The Bruges minstrels generally played outside or facing the outdoors: in processions, in the market square, as well as in front of the town hall and from its windows or belfry. These locations were less suitable for recorders. But we know that the Bruges minstrels also played indoors. They joined in dances at the Burgundian court: 'open' balls in the palace, when townswomen were invited to participate, and balls in the reception room of the new town hall. They played for banquets to entertain prominent visitors during the May Fair. For the citizens, they also did freelance work, such as playing at weddings. The necessity of such outside sources of income is implied by a vote of the city council during the war years of 1480 and 1481 to give the musicians an additional sum of money because they had 'little or nothing to do because of the sober times that now rule'.

Beginning in 1481, the city instituted *Salve* or *lof* ('praise') concerts in honour of the Virgin Mary in St Donatian's church every day of the year, performed by the succentor and choirboys with the organ.[204] Two years later, in May 1483, just after the city bought an official set of recorders for the minstrels, the city paid them to perform instrumental music inside the church after the singing in the *Salve* concerts, to entertain the populace and visitors on market days.[205] As for the repertoire, in 1484–85 Nicasius de Brauwere, master of the choirboys at St Saviour's church, was paid for writing a set of motets for the use of the 'minstrels of this city'.[206] Strohm writes that the minstrels' concerts in St Donatian's 'were held in honour of the Virgin, and one has to assume that the minstrels played sacred works . . . especially the *Salve regina* and other Marian pieces, or sections from Masses that were suitable for instrumental performance'.[207] He goes on to suggest that the celebrated Jacob Obrecht (1457/8–1505), who became master of the choirboys of St Donatian's in 1485, composed for these concerts, including such surviving secular works as *T'Andernaken*, 'a cantus firmus setting of the well-known tune, which appears in the tenor in very long notes, while the other two voices spin an elaborate counterpoint around it'.[208]

Recorder teaching is mentioned in another Flemish city. In 1492, the Ghent town archives noted that: 'Janne and Willem van Welsens, brothers, have come before the town officials and have obligated themselves to Josse Zoetink for the sum of £28 gr . . . and this for the knowledge, effort, and teaching to be done by the said Josse in daily instruction in the art of shawm playing, recorder playing, and other things . . .'.[209] Zoetink was a town minstrel in Ghent. The Van Welsens brothers were hired by the town of Tournai two years later, but by 1496 had moved on to Bergen op Zoom.[210] All these cities were under the control of Burgundy until 1477, after which effective leadership fell to Maximilian I and the House of Habsburg.

ICONOGRAPHY[211]

The recorder's iconography – its presence, symbolism, and associations in works of art – has been studied extensively by Rowland-Jones, Lander, and others. We may be tempted to take works of art as literal, almost photographic records, showing us reality 'as it was' (not taking into consideration how regularly photographs have been retouched, airbrushed, or Photoshopped since their invention). But in all eras artists have their own interpretive and symbolic reasons for depicting musical instruments, and we can only make educated guesses at their mindset. We should never assume that artists were even attempting to reproduce real instruments they had observed closely, except perhaps when the level of detail would have been unnecessary otherwise. Is that black dot a finger-hole? Is that blur a window with ramp? Such questions are compounded by reproductions of artworks, which display varying degrees of resolution, and even access to the original is no guarantee of 'authenticity': physical deterioration over the centuries, and 'restorations' by later generations, increase the difficulty of determining and separating layers of interpretation. For example, Pere Serra's *Virgin of the Angels*, one of the most important paintings in recorder history, has been subject to crude restoration, resulting in some vital features observed before restoration now being obscured.[212]

The main criteria for distinguishing a recorder from other woodwind instruments are: a window and ramp; seven finger-holes and a thumb-hole shown or implied; the lowest finger-hole perhaps doubled; the finger-holes spread along most of the body of the instrument (on shawms they are higher); and no reed, staple, or pirouette (to indicate a shawm). Since we know nothing about medieval hand and finger positions, or whether or not cheeks were puffed in recorder playing, we cannot conclude anything from their depiction. We must also bear in mind that the external profile of a recorder does not always reflect its bore, which affects the tone colour, range, and fingerings.[213] All in all, the iconography of duct flutes, and especially the recorder, is a minefield for the unwary. So let us proceed with caution, suspending our assumptions as best we can.

Representations suggestive of the recorder begin in the early fourteenth century. The earliest and most conclusive belongs to a fresco in the Church of St George in Staro Nagoričane, a village near Kumanova in the Republic of Macedonia, reconstructed by the Serbian king Stefan Uroš II Milutin between 1313 and 1318. Frescoes were painted by Mihailo and Evtihij (Michael Astrapas and Eutychios) from Thessaloniki in neighbouring Greece, starting in 1315. *Ecce Homo: The Mocking of Jesus* depicts a performance reminiscent of 'the actors' odious theatre', described by the Serbian monk Teodosije as being performed on the streets, where 'people gathered, regardless of the weather, watched and listened insanely to harmful devilish songs and indecent, rude words all the way to the end'.[214] Christ is tormented by a crew of evil-looking musicians: two blow enormous curved trumpets, one holds a huge snare drum, and a youth with a sly grin plays a cylindrical duct flute, inclined slightly downwards. The detail of the lashings, snare, and beater of the drum looks highly realistic. The duct flute appears to have three holes for the upper (right) hand and four holes for the lower hand. The lowest hole is single, and there may also be a small tuning hole towards the end of the instrument. Lander comments: 'Although the thumb of the player's uppermost hand is held awkwardly at the side of the instrument, his purpose here is to create noise rather than music.' This instrument looks as much like a recorder as most portrayals from the fourteenth and fifteenth centuries.

A couple of recorder-like instruments were depicted in Italy in the 1330s. A fresco of *St Francis in Glory* (ca. 1334), from the school of Giotto di Bondone, portrays the saint enthroned and surrounded by a throng of angels, a few playing musical instruments – four trumpets and two short duct flutes with flared bells. As Lander has pointed out, 'Although the pipes could be small shawms, the players' fingers are deployed perfectly for recorder playing, with all four fingers of their lowermost hands covering their holes.'[215] Bernardo Daddi's painted panel *Annunciation and Nativity* from his *Polyptych of San Pancrazio* (1336–38) features more musical angels, two of whom play alto-sized, flared-bell duct flutes with puffed cheeks. Again, the playing position would be suitable for recorders.

Three duct flutes, two long and one short, appear in *Coronation of the Virgin* by the Venetian painter Stefano Veneziano (1381) in the company of singers, fiddle, gittern, lute, portative organs, and psaltery. Rowland-Jones observes that 'One of the pipes has nine finger-holes, another thirteen; a third . . . has six holes with all fingers down and a seventh for the little finger of the lowermost (left) hand. These instruments could be the artist's attempt to represent recorders.'

Of the 315 works of art from Aragón before 1500 with musical subject-matter studied by Jordi Ballester, 27 include representations of duct flutes.[216] Rowland-Jones comments: 'While this is not a large part of the whole, in comparison with the scattered distribution of examples elsewhere in Europe it is exceptional.'[217]

Coinciding with the reference to *flahutes* in Aragón in 1378, two similar works of art attributed to the Aragonese painter Pere Serra (fl. 1357–1405) clearly depict recorders.[218] Their exact dating, however, is less clear. Only two works are securely documented as by him, both bearing dates (1394 and 1395), but neither contain duct flutes; all other attributions and dates by art historians are based on stylistic considerations.[219] Que Serra sera!

The central panel of the altarpiece *Virgin of the Angels*, painted around 1385 for the monastery of Sant Cugat del Vallès, now a suburb of Barcelona, shows the Virgin Mary with the infant Jesus on her knee, surrounded by six angels playing harp, lute, gitttern, organetto, psaltery, and recorder.[220] The cylindrical recorder has eight finger-holes in line higher up the instrument than the whole of the player's lower (left) hand, below which one of the paired finger-holes for the little finger is visible.

A similarly posed group, playing the same six instruments, is depicted in an altarpiece for the cathedral of Santa Clara, Tortosa, formerly dated ca. 1385 but now thought to have been painted as late as 1400.[221] The wide-profile duct flute seems to narrow gradually throughout its length, like the Tartu recorder, although that could be a product of the attempt at perspective. The walls are unnaturally thin. The window is square, with a long, thin ramp. The instrument is slightly tilted towards the viewer, as if to display it better. The right hole of the doubled seventh hole is painted black, presumably to suggest plugging with wax or some

6. Pere Serra, *Virgin of the Angels* (detail), ca. 1385.

other material. It looks as if three attempts had been made above the fourth finger-hole at boring the hole then filling it in, perhaps to tune ♯IV more accurately or even to experiment with a doubled hole for ♭IV and ♯IV.[222] The instrument has a pair of incised rings towards the end.

The Real Monasterio de Nuestra Señora de Guadelupe (Royal Monastery of Our Lady) in Extremadura, Spain, has two doors inscribed 'Paulus de Collonia' and 'Alleman fecit', implying a German craftsman. The portals are decorated with bronze reliefs that include probable recorders. In *Coronation of the Virgin*, angel musicians once more play fiddle, harp, lute, organetto, and a duct flute with a flared bell. All four fingers of both hands are placed on the instrument. In *Nativity*, a shepherd grasps a flared-bell duct flute in one hand, below which four finger-holes are clearly visible as well as two indentations that may indicate paired holes for the little finger of the lower hand. Rowland-Jones writes: 'The bronze doors were installed at the end of the 14th century, possibly around 1389, the date given for the completion of the increasingly lavish monastery church, after which attention moved to building the cloister (1389–1405). The doors, possibly ordered from Cologne, could have been a final sumptuous finish to the façade of the church.'[223]

More securely dated (1391–92), but less clearly depicted, is a cylindrical duct flute in another Aragonese *Virgin of the Angels*, this time by Enrique de Estencop (fl. 1387–1400), from the church of Longares, near Zaragoza.[224] Again the angels also play gittern, harp, and psaltery. The window and ramp of the duct flute are shown side-on, and the little finger of the lower (left) hand is raised, strongly suggesting a recorder. As in the Serra examples, the instrument has two incised rings near the end. More importantly, the window cut-up lacks side walls. Five other cylindrical recorders appear in paintings by Jaume Cabrera and Pere Vall around 1400, in the company of fiddle, gittern, harp, and lute, as well as singers.

The earliest probable depiction of a recorder in France can be dated ca. 1390–1408.[225] It is found in two sheets with music held at Windsor Castle, England, separated from a missal now in the Biblioteca Casanatense, Rome. 'The illustrator is thought to have been an unknown miniaturist from the Duchy of Guelders, of which Nijmegen was the capital. The missal originally belonged to Jean d'Armagnac, archbishop of Nemours and great-grandson of Jean, Duke of Berry. One of the Windsor sheets is a Majestas (Christ in a mandorla enthroned with depictions of the four Evangelists) bordered by sixteen musical angels. The second angel down on the right plays what is almost certainly a recorder of soprano/alto size. . . .'[226] The profile is cylindrical.

Thus in the fourteenth century, recorders, or probable recorders, are generally depicted as played by angels alongside other *bas* instruments. Two structural types – cylindrical and flared-bell – can be observed, in alto, tenor, and perhaps soprano sizes. The paired finger-holes for the little finger of the lower hand are often shown, once even filled.

In the early fifteenth century, depictions of recorders become more plentiful and less ambiguous in several western European countries. Let us look at those cases that shed some light on the physical characteristics, sizes, and symbolism of the instrument.

The Master of Fonollosa's *Virgin and Child* (1410) 'probably shows for the first time two recorders of different sizes (soprano and tenor) participating in a purely instrumental group' (with fiddle and harp).[227] Two other Aragonese works of art include medium-sized recorders, presumably altos: Ramón de Mur's *Virgin Suckling the Child* (ca. 1415–25) and the Master of La Secuita's *Altarpiece of the Virgin* (1425–40). Rowland-Jones writes that 'On the evidence of the [Aragonese] altarpieces, a [soprano], alto and tenor recorder trio corresponding in voice-ranges to a vocal trio would have been in place by 1410.'[228] His own evidence, however, suggests 1425 as a more secure date. The angels in Miquel Nadal's altarpiece for Barcelona Cathedral (1453–55) play rebec, lute, and harp, along with three recorders: tenor and either two altos or an alto and a soprano.[229]

The first (virtually) secure depiction of a recorder in England comes from the Priory Church in Christchurch, Dorset (ca. 1400): a carved stone corbel (a supporting projection jutting out from a wall) of an angel sitting in a boat playing what may be a cylindrical tenor recorder with a slightly flared bell. The hands are drawn away, as if to show viewers that the instrument is the new recorder rather than a *flageol*. At the Burgundian court, a painted miniature of a banquet before the hunt from the studio of the Master of Bedford illustrates the *Livre de la chasse* by Gaston Phoebus (dated 1405–15). A man by one of the tables plays a cylindrical recorder.

Although the surviving medieval recorders, and several fourteenth-century depictions of duct flutes, come from German-speaking lands or their immediate surroundings, obvious recorders are not shown until the second half of the fifteenth century. In one particularly fine painting by the Master of the Lyversberg Passion (ca. 1463), angels play three small recorders on one side, while other angels play three shawms and a proto-sackbut on the other side, accompanied by a variety of bowed and plucked strings.

Most of the fifteenth-century works of art depicting recorders show them played by angels, but a significant minority are placed in the hands of shepherds. In fact, the first illustration of a recorder in Flanders, in a book of hours that probably came from Bruges or Ghent (ca. 1440), shows a shepherd. Two remarkable series of book illuminations of shepherds from Bruges were painted by the Master of the *Vraie cronicque descoce*, believed to have been a follower of the celebrated Willem Vrelant (fl. 1449–81), for Virgil's *Eclogues* and *Georgics*. The shepherds Corydon, Dametas, Menalcas, Mopsus, and Thyrsis as well as anonymous bystanders have plentiful recorders suspended from their waists in bags and slings, pick up a recorder to make a point in a discussion, play recorders sitting on the grass or a rocky ledge, and engage in recorder-playing contests standing up. All the instruments are cylindrical, apparently alto-sized, with a plain profile. In *Farmers and their Livestock*, the recorder reinforces, perhaps intentionally, that some of the pigs and horses are copulating. A later series of illuminations for Virgil's *Eclogues* from France (1469) shows shepherds playing or holding alto- and tenor-sized recorders with a flared bell and a small tuning hole above the foot. In both series, the recorder is a contemporaneous substitute for the Roman *tibia*.

Surprisingly few minstrels are depicted playing recorders. The most significant are those found in the Breviary of Duke René II of Lorraine (ca. 1490), who later in life also became king of Naples and Jerusalem. One folio portrays him copying the Psalms, surrounded by people playing musical instruments. In the background three minstrels play trumpet, probably vihuela de arco, and drum. Seated with the king, a man wearing a crown, apparently representing the author of some of the Psalms, the biblical King David, plays a harp. In the foreground, a group of three well-dressed women, presumably courtiers, play hammered dulcimer, portative organ, and recorder; the recorder player wears an elaborate headpiece. Her instrument is of tenor size, with a flared bell. We have other evidence that well-born women learned *bas* instruments.[230] Another folio in the Breviary shows minstrels standing in a hall, playing together on a mixed group of sigmoid horn, two trumpets, vihuela de arco, harp, hammered dulcimer, and two recorders: apparently alto (partially hidden) and tenor with a slightly flared bell.

A reliquary of gilded silver from Girona depicts two angels playing what seem to be a tenor recorder and a basset recorder (with bocal).[231] The base of the reliquary bears the coat of arms belonging to Bishop Berenguer de Pau, who supervised the see of Girona between 1486 and 1506.[232] This leeway in the dating notwithstanding, it seems likely that the basset had been developed by about 1500, a little before being discussed by Virdung (1511).

How well do iconographical representations of recorders match surviving examples? A duct flute with a beak reminiscent of the Göttingen recorder – except that the profile is conical rather than obconical – appears in a stone carving from the cathedral in Bamberg from as early as ca. 1230. Four recorders in works of art resemble the Dordrecht recorder. The instrument we have mentioned as being played by a shepherd in a book of hours from Flanders (ca. 1440) has a cylindrical profile with elongated window and ramp. The man seems to be stopping the end with his right hand, a practice described by Girolamo Cardano in the following century. The cheek of an oak choir-stall from a Spanish cathedral (1445–79), carved by Francisco Gomar, depicts a recorder with a beaded foot. Two late fifteenth-century illuminations of Martin le Franc's *Le Champion des dames* show cylindrical recorders with beaded and flared feet, suggestive of mortise-and-tenon construction. One of the recorders is played by a girl sitting next to a pool while Freethinker and Evil Tongue argue about her virtue – presumably a commentary on females with phallic objects in their mouths.

In medieval astrology, the 'children of Venus' were born in April under the influence of the goddess, protector of courtship, love, marriage, and fecundity. They were said to be pleasing, cheerful, erotic, and pleasure-loving, and they play musical instruments, sing, and dance.[233] Three works of art from the late fifteenth century depicting Venus and her children show them playing instruments including the recorder, bathing outdoors, and cuddling.[234]

Francesco del Cossa's fresco *April, or the Triumph of Venus* (1470), probably the best-known fifteenth-century painting containing the recorder, belongs in the same category.[235] Venus arrives on a barge with Mars kneeling at her feet. The three Graces stand naked on a knoll in the background. On the bank side, rabbits abound, and fourteen people, mostly dressed like courtiers, stand or kneel in a group. A couple must be about to get married, because the man wears a coronet of myrtle, a token of conjugal fidelity; and the woman holds a lute, a symbol of fecundity. In the front, in a less sanctioned display, a young man kissing a woman slips his hand between her unlaced skirts. In the background, a questioning man stands behind two women, one holding a lute. The other woman, who because of her dress is probably intended to be a nymph or a Muse such as Euterpe,[236] grasps a pair of recorders, one slightly longer than the other, around their middle in her right hand. Both recorders have a cylindrical profile, perhaps contracting in the middle (hard to tell with the woman's hand in the way), definitely leading to a flared bell. The window lacks sidewalls, in the manner of an organ pipe. Researchers have suggested that the recorders in a woman's hand both represent an ancient double pipe and symbolize amorous union.[237] In a painting so rife with sexuality, they may just be phallic symbols. Less well-known, the companion fresco *May, or the Triumph of Apollo* depicts the god in the underworld playing a longer cylindrical recorder with a flared bell.

The Recorder Home Page: Iconography (*RHPI*) documents more than 300 depictions of the recorder in surviving fifteenth-century works of art. On forty-five occasions, the instrument appears alone. A pair of recorders, whether by themselves or with other instruments, is shown nineteen times. A trio of recorders is rarer: six times with other instruments, once alone (in Lippo d'Andrea's *Coronation of the Virgin*, early fifteenth century). In mixed ensembles, certain other *bas* instruments occur frequently with the recorder or ambiguous duct flute: lute or guitar or vihuela (92 times), harp (55), fiddle (46), some kind of organ (32), percussion (29), psaltery (23), rebec (17), and gittern (12). The sheer weight of numbers strongly suggests that the artists made this association based on some observation of contemporaneous practice, not just copying other paintings, and that recorders were played with other *bas* instruments in the fifteenth century far more often than by themselves or with each other. Yet *haut* instruments such as trumpet (18 times), shawm (16), and pipe and tabor (7) also come into the picture. Singers are depicted often (44 times).

The recorder or ambiguous duct flute is sometimes accompanied by another single instrument: fiddle, harp, organ, rebec, and tambourine. Combinations with two *bas* instruments are also common: harp and lute, fiddle and lute, lute and organ, lute and guitar, fiddle and harp, gittern and rebec, lute and psaltery, lute and rebec (as in Siena, 1468), lute and viol, lute and viola da braccio, and organ and lute. And finally, there are frequent combinations with three *bas* instruments, notably fiddle, harp, and lute; harp, lute, and rebec; and harp, lute, and psaltery. Not only was the lute by far the most frequent accompanist, recorder or ambiguous duct flute are depicted with lute alone in sixteen works of art. The players are angels, putti, or a child. Recall that the pairing of recorder and lute was also mentioned in Octavien de Saint Gelais's *Le séjour d'honneur* (1490).

A recorder with the lowest finger-hole doubled can be played readily with either left or right hand uppermost, because the holes accommodate the natural shortness of the little finger. Yet it seems that even when the lowest hole was single and even in a straight line with the other holes, small recorders could be played

7. Three recorders built into the corner pillar of the Maison des Trois Flûtes, a house built around 1490 in Bourges, France, now a pâtisserie.

with either hand uppermost. In artworks reproduced on *RHPI* for both recorders and other duct flutes, in the fourteenth century the positions are depicted about equally. In the fifteenth century the positions are about equal for recorders, but about 50 per cent more with the right hand uppermost for other duct flutes. Most of these instruments are of soprano or alto size. A couple of tenor recorders have a different feature to accommodate the little finger: the lowest hole is offset.

Perhaps the most monumental depiction of recorders is literally built into the corner pillar of a house dating from around 1490 in Bourges, France, now a patisserie: the pillar consists of three enormous cylindrical recorders, including the paired holes for the lowest finger.

WHEN AND WHERE WAS THE RECORDER DEVELOPED?

In sum, we have no evidence for duct flutes with holes for seven fingers and thumb before the early fourteenth century, although the individual elements were present as early as the tenth century.

Recorders of type-S (with a semitone as the lowest interval) from the fourteenth–fifteenth centuries have been found in Estonia, Germany, and Poland. Their bores are reportedly of three main types: cylindrical; cylindrical then contracting; or contracting then expanding. We have only the imprecisely dated Copenhagen recorder as physical evidence for the development of type-T (with a whole tone as the lowest interval) prior to Virdung in 1511, although the sets of four recorders that became common at courts and in cities of western Europe from 1408 onwards are suggestive of polyphony that would have benefited from this type.

Aside from the kind of soft duct flute sometimes played together with fiddles described by Konrad of Megenberg, writing in Paris around 1350, the first plausible references to the recorder come from Aragón (1378), Germany (1386–87), England (1388), and France (1416). Apart from a fresco in Macedonia, painted in 1315–18, which includes a probable recorder, the first clear depictions stem from Aragón, starting around the 1380s. Works of art from the fourteenth and early fifteenth centuries already show both cylindrical and obconical recorders, and ambiguous duct flutes as well as cylindrical instruments with flared bells. The annual minstrel schools, held mostly in Flanders, and extensive international contacts among the monarchy and higher nobility, would have helped to spread new instruments quickly within western Europe.

Such diverse evidence should deter those seeking simple explanations. As Lander has said: 'If we are to speculate, could it not be that the recorder family is polyphyletic [derived from more than one common evolutionary ancestor or ancestral group] rather than monophyletic [descended from a common evolutionary ancestor or ancestral group], that it emerged at a variety of different times, in a number of places, in a variety of forms, each of which underwent subsequent development and modification?'[238]

2

THE ERA OF RENAISSANCE RECORDERS, 1501–1667

DAVID LASOCKI

If the fourteenth and fifteenth centuries left us little certain information about the recorder, after the turn of the sixteenth century, the floodgates open wide for evidence of all kinds. Between 1501 and 1667, whether we are considering treatises, inventories, purchases, pay records, contracts, iconography, literature, sacred and secular music, or surviving instruments, we find signs everywhere of what has been called a Golden Age for the recorder.[1] Throughout Europe, spilling over into Spanish and Portuguese colonies in America, Africa, and Asia, the recorder was played frequently by professionals working for royal and ducal courts, towns and cities, prominent citizens, associations, cathedrals and churches, schools, theatres, and academies. It was enjoyed by amateurs of all social classes and served in music instruction for children. Accomplished makers constructed instruments in up to eight different sizes, mainly played in consorts: the recorder could therefore be employed in more registers than any other wind instrument. As well as being depicted, often symbolically, in works of art by the greatest masters, it was even cited three times by Shakespeare. The present chapter considers the era from mid-Renaissance to mid-Baroque as a unit, because the same three basic types of recorder were made throughout.

NAMES[2]

Fairly consistent terms had been established in several languages by the sixteenth century. A set of *recorders* was bought for the 'Sackbuts' at the English court in 1501 and a consort of players entitled 'Recorders' existed there from 1540 to 1630.[3] Yet the only evidence verifying the recorder's nature in England before 1679 remains Palsgrave's English–French dictionary, *Lesclarcissement* (1530), which equates it with the unambiguous French *fleute a neuf trous*. By this time only the transverse flute was called *flute* (inventory, Westminster, 1542).

Pipe could mean recorder and other members of the flute family, bagpipe, or shawm. Palsgrave gives a double definition of 'Recorder[,] a pype', also translating 'Pype [or] to pype with' as *fleuste*, a standard French verb for the recorder. John Baret's *An Alvearie or Triple Dictionarie* (1574) has entries for 'flute or pipe' and 'pipe', but not 'recorder'; nevertheless, it translates the Latin *inflare tibias* as 'To blow a pipe or recorder.' Shakespeare famously played – with words – on 'pipe' and 'recorder' in *Hamlet* (1599–1601).

The principal designation in other languages was a cognate of 'flute'. In French, *fleute* or *fleuste* was retained but also shifted its spelling to *flute* or *fluste* (*Livre plaisant*, 1529). Although *flute d'Allemagne* was used to distinguish transverse flute and recorder, as in Queen Mary of Hungary's inventory (Brussels, 1535), terms were inconsistent: *fleutte* refers to the transverse flute in a Swiss fingering chart (1536).[4]

In Italian, *flauto* continued from the fifteenth century into the eighteenth. The Este archives in Florence (1530) include a request to purchase 'a case or set of flutes (*Flauti alemani*) that are played in the middle of the flute (*flauto*) and not in the head, as we play ours', contrasting flutes and recorders.[5] The variant *frauti* was juxtaposed with *traverʒi* in Naples (1592).[6] Transverse flutes were also called *faifer* (Verona, 1548), *fifari* (Venice, 1557), *traverse* (Florence, 1564), *flauti traversi* (Siena, 1573), or *piffari* (Verona, 1593).

In Dutch, *floyt* (Mechelen, 1502–03) yielded to *fluyt* (Oudenaarde, 1531) or *fluut* (Oudenaarde, 1536–37). *Handflueten* (Bruges, 1543–44) or *handtfluiten* (Oudenaarde, 1567) must have been an alternative general name for recorders, as they came in a *cokere* (case) of twelve or *accord* (set) of eight, respectively. *Handtpipen* are mentioned in an apprenticeship contract in Utrecht (1561).[7] Scholars have assumed that *hand-fluit*, mentioned in Dutch music and instructions of the 1640s, referred only to the soprano recorder, but the term could still have been general. As in English, *piepen* (Leeuwarden, 1640) could mean recorders, contrasted with *dwarspipen*, flutes.

Besides an early instance of *flötenpfeyffen*, flute pipes (Nuremberg, 1512), the German language generally adopted *Flöte* (Virdung, 1511), found in archival records in variants including *flötte*, *Flött*, *Flöde*, *Floite*, *flöute*,[8] and *fleutte*, as well as the diminutive *Fleuttl*. The western part of Germany favoured a different vowel – *fleiten* (Cologne, 1519), *fleden* (Augsburg, 1540), *fletten* (Augsburg, 1566), *Fledten* (Karlsruhe, 1582), or *fläthen* (Stuttgart, 1589) – and yet another variant turns up in Austria and Switzerland: *Flauten* (Innsbruck, 1596; Basel, 1614). *Flutten*

(Dresden, 1629) sounds close to French and Dutch. *Handt flöten*, the equivalent of the Dutch *handfluiten*, appears once (Berlin, 1582). *Schlossflöten* (Neisse, 1625) signified keyed recorders. The transverse flute or fife, in contrast, was called *schwegel* (Cologne, 1519), *Querpfeif* (Leipzig, 1538), *zwerchpfeyff* (Nuremberg, 1539), or *Querflöte* (Naumburg, 1658). We also know two Slavic terms for the recorder: *Fletný* (Český Krumlov, 1599) and *fletów* (Kraków, 1599).

In Spanish, *flauta* had a range more like 'pipe' in English. In dictionaries, *flautas* are defined as several possible members of the flute family, the tubes of certain other woodwind instruments, and organ pipes.[9] Sometimes the term clearly meant recorder, as in Mary of Hungary's inventory (1558), contrasted with *pifano*, meaning flute or fife. *Flauta* could also refer to the transverse flute, as in the inventory of Don Íñigo López de Mendoza (1566), where the seven *flautas* from Flanders, one of them a *jabeva* (*xabeba*, Moorish flute), correlate with the seven *pifaros* in the collection of his son, Don Diego Hurtado de Mendoza (1560), who predeceased him.[10] In the Spanish colonies, *flauta* overwhelmingly meant recorder (Tlaxcala, New Spain, 1538).[11]

In Portuguese, *flauta* is first documented as tabor pipe at the court (1525), but *frauta* clearly means recorder at Braga Cathedral in 1538 and in Brazilian sources from 1552, sometimes replaced by *flauta*.[12] Brazilian sources in Latin between 1573 and 1741 use the terms *fistulis*, *tibiae*, *tibiarae*, *tibijs*, *tibias*, and their players, *tibicines* and *tibicinij*, whereas Cardano in Milan around 1546 preferred *elyma*.

The basic designation for recorder was sometimes clarified by a qualifying adjective, phrase, or prefix. As already mentioned, the French *fluste a neuf trouz* (nine-holed flute) is found in Palsgrave (1530), then the title pages of Pierre Attaingnant's chanson collections (Paris, 1533), Philibert Jambe de Fer's *Epitome musical* (Lyons, 1556), and as late as Marin Mersenne's *Harmonie universelle* (Paris, 1636), which adds two other terms. Jambe de Fer adjudges the name 'a bit silly', since one of the two lowest holes must be stopped.[13] The Spanish equivalent, *flauta de nueve puntos*, is also found (Burgos, 1548).[14] The Latin edition of Mersenne's treatise (1635) mentions both eight and nine holes: *Fistula octo foraminum*, *Fistula novendum foraminum*.

The modern German word *Blockflöte*, block flute, also spelt *Plockflöte*, is documented first by Michael Praetorius (*Syntagma musicum*, II, 1619), although the prefix is found in Dutch earlier in an inventory (Leeuwarden, 1600): *blokpijpen*, block pipes. The vertical orientation is implied in the Italian *flauto diritto*, straight flute (letter from Giovanni Alvise [Alvise Zorzi], 1505).[15] An Italian association appears in one inventory during this period: *flauti all'italiana*, Italian-style flutes (Siena, 1547). Jambe de Fer proposes 'there would be no harm or danger' in the name *fleute d'Italien* (Italian flute) or the Italian name *flauto*, because of the 'delight' the Italians take in playing the instrument. An association with England is found twice in France: *litui Anglicani* (Jesuit School, Saint-Omer, first decade of the seventeenth century)[16] and Mersenne's unique term *fluste d'Angleterre* (1636), or *Fistula Anglica* in the Latin edition (1635), probably reflecting the instruments made by the English branch of the Bassano family.

Jean-Baptiste du Val, working in Venice in 1607, used *fleustes douces* for the recorders he heard in church.[17] *Douce* can mean both sweet and soft, but Mersenne clarifies that 'These *flustes* are called *douces* because of the sweetness of their sounds, which portray the charm and the sweetness of the voice.'[18] Later he puts it that 'the sound of these *flustes* is judged so sweet by some people that it merits the name of charming and ravishing', although he believes that this manner of speaking should apply only to the pleasures of Heaven.[19] His Latin edition calls the instrument *Fistula dulcis*.

SIZES, CONSORTS, AND PITCHES[20]

Virdung's *Musica getutscht* (1511), the first published treatise to discuss the recorder in detail, depicts the *Baßcontra* or *Bassus* recorder in F (with a fontanelle, a cover made of perforated wood or metal to protect a key), *Tenor* in C, and *Discant* in G, emphasizing they are a fifth apart. (*Discant* should not be confused with *descant*, the modern British term for recorder in c^2.) His recorders sound at 4′ pitch, an octave higher than notated (F^0, c^0, g^0). As Praetorius (1619) explains, recorders can confuse the ear into believing they sound an octave lower – presumably why they were commonly notated that way.[21] *Bassus* is short for *contratenor bassus*, so for Virdung *bass* and *contrabass* are interchangeable, although the usual meaning of *contrabass* gradually changed over the sixteenth century and early seventeenth from bass to an octave below the bass. Virdung states that a consort (*coppel*) of recorders was made up of two *Bassus*, two *Tenor*, and two *Discant*; a quartet, of *Bassus*, two *Tenor*, and *Discant*, or else *Bassus*, *Tenor*, and two *Discant*, depending on the range of the alto part (*contratenor altus*).

Martin Agricola's *Musica instrumentalis deudsch* (1529; 2nd edn, 1545) depicts the same three sizes, calling them *Bassus*, *Tenor* or *Altus*, and *Discantus*. Jambe de Fer's *Epitome musical* (1556) spells out that the same size of recorder plays both tenor and alto parts.[22] He calls his sizes *bas*, *taille* or *haute contre*, and *dessus*. The same three sizes of recorder – *basso*, *tenore*, and *canto* or *sopran* – are mentioned in the Italian treatises, Ganassi (1535), Cardano (ca. 1546), and Lodovico Zacconi (1596), and likewise *Baxo*, *tenor*, *tiple* in Spanish, Pietro Cerone (*El melopeo y maestro*, Naples, 1613). Cardano also discusses a 'high' (*altiore*) recorder in D.

The names and ranges of the F, C, and G sizes in the treatises before Praetorius mimic the four parts in vocal polyphony. Most wind repertoire consisted of vocal pieces, read off the vocal part-books. Therefore, the typical four-part polyphony of the earlier sixteenth century could be played on bass, two tenors, and alto. Let us abbreviate this schema of fundamental pitches as FCCG (from low to high). If a piece called for more than four parts, the additional ones tended to duplicate the ranges of other voices, leading to combinations such as FCCCG or FCCCGG.

Renaissance composers used a number of clef combinations. In the 'natural' clefs, *chiavi naturali* (F4–C4–C3–C1 = bass, tenor, alto, and soprano clefs), the total range of the piece was covered by the FCCG combination, which played the vocal parts as written. But depending on the mode of the original chant on which the piece was based, among other reasons, pieces were sometimes notated in another clef combination later called *chiavette*, literally 'small clefs', more commonly called 'high clefs' (F3/C4–C3–C2–G2 = baritone or tenor, alto, mezzo-soprano, and treble clefs). These clefs placed the compositions in a higher range, too high for our FCCG combination as well as for the (male) singers of the day. Therefore, all the parts were transposed down either a fourth (one flat in the signature) or a fifth (no signature).[23]

From surviving treatises, with the exception of Cardano, we could gain the impression that only *Bassus* in f[0], *Tenor* in c[1], and *Discant* in g[1] existed in the sixteenth century. In contrast, Praetorius (1619) describes a *ganz Stimmwerck* or *Accort* (whole consort) consisting of no fewer than twenty-one recorders, which could be bought in Venice: one *Groß-baß* in F[0], two *Baß* in Bb[0], four *Basset* in f[0], four *Tenor* in c[1], four *Alt* in g[1], two *Discant* in c[2], two *Discant* in d[2], and two *Klein Flöttlin* or *Exilent* in g[2].[24] These instruments are now notated at sounding pitch and the names have been adjusted to accommodate the wide range of sizes. Although we could deduce that the additional sizes were recent innovations, both sixteenth-century inventories and surviving recorders prove they were already current much earlier.

In 1520, an inventory at the Medici court in Florence listed: 'three new large recorders for the bass (*contrabasso*) part'.[25] 'Large' is a relative term, but the next references are unambiguous. Among the recorders bought in Augsburg in 1535 by the celebrated wind player Wolff Gans for Mary of Hungary's court in Brussels was 'one for the bass (*contrebas*) part the height of a man'.[26] The same recorder appears as the lowest member of a consort in Queen Mary's inventory in 1559: 'four recorders, one very large about three *baras* in length, and the others each decreasingly smaller'.[27] One *bara* equalled 83.52 cm (33 in), so this recorder was about 2.5 m (8 ft 2 in) long, the height of the very tallest of men.

We also know from surviving instruments that the largest recorders were sometimes extended in length to produce two or three extra notes. Those instruments with two extended notes (Rome, Verona, and St Petersburg) have two extra keys on the back, operated by the lower thumb, to give the semitone and minor third below the normal lowest note (all holes closed). Other instruments with three extended notes (Antwerp and Munich) have a double key on the front, to give the all-holes-closed note as well as the first extended note, a semitone below, and a double key on the back to give the further notes, a minor third and a fourth below all fingers closed. A surviving extended recorder by Hans Rauch von Schratt is 2.433 m (about 8 ft) long.[28] A surviving basset by him bears the date 1535.[29] So Mary's consort would presumably have consisted, using Praetorius's terms, of extended great bass, extended bass, basset, and tenor sizes. Two similar large instruments are listed among the late Felipe II of Spain's instruments in 1602: 'A very large bass. . . . It is a contrabass (*contravajo*) of recorders', along with a merely 'large' instrument that acts as a 'tenor to the large recorders'.[30] The number of recorders in Praetorius's whole consort was close to twenty-two, the figure given for a set the Accademia Filarmonica in Verona bought in 1548; remarkably, the seven instruments that have survived from that set do correspond in size and number to the lowest: great bass in F^0, two basses in Bb^0, and four bassets in f^0.[31]

To describe the sizes unambiguously, for the rest of this chapter we employ the terms used by Adrian Brown, a leading maker of Renaissance recorders today, based on Praetorius's terms. See Table 2.

In late sixteenth-century instrumental music, which often had a larger overall compass, a fourth size of recorder would be called upon, generally the soprano in D, giving us the variant schema FCGD. Praetorius describes this practice and gives suggestions on how to deal practically with the three extra sharps that the highest instrument effectively adds compared with the bass part.[32] He even mentions a fifth size in various families of instruments, which he says makes the music difficult to play, although it could work 'if the composition is accommodated to it'.[33]

Table 2. Names from Praetorius and Adrian Brown for sizes of Renaissance recorder

SL = speaking length; > = greater than; < = less than

Lowest note	F⁰	B♭⁰	f⁰	c¹	g¹	c²	d²	g²
Adrian Brown's names and descriptions	great bass (keyed, with crook, SL >140 cm)	bass (keyed, with crook, SL <140 cm)	basset (keyed, without crook)	tenor (no key, SL >45 cm)	alto (SL 32–45 cm)	soprano in C (SL 25–32 cm)	soprano in D	sopranino (SL <25 cm)
Praetorius (1619)	Groß-baß	Baß	Basset	Tenor	Alt	Discant	Discant	klein Flötlein or exilent

Sopranino, soprano, and alto are differentiated in inventories from Graz, 1577 (*discant, khlainere discantl, khlaine flöttlen*) and Berlin, 1582 (*Altt, Dißcantt Pfeifflein, klein Dißcantt Pfeifflein*).[34] The distinction between C and D sopranos is not apparently made in an inventory until Hechingen, 1609 (*alt, discant, hohe discant*) and Kassel, 1613 (*Alt, Soprani, höhere Soprani*).[35] Even then, the terms make it hard to tell the difference between 'high soprano' and sopranino. In early seventeenth-century Italian music the diminutive *flautino* was employed as a synonym for *flauto* (alto recorder in G).[36] The *flautino alla vigesima seconda* (small recorder at the 22nd, or third octave) scored for in Claudio Monteverdi's *Orfeo* (1607) is probably a sopranino recorder in G.[37] The *Quartflöten* (fourth flutes) purchased by the city of Leipzig in 1635 were likely to have been a fourth higher than the alto in G, therefore sopranos in C, for which Praetorius had no distinguishing name.

Although Praetorius documents recorder consorts going down to great bass, in the third volume of his *Syntagma musicum* he remarks:

> If you want to use a choir of recorders together with various other choirs consisting of different instruments, I think it is better to give the bass part to a bass sackbut, or better yet, a curtal, and the tenor part to a sackbut or viola instead of the recorders, because the tenor and especially the bass recorders are far too soft in the low register; you can barely hear them because of the soprano and alto recorders, not to mention the other instruments in the additional choirs.
>
> However, if you want to use recorders alone, with no other added instruments, in a canzona, motet, or even a concerted piece for more choirs, the whole consort of recorders can be used most suitably, particularly the five types beginning with the lowest one and excluding the highest ones because of their shrillness. The recorder sound is soft and delicate, and especially pleasing in smaller rooms. But in church the basset and bass recorders cannot be heard very well, making it necessary for the other choirs placed together with them (whether viols or voices) to perform softly, assuming each choir or part is to be heard clearly among the others.[38]

Praetorius also supplies an important clue about how the lower sizes missing from earlier treatises were used in practice. In his table for the whole recorder consort, he gives four groupings of *Baß/ Ten.Alt./ Cant.*, starting with great bass,

bass, basset, and tenor sizes, respectively, explaining: 'It is thus always possible to use three sizes together . . . i.e. one size for the bass, a second for tenor or alto parts . . . and a third one for cantus parts.'[39] In other words, the FCCG schema could be used in four different registers: (1) great bass, two basses, basset; (2) bass, two bassets, tenor; (3) basset, two tenors, alto; and (4) tenor, two altos, soprano. Because these registers are a fifth apart, the players did not have to worry about what actual size of recorder they were playing, only which part they were assigned. With all fingers down, any recorder could correspond to *ut* in a particular hexachord. It should be added that in (1) the lower interval is a fourth, upsetting the system slightly. The great bass player, whose instrument is in F, not the E♭ necessary to maintain the interval of a fifth with the bass, would have to transpose down a tone, or else the others would have to transpose up a tone. In 1565, Juan de Arroyo, a minstrel at Granada Cathedral, petitioned to buy a large case of recorders in three *mixturas*: 'large recorders, medium recorders, and also small ones'.[40] Were these *mixtura*s equivalent to Praetorius's registers?

Of the pitch standards in use in the sixteenth and early seventeenth centuries, three are documented for recorders, although the second one has four different names: (1) *tutto punto*, ca. A 440 (Florence, 1564). (2) *mezzo punto*, ca. A 466 (Genoa, 1592); 'common organ pitch' (Munich, 1571); 'a large recorder for concerts, bought from Venice', probably at *CammerThon* or 'chamber pitch' (Innsbruck, 1596); 'two small recorders at *Cornedthöch*', cornetto pitch (Kremsmünster, 1606).[41] (3) Praetorius (1619) adds that 'In England they used to have, and in the Netherlands still have, most of their wind instruments about a minor third lower [A–2, ca. A 392] than our *Cammerthon* . . . . recorders and other instruments sound more lovely at such a low pitch . . . and produce at it almost a different kind of timbre to the ear (since they do not scream so much at this pitch).'[42] It perhaps represented a lower version of another pitch standard, *tuono corista*.

Brown has measured about 120 of the approximately 200 surviving Renaissance-type recorders (and cases) and made estimates of their pitch.[43] In general they were made in sizes a fifth apart, as described by the treatises. The great majority of instruments from the more important makers seem to be aligned with one of three grids, which he surmises are founded on the reality that a great bass recorder in F^0 at *mezzo punto* is the largest practical size. The first grid was built on a cycle of fifths starting from a low F, giving a great bass size in F^0, bass in c^0, basset in g^0, tenor in d^1, alto in a^1, and soprano in e^2 (no sopranino in b^2, as that would probably have been too small to make and its tone verging on the painful). The second grid is also built on a cycle of fifths but at A–2. The third grid is basically a tone lower than the first but reduces the bottom interval to a fourth: great bass in F^0 (rather than an impractically large Eb^0), bass in Bb^0, basset in f^0, tenor in c^1, alto in g^1, and soprano in d^2, along with sopranino in a^2. A later variant of the third grid adds a soprano in c^2 and the sopranino is in g^2, thus matching the set mentioned by Praetorius. In the first grid, the lower recorders in F^0, c^0, and g^0 are aligned with *mezzo punto*; in the third grid, the higher instruments in f^0, c^1, and g^1 are at this pitch.

In 1631, the inventory of the town wind band in Hermannstadt, Transylvania (now Sibiu, Romania), included: one *discant* recorder with a key, two large keyed recorders with crooks, one large bass recorder with a crook, two large *discant* recorders with keys, and three large recorders with crooks.[44] Four of them survive in the Brukenthal Museum, Sibiu: a basset, a bass in C, and part of a great bass, tuned in fifths and bearing the mark HIER•S•; and a basset marked W with a three-branched crown above it, probably made by master Vilém or Wilhelm of Rožmberk.[45] Besides showing the presence of only larger sizes in the town band's collection, the inventory confirms that *discant* refers to function within a register of recorders, not (only) to a particular size and pitch level.

Eight recorder cases have survived from the sixteenth century, six still containing some or all of their original instruments. Seven are for high sets, beginning with basset, tenor, or alto sizes. The largest case, bearing the date 1603 and the arms of the city of Augsburg, must have belonged to its wind band.[46] It held twenty-eight instruments: sixteen recorders, six flutes, and six conical instruments that may well have been cornetti. The sizes of the recorders would fit Brown's third grid (minus the great bass): a bass in Bb^0, four bassets in f^0, four tenors in c^1, three altos in g^1, two sopranos in d^2, and two sopraninos probably in a^2, all at *mezzo punto*. A couple of generations earlier, an inventory of Augsburg's instruments in 1540 revealed that a case of recorders (one basset, two tenors, two altos) had been lost from the Dance House.[47]

In the seventeenth century, new terminology began to appear. The Norwich Waits (city minstrels) owned *treble* and *countertenor* recorders (1622, 1639), both terms apparently referring to the alto, and the *treble* also turned up at court (1636). The *two alte Contraltfletten* (two old contralto recorders) inventoried at the Bavarian court in Munich (1655) were probably also altos.[48]

Despite Praetorius's new names and his recommendation about alternating fourths and fifths, Mersenne's *Harmonie universelle* (1636) still describes *basse, taille* or *haute-contre*, and *dessus* a fifth apart. He also mentions two interlocking registers, the *petit jeu* and the *grand jeu*, the latter being depicted as what Praetorius called great bass, bass, and basset sizes. 'The bass of this high *jeu* . . . serves as discant to the low *jeu*, which begins where the other ends.'[49] In other words, Mersenne had in mind a set of five sizes, all a fifth apart: great bass, bass, basset, tenor, and alto. But these two registers could not in fact be played together with the same fingerings, because, following the sequence of fifths, they are a ninth apart. To do so, instruments from Brown's first and third grids would have to be combined.

TECHNIQUE AND PERFORMANCE PRACTICE BEFORE GANASSI

Until learning an instrument began to be institutionalized during the French Revolution, professionals learned mostly by a process of oral transmission within a formal contract of apprenticeship. Content and methodology were essentially regarded as trade secrets, as in any other craft or art. Instruction books were aimed at amateurs.

By the sixteenth century, enough amateurs – adults and children – existed in several countries to warrant general instruction books that included material on the recorder, and even the first book entirely devoted to it, Silvestro Ganassi's *Fontegara* (Venice, 1535). One important caveat: all instruction books were written for people who could hear music performed at the time and absorb its nuances by ear. Without the sound, even Ganassi's comprehensive instructions are limited in helping the reader develop the artistic playing he described. Books can give us only a small idea of what recorder playing was like in a few scattered places at arbitrary times.[50]

Around 1510, someone wrote out brief instructions, almost certainly for the 15-year-old Bonifacius Amerbach (1495–1562), later a humanistic Swiss law professor with keen musical interests.[51] The book is headed only 'Discant'; in the family's estate catalogue of 1578, it is described as 'Introductio gschriben uf pfifen' (Introduction written about pipes). It depicts an alto recorder in g^1, giving rudimentary fingerings for the first octave, some explanation of mensural notation, and a series of exercises.

Sebastian Virdung (b. ca. 1465; d. after 1511), the author of the first general instruction book on music, *Musica getutscht und auszgezogen*, served as a chaplain and singer in Heidelberg, Stahleck, Stuttgart, and Konstanz, apparently having no connection with Basel, where his book was published in 1511. In writing at length about instruments for the first time in the vernacular and presenting 'everything . . . made simple',[52] Virdung spells out his amateur audience. His recorder instructions consist largely of descriptions of how to finger the instrument. He uses two systems of notation, both perhaps invented by himself: one in effect a fingering chart, the other a tablature containing one symbol for each note; contrary to later practice, the holes are numbered from lowest (1) to highest (8), and the numbers given refer to fingers you have to take off – not put on. His only other technical information: you must 'learn how to apply the tongue . . . together with the fingers, so that they move with each other exactly . . .'.[53]

Virdung explains that the bottom hole of the recorder is doubled, to allow for playing with either left hand or right hand uppermost, the unused hole being closed with wax. In sixteenth-century paintings, recorders are shown slightly more with the right hand uppermost (214 versus 177 examples).[54] The interchangeability of hands is demonstrated neatly in the altarpiece *Coronation of the Virgin* by the Bohemian artist Gangolf Herlingere (ca. 1520), in which two members of a trio of recorder players (alto and tenor) are playing left hand uppermost; the third (soprano), right hand uppermost. Virdung's treatise had great influence, as witnessed by no fewer than three translated versions published over the next half century: *Livre plaisant et tres utile* (Antwerp, 1529); Othmar Luscinius, *Musurgia, seu praxis musicae* (Strasbourg, 1536); and *Dit is een seer schoon boecxken* (Antwerp, 1568).

Martin Agricola (ca. 1486–1556) served as Cantor of the Protestant Latin school in Magdeburg. His *Musica instrumentalis deudsch* (Wittenberg, 1529), modelled on Virdung's treatise, is written in 'German rhythm and metre for a special reason, so that youths and others who wish to study this art might all the more easily understand it and retain it longer'.[55] He rejects tablature (without naming Virdung), believing that it would be beneficial for students to learn vocal notation. The middle size, because it serves for both tenor and alto parts, is called both *tenor* and *altus*, the latter confusingly being depicted a little smaller in the woodcut. Rather than describing each fingering, Agricola directs readers to his fingering charts – one for each size of instrument – which contain some differences, giving the impression, as William E. Hettrick remarks, 'that he had experimented with three individual instruments, rather than using just one size and duplicating its fingerings for the other two'.[56] For graces (*Mordanten*), which make the melody elegant, Agricola recommends observing a professional wind player.

The substantially rewritten text of Agricola's second edition of 1545 – aimed at 'our schoolchildren and other beginning singers' – includes significant differences and additions.[57] He mentions vibrato (*zitterndem Wind*) for woodwind instruments approvingly.[58] As for articulation, longer notes take the syllable *de*; semi-minims can also take *di ri*, the articulation for the shorter note values, celebrated in the rhyme '*Wiltu das dein pfeifen besteh / Lern wol das diridiride*' (If with your pipe you wish to succeed / learn well the *diridiride*).[59] Finally, in the very small note values of diminutions (*Colorirn*), some musicians are said to use the articulation *tell ell ell ell ell ell ell ele le*, which he calls the 'flutter-tongue' (*flitter ʒunge*), best learnt from a teacher.[60] Incidentally, an English play, *Ralph Roister Doister* by Nicholas Udall (ca. 1552), includes the line 'Then to our recorder with toodle loodle poope', an apparent reference to an articulation similar to Agricola's.[61] Both authors therefore anticipate Johann Joachim Quantz's *did'll* for the flute (*Versuch*, Berlin, 1752) by two centuries.[62]

SILVESTRO GANASSI AND HIS *FONTEGARA*

Silvestro Ganassi dal Fontego (1491/2–1571 or later) published his *Opera intitulata Fontegara* in Venice in 1535, probably supervising the printing of it himself.[63] The full title of this unique work still only hints at its extraordinary scope: 'Work entitled "Fontegara", which teaches how to play the recorder with all the appropriate art of this instrument, especially the art of diminution, which will be useful for any wind or string instrument as well as for those who take delight in singing.'[64]

Ganassi lived in Venice his whole life.[65] His father, Antonio, was a barber and probably also a musician. The family lived in the shops at the street level of the Fontego della Farina, the city's main granary, from which the title of *Fontegara* is derived.[66] Silvestro was hired as a *piffero* of the Doge of Venice in 1517 to play the *contra alto* part. He and at least his brothers Girolamo and Giovanni, later joined by his son Giovanni Battista, also formed the Sonadori del Fontego, documented 1516–50, who played at feasts and receptions. Ganassi subsequently published two treatises for the viol, *Regola Rubertina* (1542) and *Lettione seconda* (1543). Ganassi mentions that the dedicatee of the former, the wealthy exiled Florentine banker Ruberto Strozzi, was his student.[67] In the dedication of the latter to Strozzi's cousin Neri Capponi, another exiled banker, Ganassi notes 'the honour of having been your teacher'.[68] At Capponi's home, gatherings were held with voices and viols (doubtless including Ganassi), directed by the celebrated composer Adrian Willaert, who had been hired as maestro di cappella at St Mark's in 1527. Ganassi's teaching is also reflected in him renting a *volta*: one of a large series of rooms in the vicinity

8. Silvestro Ganassi, *Opera intitulata Fontegara* (Venice, 1535), frontispiece.

of the Rialto bridge that housed artisanal, financial, and commercial activity, as well as painters' workshops and schools of music. In 1547, Ganassi wrote to the governors of the city of Ancona, promising to send them a company of *piffari*, including 'my student who is one of the finest players there are in the whole of Italy'.[69] Several poems and books praised Ganassi's musicianship, intellect, spirit, and virtue.[70] Well-known and respected also as a painter, he presumably supplied the drawings for the illustrations and musical examples in his treatises.

Ganassi dedicated *Fontegara* to Andrea Gritti, the Doge of Venice from 1523 to 1538, and obtained a licence for the treatise from the Venetian Senate for twenty years: unusual in its long term and because such a right was normally given to the printer not the author.[71] Gritti was in the midst of a cultural urban renewal project, *renovatio urbis*, of which the treatise was an exemplary gem, doubtless inspired and perhaps even suggested by the Doge.[72]

Systematic and imaginative, the first treatise ever published about a single instrument and also the first treatise about diminutions, *Fontegara* is the only comprehensive book about recorder pedagogy before the twentieth century. Many of its features are challenging for the modern reader: the Venetian-flavoured Italian, the influence of both ancient Greek music theory and ancient Latin rhetoric, the key use of certain elusive terms, and Ganassi's description of an astonishingly well-developed style of recorder playing belonging to a powerful musical art that could surpass Nature and inspire a higher status for the arts and artists.[73]

Ganassi begins by declaring that recorder players should learn from the human voice:

> Just as the painter imitates all the actions of nature through various colours, the instrument will also imitate the utterings of the human voice with the proportion of breath [the quality of the airflow] and the shadowing action [closure of the air passage] of the tongue with the assistance of the teeth. I have had experience in this matter, and I have heard other players who could make the words understood through their playing. Consequently, one could well say that this instrument lacks nothing but the shape of the human body, as it can be said of a well-made painting that it lacks nothing but the breath. Therefore, you can be certain about its [the recorder's] aim . . . that it is possible to imitate speech.[74]

Given that, in his epilogue, Ganassi holds up 'the capable and expert singer'[75] as a model for recorder playing, the initial reference to speech (*il parlar*) seems puzzling. The explanation seems to be that the recorder player can imitate 'the emotive character of the words and the chosen manner of "pronunciation" by the singer'[76] as well as the emotive power of a fine orator.[77]

Almost all the qualities and techniques in *Fontegara* come in threes: a sixteenth-century symbol of perfection, the Holy Trinity, the authority and legitimacy of the author, and the Aristotelian concept of moral virtues as the mean or 'temperance' between two extremes.[78] The fundamental triad is the mastery of breathing, tongue, and finger technique. About the breath: 'the human voice is like a mistress that teaches where to proceed in a moderate manner; because when the singer sings a certain composition with soothing words, he makes his pronunciation soothing; if joyful, in a joyful manner. Hence, if you would wish to imitate such an action, then you should proceed with a moderate breath, so that, in the appropriate moments, you may alter it by either augmenting or diminishing [the airflow].'[79] In other words, the player learns good breath control in the service of the piece's affect.

The second member of the fundamental triad, the tongue, incorporates two further triads of its own. There are three 'basic' kinds of tonguing syllable (*lingua*).[80] And Ganassi classifies the syllables in three ways: (a) by their quality, (b) by their degree of closure of the air passage, and (c) by the placement of the closure (Table 3).[81] Note that in his syllables, the *t* is pronounced against the teeth, the *r* with the tip of the tongue brushing against the upper alveolar ridge (gum ridge), and the *ch* is equivalent to the English *k*.

Table 3. Silvestro Ganassi, *Opera intitulata Fontegara* (Venice, 1535), classification of tonguing syllables

Type of syllable	a) Quality	(b) Degree of closure of the air passage	(c) Placement of closure
1. *te che*	Raw and harsh	More articulated = direct	*te*: head = direct *che*: throat = reverse
2. *te re*	Harsh (*te*) and tender (*re*)	(Temperance)	[*te*: head = direct *re*: throat = reverse]
3. *le re*	Pleasant and easy	Less articulated = reverse	*le*: head = direct *re*: throat = reverse

The first basic kind of tonguing (a), *te che*, 'has syllables that cause a raw and harsh effect', because it is formed of two stop consonants.[82] The *degree* of closure of the air passage (b) is 'direct', because 'the syllables are more articulated',[83] presumably because of the clear interruption of the airflow at both points of closure. But the *placement* of the closure (c) is mixed, because in any pair of syllables, the first is 'direct' and the second is 'reverse' or 'contrary'.[84] Moreover, 'all actions generated by a "direct" tonguing are called "head" tonguing, because it accumulates the air below the hard palate and near the teeth. The reverse tonguing is called 'throat' tonguing, because the air occupies [i.e. is held in] the area near the throat,'[85] so articulation occurs near the soft palate.

The third kind of basic tonguing (a), *le re*, has 'pleasant and easy syllables', because it is formed by two liquid consonants.[86] The *degree* of closure of the air passage (b) is 'reverse', because 'the syllables are articulated less'.[87] The *placement* of the closure (c) is again mixed, because there is one direct (head) syllable, *le*, and one reverse (throat), *re*. Strictly speaking, in this case the second syllable is not produced by a full closure at the back of the mouth, but by a fluid movement of the tongue creating only a partial closure, further back in the mouth than the initial syllable. Perhaps the point is the importance of alternating two syllables with different areas of closure to achieve expressivity and agility.

A second, 'median', kind of basic tonguing, *te re*, bridging the first and third, 'contains in itself the temperance of both extremes: the harshness and tenderness',[88] because it is formed of one stop consonant and one liquid consonant.

Table 4. Ganassi, *Fontegara*, tonguing syllables, varying the consonants and vowels

Type 1	Type 2	Type 3
Teche teche teche teche teche	*Tere tere tere tere tere*	*Lere lere lere lere lere*
Tacha teche tichi tocho tuchu	*Tara tere tiri toro turu*	*Lara lere liri loro luru*
dacha deche dichi docho duchu	*dara dare dari daro daru*	
	chara chare chari charo charu	

Just when we may think we understand the complexity of Ganassi's tonguings, he introduces a new concept: complete (with two syllables) or incomplete (halved) actions of the tongue. The halved tonguing ('single' in modern parlance) has only one syllable or letter, so that at speed it becomes *ttttt* or *ddddd* or even *lllll*.[89] Furthermore, when it comes to a discussion of vowels, he recommends the reader to find out 'which syllable or letter Nature has granted you the ability to pronounce rapidly'.[90] At this point he changes the uniform typography for the only time in the book to present three (of course) columns (Table 4).

Ganassi gives examples of changing *t* to *d* in the first type of tonguing, to *d* or *ch* (and from what he says later, also *gh*) in the second type, in order to develop a wider range of effects, but he does not give variants of *l* and *r*.[91] Moreover, all the other vowels can substitute for *e*: the same vowel for both syllables or changing the vowel in the second syllable. Each of those vowels would lead to a different tongue position and therefore to a different ratio of speed to quantity in the airstream and a different tone colour.

Ganassi says that when one increases speed, 'the pronunciation disappears',[92] so that the second and third basic types of tonguing are reduced to one syllable of only three letters, such as *tar*, *dar*, *char*, *ghar*, or *lar*.[93] Finally, 'There is another tonguing that does not pronounce any syllable, and its movement is from one lip to the other; and because the breath occupies the area near the lips, it is called head tonguing.'[94] Although most scholars have interpreted this as a kind of legato, Pedro Couto Soares suggests that Ganassi may have intended something like a lateral movement of the tongue, similar to *ẓaghareet*, a form of ululation familiar today in the Middle East.[95]

The third member of the fundamental triad, fingering, is applied to a further triad: three relative sizes of recorder, *basso*, *tenore*, and *sopran*, for which he gives the interval of a thirteenth as the normal compass. Ganassi's basic fingerings are shown by a series of six charts consisting of schematic depictions of a recorder with the closed holes filled in – a big advance in comprehensibility from the notation of Virdung and Agricola. Five of the charts are based on the hexachords as used in the polyphonic music of the early sixteenth century: *hexachordum naturale* (natural; C D E F G A), *hexachordum molle* (soft; F G A B♭ C D), *hexachordum durum* (hard; G A B♮ C D E), and *hexachordum fictum* (fictional; B♭ C D E♭ F G). Underneath each chart Ganassi connects the fingerings with the solmization syllables (*ut re mi fa sol la*) used in note-reading. Whichever hexachord the chart begins with, in order to go higher than six notes the musician must 'mutate' to another hexachord (no more than two hexachords per staff). Under the solmization syllables is a staff showing one or more clefs with their associated flats (if any). And under the staff, he shows the solmization syllables used on coming down the staff – imaginatively, perhaps uniquely, reversing some syllables (*tu im al los*) to indicate that all the syllables are now read from right to left (and sometimes, after which syllable to mutate). The descending hexachords are the same as the ascending ones, but do not always mutate on the same syllable. See Table 5. The sixth chart includes the notes for musica ficta (C♯, D♯, F♯, G♯), outside the hexachords.

In addition to the normal compass, Ganassi famously describes his discovery of a further octave of notes, including the accidentals of ♯1, ♭3, ♯4, and ♯5 in the third octave, completing the gamut and making a total compass of two octaves and a sixth. Because this portion of his treatise has proved the most controversial, his description is worth reproducing in full:

My most dignified reader, you should know that for many years I have experimented with how to play, and that I have enjoyed watching and practising with all the foremost players of my time. In this I have never encountered a dignified man in this art who practised more than the ordinary notes [*voce*]. I mean to say, they might have added one or two notes, whereas I have examined it in such a way that I found that which others did not know – it is not that they were unacquainted with the way to proceed but, because of fatigue, they gave up – that is, seven additional notes aside from the ordinary ones, of which I will give you all the knowledge. . . . The seven notes found by me, together with the thirteen ordinary ones, make twenty, which we will divide into three parts: nine low-pitched [*grave*], seven high-pitched [*acute*], and four extremely high-pitched [*sopra acute*]. As I have said, the nine low-pitched ones are produced with a deep blowing [*grave*], the seven following ones with a sharp blowing [*acuto*], and the final four with an extremely sharp blowing [*acutissimo*].[96]

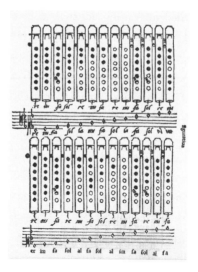

9. Ganassi, *Fontegara*, first fingering chart.

Table 5. Features of Ganassi's fingering charts
hexachords are ascending: F = fictum; H = hard; N = natural; S= soft

Chart	Starting syllable	*Sopran* in g¹ (C1 clef)		*Tenore* in c¹ (C3 clef)		*Basso* in f⁰ (F3 clef)	
		hexachords	flats	hexachords	flats	hexachords	flats
1	ut	H–N–H	0	N–S–N	1	S–F–S	2
2	re	S–N–S–N	1	F–S–F–S	2		
3	re	S–F–S–F	2				
4	ut			N–H–N	0	S–N–S	1
5	fa					N–H–N–H	0

The types of 'blowing' may not be intended to be taken too literally, as they reflect the terms used for the three registers of the gamut (as in the previous sentence).

All three charts showing the high notes use the soprano clef, which some scholars have taken to imply that only Ganassi's *sopran* size of recorder could play these notes.[97] But that is simply their place in the gamut. Moreover, the extra notes could be more symbolic than practical, as suggested by their virtual exclusion from his diminutions, and they would not have been needed to play the polyphonic music of the time. Pedro Sousa Silva points out that: 'The *gammaut* [gamut], also known as *musica vera*, is a finite set of *punti* – notes – where music happens. In the sixteenth century, it is usually considered to have 20 *punti* in earlier and more theoretical sources. . . . By expanding the range of the recorder to 20 *voci* [his version of *punti*] Ganassi is creating the most subtle and strongest statement of all: the recorder *is* the *gammaut*, the *musica vera*, the paradigm of perfection.'[98]

Ganassi comments:

> I should first warn you that the recorders made by various makers are different from each other, not only in the bore [and] the distance between the holes, but also in the air [voicing]. Some of these makers differ from each other in the way they tune their instruments, because each of them has his own distinct way of playing the instrument and also different ears. From these differences is born a variety of methods of playing instruments made by one or another maker. So I will show you the way of several makers by their different marks, which will be demonstrated in the representations of the recorder in the fingering charts.[99]

In general, Ganassi says, if a given fingering does not work on a particular recorder, 'you must experiment with covering and uncovering one or two holes, either more or less, as well as adjusting your blowing'.[100] He also mentions that intonation must be adjusted on partially covered notes, 'sometimes more, sometimes less, in accordance with the necessary maintenance of the true harmony'.[101]

It comes as no surprise that Ganassi's 'several' maker's marks turn out to be another triad. The basic fingering charts have only a Gothic A, as does the trill table, suggesting that this maker was his favourite. For the expanded range he gives three different charts, each one bearing the mark of a maker: a B, the Gothic A, and a trefoil with the tail pointing right, in that order, and presumably showing 'the way' (generally slightly different fingerings) of each maker's instruments.

The B has caused some puzzlement, because no surviving woodwind instruments bear it, although it has been suggested that it might have belonged to an unknown maker from Nuremberg. Perhaps it actually referred to the celebrated Bassano family (see the section on the Bassanos later in this chapter), whose instruments had the widest distribution of any Renaissance makers. None of the members of the family had moved from Venice to England permanently then, and it would certainly be curious if Ganassi had not referred to the mark of such outstanding recorder makers of his day, based in his city.

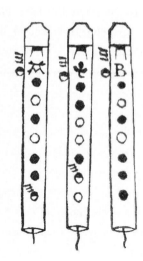

10. Ganassi, *Fontegara*, composite image of fingerings bearing the three maker's marks.

The Gothic A is associated with the Schnitzer family working in Munich and Nuremberg. Incidentally, a letter written from Tivoli by Duke Ernst of Bavaria in 1574 states, 'The Italians obtain their sackbuts, recorders, and crumhorns almost exclusively from Nuremberg.'[102] The Schnitzer instruments can often play two octaves, using the fingerings given by Ganassi. Their bores, although conical, have a more cylindrical profile, with less of a difference between their maximum and minimum diameter. As a result of this, they are slightly longer for a given pitch and have a more pronounced bell flare than similarly sized recorders by other makers. The sizes of the surviving recorders – no great bass size – tend to fit a sequence of fifths starting from F. Biographical evidence and the characteristics of these instruments suggest that most of them date from the first half of the sixteenth century.

A double trefoil with a right-pointing tail is found on two surviving recorders (extended bass, Munich; basset, Salzburg, dated 1535) that bear the name 'Hans Rauch von Schratt', a member of the Rauch family from Schrattenbach in Bavaria. The bores of the surviving Rauch recorders are conical, sometimes showing great individuality in their profile, with large gouged-out sections created to tune octaves and aid stability. Most Rauch recorders fit a sequence of fifths starting from F for the great bass.

In the 1970s, the search for any original Renaissance recorder that could be played with Ganassi's (cumulative) high-note fingerings was to result in the development of at least three new designs for so-called 'Ganassi' recorders. See box on p. 81.

According to Ganassi, *sonare artificioso*, playing 'artfully' (in the sense of 'in a skilful manner') or 'artificially' (instrumentally),[103] comprises a further triad: three necessary and interdependent elements. The first element is *imitatione* (imitation), which 'derives from artfulness' and 'must imitate the human voice' in the quality of the airflow.[104] The second element is *prontezza* (promptness), which has to do with the quick response to changing the airflow in accordance with the affect. Both imitation and promptness also occur in relation to painting in the sixteenth century, the latter referring to the dynamic movement of the artist's hand.[105] The third element is *galanteria* (gallantry), 'which derives from and emanates from the trilling of the finger upon the hole of the recorder',[106] contributing to the emulation of the human voice.[107] He mentions trills varying from (1) the 'lively and expansive' (*vivace & augumentata*) interval of a third, more or less; to (2) the 'medium' (*mediocre*) interval of a tone, more or less; and (3) the 'mild or calming' (*suave over placabile*) interval of a semitone, more or less, down to a *diesis* (quarter-tone) or even less, which we could consider a form of finger vibrato, similar to the French *flattement* of the Baroque, although the pitch variation of that went below the main note.

In his trill table, Ganassi gives different fingerings for V (*vivace*) and S (*suave*) trills on each note of the basic compass of a thirteenth, 'intended for the recorders of one specific maker. Therefore, if with others [instruments from other makers] you cannot play them, then you need to work industriously to cover or uncover one or two holes, either more or less.'[108] Some of the trills involve alternative fingerings for the notes in question: further proof – next to his remarks on correcting intonation by subtle alterations of fingering and blowing – that such refinements of technique are not a product of the twentieth century.

The final element of Ganassi's 'fingers' triad, beyond fingering and trills, consists of 'two actions that influence the agility of the hand: the action and proficiency in tonguing and the method of making diminutions'.[109] We might call the first action 'finger–tongue coordination' in fast passages. The second action is a type of melodic ornamentation, *diminutione* or *atti*, which in his later treatises he called *passaggi* or *groppetti*, the general terms in the second half of the century.[110] He disarmingly defines these diminutions as 'nothing but varying something or a process that, by nature, seems compact and simple'.[111] The idea, as we also know from extensive subsequent literature, is that the notes of a piece are divided into a number of smaller notes.

Ganassi devotes the vast majority of his treatise to illustrating diminutions, demonstrating by sheer length of treatment alone – he himself calls it an 'unbearable effort' – their central role in recorder playing.[112] He bases his method on the ornamentation of a number of *motti* (intervals) between the notes of the piece, from unison to fifth, both ascending and descending, which may be complicated by the presence of an intermediary note (*motti mediati*). These *motti* are discussed according to three elements. (1) The proportions: C, 5/4, C3, and 7/4, although 7/4 has a smaller number of examples because its proportion is said to be 'rather laborious and troublesome'.[113] Each *motto* is systematically converted into a series of figurations classified by (2) *vie* (melodic contour) and (3) *minute* (note values), subclassified as simple or compound, particular or general. 'Simple' means that the proportion, melodic contour, and/or note value remain the same throughout a given diminution; 'compound', that they do not. 'General' means that all three attributes are simple or all are compound; 'particular', that one of the attributes differs from the other two.

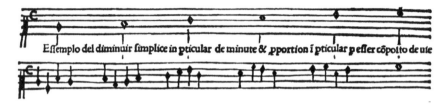

Example 1. Ganassi, *Fontegara*, Capitulo 12, paragraph 35, simple–particular

A couple of examples should help in understanding this system. In Example 1, the proportion is simple (only C); the *minuta* is simple (the semibreves are divided into only semiminime, or crotchets); but the *vie* are compound (the melodic contour changes every semibreve). So, because two attributes are simple but the third is not, this example is classified as simple–particular.

Example 2. Ganassi, *Fontegara*, Capitulo 12, paragraph 37, compound–general

In Example 2, the proportions are compound (changing from C to 6/4, 5/6, 7/5, and 8/7); the *minute* are compound (the note values change from crome, or quavers, to semicrome, or semiquavers, and semiminime); and the *vie* are compound (the melodic contour changes every semiminima). So, because all the attributes are compound, this example is classified as compound–general.

It might seem self-evident that, in diminutions, the pitches of the smaller notes into which the notes of the piece are divided always change to form melodic contours. But Ganassi presents a number of purely rhythmic figurations in which the rhythms, and sometimes added rests, are varied on a single pitch in creative ways, producing something of a *parlando* effect.[114]

Dina Titan explains the rhythmic complexity of Ganassi's diminutions by reference to the writings of two ancient Greek philosophers, Aristoxenus of Tarentum (fl. 335 BC) and Aristides Quintilianus (fourth century AD?), whose works had become available in Italy in the late fifteenth century and were circulating in manuscript translations and letters among musicians.[115] Indeed, all Ganassi's terminology, including *motti*, 'simple', 'compound', 'general', and 'particular', stems from the Greek sources.[116] As part of raising practical music from a craft to an art, he creates his own ingenious model based on great authorities of the past. Unlike the sixteenth-century rhythmic system, in which a *tactus* of a long note was divided into small notes, the Greek model was additive, i.e. progressing from small units to bigger ones.[117] This explains the frequent unusual dotted notes in Ganassi's examples: although he retains a fixed value of a semibreve for the *tactus*, the ordering of notes inside it follows Greek additive logic.[118] Similarly to the Greek poetic foot, Ganassi's *tactus* is divided into two parts, *arsis* and *thesis*, the relationship between which is not only equal (1:1) or 2:1, as already appeared in the sixteenth century, but can also display the ratios 3:2 or 4:3.[119] Within each *arsis* or *thesis*, the notes can be arranged in any of these four ratios, including their *antithesis* (reverse ratio, 1:2, 2:3, or 3:4).[120]

At the end of each of his four rules in which his diminutions are arranged by proportion, Ganassi includes many examples of cadences. Because of the implied harmonic progression involving dissonance and resolution, the cadences are longer than his standard *motti* but display the same melodic features together with trill-like figurations before the close.[121] In an extreme display of thoroughness, a manuscript appendix to a surviving copy of *Fontegara* consists of 175 diminutions on a single cadence; it was prepared by Ganassi in 1543 or later and offered for sale along with *Fontegara*, some manuscript lessons for the lira (not extant), and one or both of the viol treatises to an intermediary identified only as Domenico, but perhaps his brother-in-law Domenico Bembo.[122]

All in all, Ganassi's approach produces the most detailed and systematic treatment of diminutions in all the treatises of the sixteenth and early seventeenth centuries, lacking only a fully worked model diminution upon an entire piece.

Ganassi notates his examples of diminutions exclusively in one of the soprano clefs (C1 or C2), apparently to avoid ledger lines. This does not conclusively imply a restriction to soprano parts, because the wording on the title page promises a general collection 'that will be useful for any wind or string instrument as well as those who take delight in singing'. Yet one striking piece of sixteenth-century evidence indicates the necessity of imposing restrictions on diminution-loving professionals: at Seville Cathedral in 1586, Francisco Guerrero (1528–99), the maestro de capilla, issued an order about performance.[123] The soprano players Juan de Rojas and Alonso López were ordered that, whether they were playing shawms or cornetti, they must alternate their *glosas* (diminutions), 'because glossing together creates insufferable dissonance'.[124] Juan de Medina, playing the alto part, must not 'disturb' by exceeding the *glosas* appropriate for the alto. But when he plays the alto shawm as a *tiple* (soprano) with the sackbuts, 'he is given freedom to create all the fineries and *glosas* that he wishes, since he knows how to do them well on this instrument'.[125] Furthermore, later sixteenth-century treatises such as Adrianus Petit Coclicus (1552), Hermann Fink (1556), Girolamo Dalla Casa (1584), and Giovanni Bassano (1591) mention or illustrate using diminutions on some or all of the voices in turn.

Giulia Tettamanti has proposed that we can apply Ganassi's *sonare artificioso* triad beyond airflow.[126] For example, *imitatione* is the central tenet of Renaissance pedagogy. So in learning diminutions students imitated and emulated the teacher until they had incorporated all the substance and style of the diminutions, then went on to create their own way of expression. By repeating Ganassi's diminution patterns, students could memorize them to build up their own 'library' of patterns, then apply them to any piece they wished to ornament. Moreover, repeating these patterns also served as daily technical exercises, preparing students' hands to acquire the agility and fast response required of any good player, thus adding to *prontezza*. Finally, although Ganassi links *galanteria* to trills, dictionaries of the period define it as ornaments, jewels, or being gallant (graceful, fashionable, elegant), so we can extend his recommendations by keeping in mind the affect of the piece and choosing the most gallant diminution for each occasion.

Despite its complexity, *Fontegara* was still addressed to the amateurs of the time. In his dedication letter to *Regola Rubertina*, Ganassi says that he is using his talent, as he did earlier in *Fontegara*, to 'make the road easier for those who take delight in this virtue' (because it is praiseworthy to play an instrument).[127] We can only be grateful that he gave us far more than the crumbs from a professional's table, and that he considered the Venetian amateurs of his day sophisticated and accomplished enough to benefit from his comprehensive method.

MORE ON RECORDERS IN GANASSI'S VENICE

In 1505, Alvise Zorzi, a member of the Venetian *piffari*, wrote to Francesco Gonzaga of Mantua to offer him a motet that he had arranged for several instrumentations of cornetti, sackbuts, and shawms, as well as one for eight recorders.[128] In a group perhaps something like the Sonadori del Fontego, Bernardin son of Bortolomeo, *piffaro* of the Doge, Alvise Bassano, Gasparo son of Bernardo, and Yipolito de San Salvador played recorders as well as cornetti, trumpets, and shawms for processions of the Scuola di San Marco in 1515; the latter three musicians later worked at the English court.[129]

Francesco Sansovino wrote of Venice in 1581: 'there are many . . . *ridotti*, where the virtuous in that profession take part and make singular concerts all the time, it being crystal clear and true that Music has its own seat in this city'.[130] From the mid-1560s onwards, the well-connected Venetian lawyer Alvise Balbi held a *ridotto* at his home, a kind of salon where cultivated men rubbed shoulders with professional musicians: music was of course performed, poetry was recited, and conversations about the arts, literature, philosophy, medicine, and science abounded.[131] In 1588, Balbi's inventory included 'six large recorders for chamber music' as well as 'a new kind of large recorders, made with a lot of spirit, with the Privilege of the Most Excellent Senate, which imitate the human voice' – perhaps actually either bassanelli or curtals.[132]

As for amateurs, Gastone Vio and Stefano Toffolo have analysed the musical instruments mentioned in the probate inventories of sixteenth-century Venetians. The recorder is the fourth most frequently mentioned instrument, after the lute, harpsichord, and clavichord.[133] See Table 6. Members of the citizens and commoners presumably owned recorders for themselves to play or for music-making with their families and friends. The archbishop may have hired musicians to play for him.

TECHNIQUE AND PERFORMANCE PRACTICE AFTER GANASSI

Girolamo Cardano (Jerome Cardan, 1501–76), the great Italian Renaissance philosopher, mathematician, and physician, made a significant contribution to

Table 6. Recorders in sixteenth-century Venetian probate inventories

Date	Person	Class	Recorders	Other instruments
1555	Archbishop Pesaro	Nobili	a case of nine	clavichord
1551	Nicolò Sagondino, secretary to the Council of Ten	Cittadini	a case of ten	organ, clavichord
1560	Gerolamo da Modena, pharmacist	Cittadini	a case of five and small ivory one	small organ, two clavichords
1551	Brothers Giovanni Lorenzo and Zaccaria di Griffalconi	Cittadini	a case of	harpsichord, two lutes, four viols, a case of crumhorns
1577	Alessandro di Giustina, artisan	Popolani	two	

music theory. Also a keen musician, he took recorder lessons as a child in Pavia. In 1561, he called his former teacher, Leo Oglonus, 'an upright and outstanding man, now well over eighty years of age'.[134] In his autobiography (1575), Cardano mentions that in his youth he often spent the whole day walking around, 'dripping with perspiration from the exertion of a round of serenading on my musical instruments'.[135] Although he modestly claims 'In music I was inept in practice, but in theory I was not incapable',[136] his treatises show he must have become skilful on the recorder as well as stringed instruments.

Cardano's first Latin treatise on music, *De Musica*, written around 1546 while he was living in Milan, was published only as part of his complete works, 117 years later. It contains chapters on wind instruments and on the recorder (*Elyma*), partly based on Ganassi but filtered through his own experience. Among his conditions for the 'excellence of instruments . . . is that they sound well with the human voice and with other instruments. On this account recorders are the least praiseworthy, for hardly any other instrument blends less well. . . .'[137] In the recorder chapter, however, like Ganassi, he considers it 'a particular property' of the instrument to *imitate* the voice exactly, 'by using a relaxed tone in laments, a strong tone in excitement, a smooth, connected tone in serious moods, and so forth concerning the other emotions. . . '.[138]

On articulation, Cardano contents himself with summarizing Ganassi's tonguing syllables: 'The pronunciation is of three kinds: a gentle utterance which is formed by liquids such as *lere*, a sharp utterance formed by mute aspirates such as *theche*, and a moderate utterance which is mixed, such as *there* or *thara*.'[139] He also mentions turning the tongue up to the palate, or extending it to open or close the 'passage' (windway), producing 'either a direct or reflected flow of air. It is wonderful how much this improves the tones and also varies and colours them.'[140]

Cardano makes some sophisticated comments about breath control:

There are two general ways of considering breath: one from the standpoint of magnitude [volume], the other from the standpoint of impetus [pressure]. From the standpoint of pressure there are three varieties: relaxed and weighty, excited [intense], and moderate. From the standpoint of volume there are again three varieties: full, empty [shallow?], and moderate. We use the relaxed and weighty for larger instruments and those that are easy to blow, such as recorders, and on low notes; for if you use an intense breath, larger instruments will sound strident, and you will not be able to produce low notes. . . . A shallow breath is used for small instruments and high tones, and instruments that are easy to blow. Thus we use . . . a very full and relaxed breath on larger recorders, and a shallow and intense breath on small recorders . . . for the lower tones on small recorders, we use a shallow and relaxed breath.[141]

Moreover, he explains Ganassi's concept of *prontezza* well: 'the flow of breath must be well controlled and stable, not diffuse or unsteady, and . . . a change of breath be made incisively and without delay. This principle is called promptness (*promptitudo*).'[142]

Cardano is the first writer to mention an unnamed 'high recorder' (*altiore elyma*) in D. He describes fingerings for that size, the 'high soprano or *cantus*' (*soprani seu cantus in acutiore*) in G, the tenor (*Elyma tenoris*) in C, and the 'bass or lower' recorder (*Basso seu graviore*) in F, affirming the basic principle that 'all recorders are a fifth apart in pitch'.[143] After noting one particular alternative fingering, he remarks: 'in the best recorders there is much variety'.[144] Despite giving a basic compass of a ninth, he writes: 'With an open [thumb-hole] and a more intense breath, all tones sound an octave higher; and with [the thumb-hole] half closed and an even more intense breath, they reach two octaves.'[145] For the *cantus* recorder, 'When you want to rise into the second register, the same procedure is followed as in the other recorders. But Silvestro Ganassi adds seven more tones above *E la* [e³], which is the last and highest note of the Guidonian hand.'[146] Then he reproduces Ganassi's high-note fingerings, not always accurately, before making his own preference clear: 'But for these tones . . . I use a higher recorder [in d²]', the third register of which 'goes to *G sol re ut* beyond the hand [g⁴]. Thus only two more tones are needed to complete Ganassi's invention.'[147] In other words, he says you can play the high D-recorder up to within a minor third of the highest of Ganassi's fingerings on an alto, without resorting to his fingerings. As the normal range of an octave and a sixth on a high D-recorder takes us only to b³, however, we would still need some of Ganassi's high-note fingerings to go up to c♯⁴, a minor third below e⁴.

Extending the recorder's compass downwards seems to interest Cardano more. Half-closing the end-hole produces a tone lower: 'This is done by placing the recorder's lower end gently against the leg and using a relaxed breath. . . . But if only one-fourth of the hole is closed, only a semitone lower will be produced. Leo Oglonus, my music teacher, taught me this tone.'[148] The similar technique of half-closing the end-hole of a four-holed pipe was already described by Agricola in 1529.[149]

Cardano is enthusiastic about the micro-interval called a *diesis*, which he defines as 'a quarter of a whole tone and half of a small semitone . . . in 35:34 proportion . . . the smallest of the useful intervals that can be sung'.[150] To produce such an interval, 'only one-fourth of a hole is covered. . . . Also . . . by a repercussion of the tongue alone, for . . . a tongue that is bent back restrains the breath and lowers the tone a little so that a diesis is reached through the difference' – a further reference to the profound influence of tongue position on the quality of recorder sound and intonation.[151] He also describes how 'all tones can be turned into semitones and dieses, for if the [end] hole is half closed, whole tones will become a semitone lower, and semitones will become dieses; if one-quarter closed, a whole tone will become a diesis lower'.[152]

Cardano writes passionately about the *diesis* again in his section on trills, which goes into more detail than Ganassi did:

a trill (*vox tremula*) is used very often with a higher or lower diesis or semitone. This is a twofold action, with a tremulous quality in the breath and a trembling movement of the fingers. If this movement is made through several finger-holes, sometimes a major third results and sometimes a minor third; but very often the movement is half of that used on a fully opened hole. Therefore, when the trembling movement is made on a semitone or even on a whole tone by opening a hole very lightly, a sound running back and forth through dieses is created, a sound than which nothing finer, nothing sweeter, nothing more pleasant can be imagined.[153]

As with Ganassi, we could consider the alternation of the micro-intervals a form of finger vibrato, which Cardano combines with breath vibrato. 'Thus lively trills (*vivaces voces*) are made with a finger constantly opening and closing [a hole]; mild trills (*suaves*), with a trembling finger. But for the milder (*suavissimae*) trills, three observations are necessary: (1) lower and not higher notes should be trembled; (2) open [the hole] with the finger lightly and very little; (3) the recoiling motion of the fingers should not stop but should tremble just as a sword strongly vibrated will repeatedly rebound.'[154]

Cardano also makes some general remarks about recorders. 'The better instruments are made of wood from the plum tree; those of light white wood are harsher; those of solid wood such as boxwood are heavier and less convenient but sound more pleasant.'[155] He complains about recorders with large holes, which are harder to finger and require more breath, thus fatiguing the musician, and sound more strident. 'They show the inexperience of the instrument's maker who, having to follow a rule like a blind man led by the hand, has enlarged the size of the holes.'[156]

Finally, Cardano confirms the importance of diminution technique in recorder playing. He derives its purpose from 'two characteristics of instruments, unlike the voice: not to keep holding a single tone and not to stop playing but constantly to change pitches'.[157] Like Ganassi, he divides the written notes into groups of increasing complexity, ending when 'five equal notes are divided into seven parts, and this is very hard to do perfectly. There is no point in going any further, for if you divide four into five the very slight difference between them causes the greatest difficulty and lacks harmony, since it has been shown that whatever the ear cannot perceive does not produce pleasure.'[158]

Cardano wrote a second Latin treatise, also entitled *De Musica*, in Bologna in 1568 (revised six years later), in which he discusses ensemble playing: 'Although it is very easy for instruments of the same type to play together, they may also be joined by instruments which play intervals that are not exactly on pitch. ... Concordant sound is easier for string players than for woodwind players, because they can tighten or loosen their strings at will. Thus the best string players always adjust to other string players and to the woodwinds, but woodwind players do not adjust unless they have excellent instruments.'[159]

Two of Cardano's countrymen were more optimistic about woodwind intonation in ensembles. Hercole Bottrigari (1594) includes winds 'such as recorders and flutes and straight and curved cornetti' in his category of 'stable but alterable instruments' – that is, 'those which, after they have stability through their finger-holes . . . the accomplished player can nonetheless use a little less or a little more breath and can open the finger-holes a little more or a little less, bringing the notes closer to a good accord'.[160] Zacconi (1596) remarks: 'cornetti, flutes, recorders, curtals, cornamuses, and other [woodwind] instruments . . . by covering and uncovering somewhat those holes and bores . . . help them to adjust as best they can.'[161]

The only sixteenth-century French author to write about the recorder was Philibert Jambe de Fer (ca. 1515–ca. 1556), a Protestant composer and choral director in Lyons. The fingering chart in his *Epitome musical* (1556) has been taken as the earliest evidence of buttress-finger or supporting-finger technique – keeping down the third finger of the lower hand whenever possible – although he employs it for only three notes (VIIb, VIII, and IX). He stresses that the recorder has a more limited compass than the transverse flute ('at the most' two octaves, compared with 'a good' two octaves and a fourth); and whereas the tenor/contratenor flute in d¹ can also play soprano parts, the recorder needs a separate instrument for that range (with a compass of g¹ to g³).[162]

The otherwise unknown Aurelio Virgiliano wrote a two-part manuscript collection, *Il dolcimelo*, around 1600.[163] The first part contains instructions and diminutions 'to perform on the voice and all sorts of musical instruments'. The second part includes nine *ricercari* that can be performed on the recorder as well as other instruments; the third part, a fingering chart for an alto. Praetorius's monumental *Syntagma musicum* (1619) has been discussed earlier.

Sir Francis Bacon's posthumously published *Sylva Sylvarum* (1627), apparently based on his unfinished notes, makes the practical observation that: 'the recorder itself, or pipe, moistened a little on the inside, but set so as there be no drops left, maketh a more solemn sound than if the pipe were dry, but yet with a sweet degree of sibilation or purling'.[164]

In his *Harmonie universelle* (Paris, 1636) and its Latin predecessor *Harmonicorum libri* (1635), Marin Mersenne devotes several sections to instruments of the flute family: three-holed tabor pipe, flageolet and six-holed pipe, recorder, and transverse flute and fife. He observes that all kinds of flutes 'can make four or five different parts for an entire consort . . . which closely imitates the consort of voices, for it lacks only pronunciation, which one nearly approaches with these flutes'.[165]

In the section on the tabor pipe, Mersenne sets up the basic principle of his *tablature*, which serves as a fingering chart but also 'is used by those who do not know the value and use of normal musical notes'.[166] Later he shows the tablature for the six-holed pipe. These tablatures may well have been used as ones to play from, in the sense that we encounter in England later in the century for the flageolet and recorder. Parallel horizontal lines correspond to the holes of the instrument, a vertical bar placed on a line indicates a closed hole, and zeros placed on all remaining lines indicate open holes. Mersenne does not provide a symbol for the 'pinched' thumb-hole, using a zero instead, but noting: 'the hole that is stopped with the thumb of the left hand . . . must be half open, and not completely unstopped, as it is in the tablature, to make the notes that go beyond an octave, because the notes are better and more natural.'[167] All semitones are made by half-stopping holes; and leaving a hole more or less than half open can create quarter-tones for the enharmonic genus. (This genus in ancient Greek music theory includes two intervals of a *diesis*, about a quarter-tone, as discussed above in connection with Cardano.)

Mersenne's first engraving shows a recorder still made in one piece with apparently a slight inverse conical bore. His *tablature* uses the same way of showing fingerings as for the six-holed pipe, apart from the fingering - -2- ----, shown by means of one closed and seven open circles. The G-major and G-minor scales refer to a model recorder tuned in C, with a notated range of two octaves, c^1 to c^3 ('although some give it only the range of a thirteenth'), beginning with g^1, ascending to c^3, then descending to c^1.[168] The fingering is already completely 'Baroque', including supporting-finger technique.

On articulation, Mersenne differentiates between a 'dead' technique with the breath alone, used by 'rustics and apprentices', and a 'living' one employing the tip of the tongue, used by 'masters'.[169] He illustrates two methods of articulating a cadential trill: with *tara tara tara ta*; and with the breath alone (slurred), 'which imitates well the voice and the most excellent method of singing'.[170]

Besides the *Vertoninge*, Paulus Matthijsz in Amsterdam published another set of instructions, *Onderwyzinge*, around 1656, just before Jacob van Eyck's death.[171] See box on pp. 125–26. Gerbrant Quirijnsz van Blanckenburgh, an organist and carillonneur in Gouda, states that he wrote it 'at the request of P. Matthijsz, and at the service of all amateurs of the recorder'.[172] It explains 'how one can blow all the tones and semitones most common to the *handt-fluyt* entirely in tune, and how one can most easily make a grace on each one'.[173] These instructions, about a C instrument, are found with one of the extant copies of *Der Fluyten Lust-hof I* (3rd edn, ca. 1656). They could hardly be more different from those in *Vertoninge*. Van Blanckenburgh gives separate fingerings for every enharmonically equivalent note, the difference usually consisting of slightly more or less shading one finger-hole, and one or more trill fingerings for every pitch (again involving only one finger-hole). Ruth van Baak Griffioen notes: 'His fingerings are so nuanced . . . one suspects that they fit his own recorder but not necessarily anyone else's. He does mention, however, that for c♯[2], a closed-thumb fingering . . . is "a bit too low on all recorders." '[174] Beyond the fingerings he offers only two elementary pieces of advice: 'stop the fingers neatly, and . . . don't blow too hard or too soft, as through that you make the notes too sharp or too flat.'[175]

PHYSICAL CHARACTERISTICS

The bores of surviving Renaissance recorders can be classified into three main types, apparently used concurrently by the main makers.[176] The first type, found in the majority of surviving Renaissance recorders, has a primarily obconical bore. It follows an approximately cylindrical shape from the mouthpiece to around the thumb-hole. Then it contracts in an irregular cone to around the lowest tone-hole. From this point, where the diameter is about three-quarters of that at the mouthpiece, the bore expands gently to the bell in a conical fashion ('flared bell'). Recorders of all sizes can be made using this bore.

The second type of bore is essentially cylindrical, often with a pronounced expansion between the seventh tone-hole and the end of the bell. Recorders with this type of bore have a more open sound, richer in harmonics than those with the first type. Moreover, they can often play more notes in the higher register, although it is debatable whether this was the makers' original goal. The tone-holes are farther apart than on the first type: too far apart in fact to make larger sizes than tenor practical.

The third type of bore is cylindrical from the mouthpiece to around the seventh tone-hole. There follows a short but steep obconical section, creating an abrupt 'stepped' contraction in the bore. For this reason, Adrian Brown coined the term 'step' bore for this type, which is found in one-fifth of surviving Renaissance recorders. It tends to produce weaker lower notes than its obconical and cylindrical counterparts, but conveniently allows easy production of high notes using fingerings close to those of Baroque recorders and modern recorders with 'English' fingering, so it could be viewed as the forerunner to the Baroque bore. The larger diameter of the cylindrical section and then the abrupt contraction help to produce the third harmonic series, necessary for the higher notes. Again, sizes larger than the tenor cannot be made, as the tone-holes would be too far apart to be practical.[177]

The myth of a historical 'Ganassi' recorder

In the 1970s, several makers, notably Frederick Morgan, Bob Marvin, and Alec Loretto, sought to create a recorder that would play with Ganassi's high-note fingerings.[178] Marvin modelled his recorder on the frontispiece of *Fontegara*, then experimented with cylindrical bores and flared bells.[179] Morgan and Loretto independently took a recorder from the Kunsthistorisches Museum Vienna as a model: SAM 135 (formerly C146 and 8522), an alto by the Bassano family with the type-A !! maker's mark and a basically cylindrical bore. As Morgan noted, 'the voicing of the instrument is badly damaged', but 'a copy made from the measurements sounded well, and certainly played the fifteenth note [XV] with Ganassi's fingering, although a little too high. The notes above it were fine, and their pitch could be adjusted by small changes in fingering; but there was no possibility of adjusting in this way the note itself, which, even with the use of all the fingers, still tended to be sharp. A minor modification to the length of the bell and the amount of flare . . . gave the note, and also the fundamental well in tune.'[180] The Morgan design with this modification became the most prominent, not least because of the outstanding quality of his 'Ganassi' instruments, showcased by Frans Brüggen's performances and recordings as well as Morgan's generosity in distributing his drawing of SAM 135 to other makers.

It later emerged that SAM 135 was the middle size in a consort comprising a tenor, two altos, and a soprano, the case for which has survived (SAM 171).[181] Neither was SAM 135 a unique instrument. Many other surviving recorders, almost certainly part of consorts, have similar characteristics and could play with Ganassi's fingerings, although we have no indication that these were ever designed to specifically play his 'seven extra notes'. Neither is there any evidence of a separate type of Renaissance recorder made with the aim of increasing the upper range.

The 'Ganassi' recorder concept led to a thoroughly modern instrument, attractive to soloists for its strong tone and large range. See box on pp. 282–83.

THE BASSANO FAMILY AS MAKERS AND PERFORMERS:
THE COURT RECORDER CONSORT

In 1531, Henry VIII of England engaged four Venetian wind players using the last name 'de Jeronimo' for his shawm and sackbut consort.[182] They were in fact four of the sons of Jeronimo Bassano I (d. 1546–50?): Alvise (d. 1554), Anthony I (d. 1574), Jasper (d. 1577), and John (d. 1570). They stayed in England only a few years before returning to Venice. But in 1538, Henry attracted Anthony back as an instrument maker, followed by the other three brothers in 1539–40, along with their younger brother Baptista (d. 1576). Now the five of them made up a consort of 'recorders' – a unique professional example before the twentieth century.

This consort, expanded to six members in 1550, was employed until the amalgamation of the three court wind consorts into one group in 1630 – no less than 90 years. Its later members included Bassanos of the second and third generations in England (Arthur, Anthony II, Augustine, Edward, Henry, Jeronimo II, Lodovico), other foreigners (William Daman, Alphonso and Clement Lanier), and from 1593 onwards some native wind players (Robert Baker I and II, John Hussey, William Noake).[183] The musicians were on call daily in one of the five 'standing houses' of the monarch along the River Thames – Westminster, Greenwich, Richmond, Hampton Court, and Windsor – apparently to play for dances and dinners.

The Bassanos moved from the town of Bassano in the Veneto to Venice. Presumably Jeronimo's sons would have been trained in the highly expressive style of recorder playing described by Ganassi, including the improvisation of diminutions up to complex proportions – a good reason for Henry VIII to recruit them.

Little has survived of the court recorder consort's repertoire. The celebrated Fitzwilliam Wind Manuscript (late sixteenth–early seventeenth century) includes madrigals, motets, chansons, and a fantasia by Jeronimo Bassano II (1559–1635), all for six parts, which, if not performed by the consort, at least shows the probable kinds of pieces. Jeronimo also composed four five-part fantasias, in the free contrapuntal style of not later than about 1580, and he and Augustine (d. 1604) left some simple dances (almandes, pavans, and galliards). The vocal pieces, perhaps also the dances, would surely have come to life when performed with diminutions. Moreover, the consort would surely have mastered pieces in unusual proportions, such as some surviving instrumental pieces composed by members of the Chapel Royal, for example John Baldwine's *4 Vocum* (in 5/4 metre) and Christopher Tye's *Sit Fast* (which moves into 4:3 and 3:1).

A book about the town of Bassano published in 1577 by Lorenzo Marucini, a Venetian doctor, contains the following information about Jeronimo Bassano I:

> Maestro Gieronymo, called 'il Piva', inventor of a new bass wind instrument, most excellent *pifaro*, and employed by the Most Illustrious Signoria of Venice; he had three musician sons, trained by him, who together with their father were led to the Queen of England with a large salary and much honour; and the excellence of these great [men] was also in the making of recorders; indeed, those [recorders] marked with their mark are held in great veneration among musicians and people are willing to pay a lot of money for them where they can be found.[184]

Marucini makes some mistakes: Jeronimo had six sons, there is no record of him going to England, and five sons settled in England during Elizabeth's father's reign. Still, Marucini should have been on more certain ground about the reputation of recorders bearing the family's distinctive maker's mark. The 'new bass wind instrument' Jeronimo is said to have invented could well have been the curtal. At the court of Alfonso d'Este in Modena in 1506, a musician named Baptista da Verona was paid travel expenses for his journey to Venice to buy recorders, perhaps from Jeronimo.

The known makers among the London Bassanos begin with Anthony I, appointed 'maker of divers instruments' to the court in 1538 and presumably responsible for some of the cornetti, crumhorns, dulceuses (probably curtals), fifes, flutes, recorders, shawms, and a tabor pipe listed in Henry VIII's inventories (1542 and 1547). Alvise, the eldest of the brothers in England, had a 'working house' as well as a dwelling house in the family's living quarters at the dissolved Charterhouse monastery in 1545.

A sixth brother, Jacomo (d. by 1566), came to England with the other five but was not appointed to the court. Perhaps he made instruments privately; in any case he had returned to Venice by 1544. In 1559, three members of the Doge's *Pifferi* who also had their own independent company made an agreement with Jacomo and his son-in-law Santo Gritti de Sebenico (ca. 1530–86) to supply instruments, including recorders, to them and act as the makers' agents. John visited Venice in 1566–67, just after Jacomo's death, and a document in 1571 shows that he had been in a 'brotherly company' with Jacomo.[185] Probably the traffic went both ways between London and Venice, including the London brothers supplying Jacomo with instruments to sell in the larger Italian market.

Santo seems to have changed his last name to Bassano. In 1582, he took out a patent for new instruments, probably bassanelli. In 1572, Girolamo Dalla Casa, 'musician and *piffaro* at San Marco' in Venice, arranged for the sale to Diego de Guzmán de Silva, Spanish ambassador to Venice, of a large number of instruments and music (by Cipriano de Rore, Orlando di Lasso, Vincenzo Ruffo, and Pedro Guerrero) intended for the 'service and Galley Royal' of the Spanish king's half-brother, Don Juan de Austria, including a case of large recorders, perhaps made by Santo.[186] Juan was the commander of the Spanish armed forces and had his own budget in the royal household.

Santo's son Giovanni (1560/61–1617) became a *piffaro* of the Doge in 1576, as well as *maestro de canto* (singing teacher) at St Mark's from 1583, and he provided companies of musicians for churches and monasteries from 1586. He published a famous book of solo instrumental music and diminutions, *Ricercate, passaggi et cadentie* (1585), a collection of fifty diminished pieces, *Mottetti, madrigali et canzoni francesi* (1591), and several books of pieces.

The only member of the second generation of the Bassano family in England who undoubtedly made instruments was Arthur (1547–1624), who bequeathed to his son Anthony II (1579–1658) 'all my instruments, working tools and necessaries belonging to the art of making of instruments'. So Anthony or his son may well have been responsible for making the very large recorders depicted by Mersenne (1636) with the remark that they 'have been sent from England to one of our kings'.[187]

Further instruments made by the Bassanos in England can be traced in Spain and Germany.[188] In 1562, Toledo Cathedral bought a case of eight recorders: two altos, four tenors, and two bassets, 'made in England and bearing the mark of a fly's wings'.[189] In 1567, Burgos Cathedral bought unspecified instruments from England, facilitated by the Spanish ambassador, and Ciudad Rodrigo Cathedral bought recorders and crumhorns from England. Seville Cathedral owned a set of twelve recorders – two sopranos, four altos, four tenors, and two *contrabajos* – plus two curtals that had been purchased from England in 1607. An expensive set of recorders and cornetti was bought in England for the Porta Coeli convent, Valladolid, in 1618, facilitated by a later Spanish ambassador.[190] Sometime before 1626, Huesca Cathedral had bought a set of eight recorders and an additional large one in England.

The banker Raymund Fugger Jr owned 'a large case, in it twenty-seven recorders, large and small, made in England' in 1566.[191] Five years later, his relative

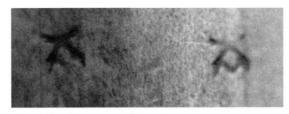

11. Renaissance recorder makers' marks: 1. 'Fly' (silkworm moth) mark of the Bassano family; 2. Gothic A mark of the Schnitzer family; 3. Trefoil mark of the Rauch von Schratt family; 4. HIE.S mark; 5. HIERS.S. mark.

Johann (Hans) Jakob Fugger, artistic adviser and superintendent of the music at the Bavarian court in Munich, offered for sale a remarkable chest containing forty-five wind instruments made by the Bassano brothers in London. The otherwise elaborate descriptions of these instruments neglect to name some precisely, but they probably consisted of thirteen shawms (in two sets), ten cornetti, a tabor pipe or flute, twelve crumhorns, and nine recorders. It was apparently unusual that these different instruments 'are all tuned together at common organ pitch',[192] a standard probably equivalent to *mezzo punto*.[193] An accompanying letter mentions an additional chest of six large viole da gamba and a chest of three lutes – evidence that the Bassanos also made stringed instruments.

I proposed in 1983 that the Bassano family's maker's marks were variants of ‼, representing the silkworm moth found on the family's coat of arms, and also perhaps HIERS.[194] The primary theory was proven in 2021 by the Toledo reference to 'fly's wings'.[195] About 150 woodwind instruments with ‼ marks survive: cornetti, curtals, flutes, shawms, and no fewer than fifty recorders. Maggie Kilbey has divided the variant marks into eighteen types plus some unclassified ones.[196]

Adrian Brown assesses the ‼ instruments as:

the masterpieces among surviving Renaissance recorders. The majority of them are beautiful, well-proportioned instruments, and their technology is more advanced than that found on many of the other surviving recorders. Their tone-holes are standardized in that like sizes in different collections follow the same pattern; on larger sizes, they are often angled up or down the bore, giving the player an easier stretch for the hands. The caps are attuned to the instrument, in that the space inside the cap is made to dictate the size of the air reservoir thus created, giving the recorder a better sound and control. The crooks and holes inside the caps show similar ingenuity, the holes having a taper towards the inside space of the cap which softens the flow of air into the recorder and reduces problems with the stability of the attack. The variants of the mark often accompany subtle differences in making: different shapes of windows, drilling of tone-holes, styles of keywork and so on, suggesting that they may represent the different generations or workshops.[197]

His last argument is strengthened by his research in the Accademia Filarmonica of Verona, where the !! recorders, survivors of three separate sets, show three different styles of making and are tuned in three slightly different pitches.

Most !! recorders fit the third grid of pitch-sizes mentioned above: bass in Bb^0, basset in f^0, tenor in c^1, and alto in g^1. These instruments clearly represent a long period of recorder making, from the 1540s or earlier to the end of the century and beyond. The bores are generally obconical, although the two surviving altos are more cylindrical.

Twenty-nine woodwind instruments with HIERS or HIES marks survive, including thirteen recorders (also cornetti, crumhorns, and curtals). Recent research suggests that the maker was not a member of the Bassano family but probably Gerolamo Salbrun 'dalli flauti' of Venice (fl. 1581–1607).[198] These instruments, ranged in fifths starting from F, have a crude or rustic design, with great irregularity among instruments of the same size.

REPERTOIRE, 1500–1600

VOCAL

The earliest music mentioned in connection with recorders consists of vocal repertoire, playable at the notated pitch or requiring transposition. As mentioned above, in 1505, the Venetian *piffaro* Alvise Zorzi offered Francesco Gonzaga of Mantua a motet he had arranged for eight recorders.[199] In Nicole de la Chesnaye's morality play *La Condamnacion de banquet* (1507), Bonne Compaignie (Good Company) addresses the musicians: 'Come on, you galants who usually play harps and other instruments, you've been good too long. A song goes best with recorder playing,' followed by a list of no fewer than seventeen songs of the day.[200]

The title page of the collection *LXXV. hubscher Lieder myt Discant. Alt. Bas. und Tenor. lustick ʒu syngen* (Cologne, Arnt von Aich, 1519) states that the songs are suitable for recorders (*fleiten*), flutes (*schwegelen*), and other instruments. All but two of the seventy-five pieces are notated in the *chiavi naturali*, including thirty-one in the clef combination C1–C3–C4–F4 and fourteen in the slight variant C1–C3–C3–F4. As Peter Van Heyghen has pointed out, 'almost all the songs can be played comfortably on a standard four-part recorder consort' (alto, two tenor, and bass parts).[201]

A collection of twenty-eight four-part French chansons and two Italian songs published by Pierre Attaingnant in Paris in 1533, *Chansons musicales a quatre parties*, indicates four that can be played on recorders, seventeen on flutes, and seven on both. Only the soprano part-book survives, but some of the chansons can be completed from concordances.[202] A second collection published by Attaingnant that year, *Vingt et sept chansons a quatre parties desquelles les plus convenable a la fleuste dallemant . . . et a la fleuste a neuf trous*, also of twenty-eight four-part chansons despite the title, contains two marked for recorders, nine for flutes, and twelve for both. The French and Flemish composers of the chansons considered suitable for recorders are both well-known and obscure: Bourguignon, Bridam, Jean Guyon, Jacotin, Josquin des Prez, Guillaume Le Heurteur, Johannes Lupi, Pierre Passereau, Claudin de Sermisy, and Pierre Vermont.

Georg Forster's *Ein Ausʒug guter alter und newer teutscher Liedlein* (Nuremberg, 1539) states that it is 'appropriate to use on all sorts of instruments'.[203] A copy of the fourth edition (1552) contains handwritten annotations by an anonymous musician indicating possible instrumentation, including twenty songs for flutes, six for recorder, and two for both.[204] A madrigal and a motet suitable for recorders were sent to the Accademia Filarmonica di Verona in 1552. See p. 115 below.

Printed or manuscript music of songs is depicted in some sixteenth-century works of art that include the recorder. In the *Allegory of True Love* by Pieter Jansz Pourbus (ca. 1547), two soprano recorders facing in opposite directions are placed on the tenor part of an explicitly sexual, pastoral four-part chanson by Thomas Crecquillon, *Ung gay bergier* (published by Tielman Susato in 1543), which is sitting on a dining table; next to it the shepherd Daphnis holds another soprano recorder – two associations of the recorder in one painting.[205]

DANCE

The cover of a set of dance choreographies, *Sensuyvent plusieurs basses dances*, probably published by Jacques Moderne in Lyons (1530s), depicts a four-part consort of recorders. Moderne's *Musicque de joye* (ca. 1550) contains ricercars and dances intended primarily for instrumental performance on 'spinets, violins, and recorders'.[206] *Le Piacevoli notti*, a piece of imaginative literature published by Gianfrancesco Straparola in Venice (1550–53), describes an aristocratic company partying in an empty palace on an island in the lagoon.[207] Recorders (*flauti*), also sweet recorders (*soavi flauti*), are mentioned in connection with dance music.

In 1532, the charter of the town musicians of Reval (Tallinn), Estonia, mentions that 'after the evening meal they should play four popular double dances and then they can play a double dance with recorders (*flouten*) or crumhorns'.[208]

At the wedding of Count Johann Georg of Hohenzollern in Hechingen in 1598, at a dance, 'The trumpets were no longer used, but viols, flutes (*Zwerchpfeifen*), and recorders (*Flöten*) as quieter instruments. The same was the case with dinner and after it.'[209] The inventory of his instrument collection in 1609 includes 'A consort of twelve recorders, consisting of a large bass, three tenors, three altos, three sopranos, and one higher soprano; the other high soprano is lacking. Five recorders, namely two tenors and three tenors [sic].'[210]

Recorders are documented several times in the French ballet of the period. In the first ballet de cour, the celebrated *Ballet comique de la royne* (1581), a scene depicts Tritons, represented by the singers of the Chambre du Roi playing lyres, lutes, harps, recorders, and other instruments, mixed with the voices.[211] Later an intermezzo 'is composed of eight satyrs, seven of whom are playing recorders, and only one singing, who is M. Saint-Laurens, singer of the Chambre du Roi'.[212]

The instrumentalist and composer Michel Henry the younger (1555–1625 or later), who eventually became *violon de la chambre du roi* (ca. 1616), copied a collection of ballet airs around 1620.[213] Seven airs towards the beginning of the collection are described as having been performed in 1587 'around the town' by his father and others on lutes, spinets, mandores, violins, recorders (*flutes à neuf trous*), pipe and tabor, tambours de Basque, and larigaux.[214]

The eighteenth-century author Henri Sauval, writing about Jacques Mauduit, who took over the direction of the Académie de Poésie et de Musique after the death of Antoine de Baïf in 1589, remarked: 'Sometimes we get together beforehand to sing chansons, and where recorders are welcome. . . .'[215]

MIXED CONSORTS AND TABLE MUSIC

Mixed consorts, some large, involving the recorder, are described in several sources about celebrations in the sixteenth century. See Table 7. Besides the wedding banquets listed there and in relation to Hechingen above, recorders are documented as taking part in other table music.

An otherwise unknown author named Simeon Zuccollo da Cologna published a book called *La pazzia del ballo* (The insanity of dancing, Padua, 1549), which rails against the evils of dancing, perhaps satirically. After lambasting the musicians around the biblical King David, as observed by the prophet Amos, Zuccollo turns

Table 7. Mixed consorts and ensembles

Year	Place	Information	Instrumentation
1529	Ferrara	Wedding banquet for Cardinal Ippolito II d'Este	Prelude: *cetera* (cittern?), lute, harp, and recorder (*Flauto*); four dancing couples in *balli alla gagliarda*
			3rd course: harp, recorder (*Flauto*), and harpsichord
			8th course: 3 recorders (*tre Flauti*) and 3 cornamuses (alternating or in octaves) with viola da gamba; 2 people doing tricks
			17th (last) course: Alfonso della Viola conducted a composition with 6 voices, 6 viols, lira, lute, *Cittara*, sackbut, tenor recorder (*Flauto mezzano*) and bass recorder (*Flauto grosso*), flute (*Flauto alla Alemana*), *sordina*, and 2 keyboard instruments
1529	Ferrara	Similar banquet	1st course: Composition by Alfonso della Viola performed by 11 singers with 5 viols, harpsichord, lute, and tenor and bass recorders (*Flauto grosso, & un mezzano*)

Year	Place	Information	Instrumentation
			4th course: another composition by Alfonso performed by 5 singers with 6 viols, violin, *dolʒaina*, capless crumhorn, 2 tenor recorders (*Due Flauti meʒani*), organ, and mute cornetto
			9th (last) course: music performed by 5 voices with 5 viols, harpsichord, bass recorder (*Flauto grosso*), lira, sackbut, and flute (*Flauto all'Alemana*)
1565	Florence	Wedding of Francesco de' Medici; intermedii for Francesco d'Ambra, *La Cofanaria*, composed by Alessandro Striggio and Francesco Corteccia	A1. Instrumental music for opening of Heaven, Striggio: 4 double harpsichords, 4 viols, 2 sackbuts, 2 tenor recorders (*tenori di flauti*), mute cornetto, flute (*traversa*), and 2 lutes
			A2. Ballata, 'A me, che fatta', Striggio, sung by Venus, 3 Graces, and 4 Seasons with 2 harpsichords, 4 bass viols, alto lute, mute cornetto, sackbut, and 2 recorders (*flauti diritti*)
			A3. 'Ecco Madre', Striggio, sung by Cupid (Amore) and four Passions with 2 harpsichords, bass lute, violone, treble viol and recorder (*flauto*) playing *passaggi* (*aggiunto*), 4 flutes, and sackbut offstage
			B. 'Oh altero miracolo novello', Striggio, sung by Cupid, Zephyrus, Playfulness, and Laughter with 4 lutes, viola da gamba, and lirone onstage; 3 harpsichords, bass lute, treble viol, alto flute (*traversa contr'alto*), bass? recorder (*flauto grande tenore*), bass sackbut, and mute cornetto playing *passaggi* offstage

1568	Florence	Baptism of Leonora de' Medici; intermedii for Lotto Del Mazza, *I Fabii*, composed by Alessandro Striggio	B1. 'Perche giovine', sung by Hercules and Pleasure with 3 harpsichords, 3 lutes, 4 sackbuts, 4 viole da gamba, 2 recorders, and flute
			E2. 'O che non sol', sung by Love, Fear, Glory, and Honour with 2 sackbuts and 3 recorders
			E3. 'Se de'un medesmo germe', 21 voices with 2 sackbuts and 3 recorders plus 4 viole da gamba, mute cornetto, lira da braccio, and lute
			E4. 'Vattene ò bella schiera', 9 voices with 2 sackbuts and 3 recorders
			F. 'O lieto, ò vago Aprile', 12 voices with 2 cornetti, 4 sackbuts, 6 lutes, treble and bass viols, 2 recorders, and flute
1568	Munich	Wedding of Wilhelm V, Duke of Bavaria	Normal dinner music at the court: cornamuse, recorders (*flauti*), flutes (*fifferi*), sackbuts, and cornetti; canzoni francesi and other cheerful works
			6th course: 6 violoni, 6 recorders (*flauti*), 6 voices, and keyboard instrument
			Festive tables in the middle of 3 labyrinths: harpsichord, sackbut, recorder (*flauto*), lute, cornamusa, mute cornetto, viola da gamba, and flute (*fiffaro*)
			Dessert: 3 choirs of 4 parts: 1) 4 viole da gamba; 2) 4 large recorders (*flauti grossi*); 3) dolzaina, cornamusa, flute (*fiffaro*), and mute cornetto
			Lunch: unknown motet in 40 parts by Striggio, directed by Orlando di Lasso: 8 sackbuts, 8 viole de arco, 8 large recorders (*flauti grossi*), keyboard instrument, large lute; other parts taken by voices
1575	Stuttgart	Wedding of Duke Ludwig of Württemberg	Procession to the church: 'loud symphony of bright sackbuts and cornetti, fast recorders (*Flöten*) and flutes, in four, five, and six parts, with strings, harpsichords, crying pipes, and shawms, which the heart likes to delight in'

Year	Place	Information	Instrumentation
			Banquet: table music included even more instruments: strings, lutes, harps, virginals, positive organ and regal, violins, flutes, and recorders, bombards, cornetti, curtals, sackbuts, and bass viol
			Later 'a piece in four voices soon changed freely, for recorders, cornetti, and flutes, which can be played so fast'
1586	Florence	Wedding of Cesar d'Este; intermezzi for Giovanni Bardi, *L'Amico fido*	VI. E2. 'Squarciasi il velo oscuro', Striggio, sung by 14 nymphs with lute, harps, harpsichords, sackbuts, and bass recorders (*flauti grossi*)
			VI. F1. 'O noi lieti, e felici', Bardi, sung by 2 choruses with lutes, harps, *dolʒaine*, bagpipes, 3 viole da gamba, recorders (*flauti*), flutes, sackbuts, regular and mute cornetti, violins, and bass recorders (*flauti grossi*)

Sources: Brown 1973, 97–107; Brown 1975, 238–40; Messisburgo 1980, ff. 10, 11, 12, 14v, 16v, 17v, 19; Moroney 2007, 11; Pietzsch 1960, 49–51; Troiano 1980, ff. 44v, 65v, 66v, 68v, 146v; Weaver 1961, 366–76.

his attention to what seem to be contemporary priests who enjoy their drink too much, and 'immediately they start singing, and with recorders, cornetti, cornamusas, and their other instruments, start to play madrigali, sonetti, and amorous canzoni, lascivious and very dishonest'.[216]

During festivities at the Inner Temple, one of the four Inns of Court in London, in 1562, 'The Prince so served with tender meats, sweet fruits, and dainty delicates confectioned with curious cookery . . . and at every course the trumpeters blew the courageous blast of deadly war, with noise of drum and fife, with the sweet harmony of violins, sackbuts, recorders, and cornetts, with other instruments of music, as it seemed Apollo's harp had tuned their stroke.' The 'prince' in question was the satirical part of Prince of Pallaphilios, acted by the royal favourite Lord Robert Dudley.[217]

At a Carnival dinner at the court of Charles IX in France in 1564, 'Each course was brought in with music: a concert of trumpets and sackbuts; or four voices accompanied by "a spinet, a treble viol, an alto recorder, and a bagpipe."'[218]

When the Portuguese king Sebastião I met Felipe II of Spain at the monastery of Guadalupe in 1576, Rodrigo de Beça, Sebastião's chaplain, wrote: 'we had at the table two musicians who went with us, with their Castilian guitars. They sang very well, and there were recorders.'[219]

A miniature by Hans Mielich of the Bavarian court Kapelle around 1570 shows a hall of the palace with Orlando di Lasso standing by Duke Albert V on the extreme left, listening to an ensemble of musicians. There are about twenty singers, and the instruments include virginals, strings, curtal, flute, sackbut, cornetti, and what seem to be alto, tenor, and bass recorders.[220]

During the second half of the sixteenth century, consorts of unlike instruments became common in England, the practice perhaps having been transmitted through Italian musicians at court. The English mixed consort (sometimes anachronistically called 'broken consort') usually consisted of treble viol or treble violin, bass viol, lute, bandora, cittern, and flute. The Matthew Holmes consort books (ca. 1595) are alone in specifying a recorder. [221] This would have been a tenor, notated in G2 clef, in the same register as the flute, except for one piece in C2 that fits the alto.

Praetorius (1619) gives a much broader range of instruments for 'a whole consort in the English manner': harpsichord, two or three lutes, theorbo, bandola, cittern, bass violin, recorder or flute, muted trombone, viola bastarda, and a small treble violin.[222] Two Continental depictions of the mixed consort include the recorder: Adriaen Pietersz van der Venne's *Celebration in Honour of the Truce between the Spanish and the United Provinces of the Netherlands* (1619): lute, violin, harpsichord, bass violin, orpharion, perhaps curtal, xylophone, and tenor recorder; and Simone de Passe's *Musical Company* (1612): cittern, violin, viol, bandora, and a small recorder.

THE RECORDER IN SPAIN AND PORTUGAL

Almost everything we know about the recorder's participation in European sacred music during the sixteenth century comes from the religious institutions of Spain and Portugal.[223] Such a development could happen in those countries because of the perspective, belatedly articulated in Father Martín de la Vera's treatise *Instrución de eclesiásticos* (Madrid, 1630), that because recorders, shawms, and crumhorns could be imitated on the organ, it was permissible to use them to accompany sacred polyphony.

Salaried minstrels were attached to a cathedral first in Seville, starting in 1526. Initially, there were five minstrels, three shawms and two sackbuts, augmented by another sackbut in 1546, although these designations did not preclude them from playing other instruments. Douglas Kirk has called the introduction into the church liturgy of secular instruments, especially loud ones, 'churching the shawms'.[224]

The first reference to cathedral minstrels 'churching the recorders' comes from Toledo in 1532 when it started employing six minstrels: an order 'for nine recorders in a case covered with black leather'.[225] Two dozen other cathedrals, large and small, followed suit in adding sets of recorders for their minstrels – an impressive list: Braga, Portugal (first documented 1538), Jaén (1545), Burgos and León (1548), Valencia (1560), Granada, Seville, and Évora, Portugal (1565), Ciudad Rodrigo (1567), Ourense (1568), Oviedo (1572), Plasencia (1575), Calahorra, Huesca, and Zamora (1578), Calatayud (1581), Sigüenza (1598), Zaragoza (1599), Palencia (1602), Barbosa (1618), Teruel and Valladolid (1631), Cuenca (1633), and Badajoz (1673).

Other religious institutions did the same: the Jesuit College in Évora, Portugal (1559), the church in Úbeda (1568), the Royal Monastery in Guadalupe (1576), the church of Pilar in Zaragoza (1579), the church in Valdemoro (1582), the Augustinian monastery of Santa Cruz in Coimbra, Portugal (by 1618), and the Porta Coeli convent in Valladolid (1618). Two churches hired musicians from Toledo, attached to the cathedral as well as independent, to play wind instruments including recorders: La Puebla de Montalbán (Divine Office, 1585) and Casarrubios del Monte (Vespers and Masses, 1590).

The number of recorders in a case or set varied from two (basses) to four (five times), then up to fourteen, as well as two cases jointly holding seventeen plus an extra three basses. Probably the sets of four consisted of alto, two tenors, and bass. The instruments were used intensively: in Seville (1565), a new case of recorders was ordered to be bought if the old one could not be repaired; in Granada (1578), recorders were repaired; in Calatayud (1581), a case for the recorders was ordered to be repaired or replaced; and in Sigüenza (1598), old recorders kept in a chapel were checked to see if they were in good enough condition to replace ones missing from the main set. The origins of the instruments are listed in Table 8.

The first recorder maker documented in Portugal was João Gonçalves, a shawm player at the Cathedral of Braga by 1532, paid in 1538 'for making the recorders and shawms', presumably for himself and his five colleagues to play in the services.[226] He was employed as a shawm player at a salary of 4,000 reales and as 'official maker of recorders and shawms' for an extra 2,000 reales in 1538–40 and 1543.[227]

One of the Spanish royal minstrels, called Gaspar de Camargo (Senior or Junior), lamenting the dearth of makers and suitable wood for instruments in the

Table 8. Origins of Spanish recorders

Date	Place	Origin	Recorders
1549	Toledo	purchased in Seville	a case of
1565	Granada		large, medium, and small in *mixturas* for 12 ducats plus 7 *reales* shipping
1550		Prince Felipe purchased on Grand Tour in Augsburg	a case of
1551	Toledo	purchased from former minstrel now serving Felipe	a case of
1562	Toledo	purchased from the Bassanos in London	a case of eight (2A 4T 2B)
1567	Burgos		unspecified
1567	Ciudad Rodrigo		recorders and crumhorns
1614	Seville		a set apparently bought in 1607 (2S 4A 4T 4B with 2 curtals)
1618	Valladolid convent		recorders and cornetti for 600 ducats including shipping
1626	Huesca		a case of eight very fine and outside another very good big one serving as bass
1599	Ourense	brought from Braga, Portugal	'various'
1607	Sigüenza	brought from Zaragoza	unspecified
1631	Valladolid	purchased in Madrid	to replace recorder missing from set for 5½ ducats

Sources: Borgerding 1997, 99; Duro-Peña 1996, 227; López-Calo 1963, I, 225–26; *LMR*; López-Calo 2007, VII, 121; López Suero 2021a, 135–36; Miller 2018, 343; Ruiz Jiménez 2021a.

country, bought tools at a cost of 200 ducats – about two-and-a-half times his annual salary at court – for a talented local maker called Peri Juan, presumably to set him up in business, and arranged a licence for him to cut wood in several Spanish forests.[228] Bartolomé de Selma (d. 1616), wind-instrument maker to the Royal Chapel in Madrid, left no instruments, but tools and supplies for making recorders are listed in his probate inventory, and he put ferrules (probably thumb-bushings) in three alto recorders for the court.

The sets or consorts of recorders sometimes came with other instruments and were presumably customarily played with them. In Seville in 1590, a cathedral minstrel named Luis Albánchez sold to Juan de Villarrubia, a musician in Cádiz, a curtal and a case of eight recorders said to be at the same pitch as the curtal. The set in Seville in 1614 originally with two curtals has already been mentioned. In the same year, Barbosa Cathedral bought a set of recorders with a sackbut for the bass part. This last reference especially confirms Praetorius's comment that for the bass part of a recorder consort, sometimes a curtal or sackbut was used rather than a large recorder.

The recorders were used in Spanish sacred music primarily in the Divine Office, especially at Vespers and Compline, although also in the Mass; the festivities of Christmas and Corpus Christi are each cited twice. At Jaén in 1545, the authorities issued an order 'that the motet sung after the Elevation of the Host' in the Mass 'be played by the minstrels on the recorders'.[229]

The comprehensive rules governing musical practice formulated for the cathedral of León in 1548, four years after its band of minstrels was founded under the direction of the former royal musician Juan de Torquemada, mention one specific example of instrumentation: on 'Holy Saturday at the Mass . . . at Compline [the minstrels play] the first psalm, the last, and the *Nunc dimittis* with the recorders in *fabordón*.'[230] *Fabordón*, the Spanish equivalent of the Italian *falsobordone*, was 'a chordal recitation based on root-position chords, with the form and often the melody of a Gregorian psalm tone. . . . Instrumentalists usually embellished the repeated chords of the recitations, just as soloists embellished the cadences.'[231]

At the inauguration of the Jesuit College in Évora, Portugal in 1559, a solemn Mass included recorders. The regulations for musical practice at Évora's Cathedral for 1565 stipulate: 'When singers perform alongside instrumentalists, they take one or more parts in polyphonic pieces while the other parts are assigned to either the organ or the recorders.'[232] In the 1560s, four shawm players were employed there who doubtless played the recorders. Because the singers were usually placed at a distance from the organ or instrumentalists, the chapelmaster had to direct when singers were sent to perform next to the organ or recorders. One-to-a-part singing accompanied in this way was mostly used in *alternatim* performance of psalms, canticles, and hymns: the singers and recorders on one side, the choir on the other, as the regulations for 1569 specify.[233] Some later regulations, possibly from the 1590s, give instructions for performing the verses of the first Compline psalm for Sundays and Holy Days in Lent; in two of them the recorders play with the vocal soloist(s). By that time, the wind instruments had expanded to include cornetto and curtal, and as many as nine players were employed.

At the meeting of Felipe II of Spain and Sebastião I of Portugal at the Royal Monastery in Guadalupe in 1576, recorders were played not only in a secular context in the table music (see p. 93 above), but also later during the Elevation of the Host in the Mass.

At Seville Cathedral in 1586, the maestro de capilla Francisco Guerrero, whose order about *glosas* in performance is mentioned above, also stipulated in relation to Compline: 'that in the choral festivities there always be a verse with recorders. That in the three verses that are played in the *Salve Regina*, one be with shawms, the other with cornetti, and the other with recorders, because using one instrument all the time is annoying.'[234] These regulations were still in effect in 1611.

In 1610, at a celebration of the beatification of Ignatius of Loyola in Seville, Alonso Lobo (1555–1617), then maestro de capilla, wrote incidental music, evidently for two choirs, one of them instrumental. In the Vespers, 'Lobo . . . put singular diligence into all sorts of singing; thus in the psalms, with several shawms and sackbuts, curtals, cornetti, recorders, and two organs, as in *chanzonetas* composed on purpose for the Saint. . . . The Mass continued with the same variety of music, and all the instruments we spoke of at Vespers, plus motets, villancicos, and other similar compositions in which the master wishes to take special care.'[235]

In Sigüenza, province of Guadalajara, the *Directorio de Coro* in 1594 ordered in connection with Christmas: 'At the same time that the words *Nativitas Domini nostri Iesus Christi secundum carnem* have just been sung, the minstrels have a short and devout verse with the instruments that seem most appropriate to them, recorders or [corna]musas.'[236]

At Zaragoza Cathedral, the musicians were instructed in 1599 that *chanzonetas* and villancicos should not be sung on Christmas Day or Epiphany during Matins or Mass, as they interrupt the Divine Office and mix the sacred with the profane. Instead, 'a lot of solemnity and music should be added in the said festivities of Christmas Day and Epiphany, choosing a verse in each psalm, the one that seems most appropriate to the festival, and that said verses are composed by the chapel master in polyphony, using great variety in them: sometimes with simple voices, others with voices and recorders . . .'.[237]

In Palencia in 1602, during the Corpus Christi festivities, the cathedral authorities prescribed that after the Divine Office during the day, the singers should gather in the chapel, sing with small organ, 'and the minstrels play shawms, recorders, and violones'.[238] During Corpus Christi in 1627, 'at one o'clock everyone will be in the church – chapel master, organist, singers, and minstrels – and the minstrels will begin with the shawms, and then with the recorders and other instruments . . .'.[239]

The *Constituciones* of the Cathedral of Valencia, published in 1636, specify: 'on all Thursdays of the year, when the Office of the Holy Sacrament is made, the Mass will be said as a first-class feast, and the Compline of said Thursdays with the greatest possible solemnity; singing a verse with one voice and the organ, another verse with *fabordon* in four parts, and another verse with recorders and one voice; and all of them getting together, joined by some minstrel, when they will say *Gloria Patri*, etc.'[240]

In 1607, services commenced at the partly completed church of San Pedro in Lerma. Francisco Gómez, the Duke of Lerma, hired four musicians who had evidently been playing at the court in Madrid, on alto shawm, two sackbuts, and curtal. A soprano player was added the next year: Andrés de Alamillos from León, on cornetto, soprano shawm, recorder, and cornamuse,[241] paid more than the others, so probably he served as the band leader. Alamillos seems to have brought with him a surviving manuscript consisting of fabordones by Philippe Rogier, Guerrero, and Cristóbal de Morales; hymns by Juan de Urrede and Guerrero; motets by Lobo, Guerrero, and Giovanni Palestrina; chansons by Clemens non Papa, Crecquillon, Lasso, and Rogier; and madrigals by Lasso, Philippe Verdelot, and Striggio. Kirk argues that this manuscript was probably produced at the Royal Chapel in the early 1590s and intended for the Hurtado de Mendoza family in León.

The minstrels stayed for only a year or two; thereafter the duke used the nuns of the Dominican convent of San Blas, which was moved to Lerma in 1611. They could sing and play well on a variety of stringed and wind instruments. The duke lent them books of music that the minstrels had played: motets by Guerrero and Tomás Luiz de Victoria as well as sacred music by Juan Navarro.

THE RECORDER IN THE SPANISH AND PORTUGUESE COLONIES

One of the most remarkable stories in the recorder's history is the export of the instrument and players by the Spanish and Portuguese as part of the colonisation and enforced Christianization of the Americas and elsewhere.[242] Throughout what are now South America, Central America, and southern North America, from

Mexico to Argentina and from Ecuador to Brazil, as well as in isolated places in Africa and Asia, missionaries discovered that the indigenous people – whom they called *indios* in the Americas – delighted in music and readily learned to sing and compose Western polyphony and play it on Western instruments, especially the recorder. The instrument was taught in schools, employed in the liturgy as well as in secular festivals, and in Spanish colonies made by the *indios* themselves. The musical practices are similar but not identical to those in Spain and Portugal.

In their zeal to Christianize the 'heathen', the Spanish and Portuguese enslaved, exploited, expelled, and exterminated millions of people, employing the recorder as a tool for conversion. From the perspective of the colonized, ancient cultures were savaged by foreigners with superior weaponry, their own instruments and music were largely suppressed and replaced, and their musical ability was used against them in their own downfall. In short, the recorder was co-opted in the imposition of European cultures. We would do well to remember that the following accounts, so sweet on the surface, are all from the colonizers' perspective.

SPANISH COLONIES

The earliest reports come from the city of Tlaxcala, New Spain (later Mexico). The Franciscan missionary Father Toribio de Moura Benavente (aka Motolinía) (1482–1568), quoting a letter from an anonymous friar, wrote about two celebrations. In 1538, a Corpus Christi procession, so splendid that 'if there was the Pope and the Emperor with their court, they would greatly rejoice to see it', ended with the musical ensembles joining up: 'a polyphonic choir of many singers and its recorder music played together with singers, trumpets, and drums, small and large bells, and this all sounded next to the entrance and exit of the church, so that it seemed the sky was falling down'.[243] Note that recorders were even played in the open air. An Easter celebration in 1539: 'These people of Tlaxcala have greatly enlivened the Divine Office with songs and music. For polyphonic music they have two choirs (*capillas*), each with more than twenty singers, and two choirs of recorders, where they also played the rebec and Moorish flutes, and have very good masters of drums played together with small bells, which sound delightful.'[244] In 1549, the cathedral in Ciudad de Guatemala bought 'a case of large recorders'.[245]

Quito, in what is now Ecuador, was founded in 1534; a year later, the first Franciscan monks arrived, including Father Jodoco Rique (1498–1575; original name Joos de Rijcke), a native of Mechelen. In 1551, the monks began to build a church and monastery that incorporated a school, entitled the Real Colegio de San Andrés in 1559. A manuscript of 1575 relates: 'In addition to teaching the *indios* children to read and write, Father Jodoco taught them to play all the [European] musical instruments, keyboard and strings, as well as the sackbut and shawms, recorders, trumpets, and cornetti, and the knowledge of polyphony and plainchant.'[246] Jodoco himself wrote in a letter dated 1556 that the *indios* were 'Extremely intelligent; they easily learn reading and writing, singing, playing recorders and other similar instruments.'[247] A document of 1568 describes the teachers at the school, three of whom were *indios* and associated with the recorder.[248] A request for more funds from Spain in 1573 incorporates testimony from witnesses. One Captain Pedro de Ruanes reports that the *indios* 'have shown and taught in the said school to play music of organs, trumpets, recorders, and shawms, from which . . . many churches and monasteries of this land have been provided with singers and musicians and players, of which great good has come and continues'.[249] Bishop Reginaldo de Lizárraga (1540–1609), describing Quito in 1605, observes: 'I met at this school an *indio* boy named Juan, and because he was red [*bermejo*] by birth they called him Juan Bermejo, who could be a *tiple* of the chapel of the Supreme Pontiff; this boy came out so skilled in polyphony, recorder, and keyboard that, as a man, they took him out to the main church, where he served as a chapel master and organist.'[250]

In the Viceroyalty of Peru, the Jesuit Father Juan de Matienzo (1567) recommended that instruction in singing and playing recorders should be aimed at the sons of *caciques* (leaders) to foster the programme of Christianization.[251] In the Philippines, also considered part of New Spain, between 1581 and 1596 the Augustinian Father Diego de Rojas worked in the provinces of Cagayán, Ilocos, and Pangasinán, spreading Christianity. In various places he resided, he had a 'school for the children of the natives, whom he clothed and took care of, and taught to read and write and play recorder and shawm and learn plainchant and polyphony'.[252]

So popular had recorders and other Western instruments already become by the 1560s that the authorities issued limiting orders. In Mexico City (1566), the Dominican Archbishop Alonso de Montúfar called a church council meeting, which issued the following: 'The great excess in our archdiocese of musical instruments, of shawms, recorders, viols, trumpets, and the great number of *indios* who spend their time in playing and singing obliges us to apply a remedy and to place a limit on all this superabundance. We therefore require and order that . . . as for the shawms and recorders, we require that they be stored in the principal towns and distributed only for use in the villages on festival days of their patron saints. . . .'²⁵³ Five years later, Felipe II of Spain reinforced the council's provisions by issuing the following order to the president and ombudsmen of the royal *audiencia* of Mexico:

> Because of the cost of maintaining the present excessive number of instrumentalists who consume their time playing trumpets, clarions, shawms, sackbuts, recorders, cornetti, dulzainas, fifes, viols, rebecs, and other kinds of instruments, an inordinate variety of which are now in use in the monasteries . . . and because the number of musicians and singers is reported to be increasing constantly in both large and small towns . . . and because very many of those reared simply to sing and play on instruments soon become lazy scoundrels whose morals are reported to be extremely bad . . . and because in many places they do not pay tribute and resist lawful authority, we require a reduction in the number of *indios* who shall be permitted to occupy themselves as musicians.²⁵⁴

But Steven Barwick observes that 'not all of the proposed restrictions were effective, and the proliferation of Indian musicians continued'.²⁵⁵

Indeed, there were numerous reports of recorders participating in vocal music, both sacred and secular. In Cuzco, Viceroyalty of Peru (1560), Garcilaso de la Vega reported that he knew five *indios* who could sight-read any book of part-songs on recorders. In Mexico City (by 1568), Juan de Ovando wrote that recorders were commonly used to accompany polyphony in all the churches. In Lima, Viceroyalty of Peru (1583), the Third Council recommended that recorders should be included with choirs. At the Colegio of San Ignacio de Loyola in Cuzco (1600), Father Antonio de Vega observed that every Saturday in the chapel, the *Salve Regina* was accompanied by crumhorns, recorders, shawms, and trumpets, as used in festivals and processions. Also in Peru (1615), 'Guamán Poma de Ayala, writing about Andean church organization mentions a standard number of four *cantores* (literally, singers) who received a salary, food and exemption from tribute and labour levies, paid by the administrators and priests of the church. His drawing shows five such *cantores* playing the *Salve Regina* on recorders, indicating a flexible definition of the word *cantor*, as well as of the optimal number of musicians.'²⁵⁶

In Córdoba, then part of the Viceroyalty of Peru, later Argentina (1637), Father Antonio Ripario mentions that the *indios* came in from the *reducciones* (urban settlements) to perform songs and motets accompanied by recorders and other string and wind instruments. In Santafé (now Bogotá, Colombia) in 1646,

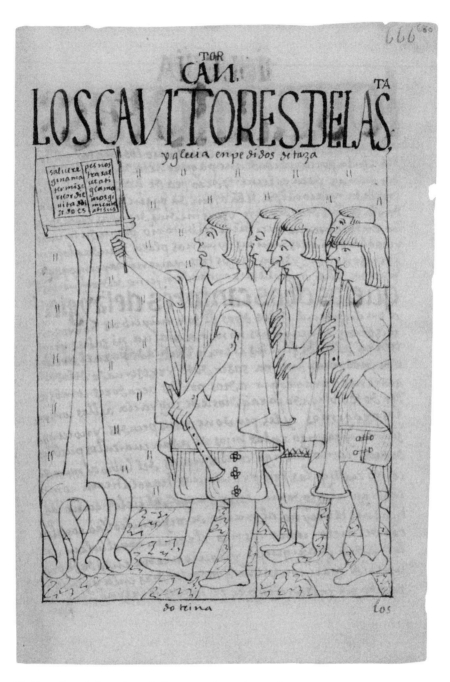

12. From Guamán Poma de Ayala, 'Nueva corónica y buen gobierno' (Peru, ca. 1615).

the Jesuit Father Francisco Ellauri asked for exemption from taxes for four *indios* who served the church as singers: 'the Divine Offices are made and celebrated with the decency and cleanliness that could be in the most careful of Spaniards, [and] there assist, ordinarily, a very good number of singers so skilled in polyphony and in a variety of instruments . . . [including] recorders . . . that can compete with the good or the best of the Kingdom'.[257] The church in Fómeque, east of Bogotá, owned 'four recorders for the season of Lent' (1676).[258]

The instruments naturally came from Spain at first. Father Juan de San Román, provincial vicar of the Order of St Augustine in Mexico, went back to Spain in 1551; on his return he was allowed to bring 'some recorders and shawms' for the monastery free of taxes.[259] Yet by 1568, Motolinía could note that in Mexico the *indios* 'make well-tuned recorders of all sizes, as are needed to accompany vocal polyphony'.[260] Pátzcuaro, the capital of Mexico until 1575, was a centre of instrument-making, including recorders.[261] Juan de Torquemada summarized in 1615:

> The first instruments of music made here were recorders, then shawms, and afterwards viols and curtals and cornetti. After a while there was no single instrument used in churches which *indios* in the larger towns had not learned to make and play. It became unnecessary to import any of these from Spain. One thing can be asserted in truth: in all the kingdoms of Christendom (outside the Indies), nowhere are there so many recorders, sackbuts, trumpets, crumhorns, and drums as in this kingdom of New Spain.[262]

PORTUGUESE COLONIES

The recorder was used more extensively in Brazil, partly because, besides tabor pipes, the other wind instruments common in the Spanish colonies are not documented as having been imported until at least the late sixteenth century.

In 1549, when the Portuguese decided to concentrate the administrative power in their colony of Brazil, they installed a General Government and made Salvador, in the present-day state of Bahia, the country's capital. Six priests and brothers of the Society of Jesus (Jesuits) under Father Manuel da Nóbrega came with the armada of the incoming governor, Tomé de Sousa, that year, encouraged and supported by the king, and started to build a church. As a religious order strongly oriented towards education and peaceful means, the Jesuits' task was to convert and catechize the *Brasis* (the local term for *indios*) – and to create a useful pool of labour at the service of the Portuguese. The priests focused on teaching the sons of the *Brasis* chiefs (*principais*), knowing that would sow the seeds of cultural change. Singing and playing instruments were added to the programme of the houses (residences) of reading and writing they created, and also to all celebrations of the liturgy. These places of learning were converted later into the colleges (*colegios*) of the Society of Jesus.

In 1550, the Jesuits in Portugal sent to Salvador seven orphan boys who had already sung in the ceremonies at the Colegio dos Meninos Orfãos in Lisbon, as it was envisioned that the boys would be useful in the conversion process.[263] The boys must have brought recorders (*frautas*) with them. That year Father Leonardo Nunes and ten or twelve boys were sent to São Vicente (in the present-day state of São Paulo) – a distance of more than 2,000 km – together with the armada of Pero de Góis.[264] A letter to the Jesuit College in Coimbra reported that the first Mass in the new church of São Vicente on 1 January 1551 was held 'with all the polyphonic music and music for recorders, just as it is there [in Coimbra]'.[265] More boys arrived in Salvador in 1551.[266] All these boys learned *Tupi*, the local language of the *Brasis*, and served as translators. Curiously, almost as if recorders were not already known, Father Francisco Pires wrote a letter back to Lisbon on behalf of a Portuguese orphan in Salvador in 1552, saying of the *Brasis*: 'It seems to me that, since they are friends of musical things, we would win them over by playing and singing among them, because there is a difference between what they do, what we do, and what we could do if Your Reverence provided us with some instruments for us to play here (sending over some boys able to play), such as recorders, tabor pipes, bells, and triangles, and a couple of tambourines and rattles. . . .'[267] Perhaps this letter was just reiterating the usefulness of the boys and pleading for more instruments. In this whole period, there is no evidence of recorders being made in Brazil.

In 1553, a school in São Vicente was already operating, started with four orphans that Nóbrega brought from Salvador, joined by local *Brasis* children, as he reported: 'In this house the boys have their exercises well ordered. They learn to read and write and go on far; others, to sing and play recorders. . . .'[268] The Portuguese boys are last mentioned in 1557, when Father Antonio Blasques noted that the music-loving *Brasis* were astonished at their performance.[269]

In Salvador itself, in 1564, on the Feast of the Holy Name, a priest described a Pontifical Vespers followed by the ordination of priests, a procession, and a solemn Mass. The Vespers were extremely long, because:

There were three different choirs: one of sung polyphony, another of a harpsichord, and another of recorders, so that when one ended, the other began, and all of course with great order when it came to their turn . . . When they played the recorders, the spectators enlivened and rejoiced even more, because, besides them playing moderately well, those who played were the *Brasis* boys, whom Father António Rodrigues has taught for a long time. This spectacle was so joyful for the people that I don't know how I can praise it more . . . they talked of nothing else in the city than the good upbringing and teaching of these children.[270]

Rodrigues (1516–68) was a former soldier, who had helped to found both the original Buenos Aires, now the capital of Argentina, and Asunción, now the capital of Paraguay, then part of Brazilian territory.[271] He later moved on to the Colegio do Rio de Janeiro, where it was reported that:

He was a connoisseur not only of the Brazilian language, but also of music, including the art of playing the recorder. He taught it to countless Brazilian boys, and from that granary, so to speak, the knowledge of playing the recorder spread in Brazil through the villages of the Christian *Brasis*. The spirits of the *Brasis*, deeply captivated by the charm of these instruments, have developed a sense of devotion and worthy conceptions of divine matters. Because of this, the *Brasis* held Father Rodrigues in high esteem.[272]

After the celebration in 1564, 'A merchant had a very good wrapping of recorders, and he, seeing the Brazilian boys playing, sent it to them, saying that it would be much better used by them than by him.'[273] This 'wrapping' implies a set or consort. Two other pieces of evidence are more explicit about numbers. A report on the villages around 1590 by Father Francisco Soares mentions a polyphonic Mass in which boys played 'viola, seven recorders together, harpsichord, and organs'.[274] In Maranhão in 1612, at a Vespers for the baptism of a local chief, 'There were recorders disposed in the harmony of voices, which from time to time were accompanied by small drums.'[275]

In the liturgy, recorders are cited in connection with the Mass and Divine Offices in general, as well as an astonishing number of special occasions: saints' days and patrons' days, Divine Offices in Holy Week, Divine Offices on Fridays in Lent, Compline, Epiphany, presentations of holy relics, visitations, the reception and deposit of relics or saints' images in churches, Calends (the first day of the month), Pontifical Masses to ordain new priests, inaugural Masses and blessings for new churches, supplications, doctrines each Sunday at colleges to bring people in, baptisms, and marriages. The musical repertoire included hymns, especially the *Te Deum laudamus* and *Laudate Domino*, psalms, motets, litanies to bless new churches, cantigas, and the Marian hymn *Salve Regina* on Saturdays. There is also copious documentation of recorders being used in processions and other outdoor events.

The combination of recorders and shawms is documented first in 1607 in a book about the life of Saint José de Anchieta (1534–97), discussing the daily routine of boys in the colleges: 'the boys go to the school . . . some to read, others to sing plainchant and polyphony, and others to play recorders and shawms to celebrate the Masses on feast days, and to adorn the processions in the villages, in the city, and in other public events, such as when they examine the students of the bachelor's degree course or licentiate, and when they graduate.'[276] But probably that referred to the practice around 1607, because shawms are otherwise mentioned in documents only from 1602–03; curtal and sackbut, from 1614.[277]

The recorder was also taken to Portuguese colonies in Asia and Africa. In 1554, a fleet of six ships sailing from Lisbon to India under Viceroy Dom Pedro de Mascarenhas took singers who had belonged to the recently deceased Prince Dom João, as well as instrumentalists, who provided music for devotional acts. A passenger, Father Soveral, mentions 'sackbuts and recorders' accompanying the singers.[278] Among the instrumentalists was André de Escobar, a wind player who had been working at Évora Cathedral since 1542. He settled in India and was the first to teach the shawm there, and presumably other wind instruments including the recorder. Then, 'leaving many disciples in the art of music', he returned to Portugal by 1564 and worked at Évora and Coimbra. A few years later, in 1568, on a ship sailing from Lisbon to Goa (India), 'The Viceroy brings very select singers who officiate the Masses and Vespers very well, and recorders and shawms that cheer the sailors a little.'[279]

In 1561, in the Portuguese capital in India, now called Kochi, a priest wrote that 'I preach here in this house of the Mother of God, where so great is the devotion among the people of Cochin that, for the greater part of the year, during all the Sundays and Holy Days of the year, they come here without being paid to celebrate our Masses with polyphony, recorders, and shawms.'[280] The musicians that Captain Rui Gonçalves da Câmara III took with him to Africa in 1574 'played *frautas* delicately'.[281] The Portuguese explorer Paulo Dias de Novais founded Luanda in

Angola in 1576 as São Paulo da Assumpção de Loanda, becoming governor. Two years later, he sent a letter to his sister Guiomar in Lisbon, thanking her for what she had sent: 'I greatly rejoiced at the recorders, which came at a very good time. The natives sang all the short Mass [*Missa Cortilla*] of Cristóbal de Morales, the motet to St. Andrew in five parts [*Andreas Christi famulus*], and a *Pange Lingua* of Francisco Guerrero. They played it [the *Pange Lingua*] on the recorders with other ordinary things [perhaps simple pieces] with great ability and very well in tune.'[282]

SOCIAL HISTORY

PROFESSIONALS

Although professional use of the recorder goes back to the fourteenth century, it begins to be documented in earnest towards 1500 when, with the mixing of the traditional *haut* and *bas* instruments, it emerges as one of the regular ones used by professional wind players (along with shawm, sackbut, and cornetto, sometimes flute, trumpet, curtal, crumhorn, etc.).

CITY MINSTRELS AND MUSICIANS

The inventory of the Antwerp city band in 1532 provides detailed information about their instruments.[283] Twelve new recorders listed in it were in the hands of one of the minstrels, Peeter Baninck; nine more recorders were with Tielman Susato; and a further seven with Jan de Brasser (a soprano belonging to the set having been lost by his predecessor, Hans Nagel). The band also played crumhorns, shawms, trombones, and a field trumpet. Both Nagel and the fourth member of the band, Jan van Arthem, had recently died – clearly a good time to take an inventory.[284] Susato (ca. 1510–ca. 1570) later established himself as a composer and one of the most famous music publishers in Europe.[285] The recorders associated with other city minstrels in the Low Countries, Germany, and Italy are shown in Table 9.

In 1568, the group of then six Waits (city minstrels) in London acquired a 'whole set of recorders', presumably made by the Bassanos.[286] The Waits would have used recorders for their indoor performances: at private functions given by the Lord Mayor, sheriffs, and aldermen, City companies such as the prestigious Merchant Tailors, and for noblemen and gentlemen such as Sir Thomas Kytson, as well as in playing music for the London theatres and for dramatic performances at court.[287]

Table 9. Recorders associated with city minstrels

City	Date	Recorders
Low Countries		
Mechelen	1502–03	bought a case of from widow of late city *piper*, Thomas van Luypeghem
	1508–09	paid Adriaen Cools, city *piper*, for tuning and repairing six recorders
	1510–11	paid Hans Nagel for acquiring a case containing various recorders
	1533–34	paid Pierre Alamire for a case of recorders and two shawms
Bergen op Zoom	1505–06	paid Pieter Noyts, *stadt piper*, for certain recorders and shawms
Oudenaarde	1531	bought a case of German recorders
	1536–37	bought a case of
	1567	lent a case of eight (one cracked) to Meester Pauwels Maes
Bruges	1543–44	paid Clays Jolyt, city *menestruel*, for a case of twelve for four minstrels
Germany		
Nuremberg	1512	bought eight
	1539	bought another case of ten from city's own famous maker Sigmund Schnitzer
	1575–1609	inventory: a large case of ten, a very old case, a case of nine, and a flute
	1621	Friderich Lang, *Stattpfeiffer*, had two repaired by covering labium with brass
Leipzig	1523	bought six
	1526	bought nine from Nuremberg
	1543	bought a case of eight
	1555	inventory: eight old; bought ten with great bass
	1563	bought a case of; another case of bought from Konrad Rude, *Stadtpfeifer*
	1587	bought a case of
	1617	bought unspecified from maker Hans Drebs

	1620	bought three tenors and discant
	1635	bought two *Quartflöten*
Italy		
Siena	1547	inventory: a case of
	1556–58	inventory: a case of; another case of in hands of Niccolò di Maestro Cristoforo, *piffaro*
	1573	inventory: a case of six
	1602	heirs of late *piffaro* Simone Nodi returned two cases of

13. Manuscript table-book of five-part 'Phancy' by Edward Blancks, laid out to be read by the players sitting around a table.

A surviving five-part 'Phancy' (Fantasy) by Edward Blancks, a member of the London Waits in 1582–95, fits a consort of recorders (two alto, two tenor, and one bass).[288] The parts are arranged to be played around a table: four people sitting, one standing. The celebrated composer Thomas Morley described the Waits as 'excellent and expert musicians', and referred to their 'careful and skillful handling' of music and their 'melodious additions' (that is, divisions). Ten members were eventually promoted to the court, including the known recorder players John Adson, Robert Baker I, Ambrose Beeland, and William Saunders. Candidates for

Table 10. Apprenticeships in Spain, 1586–1613

Date	City	Master	Apprentice	Term	Instruments
1586	Medina del Campo	Pedro Sánchez	Baltasar González	6 years	recorder and harp; at end of apprenticeship will receive a recorder
1590	Toledo Cathedral	Gerónimo López de Velazco	Gaspar de Villegas	3 years plus 1 extra	Villegas hired in 1593, when recorder, cornetto, shawm bought for him
1592	Medina del Campo	Pedro Sánchez	Esteban Sánchez	4 years	shawm, recorder, sackbut
1594	Valladolid Cathedral	Roque de Fuentes	Blas Ortega	2½ years	recorder and tenor shawm
1598	Medina del Campo	Pedro Sánchez	Vicente Pérez, adult tailor	4 years	shawm and recorder
1613	Seville Cathedral	Alonso de Machuca	Francisco de Hermosa	4 years	treble shawm, cornetto, recorder

Sources: Bejarano Pellicer 2013a, 66, 82; López Suero 2021a, 81, 83; Reynaud 1996, 208, 210, 231–32, 267.

a place in the group were tested, sometimes by competitive examination, as in 1601 when two or three members of the Bassano family were the judges.

Recorders are also mentioned among the instruments of the Waits of Exeter (a case of four, 1575), Norwich ('Five recorders, being a whole noise', from 1584–85),[289] Chester (provided their own, 1591), Boston, Lincolnshire (1607), Oxford (1630), and York (1640).

THEATRE MUSICIANS IN ENGLAND

By the end of the sixteenth century and up to the beginning of the Civil War in 1642, ensembles of recorders were being used by the six-member consorts of musicians attached to all the London theatres.[290] These musicians had to be versatile, being called upon to play virtually all the wind instruments (shawm, sackbut, cornetto, recorder, flute, curtal) as well as bowed and plucked stringed instruments, and sometimes to sing and to take small parts in the plays. The instrument is mentioned in Hamlet's famous lecture to Rosencrantz and Guildenstern in Shakespeare's tragedy (1600): 'It is as easy as lying. Govern these ventages with your fingers and thumb, give it breath with your mouth, and it will discourse most eloquent music. Look you: these are the stops' – just beforehand, the 'players' (i.e. actors) have brought in recorders. The first certain occurrence of recorders in stage music occurs in John Marston's *Sophonisba* (1605). The stage directions of many plays indicate the instrumentation, but not the identity, of the incidental music. 'Recorders' – presumably a whole consort of up to six parts – are called for in specific contexts mentioned in the section on Symbolism and Associations later in this chapter.

APPRENTICESHIPS IN SPAIN

Six Spanish apprenticeship contracts mention recorders being taught, usually in conjunction with other wind instruments but once with a *bas* instrument, the harp. Pedro Sánchez was a member of a company of musicians in Medina del Campo, near Valladolid, who contracted with the town authorities to play both wind and stringed instruments for town festivities and entertainments between 1566 and 1593.[291] See Table 10.

AMATEURS

In Spain, recorders are mentioned in the probate inventories of two Toledo citizens: a barber in 1545 and Francisco Sánchez de la Fuente, who had had a hand in conveying two books of Masses by Francisco Guerrero from Seville to Toledo in 1592.[292] In Valladolid, as found in probate inventories between 1553 and 1592, members of all social classes owned *flautas*, which seem consistently to have been recorders.[293] The cases and sets were presumably for domestic music-making: a hosier, a barber (a 'large recorder'), a renter of donkeys (three *flautas*), a silver confectioner of the Bishop of Coria (1562), the mayor of the city (a case of),[294] the mayor of nearby Medina del Campo (seven *flautas*), the wife of a judge (two *flautas*), a notary, and an officer in charge of lodging royal troops. Strikingly, in 1593, the merchant Miguel Navarro left twenty-four *flautas* and fifteen *flautas de salterio* (tabor pipes), a large stock for him to have expected to sell in the area.

In Leipzig, recorders were bequeathed by a fencing master named Steffan Lackner (one, 1547); Görg Gengelbach, occupation unknown (five, 1548); the itinerant merchant Hans Siniger (two, 1548); another merchant named Bartel Jeger (one, 1549); the instructor Nicolaus Fidler (two, 1551); the city comptroller Georg Dockler ('a case with three *garkleins*', probably in c³, 1577),²⁹⁵ and the storekeeper Sebastian Cunrad (a case of five, 1590). In seventeenth-century Dutch art the recorder was one of the most frequently represented instruments, shown being played by both sexes and all social classes (beggars, drunkards, street musicians, artists, ladies, and gentlemen). It is depicted alone and in ensembles, indoors and outdoors, but rarely with an audience. In 1600 in Leeuwarden, capital of Friesland, a medical doctor and mathematician named Johannes Wilhelmi Velsius bequeathed music books and instruments, among them six recorders.²⁹⁶

THE RECORDER IN EDUCATION

Hints at the recorder's value in music teaching are found in the recorder treatises and tutors of the Renaissance and early Baroque. Recall that the second edition of Agricola's treatise (1545) was aimed at 'our schoolchildren and other beginning singers'. That not all the sounds produced by beginners are harmonious was clear to Shakespeare: 'Indeed he hath play'd on this prologue like a child on a recorder: a sound, but not in government' (*A Midsummer Night's Dream*, ca. 1594, V, i).

In England at Eton, a combination of public (i.e. private) school and choir school, boys started learning instruments in the 1520s; 'two new recorders' were bought in 1553.²⁹⁷ At Christ's Hospital, now known as the Bluecoat School, a music lover named John Howes urged in 1587 that the children 'learn to sing, to play upon all sorts of instruments, as to sound the trumpet, the cornett, the recorder or flute, to play upon sackbuts, shawms & all other instruments that are to be played upon either with wind or finger'. But two years later the governing body ordered that only children 'such as be blind, lame, and not able to be put to other service' should be apprenticed to a musician.²⁹⁸

In the early seventeenth century, at the English Jesuit college at Saint-Omer in France, where the students learned vocal and instrumental music, it was said that 'The music of wind instruments is full of majesty, especially for church services, for the reception of persons of high rank, and for the theatre. Such instruments are the shawm, which does not over-tax young performers, and the recorder; but the former is the more majestic.'²⁹⁹ With the permission of the Rector, children could take a daily lesson from the music master.

Thiemo Wind points out that children are portrayed holding a recorder in a number of Dutch paintings of the seventeenth century.³⁰⁰ 'Disregarding the possible symbolism and despite not knowing for sure if the child indeed played the recorder, these paintings do suggest that the recorder belonged to the musical experiences of childhood.' David Beck (1594–1634), a schoolteacher in The Hague, left a diary for the year 1624 in which he mentions playing psalms on the recorder and violin, a common expression of piety, for himself and on his friend Herman Breckerfelt's instrument for Herman's family while they sang.[301] Beck may well have also used these instruments in his teaching. The Leiden lawyer Johannes Thysius (1622–53) – famous as the possessor of the Thysius Lute Book, the largest surviving lute manuscript in the world – wrote to his uncle at the age of 15, 'I practise in the privacy of my home in singing and playing stringed instruments and also recorder and harpsichord, especially when I am tired of my studies.'[302]

NOTABLE COLLECTIONS

A chronicler reported that in 1510, during his summer Progresses – visits to noble households around the country – Henry VIII of England was 'exercising himself daily in shooting, singing, dancing, wrestling, casting of the bar, playing at the recorders, flute, [and] virginals, and in setting of songs, making of ballads, and did set two goodly Masses'.[303] His inventories include a large number of recorders.[304] The celebrated inventory on his death in 1547 was preceded by a less developed one of 1542 in which we find the following cases: six recorders of ivory, four of walnut, nine of unspecified wood, six of boxwood, seven of unspecified wood, and two of eight (great and small); plus a 'great bass' of wood, two 'basses' of walnut, and four unspecified of oak (a total of fifty-five). A marginal note observes that 'the said case with seven recorders' was checked out 'to the King's Majesty's own use' in the regnal year 1542–43. Presumably at least some of these recorders were made by Anthony Bassano I. The inventory of 1547 includes the same recorders (if the case of eight ivory including two basses, plus the case of eight great and small were the same as the earlier two cases of eight) in addition to cases of eight, nine, and four ivory instruments (a total of seventy-six in all) almost certainly made by Anthony. The inventory also notes that eight recorders and five flutes were 'checked out to' the Lord Protector, presumably Edward Seymour, in the regnal year 1547–48.

The probate inventory of Cardinal Ippolito I d'Este in Florence in 1520, revealed a new recorder that had previously been in the Este estate in Castel Nuovo, a new large recorder, and three large recorders for the *contrabasso* and a set of recorders that had been at the Palazzo Belfiore. In 1564, Cosimo I de' Medici, duke of Florence, owned eighteen recorders at *tutto punto* pitch, including three with crooks. His probate inventory in 1574 lists them and also a case of fifteen, a very large recorder, and five more crooks for the large recorders. In 1622, a year after Grand Duke Cosimo II de' Medici died in Florence, his court had even more recorders than in 1574: a case of ten in boxwood, one large with crook, and cases of eleven and sixteen, large and small, of boxwood.

The Baden-Württemberg court in Stuttgart employed some of the leading wind players of the century, notably members of the Gans family.[305] The first inventory in 1576 is now lost; a summary made by a scholar in 1890 mentions sixteen recorders, including one *Concertflöte*. Also in 1576, the court bought a case of recorders from Breslau, probably made by Bartholomeus Hess (1515–85); he and his brother Paul had received a privilege from the Holy Roman Emperor Ferdinand I in 1553, renewed for eight years in 1560, against counterfeiting of their wind instruments in Bohemia and incorporated lands (presumably Silesia, Moravia, and Lusatia).[306] In 1581, the Stuttgart court purchased from the widow of Hans Thanner, who founded the instrument-making workshop there, ten *Colonen* (columnar recorders) and eight flutes 'belonging to them'. The major inventory of 1589 completes the identification of the Breslau instruments as 'A large case with fifteen recorders, small and large' and adds to them a case of eight from Ulm, an old case of seven, 'In a case seven recorders and a flute, which were all made by the Netherlands *Pfeiffenmacher* and were bought with other things from Sebastian Gans's widow in December 1586', an old case of seven, 'A consort of transverse recorders, namely four tenors and one bass, which are used like flutes', and a consort of eleven.[307] Melchior Billingkheim, from Antwerp, had come to the court from Nuremberg in 1586 as an official *Pfeiffenmacher* but was released in 1588; he was offered the place again in 1589 but refused. Sebastian Gans was a court wind player from 1566 until his death in 1586.

In Innsbruck in 1596, the instruments belonging to Archduke Ferdinand of Tirol in the instrument room at Schloß Ruhelust included two large recorders *per concerta*, seven recorders (two bassets, three tenors, an alto, and a soprano) made in Germany, seventeen recorders (two basses, four bassets, five tenors, four altos, and two sopranos) made in France, and one large recorder *per concert* bought from Venice.

Matching Henry VIII, the probate inventory of Ferdinando d'Alarçon, Marchese della Valle in Naples (1592), includes seventy-six recorders: sets of sixteen, three, twelve, eight (one missing), eleven, seven, and five – all described as 'large and small'; plus a consort of seven in a case containing crumhorns, three large, two large, one small, one of Indian (American) walnut, and nine copper recorder crooks.[308] The third largest collection of recorders in the Renaissance belonged to a wealthy citizen rather than royalty or nobility: Raymund Fugger Jr (1566), which we have discussed in the section on the Bassanos earlier.

In Verona, three academies were associated with recorders.[309] The first, the Incatenata, owned cases of two and fourteen as well as two crooks in 1543, the year it merged with the newly formed Filarmonica.[310] The revised Filarmonica, the first purely musical academy in Italy, had as members young noblemen with artistic, literary, and of course musical interests. In addition to holding private meetings, they gave public performances of madrigals, sometimes incorporating instruments. The Accademia had a large library of music and a collection of instruments. A case of twenty-two recorders mentioned in the inventory of 1562 seems to have been deposited there in 1544 by the commander of the Venetian *milize* Captain Paolo de Naldo, who had a musical *ridotto* at his house, then donated by him to the Accademia in 1548. A letter to the Accademia in 1552 from its former chapelmaster Jan Nasco (also formerly employed by Naldo) mentions him sending it a madrigal that 'will be appropriate for your large recorders' and a seven-part motet that could be played on recorders.[311] Later directors included the composers Vincenzo Ruffo, Alessandro Romano, and Lambert Courtois. Another academy, Alla Vittoria, owned cases of fourteen and eleven recorders in 1559, five years before it also merged with the Filarmonica.[312] By 1569, the Accademia had added a case of eleven (already lacking four) and a case of ten (lacking three in 1572). Clearly, the recorders were actively played. The academy was bequeathed a collection that included a case of seven large recorders and a case of nine recorders, large and small, by one of its members, Count Mario Bevilacqua, sponsor of a famous *ridotto* in Verona, on his death in 1593, but his wishes were not respected.[313]

At the Bavarian court in Munich, Elector Maximilian I (1573–1651) had a large collection of instruments, some a century old. The recorders inventoried four years after his death consisted of: three tenors; a case of eighteen, small and large, plus a small soprano that had been given to Maximilian 'for learning';[314] a case of eight, small and large in a case dated 1574; nine columnar; a case of five from Berchtesgaden; two new small sopranos; and two old altos (*Contraltfletten*). A woodwind-makers guild had existed in Berchtesgaden since 1581.[315] Maximilian's daughter-in-law, the Electress Henriette Adelaide (1636–76), was a talented singer who also played the recorder.[316]

SYMBOLISM AND ASSOCIATIONS

In the Renaissance and early Baroque, the recorder had a series of strong symbolisms and associations in theatrical and vocal music and in works of art.[317]

THE SUPERNATURAL AND DEATH

The earliest surviving sacred music that specifies recorders brings together several of the instrument's most important associations – (im)mortality, transcendence, and the supernatural – in the context of a central tenet of the Roman Catholic faith: the 'blessed' quality of the Virgin. This short section for two recorders in the 'Quia respexit' of the *Magnificat à 7* from Monteverdi's Vespers (1609?) comes at the words 'Ecce enim ex hoc beatam me dicent' ('For behold from henceforth all generations shall call me blessed').[318]

Recorders are mentioned in two plays published in 1615 by Miguel de Cervantes. In the comedy *La casa de los celos y selvas de Ardenia*, the adventurer Bernardo del Carpio is discovered asleep. 'Sad music of recorders plays', then a phantom appears and speaks.[319] In *El rufián dichoso*, a priest who has just died of leprosy is laid out on a table, then 'music of recorders or shawms' sounds in the distance.[320] In Lope de Vega's *La gran columna fogosa* (1596–1603), *flautas* accompany the discovery of an altar, where St Basil the Great is ministering to the Christ child; and in *El truhán del cielo y loco santo* (1620–30), as pilgrims have a vision of the Virgin, *flautas* play and are not recognized: 'What concerted instruments are these that I listen to now?'[321]

In the London theatre during the Jacobean (1603–25) and Caroline (1625–49) periods, recorder music is likened to the music of the spheres or 'heavenly harmony' in three plays.[322] In several other plays recorders perform after characters die, especially for their funerals. Curiously, recorders are also associated with fake funerals, after which the deceased is discovered alive. The association with the supernatural could be a portent, or else the entrance, exit, or simply presence of a god.

In a rare example in art, the shadowy recorder player in Rembrandt's *Belshazzar's Feast* (ca. 1636–38), presumably there to provide soft music associated with the sensual indulgence of the Feast, also symbolizes Belshazzar's impending death and the supernatural 'writing on the wall'.

LOVE AND SEX

Rowland-Jones points out an important difference in symbolism in paintings of the fifteenth–seventeenth centuries: 'While a recorder on its own may represent a self-gratifying aspect of sex, two recorders, which together give forth a sweet harmony, are more likely to indicate a shared union, equally meaningful to both partners.'[323] Titian painted several fine examples. In *The Three Ages of Man* (ca. 1510–15), a girl presents two recorders to a youth holding a recorder in his right hand, perhaps an interpretation of the Daphnis and Chloe legend. In *Venus and Cupid with a Lute Player* (ca. 1560), Venus holds a recorder, representing both sacred and profane love.

Raphael's altarpiece *The Ecstasy of St Cecilia* (1515) includes three broken and discarded recorders, apparently representing the unconsummated marriage of the saint and Valerian. A fresco by Girolamo Romanino at Trento (1531) shows a courtesan holding a recorder, symbolizing the erotic, whereas Chastity beneath caresses a unicorn.

Count Baldassare Castiglione, in his celebrated *Il Cortegiano* (1513–18), promotes members of the flute family as instruments of seduction.[324] In several Jacobean and Caroline plays, recorders express love, whether supernatural or mortal.[325] Two other plays link the associations of recorders with both love and death. On another occasion, recorders prophesy love between mortal and immortal. In other plays, however, the love represented by recorders is clearly worldly – between man and woman, whether they are married, about to be married, or would like to be married.

In *Le grand ballet* (Paris, 1632), a recorder consort accompanies the consummation of a marriage: 'Then the bride is put to bed, where all the tricks and galanteries that are customary to practise on similar occasions are not forgotten. While that is happening a *concert* of *flûtes* will avowedly assist, that all the marvels which stories report about the ancient *flûte* player Ismenias are never a shadow of what they hear.'[326]

In Dutch painting of the seventeenth century, the recorder often has a clearly erotic symbolism, based on its phallic appearance. The meaning is spelt out in a verse on a painting of a flute player by Bartholomeus Dolendo (1571–ca. 1629), based on an engraving by Lucas van Leyden (1494–1533): 'Well, lusty little flutist, won't you cool my lust, / Flute with your little lute, so that I too may feel it.'[327] The lute here symbolizes the woman's sexual receptivity. In a pastoral scene painted by Abraham Bloemaert (1564–1651), a shepherd is slipping his recorder under the skirt of his shepherdess, clearly showing what is on his mind.[328]

A song from the *Nieu-Amsterdam lied-boek* (ca. 1640) is explicit: 'He stuck the pleasant little recorder / In between my breasts. / Away, away, I said, little chum / What does this amorous play mean? / If you want to play on the little recorder, /

Then play it the right way! / That won't bore me: / It's bored well enough!'[329] In other songs, the coupling of recorder and fiddle represents sexual intercourse. In Gerbrand Adriaenszoon Bredero's *Klucht van de koe* (1612), the farmer says: 'But all Holy Days the fiddle gets on board the recorder, / It's beautifully naughty – you want to become wild, so that you hear it.'[330]

The recorder's frequent presence in numerous *Vanitas* paintings, depicting the vain pleasures of this world, presumably represents the transience of sexuality. An early *Vanitas* painting by Evert Collier (1662) includes the music for Van Eyck's 'Questa dolce sirena', apparently using 'the temptations of the mythical Sirens to express earthly lust'.[331] As late as 1684 another *Vanitas* of Collier's includes Van Eyck's '[Onan or] Tanneken', relating to the biblical Onan who practised *coitus interruptus*, perhaps a discreet reference to the recorder in the picture as a phallic symbol.[332]

THE PASTORAL AND SLEEP

The recorder could also express the pastoral (and its gods), related states such as freedom, security, and peace, as well as sleep. In Renaissance and Baroque art, duct flutes – often clearly recorders – are placed in the hands of shepherds in Nativity scenes and landscapes, courtiers and others in Arcadian guise, and nymphs of the pastures and meadows (as in the Giorgione/Titian *Concert champêtre*, 1508). In several paintings, Mercury plays his recorder to lull Argos to sleep – before putting him to death, as we have already noted in medieval literature.

In seventeenth-century French theatre and opera, recorders generally represent the pastoral. In the *Grand Ballet du Roy . . . sur l'Adventure de Tancrède en la forest enchantée* (1619), a 'Ballet des Dieux bocagers' (Ballet of the gods of the groves) has six satyrs playing *fleutes*.[333] The musical play *La centaura*, by a visiting Italian, Giovanni Battista Andreini, performed in Paris in 1622, included a 'Symphony of recorders (*flauti*), crumhorns, or shawms' to represent the god Pan.[334]

In the first ballet in which Jean-Baptiste Lully took part at the court, *Ballet de la nuict* (1653), he danced in an *entrée* described in the *livret*: 'Two shepherds and two shepherdesses return to the fields playing their *flustes* and their musettes, each guiding their flocks to the village because of the night.'[335]

AGGRESSION

Rarely, the recorder is also associated with war, presumably because of its family resemblance to the fife or the perennial confusion of flutes in general with the ancient Greek *aulos*. In John Milton's *Paradise Lost* (1667), for example, the angels defeated in Heaven 'move / In perfect phalanx to the Dorian mood / Of flutes and soft recorders.'

WATER

The recorder is often depicted being played near water. In Albrecht Dürer's engraving of *The Men's Bath House* (ca. 1496), one of the bathers plays a flared-bell recorder, accompanied by a rebec. In the tapestry *Le bain* from the series *La vie seigneuriole* (Musée de Cluny; early sixteenth century), the lady bathing is apparently singing to the accompaniment of another flared-bell recorder and a lute.

Combining sex and water, Hans Sebald Beham's woodcut of *The Fountain of Youth – Bathhouse* (ca. 1530) shows people bathing in the Fountain of Youth in the left-hand part, then engaging in erotic behaviour in the Bathhouse in the right-hand part,[336] while above among the entertainers and merrymakers on a balustrade, a youth holding an erect recorder is standing ignored. In case we miss the reference, the text underneath the woodcut declares, 'He who is lacking in his eleventh finger should bathe in the bath, for it will make him fresh, hard, long, and straight.'

TORTURE

Anticipating a modern perception of the instrument, in one painting the recorder is used as an instrument of (mild) torture. For the new studiolo of Isabella d'Este in Mantua around 1530, Correggio painted the Allegories of Virtue and Vice, two themes important to Isabella. In the Allegory of Vice, three Vices torture a bearded man, perhaps Marsyas. The Vice of Flattery – a nearly nude woman with distorted, puffed cheeks – blows the recorder in his ear.[337]

REPERTOIRE, 1601–67

After the turn of the seventeenth century, consorts of recorders, cases implying various sizes, and listings of multiple sizes are found in inventories, bequests, and purchases made by people from many walks of life. Nonetheless, the surviving repertoire consists mainly of solo and chamber music, original works for consort being found only in France and Moravia.

ITALY

The recorder was called for in only seventeen surviving works published in Italy between 1600 and 1670, although it was presumably used in similar pieces that never found their way into print.[338] In Florence and Mantua it appeared predominantly in pastoral scenes: Jacopo Peri's *Euridice* (1600), Emilio de' Cavalieri's *Rappresentatione* (edition of 1600), Claudio Monteverdi's *Orfeo* (1607), Monteverdi's 'A quest'olmo' from his *Settimo libro de madrigali* (1619), and Francesca Caccini's opera *La Liberazione di Ruggiero* (1625).

In Venice, the recorder was not found in opera but in the more conservatively scored music by organists at the *Scuole Grandi* and monastic churches, such as Francesco Usper's *Synfonia prima a 8* from his *Compositioni armoniche* (1619).

Few works in the substantial repertoire of instrumental music from early seventeenth-century Italy specifically call for the recorder. The canzonas and sonatas of Girolamo Frescobaldi, Dario Castello, Giovanni Battista Fontana, Tarquinio Merula, and others, widely played today (and by Adriana vanden Bergh in the 1640s, as we will see), are either unattributed or else borrowed from the cornetto or violin. Among the few exceptions are two canzoni – one for recorder and bass, the other for two recorders and bass – in Giovanni Battista Riccio's *Il primo libro delle divine lodi* (R/1612). Riccio's *Il terzo libro* (1620) features the recorder in two further canzonas and a motet.

There are two sonatas and a canzona in Giovanni Picchi's *Canzoni da sonar* (1625), and a solitary work by Biagio Marini, his *Sonata sexta* for two recorders or cornetti and continuo from *Sonate symphonie canzoni . . . opera ottava* (1629).

GERMAN-SPEAKING LANDS

Michael Praetorius uses recorders in nine out of his forty multi-choir works called *Polyhymnia Caduceatrix et Panegyrica* (1618–19), giving general directions that apply to two more, and apparently deploying four sizes: sopranino, soprano (in C and/or D), alto, and tenor, perhaps also basset.[339] The engraving on the title pages of most of the parts depicts a large number of musicians, among them a consort of five recorder players apparently playing soprano, two altos, tenor, and extended bass. Instead of bass recorder, however, the choir of recorders in six works uses a dulcian or trombone, following Praetorius's own recommendation in *Syntagma musicum*. In two other works, the *Choro di Flauti* serves as an alternative to a *Choro pro Testudine* (choir of lutes).

JACOB VAN EYCK AND HIS CONTEMPORARIES:
THE RECORDER IN DUTCH SOCIETY

Between 1644 and ca. 1656, the Amsterdam music publisher Paulus Matthijsz (ca. 1614–84) issued a handful of volumes by Jacob van Eyck and other composers for the recorder and other instruments that conjure up a unique vision of amateur music-making in mid-seventeenth-century Dutch society.[340]

Van Eyck (1589/90–1657) was a blind musician from a noble family whose career was focused on the carillon – a series of tuned bells linked to a keyboard played with the fists and pedals played with the feet.[341] Carillons graced the bell towers of countless churches all over the Low Countries, providing citizens with their commonest experience of public music. In 1625, Van Eyck was given a permanent post 'to maintain the bells and the clockwork of the Dom [cathedral] tower', and he was also expected to perform on that carillon on Monday, Thursday, and Saturday mornings plus holidays. After four years of distinguished service, he was elevated for life to 'Director of the Bell-works of Utrecht', also overseeing the carillons and swinging bells of the other churches of the city.[342] In 1632, his contract was extended to include playing the carillon at the Janskerk, the choir part of which had become the city library, later university library, after the Reformation.

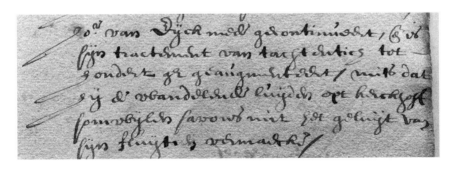

14. Archival reference to Jacob van Eyck having his salary raised in 1649 by the Janskapittel (Chapter of St John): 'mits dat hij d' wandelende luijden opt kerckhoff somwijlen savons mit het geluijt van sijn fluijtien vermaecke' (provided he occasionally in the evening entertain the people strolling in the churchyard [of the Janskerk] with the sound of his little recorder).

Eventually, Van Eyck was recognized for entertaining the citizens beyond the bells. In one of the most famous quotations in recorder history, his salary was raised in 1649 'provided he occasionally in the evening entertain the people strolling in the churchyard' of the Janskerk – a tree-lined park of brick-paved paths – 'with the sound of his little recorder (*fluijtien*)'.[343] That he was not being given licence to play the recorder but recognized belatedly in this role is shown by a poem by Regnerus Opperveldt (1640), which already lauded Van Eyck as both carillonneur and recorder player: 'There he begins on his little recorder (*fluydtje*)! / Oh what joy comes to our order! / (Lazy sloth now flee away!) / Am I in the heav'ns today? / Oh! boxwood holes, exalted treasures, / Oh! what superhuman measures / flow from thee artf'lly around, / from thy agile mouth they sound.'[344]

In one of the few descriptions of the early recorder's effect, Lambertus Sanderus wrote in a poem on the death of Van Eyck: 'Lovers of the art of measured song and recorder, whose lovely, magically sweet, soul-tugging sound can compel hearts of metal, rock, and stone . . . cease your joy.'[345] Then of Van Eyck himself: 'Who made recorder and bells speak such a sweet language that drew heaven and earth; and lured each person's ear so powerfully that the soul lost itself completely; burden and sorrow ran off the heart like water.'[346]

In 1644, Van Eyck published a collection called *Euterpe oft Speel-goddinne* (Euterpe or goddess of instrumental music), 'profitable and useful for all art-loving amateurs of the recorder, wind, and all sorts of instruments'.[347] This volume appeared simultaneously with the anthology *Der Goden Fluit-hemel* (The gods' recorder heaven), which includes music by other composers, intended 'for the violin as well as the recorder, or any wind instrument'.[348] In 1646, a second volume by Van Eyck appeared, with a striking change of title to *Der Fluyten Lust-hof* (The recorder's pleasure garden), Volume 2, and addressed to the same audience as *Euterpe*. An edition of *Euterpe* in 1649 maintained the title change: *Der Fluyten Lust-hof*, Volume 1, and modest corrections and additions were said to have resulted because the music had been 'newly listened to, improved and expanded by the composer'; although twenty pieces were added, three were omitted, apparently for reasons of layout.[349]

The two volumes of *Der Fluyten Lust-hof* make up probably the largest collection of solo music ever published for a wind instrument: no fewer than 148 pieces. Apart from two preludes (one to open each volume), three fantasias, a battle piece called 'Batali', and five duets, the other 137 pieces constitute sets of variations on a theme. (Thiemo Wind demonstrates that the crudely constructed duets are in fact arrangements made by Matthijsz.[350]) Some of the pages are actually headed 'gebroocken van J. Jacob van Eyck' (broken by Jacob van Eyck), 'breaking' being synonymous with what the English of the period called divisions and earlier was known as diminutions, in which the melody is systematically broken down into smaller note values. In other words, as Wind writes, 'the technique of "breaking" plays an essential role in the variation process'.[351] The themes consist of psalms and hymns, other sacred songs, and melodies of French, British, Italian, Dutch, German, and Spanish origin.[352]

Wind shows how the earliest variations on the psalms and hymns from the Genevan Psalter, the melodies of which consist of whole and half notes, were influenced by carillon technique, in which the playing fists tend to create harmonically oriented figures and lines. Therefore, these pieces were probably not part of Van Eyck's standard recorder repertoire, but created especially for publication. In the later psalm and hymn variations as well as in his other pieces, Van Eyck creates a consistently idiomatic, sometimes brilliant, division style for the solo recorder. Moreover, 'In the "Fantasia & Echo" Van Eyck proves himself a worthy heir to Jan Pieterszoon Sweelinck, producing a monophonic variant of Sweelinck's echo fantasias for keyboard.'[353] The most popular sets of variations today are those based on the 'greatest hits' of the seventeenth century, such as Giulio Caccini's 'Amarilli mia bella', John Dowland's *Lachrimae* ('Flow My Tears') and 'Come Again', Pierre Guédron's 'Est-ce Mars', the broadside ballad 'When Daphne from Faire Phoebus Did Flie', and 'Engels Nachtegaeltje' (English Nightingale). Some of the inevitable sameness of the division technique over the course of so many pieces is mitigated by Van Eyck's use of both 'cumulation' (referring back to preceding variations) and 'parataxis' (referring back only to the theme).[354] Furthermore, the overall form of the sets of variations is diverse.

Other Dutch composers of the period also wrote music for solo recorder. *Der Goden Fluit-hemel* (1644) contains pieces by 'Meester Willem', 'P.M.' (Matthijsz himself), the blind organist Pieter Alewijnsz de Vois (1580/1–1654) from The Hague, and even one piece by Van Eyck, as well as Anonymous. Matthijsz dedicated the volume to Adriana vanden Bergh (1631–68?), whose 'full mastery of the *hand-fluyt*' he praised in the preface, observing that on her recorder she played (violin) music by the Italians Giovanni Battista Buonamente, Tarquinio Merula, Marco Uccellini, 'and other excellent Phoenixes' with 'noble artistry'.[355] Wind has shown that Adriana, the daughter of a wealthy lawyer, was only about 13 at this time.[356] In 1650, probably for her wedding, she was the subject of an impressive portrait painted by Jacob Adriaensz Backer, depicting her as the muse Euterpe, with two small

15. Portrait of Adriana vanden Bergh by Jacob Adriaensz Backer (1650), from a private collection.

recorders, a basset recorder, a shawm, and a part-book of more violin music: Salamone Rossi's *Il quarto libro de varie sonate, sinfonie, gagliarde, brandi, e corrente per sonar per due violini et un chitarrone o altro strumento* (Venice, 1642).[357] The identification of Adriana with Euterpe suggests that Matthijsz may have switched titles before publication: perhaps *Euterpe oft Speel-goddinne* was the original title for *Der Goden*

Fluit-hemel, and the latter was intended to be the name of Van Eyck's collection, rejected because a reference to a 'heaven' of the 'gods' was considered too daring for the composer's strict Calvinist Utrecht.

Matthijsz's other anthologies, *'t Uitnemend Kabinet* (The excellent cabinet), Volume I (1646) and Volume II (1649), also had some connection with the recorder. Although *UK* I is said 'to be used by 2 and 3 violins or viols, or other instruments',[358] the recorder is mentioned in a poem included by one de Rieu: 'Come, art-lovers, and buy, each his taste satisfy, It's for recorder, violin and other instruments here. . . .'[359] Three of the solo works fit the range of the soprano recorder: two fantasias by De Vois and a composite work by him, Steven Harmensz van Eyck (De Vois's assistant), and Jacob van Eyck. *UK* II was again dedicated to Adriana vanden Bergh, to whose 'esteemed recorder' is added 'the sweet strings of Your Ladyship's viola da gamba, with their purity of sound'.[360]

All the Dutch solo pieces were intended for a recorder in C, and the references to Van Eyck playing a small recorder point to the soprano. Moreover, Dutch paintings through the 1660s almost invariably depict small recorders,[361] which may have become so popular in the Dutch Republic because they were suited to children's hands.

The myth of a 'Van Eyck' recorder

Apparently because the publisher Paulus Matthijsz was hoping to sell *'t Uitnemend Kabinet* II in conjunction with *Der Fluyten Lust-hof* I, the former included a four-page 'brief instruction'[362] called *Vertoninge en onderwyѯinge op de Hand-fluit* (Presentation and instruction on the recorder), put together by Matthijsz. The pamphlet has become associated with Jacob van Eyck himself in the public's mind today, because most of the surviving copies were bound with *Der Fluyten Lust-hof* I, and Gerrit Vellekoop reproduced it in the first complete modern edition of *Der Fluyten Lust-hof* (1958),[363] leading many makers to search for a historical soprano recorder with 'Van Eyck' fingerings, which they assumed had been endorsed by the composer himself.

An engraving of the same recorder, cylindrical with a slightly flared bell, appears in both *Vertoninge* and another set of instructions published by Matthijsz, that of Blanckenburgh. Eva Legêne has argued persuasively that it was modelled on the illustration in Virdung's *Musica getutscht* (1511);

Matthijsz simply followed 'the printer's old habit of copying material from other sources'.[364] She reports that the twentieth-century maker Frederick Morgan made a prototype and 'concluded that only with alterations contradicting the drawing could a cylindrically bored instrument play the high notes in tune with Matthijsz's fingerings' in *Vertonige*. A special 'Van Eyck' recorder', then or now, is therefore a myth.

Where did recorders played in the Dutch Republic originate? Praetorius (1619) implies that they were made locally, at a low standard pitch.[365] Wind has discovered a reference to a *Fluitemaker* named Andries Hillebrandsz working in Amsterdam between 1663 and 1680.[366] No other makers are known so far before Richard Haka (b. ca. 1646), who was clearly not active until after Van Eyck's death.[367]

Another source was vital. By 1635, Elias Tael, a merchant in Amsterdam, had become a *Neurenbergier* who specialized in importing goods from Nuremberg. In 1649, he and three similar merchants declared to a colleague that they were allowed to sell their wares freely in Amsterdam, making the usual payment to the merchants' guild, including 'all turned wooden products . . . all things turned from ivory or horn . . .'.[368] Tael's probate inventory of 1673–74 includes an astonishing number of woodwind instruments, including 382 large recorders, 72 medium, 120 small; 38 large boxwood recorders, 12 medium, 27 small; 22 large ivory recorders, 36 small; and 15 ebony recorders – no fewer than 724 altogether, as well as 22 recorder consorts. The inventory also includes about 18,000 whistles, 75 flageolets, and almost 200 flutes. An inventory of another *Neurenbergier*, Frans van Bercken (1644), includes 300 consorts from France (210 five-part, 90 seven-part) and 50 other consorts probably from Nuremberg. Such numbers – from just two dealers in Amsterdam – suggest large workshops in Nuremberg and France capable of an early form of mass production, perhaps with apprentices or other cheap labour to do the rough work.[369] As confirmation of Nuremberg instruments in the Dutch Republic, in 1653 Cornelis Graswinckel, a wealthy brewer in Delft, bequeathed a consort of recorders made in Nuremberg as well as other recorders at a different standard pitch.

Wind argues that 'a consistently even tone is an essential quality an instrument should possess in order to best execute the music of *Der Fluyten Lust-hof*. . . . [it] would also have to be easily articulated and flexible. . .'[370]

FRANCE

In 1659, Robert Cambert (ca. 1628–77) composed the music for the first French opera, *Pastorale d'Issy* (1659), for which no score has survived. The *philosophe* Charles de Marguetel de Saint-Denis, seigneur de Saint-Évremond, reported: 'This was like an essay in opera, which had the approbation of novelty; but it had something even better: that is, *Concerts de Flûtes* were heard which had not been heard in any theatre since the ancient Greeks and Romans.'[371] Clearly, he was unaware of the *Choeur de Flustes* that performed on stage to accompany a 'rustic concert' in Lully's *Ballet d'Alcidiane* performed the year before, 1658,[372] not to mention other French ballets earlier in the century. In Lully's *Les plaisirs de l'île enchantée* (1664), written for a three-day entertainment at Versailles, 'Fourteen musicians of Pan and Diana go before these two gods with a pleasant harmony of recorders and musettes';[373] later a large tree arises from beneath the stage which is filled with sixteen fauns playing recorders and violins 'with the most pleasant *concert* in the world'.[374]

MORAVIA

Besides the French ballet, the consort tradition was continued by some pieces written for the court of Karl Lichtenstein-Kastelhorn, Prince-Bishop of Olomouc, at his palace in Kroměříž, Moravia, in the 1660s and 1670s.[375] They were used as dinner music, to judge by the titles of three of them: *Sonata 'pro tabula'* by Heinrich Ignaz Franz von Biber for five recorders, strings and continuo; *Sonata 'ad tabulum'* by Johann Heinrich Schmelzer for two recorders, two violins and continuo; and *Sonata 'pro tabula'* by Giovanni Valentini for three recorders, curtal, strings and continuo. Schmelzer wrote two other sonatas for recorders and strings, and one for seven recorders and continuo. This group is completed by a *Sonatella* of Antonio Bertali for five recorders and continuo, and an anonymous sonata for two recorders, strings and continuo. Van Heyghen has observed, 'Since the few pieces that were specifically composed for recorders have many similarities to south German and Austrian literature for string ensemble, [string] compositions by [Johann] Rosenmüller, Schmelzer, and Biber may also have been part of the mid- and late seventeenth-century repertoire for recorder consort.'[376] The ranges and clefs of the pieces from Kroměříž imply that the sizes of recorder involved were soprano in d^2, alto in g^1, tenor in d^1, and bass in g^0. So the addition of a fourth to the fifths between the instruments associated with Baroque-style recorders, discussed in the next chapter, had already been established by the 1660s.

3

THE ERA OF THE BAROQUE RECORDER, 1668–1800
DAVID LASOCKI

The Baroque type of recorder was developed primarily at the court of Louis XIV of France, almost certainly by the Hotteterre family for their performances in Lully's ballets and comédies-ballets, then spread around Europe and colonial America. The instrument also seems to have undergone parallel physical developments in Germany and Italy. Although no longer a first-line instrument for professionals, the recorder remained an important second-line instrument for oboists and other woodwind instrumentalists as well as string players, in opera orchestras, theatre bands, church ensembles, court *Capelle*, and wind bands. Concertos were written to show off these musicians' virtuosity, especially but not only on small sizes of recorder. The alto recorder became a highly fashionable instrument for the gentleman amateur, and substantial quantities of music for it were composed and published, particularly in England and the Dutch Republic. Most of the greatest composers of the late Baroque – Lully, Charpentier, Purcell, Keiser, Vivaldi, Handel, Telemann, and J. S. Bach – wrote memorable music incorporating the recorder, in a variety of vocal and instrumental genres.

NAMES[1]

ENGLISH

In England, after the Baroque type was brought over from France by James Paisible and others in 1673, the traditional name *recorder* began to be replaced by the French *flute douce*, then plain *flute*.[2] The switch was possible only because the Renaissance style of transverse flute had become almost obsolete in England. The first English tutors employed *rechorder* or *recorder* (John Hudgebut, 1679; Humphry Salter, 1683), *flute* and *recorder* (John Playford, ca. 1680), *recorder* or *flute* (John Banister II, 1681; John Clarke, ca. 1683; Robert Carr, 2nd edn, 1686), and *flute* . . .

rechorder (John Walsh, 1695). The first tutor to use only *flute* was *Auto-Melodia* (John Clarke, ca. 1686), and from about 1697 the term was the norm up to Richard Bremner's *The Compleat Tutor for the Flute* (ca. 1765). In 1737, the *New General English Dictionary* of Thomas Dyche and William Pardon could already cite *recorder* as 'the ancient name of a musical instrument, now called the flute'. Calling the recorder a *flute*, which had meant transverse flute in English since the fifteenth century, still causes endless confusion among modern English speakers, because the word signals 'transverse' even to those who know history.

When the Baroque style of transverse flute, nowadays called *traverso*, was imported from France around 1695 and took hold in the following decade, it was given the French name *flûte d'Allemagne*, before long translated as *German flute*. As the traverso's popularity grew, *flute* as recorder picked up new qualifying adjectives. *Common flute* alone is first documented in John Loeillet's Op. 1 (Walsh, Hare & Hare, 1722). (An isolated instance of *Treble common flute* goes back to a manuscript by Thomas Britton, ca. 1674, for the alto recorder.)[3]

The near-homophones *consort* and *concert* were used interchangeably, sometimes confusingly. In Paisible's will (1721), *consort flute* referred to the alto recorder; a manuscript by Edward Finch (by 1738) used *concert pitch flute* for the same instrument, evidently a recorder of the size or prevalent pitch for concerts. William Tans'ur in 1746 called the alto recorder *Consort-flute*, then in 1772 switched to *Concert flute*. The expression *German and concert flutes* (advertisement, 1731) seems to mean traversos and recorders; and a traverso could be a *concert German flute* (1788); so *a set of Concert flutes* (1767) may have meant recorders of different sizes in concert quality. Terminology is rarely consistent or perfectly clear.

Thomas Stanesby Jr's proposal for elevating the tenor recorder (ca. 1735) called the recorder *Flute a'bec, or common English flute*. Finally, *English flute* appeared in an advertisement in 1745. The two major terms persisted to 1800 and beyond: *New and Complete Instructions for the Common Flute* (George Goulding, ca. 1794) and *English flute* (George Astor, 1799; Goulding, 1800; N. Swaine, ca. 1818). Although *flutes* could still refer to recorders made by the late Peter Bressan in an advertisement of 1774, the term could be generic (recorders and traversos) as early as 1720 and ambiguous by 1730. The first unequivocal designation of a transverse flute as *flute* appeared in an advertisement by the woodwind maker John Mason (1760), although the adjective *German* remained prevalent until at least 1800.

Terminology in the American colonies was broadly contemporaneous. A probate inventory from Virginia in 1679 still used the older terms to distinguish them: '1 Recorder, 2 flutes'. By 1716, recorders imported to Boston by Edward Enstone, an organist who had emigrated two years earlier, were called *flutes*. *English flute* for recorder is first documented in 1743, two years ahead of British sources, and continued to be employed in this way in American advertisements until 1815, although by the first decade of the nineteenth century it began to signify transverse flutes from England. In 1749, the alternative name *common flute* also turned up, persisting to the end of the century. Other stray terms are found: *Italian flute* (1742), *flauto a bec* (1773), *English, or common Concert Flute* in several sizes (1777), *English common Flute* (1785), *common English flute* (1787), and *flute doux* (1794). The usage of *flutes* as transverse flutes was well established by the 1780s. Finally, in the mid-1790s, *common flute* came to mean the one-keyed transverse flute as opposed to one of the newer varieties with up to six keys.

FRENCH

Jean-Baptiste Lully called for *flute* or *fluste* starting from *Ballet d'Alcidiane* (1658), not adding an adjective until *fluste douce* in *La grotte de Versailles* (1668).[4] For Lully, *flute* may have embraced the transverse flute as early as 1671; *Flûtes d'Allemagne* he used only once, in *Le Triomphe de l'Amour* (1681). Marc-Antoine Charpentier also overwhelmingly employed the term *flûte* for the recorder (from 1670), later in life also for parts in ranges and keys that imply transverse flute.[5] Occasionally, he distinguished the recorder as *flûte à bec* (*Orphée descendant aux enfers*, 1683–84) or *flûte douce*, and the transverse flute as *flûte d'allemand* (both in *Messe pour plusieurs instruments au lieu des orgues*, 1674).

A few inventories in 1702–11 still used *flûte* to mean recorder. The clearest is that of the court musician Philippe Breteuil (1709), which distinguishes: 'four boxwood recorders (*flustes*) with a soprano recorder (*fluste haute contre*) . . . three tenor recorders (*quintes [de] flustes*), three flutes (*flustes allemandes*) . . . a recorder (*flute*), another flute (*flutte Allemande*) . . .'.[6] Jacques Hotteterre's celebrated *Principes* (1707) called the recorder both *flute a bec* and *flute douce*, in contrast with *flute traversiere*, a new name for the transverse flute. *Flûte douce* quickly fell by the wayside, except for Diderot's *Encyclopédie* (1766) and its successor, the *Encyclopédie méthodique* (1785). But *flûte à bec* appeared sporadically in inventories up to 1795 as well as in numerous editions of music. The word *flûtes* on a title page that offered several instrumental options could sometimes imply both recorder and transverse flute, depending on the range and keys.

DUTCH

The Dutch Republic had its own versions of these French terms in a delightful variety of phonetic renditions. Either they were close to the French: *flûte*, documented 1705–18; *Fleutte deuse* or *Flute doux*, 1685–1759; and *Flute abec* or *flute a becq*, 1741–71; or else they replaced *flûte* with the Dutch equivalent: *fluit dous* or *fluit doux*, 1705–1827; and *Fluit a Bek*, 1739–1834.

In addition, the Dutch Republic still used earlier terms of its own: *fluit* or *fluyt*, documented until 1792, and *handfluyt*, documented until 1698. The Dutch also coined four new ones: *sachtefluit* (soft flute), 1678;[7] *Block-fluyt*, 1672 and 1686;[8] *regt fluyt* (straight flute), 1690 and 1835; and *bekfluit*, 1763–1847. We also find Italian influence: *flauta bocca* (Reynvaan, 1795); and mixed French and Italian: *Flauto a bec* (1770).

ITALIAN

Bismantova's 'Compendio musicale' (1677/94) used both *flauto* and *flauto italiano* for the recorder. A Venetian manuscript tutor, 'Tutto il bisognevole per sonar il flauto da 8 fori con pratica et orecchia' (ca. 1700?), introduced the Italian term for 'flute with eight holes'. The days of doubling the lowest hole were now past, because on a three-piece instrument, the bottom piece could simply be rotated to accommodate either hand being lower. 'Tutto il bisognevole' also employed *flauto* for both duct flutes in general and the recorder in particular. An inventory in Florence (1700) stuck to the old-fashioned terminology *flauto* or *zufolo*.

In Italy rather than Germany, *Flauto dolce* was so rare that only two manuscript collections in Venice mention it.[9] *Flauto a becco* appears once, in a petition by Andrea Fornari (1791). Otherwise, *flauto* was the standard Italian term of the late Baroque.

GERMAN

The German language had its own terms, *Flöt* (Daniel Speer, *Grund-richtiger kurtz-, leicht-, und nöthiger jetz wolvermehrter Unterricht der musicalischen Kunst*, 2nd edn 1697), *Flöte* (Johann Mattheson, *Das Neu-Eröffnete Orchester*, Hamburg, 1713), or *Flöthe* (Stuttgart, 1718), and significant changes of vowel: *Flaute* (Jacob Denner, 1710), *Flaude* (Denner, ca. 1720), or *Flautte* (Kremsmünster, 1739); and the diminutive *Flettl* (Kremsmünster, 1739–47). Otherwise, German musicians largely borrowed from French and Italian: *flutes* (Schlegel, 1708), *Fleutes Douces*

(Anhalt-Zerbst, 1699), *Flutte douce* or *Fletuse* (Johann Gottfried Walther, 'Praecepta der musicalischen Composition', 1708), *Flaute douce* (Danzig, 1731), *Flaute doulce* (Christian Daniel Friedrich Schubart, *Ideen zu einer Ästhetik der Tonkunst*, written 1784–85), *Flûte à bec* (Walther, *Musicalisches Lexicon*, 1732), *Flöte a bec* (Darmstadt, 1768), *flauto* (Agostino Steffani, *Alarico il Baltha*, 1687), *flauto dolce* (Johann Sigismund Kusser, *Erindo*, 1694), and *Flauto . . . a bec* (Stuttgart, 1783). The malleability of terminology in Germany is perfectly illustrated by successive inventories at the court in Cöthen: *Flauti à Bec* (1768), *flaute douce* (1773), and *Flauto douce* (later). Even within the same manuscript, the composer or copyist could switch terms amusingly, without apparently causing puzzlement, as in a cantata by Michael Rohde (by 1732): *Fleutdoux 1, Flutedoux 2, Fluto*.[10]

Manuscripts of Georg Philipp Telemann's music often used *flauto*, as well as *Dusflöte* (derived from *flûte douce*), but in his published works we find *flûte à bec* (*Six Trio*, 1718), *flûte douce* (*Harmonischer Gottes-Dienst*, 1725–26), and *flauto dolce* (*Essercizii musici*, 1726; *Der getreue Music-Meister*, 1728; and *Musique de table*, 1733). In his scores, Johann Sebastian Bach employed the following terms for the recorder: *Flauto, Flaute, Flaut:, Fiauto, Fiaut:*, and *Flutto*.[11] In a memorandum he submitted to the Leipzig Town Council in 1730, however, he referred to recorders as *Flöten . . . à bec*.[12] For his *Fiauti d'echo*, see the section on Repertoire below.

The term *englische Flöten* in a letter by the famous woodwind virtuoso Johann Michael Böhm in 1729 probably just meant recorders from England. In a German-language newspaper in Philadelphia in 1772, recorders were called *gemeine Floeten*, a direct translation of *common flutes* in the parallel English advertisement. *Blockflöte* does not seems to have been used during this period, reappearing only in the recorder revival of the 1920s.

OTHER LANGUAGES

In Spain, *flauta* for an instrument presented as a novelty at the court in 1692 clearly referred to the Baroque type of recorder.[13] The new Spanish term *flauta dulce* (the equivalent of *flûte douce*) is documented from Pere Rabassa's *Miserere* (1715) up to the holdings of the Panama City Cathedral in 1798.[14] Another new term, *flauta de pico* (parallel to *flûte à bec*), was specified in a cantata by Juan Francés Iribarren (by 1767).[15] A stray *flaute*, reminiscent of the Middle Ages, appeared in an advertisement in 1766.[16] *Flautas Dulzes* were mentioned among instruments bought for the Mexico City Cathedral in 1759.[17]

In Portugal, *frauta* is found in a dictionary of 1713, *flauta doce* in a poem from 1768, and *frauta doce* in a poem from 1787 and dictionaries from 1773 and 1789.[18] In Brazil, *flauta dose* turns up in an inventory in Rio de Janeiro (1768).[19]

Instruments to be made for the Swedish army by Johan Kiörning in 1691 were called *flöjter*.[20] As for Norwegian, Johann Daniel Berlin's *Musicaliske Elementer* (Trondheim, 1744) used the term *Fløite*.

PHYSICAL CHARACTERISTICS

By the 1660s, alto and lower sizes of recorder began to be made in three pieces: head, middle with six finger-holes, and foot with the remaining finger-hole. Sizes higher than the alto usually had only two pieces: head and body. This familiar Baroque type has a nearly cylindrical head piece, a slight contraction to hole 4 in the middle piece, followed by a much steeper taper, prolonged into the foot piece, which misleadingly flares outwards externally. A tapering bore has three benefits. It permits a shorter speaking length for a given pitch of instrument. It enables tuning the basic harmonic relationships of the instrument (III/X/XIV, V/XII, and VI/XIII) by local bore adjustments, not solely the diameter and position of the finger-holes. And it allows finger-holes to be placed in more convenient positions, more easily reached by the hands.[21] This new bore is not identical to the Renaissance step bore, but behaves in a similar way, responding to the same fingerings for XIV and XV in the relatively easy high register, and creating weaker low notes.

The middle piece has a tenon at each end, fitting into sockets on the head and foot pieces, these two joints generally being strengthened by elegantly turned bulges in the wood, sometimes reinforced with ivory rings. On sizes smaller than the bass, the top end of the head piece was transformed into the characteristic rounded beak, leading to a new designation, *flûte à bec* (beaked flute).

The Baroque recorder could play more than two octaves, be tuned more readily to match other instruments, and had a tone richer in upper partials than its predecessors.[22] Its greater evenness of tone colour between adjacent semitones served well for employment in solos and mixed-instrument ensembles. The alto was now almost exclusively in F rather than G, and the basic sizes were made in a combination of fourths and fifths (CFCFC).

When and where did these changes to the Renaissance designs happen? Although scholars long took it for granted that the Baroque model was developed in France by the Hotteterre family, recent evidence reveals a more complicated situation, in which some of the elements were in place earlier.

First, the fourths–fifths principle was already mentioned by Praetorius (1619), in conjunction with shawms; his documentation of a soprano in c^2 as well as the older one in d^2 follows that principle.[23] Independent confirmation of two pitches of soprano is furnished by the case in Frankfurt bearing the maker's mark HD, made for a bass in f^0, two tenors in c^1, two altos in g^1, two sopranos in c^2, two sopranos in d^2, and two sopraninos in g^2 at *mezzo punto*.[24] HD may refer to Hans Drebs or Drebes (fl. 1598–1636), who worked in Leipzig.

Second, Praetorius, observing the difficulty of tuning recorders made in one piece, offered the following solution:

> cut the body in two at a point on the upper half, between the beak and the first finger-hole; lengthen the top piece by about an inch and a half; this can then be inserted in the bottom half and used to make the total tube length greater or smaller, as much as one desires or requires. This treatment will always correct a recorder immediately, making it sound fresher or duller as required. Some renowned makers do maintain that some of the holes on a recorder treated in this way may be put out of tune, but the only genuine fault they can find is that some of the top notes will not speak so easily. The procedure has also been successfully applied to bassanelli. . . .

In other words, he envisaged creating two pieces and a tenon of the type that had been used on the bassanello – a quiet shawm adjustable in pitch by pulling out the tenons on no fewer than five pieces.[25] Praetorius attributed the invention of the bassanello to Giovanni Bassano, otherwise undocumented as a maker, so more likely it stemmed from his father, Santo. Given this experience, probably the Bassanos were among the 'renowned makers' who tried out tenon joints on the recorder. Furthermore, socket-and-tenon joints had been used for the foot pieces of great bass recorders since the sixteenth century and on bagpipe drones for several centuries.

Third, Mersenne gave fully Baroque fingerings including buttress- or supporting-finger technique as early as 1635–36.

Fourth, a Baroque-looking beak appears in a Dutch woodcarving on the casework of the organ in the Grote Kerk in Alkmaar, signed by the town sculptor Pieter Mathijsz and dated 1641.[26] Although this organ has been through many repairs and renovations, the casework seems to be original and the date is well established. Gerard de Lairesse (1712) later documented that artists working on organs often depicted the latest models or inventions.[27]

THE FRENCH EVIDENCE

The change from alto in G to alto in F can be traced in the ballets at the court of Louis XIV.[28] An f♯[1] already appears in Louis de Mollier's *Ballet de la Nuict* (1653), in which Jean-Baptiste Lully danced. It is clearly not an error, because it belongs to the opening melodic profile, forming part of a V_2 chord. In Lully's own parts designated for the recorder, g[1] is the lowest note until *Les Amours déguisés* in 1664, when f♯[1] appears for the first time. Again, it was not an error because it forms part of the dominant chord at the end of the first four-bar phrase. The G1 clef of the part implies alto rather than voice flute (alto in d[1]) or tenor, and Lully calls for the half-holed or double-holed notes f♯[1] and g♯[1] on the alto in F elsewhere. The earliest definitive f[1] comes in 1668 in *George Dandin*, also the first work in which Lully uses the key of F major for the recorder. If we also consider Lully's parts that *may* have been for the recorder, then f♯[1] is already found in *L'Amour malade* (1657) and f[1] in *Ballet de la Raillerie* (1658). So we may conclude that the F-alto could have been developed already by 1653 or 1664, but certainly by 1668, the year in which – as we shall see – Lully changed from writing for consorts to a trio texture, probably used a voice flute on the second line, and referred to *fluste douce* for the first time. In parallel, a developed Baroque oboe had been created by 1667.[29]

Further evidence that a new model of recorder was developed in France is provided by the way it spread around northern Europe. By 1673, it had reached England, when some French woodwind players, including James Paisible, who had played for Lully, came over to join the opera composer Robert Cambert. As mentioned above, the designation *recorder* rapidly gave way to the French *flute douce*, and soon plain *flute*. Although in his *A Vade Mecum* (London, 1679) John Hudgebut uses the term *rechorder*, he describes his 'zeal' for the instrument's 'improvement'. Perhaps the earliest depiction of Baroque recorders in England, the frontispiece of Salter's *The Genteel Companion* (1683), shows two elaborately turned instruments, one played by the gentleman on the left, the other lying on the table.

In 1685, when the Dutch maker Richard Haka sold some instruments to the Swedish navy, he called the recorders *fleutte does*, the first documented use of the

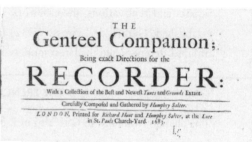

16. *The Genteel Companion* (London: Humphry Salter, 1683), frontispiece.

French name by a maker in the Dutch Republic. In Nuremberg in 1696, Johann Christoph Denner and Johann Schell applied for master's rights as woodwind makers and permission to make 'French musical instruments, mostly consisting of oboes and recorders (*Flaudadois*)', which they claimed had been invented (*erfunden*) only 'about twelve years earlier', or around 1684, a puzzling discrepancy with the evidence from England and the Dutch Republic.[30]

Which French makers were responsible for the new model? The celebrated French flautist Michel de La Barre (ca. 1675–1745), writing long after the fact, perhaps as late as 1740, claims that Lully's 'promotion meant the downfall of all the old instruments except the hautboy, thanks to the Philidors and Hotteterres, who spoiled so much wood and played so much music that they finally succeeded in rendering it useable in ensembles. From that time on, musettes were left to shepherds, and violins, recorders, theorboes, and viols took their place, for the transverse flute did not arrive until later.'[31] This account maintains that both the Philidors and the Hotteterres were responsible for transforming the shawm into the oboe. No development of the recorder is mentioned and it is considered only among the instruments that replaced the musettes, which may have been musettes de Poitou (windcap shawms), given that Lully composed for musettes de cour (bagpipes) up to at least 1672 and the instrument remained popular in the first half of the eighteenth century. Nevertheless, the Philidors and the Hotteterres are prime candidates to have developed both the oboe and the Baroque recorder.

The earliest member of the Philidor family documented as making woodwind instruments was Jacques Danican Philidor (1657–1708), discussed below. But he would have been too young to participate in the development of the Baroque oboe and recorder. His father, Jean (ca. 1610–79), the first member of the family whose last name appears in documents as 'Danican dit Philidor', and Jean's brother Michel Danican (ca. 1610–59) are both documented only as instrumentalists, although Jean also seems to have composed.[32]

Still, there is indirect evidence of the Philidors as makers, at least of *cromornes*. These new instruments (different from the Renaissance windcap crumhorns) came on the scene in 1651, causing such enthusiasm that a new group at court was created to play a consort of them: the *Cromornes et Trompettes Marines*, led by Michel Danican.[33] Jean Danican Philidor joined in 1655,[34] but no member of the Hotteterre family ever belonged. Conceivably, therefore, the Philidor brothers invented these instruments. French court records show that *cromornes* came in four sizes: *dessus*, *taille*, *quinte*, and *basse*. Vincent Robin argues persuasively that they were double-reed instruments, made in several pieces, with strongly conical bores, the lowest two sizes having extension keys, and all except the *dessus* being played with a bocal.[35] Were these instruments a reinvention of bassanelli? One of the novelties of the *cromorne* seems to have been that, unlike the treble shawm, the *dessus* size was divided into pieces. Robin has hypothesized that the *dessus de cromorne* was the original prototype of the Baroque oboe – perhaps even what Bruce Haynes called the 'protomorphic hautboy' – and after more development took on the name *dessus de hautbois* previously used for the treble shawm but now signifying oboe.[36] The *basse* survived until the late eighteenth century, exclusively retaining the name *cromorne*.

The *pater familias* of the Hotteterre family was Jean Hotteterre I (fl. 1628–92?), about whom Pierre Borjon de Scellery wrote in 1672 that he was 'unique as maker of all kinds of instruments made from wood, ivory, and ebony, such as musettes, recorders, flageolets, oboes, cromornes, and even for making complete consorts of all these same instruments. His sons are hardly inferior to him in the practice of this art, to which they have added a complete knowledge and an even more admirable execution of musette playing, in particular.'[37] This quotation establishes that the Hotteterres were important makers of woodwind instruments, including of recorder consorts – Jean's sons, Jean II (ca. 1630–68) and Martin (ca. 1635–1712), no less than him; and they played the musette even better. Both oboes and cromornes are mentioned in Borjon's testimonial, possibly making a distinction between *hautbois* (higher sizes) and *cromornes* (lower). In any case, musettes and flageolets were not made in complete consorts. Borjon added that '*hautbois* and cromornes also make a pleasant effect when mixed with musettes'.[38]

Jean I, born in La Couture-Boussey, Upper Normandy, moved to Paris in 1628 and set up a workshop there around 1635. In 1657, a contemporary observer reported that 'some listeners have been ravished by . . . the recorder (*flute douce*) of La Pierre and the flageolet of Hotteterre'.[39] Jean I's grandson, Jacques Hotteterre le Romain, states that Jean improved the small drone on the musette.[40] Tula Giannini has written that 'Jean [I]'s sons Jean *fils* [II] and Martin worked with him. When Jean *fils* married in 1654, an inventory of the workshop listed *flûtes*, flageolets, musettes, and tools for their manufacture. . . . A list of the instruments and tools that Jean *père* [I] gave to Jean *fils* on his marriage includes: three musettes . . . and tools for making flutes, shawms (*hautbois*), and flageolets.'[41] At that time Jean II became a partner in his father's workshop, inheriting half its contents. After Jean II was killed in 1668, Martin joined the workshop in his brother's place. Jean I and his descendants seem to have used the maker's mark 'Hotteterre' with an anchor below.[42]

Strong evidence places the Hotteterres close to the Baroque oboe and recorder. Seven members of the family were foremost among Lully's recorder players, taking part in performances of his works at court a collective total of sixty-seven times.[43] Jean I and his sons alone participated thirty-two times. But Lully's named musicians include neither Jean Danican dit Philidor nor Michel Danican. And although the brothers André and Jacques Danican Philidor were frequently employed (twenty times), this started only in 1670, by which time the Hotteterres had already appeared a total of thirty-eight times.

We also have three payment records for instruments that the Hotteterres made for the court. Jean I was paid 620 livres for 'the *hautbois* and other instruments' that he 'furnished to the *hautbois* players of the two companies of musketeers of the king' in 1667, when they switched from playing fifes.[44] Thus two years before Lully scored for the instrument, the term *hautbois* had already been established for military oboes. Martin Hotteterre and his cousin Louis V received the sum of 300 livres from the royal coffers 'as payment for several instruments' they furnished for Lully's *Isis* in 1671.[45] Finally, 'to Martin Hotteterre, *hautbois* and musette of the king, the sum of 200 livres, given to him for the instruments that he furnished for the said ballet of *Psyché*' by Lully in 1677.[46]

The only other notable French woodwind maker active in the 1660s was Claude Lissieu in Lyons, whom Borjon praises: 'I know of no one who approaches so closely the skill of the sieurs Hotteterre.'[47] Lissieu's only surviving musette is of the type with two keyed and fully chromatic chanters which, according to his son

Jacques Hotteterre le Romain, Martin Hotteterre was responsible developing. This implies that Lisseu's musettes, and presumably other woodwind instruments, were strongly influenced by the Hottetterres.[48]

The members of the Grande Écurie at the court, to which almost all of Lully's recorder players belonged, played at the *Ton de l'Écurie*, which Haynes places at about A 469, approximately a semitone above A 440.[49] Therefore, the recorders played by them would have been at this pitch. Beginning with *Ballet de la Raillerie* in 1658, Lully began to combine recorders with *violons*, members of the violin family in five sizes. At first, he used the group he directed called the *Petits Violons*, or *Petite Bande*, which seems to have also played at A 469. But after he became *surintendant* of the court's entire music in 1661, he merged the *Petits Violons* with the *Vingt-Quatre Violons* (Twenty-four *violons*), who played at what was soon called the *Ton de l'Opéra*, a whole tone below A 440 at approximately A 392, and considered the most suitable pitch for singers. This merging would have required some rebuilding of old instruments (both strings and woodwinds) and the creating of new ones, another possible stimulus for the development of the Baroque recorder.

The Philidors may have invented *cromornes* by 1651, and it is possible that the higher instruments of this family were developed into Baroque oboes within about fifteen years. But the only evidence of the Philidors continuing in the development of the Baroque woodwinds is that Jacques Danican Philidor's widow had 'several tools and reamers useful for making instruments' in her probate inventory (1709).[50] The Hotteterres, however, were prominent among Lully's musicians and sold oboes to the court beginning in 1667. Anthony Baines points out the similarity of the irregular bore of this instrument, the socketed joints, and even the cylindrical head piece to the construction of the musette, an instrument primarily associated with the Hotteterres as makers.[51] It therefore seems highly probable that it was the Hotteterres who developed the French Baroque recorder, although we cannot rule out participation from the elder Philidors, especially Jean.

Étienne Loulié (late 1680s) was already familiar with recorders that 'have certain holes double', but he does not say which holes.[52] Jacques Hotteterre (1707) documents double holes for fingers 6 and 7, and even for 3, to facilitate the trill on XII♯. Several surviving instruments by Bressan have double holes for fingers 6 and 7, to ease and strengthen I♯ and II♯, and one of the altos also has double holes for finger 3.[53] Several examples by makers from other countries (N. Castel, Johann Christoph Denner, Thomas Stanesby Jr, and Jan Steenbergen) have double holes on 6 and 7.[54] They were not, however, universally adopted, perhaps because they subtly altered the sound and feel of the low register.

We have seen that some features of the Baroque recorder may pre-date the innovations of French makers in the 1650s–60s. The idea of dividing the recorder into pieces with socket-and-tenon joints goes back to the sixteenth century, and further impetus for the application of this technique to the recorder may have come from French makers' recent experience with *cromornes* and the oboe. The beak may have been developed already and something like an obconical bore probably already existed. Nevertheless, the sum of details of design, including the French Baroque bore, elaborate turnery, the decrease in the size of finger-holes, and the switch from an alto in G to one in F, marked a paradigm shift to a profoundly new kind of instrument.

THE ITALIAN EVIDENCE

Our understanding of the Baroque recorder's development is complicated by an Italian treatise: the manuscript 'Compendio musicale' of Father Bartolomeo Bismantova, a musician at the cathedral in Ferrara and cornetto player to the Accademia dello Spirito Santo. The treatise includes an extensive section on the recorder, 'Regola per suonare il flauto italiano'.[55] The title page of the carefully copied manuscript is dated 1677 – a grander initial title page bears the dates 1677, 1678, 1679 – although we are apparently dealing with a version prepared for the printer later: a note on the verso of the title page dated 1694 says it was 'not sent to print because of the death of the above-mentioned gentleman' (Bismantova's patron, the abbot Ferrante Bentivoglio), 'rules for the *violoncello da spalla*, the bass, and the oboe having been appended'.[56] The oboe instructions are not included, but a manuscript copy of them that has survived separately, along with some trumpet duets dated '1688, 1689', refers readers to 'le Regole del Flauto' for 'the hand and fingers, as well as the breath and tonguing syllables, and everything else that can occur'.[57] So we have independent verification that some version of the recorder instructions was in existence by 1688–89.

The question of dating is critical for our purposes, because Bismantova presents us with new information. First, his recorder instructions, which according to the title page pre-date the otherwise earliest known tutor (Hudgebut) for the Baroque recorder by two years, nonetheless depict a Baroque alto made in three parts, with a beak, turnery, and obconical bore, played with Baroque fingerings.

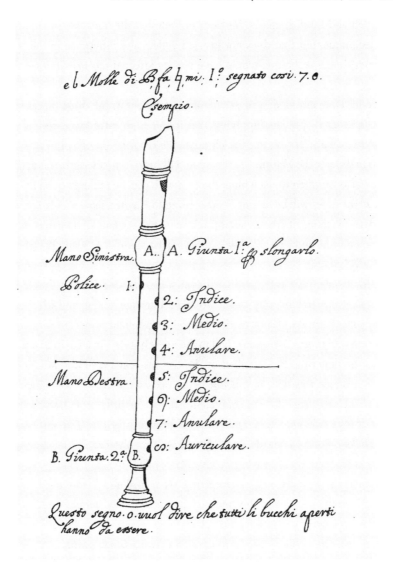

17. Drawing of the recorder from Bartolomeo Bismantova's manuscript 'Compendio musicale' (Ferrara, 1677/94).

This alto is, however, not in f¹, like those used in France and England, but in g¹, the size of the Renaissance and early Baroque. As in Renaissance practice, in his two fingering charts he notates the recorder an octave below sounding pitch (using the C1 clef, although in his musical examples he switches to the treble clef). Unlike all the French and English charts, his does not employ the buttress- or supporting-finger technique, but that does not in itself reflect any difference in the bore, as supporting-finger technique would have merely affected the size of some finger-holes.

Second, Bismantova describes such an instrument as 'of three pieces such as those used today', perhaps implying that it had been introduced recently.[58] He goes on to explain: 'If you need to elongate the recorder on occasion to lower its pitch to make it at the *chorista* . . . then you will need to first lengthen it at the top, and then also lengthen it just a bit at the foot with [i.e. by pulling apart] the joints, so that all the notes will be in tune.'[59] According to Haynes, *tuono corista* could have its modern meaning of 'the general pitch standard', or one of two specific pitch levels, a semitone and a tone below *tutto punto*, or about A 413 and 392 (the latter being Lully's pitch).[60]

Third, Bismantova calls his instrument *flauto italiano* (Italian flute). But in what sense was it Italian, why was it already a Baroque model, and why was it in g^1, rather than f^1 like the French model? Marcello Castellani points out Bismantova's description of a *trillo alla francese* (trill in the French style), from a^2 to b^2, for which he gives the fingering 23 45 (trilled on 3), and his remark: 'if the *Flauto* cannot make or produce this trill, it will not be an accurate *Flauto*'.[61] The fingering is identical to Hotteterre's for the equivalent trill on a recorder in f^1, namely g^2 to a^2, so Bismantova was evidently familiar with French practice. The difference, as Bruce Dickey, Petra Leonards, and Edward H. Tarr observe, is that 'Bismantova calls it an ornament on b^2 moving downwards while [French practice] considers it to be a trill on a^2 (actually on g^2 . . . referring to a recorder in F) moving upwards.'[62] Castellani comments: 'From this one may presume the existence of recorders of the Italian type (in g^1) and of the French style (in f^1) with probable differences of fingering apart from the *trillo alla francese*.' D'Avena Braga points out, however, that there is only modest evidence for the continuation of the alto in G in Italy in the eighteenth century: only one of the fourteen surviving Italian Baroque altos is in G; and the vast majority of the repertoire – with the probable exception of Vivaldi – favours flat keys and often goes down to f^1.[63]

On the broader implications of Bismantova's information, Castellani sets out a plausible hypothesis:

It is not totally out of the question to suppose that the transition from the Renaissance form to the Baroque form of the recorder could have taken place in Italy and France independently of any reciprocal contacts and influences. The transition was not *ex abrupto* but gradual: first the change in the bore (from cylindrical to obconical) and then the subdivision into three pieces, and hence the new design arising from the need to reinforce the joints between the sections of the instrument.[64]

He sees motivation for development in Italy in 'the new instrumental language' of the Baroque and the need to imitate the expressive qualities of the violin 'within the recorder's limits'.[65]

A parallel development in Italy would depend on woodwind makers being present there by 1677 to make the instruments. So far, however, little evidence has been found of Italian woodwind makers between the Bassanos and Giovanni Maria Anciuti (1674–1744). The money that Anciuti borrowed from his uncle Tomaso in 1693, to be repaid partly in '*piferi et flauti*', implies that he probably apprenticed with Tomaso, who is listed as a member of the Arte de' Tornidori (turners guild) in Venice from 1692. Battista Anzuto (also spelt Anciuti and Anzutto), possibly their relative, appears in the records of the guild from 1675, but nothing is mentioned about instrument making.[66]

Another manuscript tutor, 'Tutto il Bisognevole', preserved in the Biblioteca Nazionale Marciana, Venice, is dated 1630 on its cover.[67] It depicts a recorder in three pieces with Baroque turnery at each tenon, although the profile is drawn, perhaps schematically, as completely cylindrical. The fingering chart is for a recorder in f¹, showing fingerings up to g³ (not including f♯³), with supporting-finger technique. If the treatise were really from 1630, it would change recorder history. But it contains a number of anachronistic elements, so it was probably written towards 1700.[68]

NUREMBERG

Surviving instruments from Nuremberg, an important centre for woodwind making since the early sixteenth century, suggest a brief parallel development to France. Makers belonged to one of two guilds: the master turners' guild (e.g. Hieronymus Franciscus Kynseker and Johann Benedikt Gahn) and the hunt-lure and bone turners' guild (e.g. Johann Christoph Denner and Johann Schell).

Kynseker (1636–86), who had become a turner by 1662, was first mentioned as a woodwind maker in 1673. An almost complete set of his recorders survives, made in plumwood: one basset in f⁰, two tenors in c¹, two altos in f¹, and two sopranos in

c^2 (the sopranino in f^2 and case are missing) in the new alternation of fourths and fifths, at A 466. The head pieces are all turned with a distinctive 'wave profile'. The bores of the smaller instruments have the step-bore profile, whereas the basset size has a more obconical bore. The instruments are made in two pieces, the socket being reinforced by a bulge and a horn ring, but not recognizably with the decoration of the Baroque model. Kynseker was apprenticed in the workshop of the turner Johann Herbst, headed by his widow Margarete Herbst. No instruments reliably attributed to the Herbsts have survived for comparison with Kynseker's work, although an *exilent* recorder with wave profile and the maker's mark 'H' in Leipzig could have been one of theirs.[69]

Gahn (working period 1698–1711) made recorders with two distinct types of bore.[70] The first type is similar to the Renaissance step bore, albeit redesigned for a three-piece recorder: the obconical section of the middle piece starts relatively late, approximately halfway down, before contracting sharply to meet the foot piece's cylindrical bore. Adrian Brown comments that in comparison with the Kynseker bore, because the Gahn instrument is 'made from three pieces, it is possible to make more local bore changes to affect tuning issues and problems of note stability, but I feel the general idea of the design is the same and probably stems from the same tradition of making'.[71] He adds that this type of bore is more problematic than the usual Baroque design, in that accurate tuning of the basic harmonic relationships has to be achieved in part by the finger-hole positions and the diameter at the top of the middle piece, rather than by the bore profile itself. He is doubtful how successful such a bore profile would be on larger sizes of recorder.[72] The second type of Gahn bore resembles the French Baroque design, perhaps showing the influence of the makers from the rival hunt-lure and bone turners' guild. Indeed, Gahn married the widow of the turner Franz Zick (1660–98), none of whose instruments seem to have survived.[73]

Johann Christoph Denner (active 1678–1707) made a soprano recorder stamped I D FELBINGER 1682 on the base, suggesting that he might have been working in another maker's workshop at the time.[74] The bore is Renaissance type 1 (primarily obconical), but the beak is rounded. Two basset recorders by Denner are in Renaissance style: one in two parts with a detachable foot; the other in three parts with 'fontanelle' mounts on the foot.[75] As we have already seen, in 1696 he and Schell applied for permission to make oboes and recorders of the French types. After that, it seems that they and the other Nuremberg makers concentrated on recorders influenced by the French Baroque bore.

TECHNIQUE AND PERFORMANCE PRACTICE

Virtually everything we know about recorder technique and performance practice in the late Baroque and Classical periods comes from tutors and general music books addressed to the amateur. The term 'tutor' has been preferred to 'method' here, because the books are, by modern standards, rarely methodical. It is worth noting that although most surviving recorder music from the first half of the eighteenth century is German and Italian, the tutors are mostly English and French.

ENGLISH WRITINGS

In England, after the Restoration of the monarchy under Charles II in 1660, the taste for French music and instruments brought first the flageolet, then the Baroque type of recorder into vogue. The flageolet had by this time settled down to a form with four finger-holes on top and two thumb-holes behind. Thomas Greeting (d. 1682), who taught the celebrated diarist Samuel Pepys and his wife to play the flageolet in 1667–68, published a tutor called *The Pleasant Companion: or New Lessons and Instructions for the Flagelet* (by 1672, perhaps as early as 1667). Greeting was at first a 'professor of music', or private music teacher, then a royal violinist and sackbut player from 1674 until his death. Greeting's tutor, which went through several editions, served as a model for English woodwind tutors for over a century: a few rudiments of music are accompanied by fingering charts, brief instructions on ornaments, and a selection of 'lessons', or tunes of the day. Greeting wrote: 'The flageolet is an instrument that may very fitly be termed "a pleasant companion", for it may be carried in the pocket, and so without any trouble bear one company either by land or by water. It has this advantage over other instruments, that it is always in tune, which they are not. And for those whose genius leads them to music, I know not a more easy and pleasant instrument.'

Of the thirteen tutors for the recorder known to have been published in London in the last quarter of the eighteenth century, only five survive.[76] The first, *A Vade Mecum for the Lovers of Musick, Shewing the Excellency of the Rechorder*, was printed in 1679 for John Hudgebut, a music seller and musical instrument dealer. He writes: 'I have attempted to shew my zeal for [the recorder's] improvement, hoping all ingenious gentlemen will pardon the deficiency of the performance, considering it is the first essay in this kind. . . . As all instruments have found great access as well as improvements of late years in this nation, this of the recorder has not found the least encouragement [i.e. has not been encouraged the least], being received into the favour of ladies, and made the gentleman's *vade mecum'* – a constant companion. He does not acknowledge the French origin of the 'improvement'.

Although Hudgebut advertises that he sells both flageolets and recorders at his shop, he makes a case for the reader to choose the recorder, directly addressing Greeting's claims for the flageolet:

> Of instruments (though there be several species) there is none which comes nearer in imitation to the voice (which is the design and excellency of all music) than that which we call wind instruments, as the flageolet, recorder, etc. as taking its inspiration immediately from thence, and naturally dissolving into the same. Of these, though the flageolet like Esau has got the start, as being of a more ancient standing, the recorder like Jacob has got the birthright, being much more in esteem and veneration with the nobility and gentry, whilst the flageolet sinks down a servant to the pages and footmen. . . .
>
> We will allow the flageolet all its just attributes, and see if the recorder do not equal or excel them. The flageolet is a good companion, being easily carried in the pocket; so is the recorder. The flageolet is always in tune; so is the recorder – besides the sweetness of the sound, which is much more smoother and charming, and the extent and variety of notes, in which it much excels the flageolet.

Surprisingly, he ignores the very high pitch of the flageolet – variable, but usually d^2 or above – in comparison with the more vocal alto recorder in f^1.

The next tutor, *The Most Pleasant Companion, or Choice New Lessons for the Recorder or Flute* (1681), was also printed for Hudgebut, evidently referring to, and trumping, Greeting's *Pleasant Companion*. The title page names as author 'J. B., Gent.', who has generally been identified as John Banister II (1662–1736), a violinist and flageolet player in court service.

Although its first edition (1682), has not survived, the second 'corrected' edition of *The Delightful Companion: or, Choice New Lessons for the Recorder or Flute* was published by John Playford and John Carr in 1686. Its preface is signed by Carr's son Robert (d. 1696), a royal viol player, although he acknowledges 'the assistance of several able masters'. He begins by noting: 'This delightful companion, the pipe recorder, has been for a long time out of use; but now it's beginning to be in a greater repute than ever it was before. And indeed, there is no music so near a natural voice; it admits of excellent harmony in consort of two and three parts.'

The Genteel Companion; Being Exact Directions for the Recorder, printed for Richard Hunt and Humphry Salter in 1683, was compiled by Salter. Like his predecessors, Salter vaunts the vocal quality of the recorder: 'Of the kinds of music, vocal has always had the preference in esteem; and by consequence the recorder (as approaching nearest to the sweet delightfulness of the voice) ought to have the first place in opinion, as we see by the universal use of it confirmed.'

When John Walsh and Joseph Hare entered the music publishing business in 1695, they immediately issued a recorder tutor that makes the most extravagant claim of all: *The Compleat Flute-Master, or, The Whole Art of Playing on ye Rechorder, Layd Open in such Easy & Plain Instructions, That by them ye Meanest Capacity may Arrive to a Perfection on that Instrument*. Their amusing preface includes a shrewd commentary on their predecessors' tutors and a fond hope for their own:

> Many of our employ have been very industrious to oblige the public in this manner; though they were not very full in their instructions, yet they found their endeavours very successful. Since therefore their imperfect rules have proved thus fortunate, we have reason to hope that this attempt of ours (being more correct than any yet extant, having all the rules that can possibly be expressed by way of printing) will have an effect answerable to its design, the main end we aim at being only the public advantage.

Walsh and Hare certainly attracted a host of imitators: their fingering chart and ornament instructions were pirated and incorporated into most English tutors (as well as *The Bird Fancyer's Delight*) until at least 1794, by which time the instructions must have greatly puzzled the performers of Classical songs and dances.

ENGLISH FINGERINGS AND DOT WAY

A special tablature for the flageolet, usually called 'dot way', was already depicted in Laurent de La Hyre's painting *Allegory of Music* (1649).[77] Some twenty years later, Greeting deploys this tablature not only for the instrument's fingering chart but also to notate its music. The flageolet's six holes are represented by six horizontal lines. A 'dot' (a black vertical rectangle) placed on a line shows that the

18. *A Vade Mecum* (London: John Hudgebut, 1679), showing two examples of dot way: fingering chart (left) and a Minuet by Nicholas Staggins.

appropriate finger should cover the hole in question. When adjacent fingers are placed down, the dot extends from the highest to the lowest of the horizontal lines involved, becoming a continuous thick vertical line. A plus sign (+) indicates a half-closed hole; a comma or hook, an ornament. Rhythm is shown by means of a line of rhythmic values above the uppermost finger-line, one particular value being assumed to repeat until replaced by another.

Hudgebut (1679) begins his section 'Directions for Playing on the Rechorder' by explaining the instrument's own dot way: 'All tunes or lessons set by characters called dots ought, according to the eight holes of the instrument, to be set eight dots upon eight lines. But by reason too many lines blinds the sight, there is but seven lines made use of, setting seven dots upon seven lines, and the eighth dot below the seventh line.' In his first fingering chart, he adds a ledger line below the dot under the bottom line. This chart was intended for an alto with a fully chromatic range from f^1 to d^3, using buttress- or supporting-finger technique, leaving finger 6 down for all notes from c^1 to g^2. The first twenty-six lessons appear in both standard musical notation ('violin-notes') and dot way; the last ten lessons only in notation, the student presumably having been expected to master it by this time. Two years later, an announcement for *The Most Pleasant Companion* makes explicit that recorder tablature was derived from that for the flageolet: 'being a new collection of lessons, some of which are set the flageolet way, others the violin way'.

Salter (1683) extends the range of the recorder all the way up to g^3, but only in diatonic steps: 'finding that some of my tunes required higher notes, I have here given you the true and full compass of the flute'. He prefers the six-line dot way to the seven-line, adding the line underneath when necessary. Like Carr (1686) he considers dot way only a method for beginners 'that have not the help of a master to instruct them'.

By *The Compleat Flute-Master* (1695), dot way was no longer used for tunes. The preface to the Walsh edition of *The Bird Fancyer's Delight* (1717) tells us why: 'it being so impracticable and never to be attained at sight that the use of the instrument was almost lost till introduced by the gamut rules, which has not only brought it much in vogue but the performers on it are ready at sight, as on any other instrument'.

ENGLISH GRACES

Greeting's flageolet tutor gives a little table of 'graces' (ornaments): the *beat* (trill: upper auxiliary), *shake* (mordent: lower auxiliary), *slur*, and *slur & beat*. Greeting's terminology is opposite to that discussed in string treatises, where *beat* is mordent and *shake* a trill – closer to the French *battement* ('beating' = mordent) and *tremblement* ('trembling' = trill). Neither Greeting nor any recorder tutor specifies the number of oscillations for the trill or mordent, although the table by Charles Coleman in Christopher Simpson's *The Division Viol* (1665) shows seven for each of these graces. The meaning of *slur* for Greeting is the same as in later sources: moving from one note to another on the same breath without tonguing again. His *slur & beat* seems to be what we would call a prepared trill (with long appoggiatura) or simply an upper-note trill. Hudgebut presents the same four types of ornament as Greeting, in an example clearly modified from his: *beat* (trill, notated ⊙), *shake* (mordent, notated //), *slur*, and *slur and beat* (slurred trill).

The Most Pleasant Companion reproduces Greeting's paragraph on graces virtually word for word, not even bothering to change the six-line flageolet tablature in the example of graces for the recorder, but adds one new grace: 'The other shake is the *double shake*, and is played by shaking your fourth finger of your left hand, holding those fingers on that the dots belong to [23 45, trill on 3], both in the example and in the following tunes.' This curious, warbling trill across the registers was of course the standard French trill from g² to a² – Bismantova's *trillo alla francese*. The adjective 'double', which makes no sense in this context, is apparently derived from flageolet practice where, as *The Innocent Recreation* (2nd edn, 1699) explains colloquially, the ornament 'is marked with two of them dashes . . . And both them fingers must be shak't at once.'

The dot-way tablature of the 'lessons' in these tutors shows how the graces were used in practice. Marianne Mezger has illustrated this by an excerpt from the same piece, Henry Purcell's song 'Ah Cruell Bloody Fate' (from *Theodosius*,

149

1680), ornamented by J. B., Salter, and whoever was responsible for preparing the 1683 edition of the flageolet tutor by the recently deceased Greeting.[78]

Mezger describes Carr's instructions for graces in 1686 as initiating a 'second phase' in the English recorder tutors.[79] He adopts string terminology: *beat* (notated U) for mordent; *shake* or *back fall* (notated // or a seven-line squiggle) for trill. According to Carr, the *beat* is 'fetched from the half note below the note it stands over', or in other words, begins with the semitone below the main note. He remarks that the *shake* is 'fetched from or shaked in the proper note above it': that is, begins on the upper auxiliary. Virtually all the instances of the *shake* notated in the dot-way examples begin with the upper auxiliary. These examples also show many instances of a turn at the end of the *shake*, the two auxiliary notes being slurred in two ways: to the trill or only to each other. A trill table – the first comprehensive one for the Baroque recorder – gives fingerings throughout the chromatic range of the instrument.

Nine years later, *The Compleat Flute-Master* confirms that the trill (*close shake*, notated //) 'must be played from the note or half note immediately above', the choice

Ah Cruell Bloody Fate

19. Henry Purcell's song 'Ah Cruell Bloody Fate' (from *Theodosius*, 1680), with three sets of ornaments in dot way.

of upper auxiliary presumably depending on the key. After giving the symbol for 'An open shake, beat, or sweetening' as +, the tutor describes how to make only the *open shake* or *sweetening*: 'by shaking your finger over the half hole immediately below the note to be sweetened, ending with it off'. It does not mention the *beat* again, although, as in Carr, the name certainly sounds like a mordent. Probably *open shake* and *beat* were equivalent terms for mordent, and *sweetening* a fingered vibrato like the French *flattement*. After giving a description of the *double shake* (symbol / : /), *The Compleat Flute-Master* introduces two new ornaments: the *sigh* (equivalent to the French *accent*) and the *double relish* (trill with two-note turn). This tutor and the manuscript 'Rules for Gracing on the Flute' (1690s?)[80] each give a series of rules – similar to French practice – for adding ornaments when they are not marked in the music.

FRENCH TUTORS

The first published French tutor to include the Baroque recorder, *La veritable maniere d'apprendre a jouer en perfection du haut-bois, de la flute et du flageolet, avec les principes de la musique pour la voix et pour toutes sortes d'instrumens* (Paris, 1700), was written by the otherwise unknown Jean-Pierre Freillon-Poncein. The tutor was dedicated to his patron, Pierre Bérulle, Viscount of Guyancourt, an official in the province of Dauphiné, strongly suggesting that Freillon-Poncein was based in Grenoble rather than Paris. He apologizes for his lack of skill in language, and indeed the wording and organization of the tutor are often confusing.

Étienne Loulié (1654–1702) began writing his unpublished 'Méthode pour apprendre à jouer de la flûte douce' before seeing Freillon-Poncein's work, then revising and simplifying it in 1701 or 1702, expressly noting what the other author did or did not include.[81] After serving as senior musician in the Guise Music under Marc-Antoine Charpentier's direction (see p. 160 below), and teaching at the Guise-protected Academy of the Infant Jesus, Loulié became music teacher to the Duke of Chartres, a royal prince who eventually became regent of France.[82] The dot way and some wording in Loulié's recorder tutor apparently derive from English tutors of 1679–83, which he could easily have obtained from his contacts in England.

As the order of instruments named on the title page suggests, *Principes de la flute traversiere, ou flute d'allemagne, de la flute a bec, ou flute douce, et du haut-bois, divise{ par traite{* (Paris, 1707) by Jacques Hotteterre le Romain (1673–1763) was conceived primarily as a tutor for the transverse flute, which had recently become 'one of the most fashionable instruments' in France.[83] Although, as Hotteterre says, the recorder has 'its merits and its partisans, just like the flute',[84] he accords it a secondary role by placing its section after that of the flute and referring recorder players to the flute section for information on articulation and ornaments. Nevertheless, the exquisite engraving in his tutor of two hands playing a recorder has achieved canonical status in modern times as a precise depiction of the Baroque type of instrument.

A scion of a celebrated family of woodwind makers and musicians whose contribution to the Baroque recorder has been discussed in detail above, Hotteterre had recently assumed the duties of *Flûte de la chambre du roy* (Flute of the King's chamber), concentrating on playing the flute and the musette.

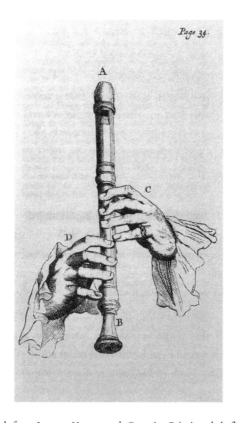

20. Recorder and hands from Jacques Hotteterre le Romain, *Principes de la flûte* (Paris, 1707).

FRENCH FINGERINGS

Loulié's basic fingering chart goes from f¹ to d³. Later he gives fingerings for e³, f³, g³, g♯³, b³, and c⁴ – 'notes little used on the recorder – that is to say, those that ascend above its normal range, and which are used only in transpositions'.[85] The fingerings for b³ and c⁴ make use of the partial venting of a finger-hole (3) as well as the thumb-hole, a technique that also turns up in the mid-eighteenth century. The notes f♯³, a³, and b♭³ are notated but the fingerings are missing, although two for f♯³ appear as parts of *tremblements*.

Freillon-Poncein's fingering chart, shown by means of schematic figures of a recorder, uniquely acknowledges the existence of major and minor semitones, although like the other charts it has the same fingering for each enharmonic pair (such as D♯ and E♭). Trill fingerings are described for the first octave only.

In his fingering charts, Hotteterre seems to have been the first to use systematically the now familiar symbols – black circles for closed finger-holes, white circles for open finger-holes, and half-blackened circles for half-closed or 'pinched' finger-holes – divorced from the representation of an instrument (which appears only at the left-hand side of the charts). Although his method of showing trill fingerings is similar to Carr's, Hotteterre's adoption of these symbols makes the fingerings easier to comprehend.

FRENCH ORNAMENTS

Loulié explains and gives fingerings for three main types of ornament: *battement* or *martellement* (mordent; both *simple* with one oscillation, and *double*, with two); *tremblement* (trill); and *flatté*, *balancement*, or *tremblement mineur* (fingered vibrato). The *battement* and *flatté* were generally shaken with the same finger, but the latter was beaten on the edge of the hole and slowly, 'so that the [pitch of the] main note is not changed'.[86] He also illustrates four other ornaments: *port de voix* (ascending appoggiatura), *coulé* (descending appoggiatura), *chute*, and *accent*. Freillon-Poncein's ornaments are similar to Loulié's – *port de voix ou de son* (ascending appoggiatura, both single and double), *descente de voix ou de son* (descending appoggiatura), *accen[t]*, *battement* or *pincé* (mordent), and *tremblement* (trill) – except that he does not mention the fingered vibrato.

For the recorder, Hotteterre gives a table of fingerings for trills (*cadences* or *tremblements*) coupled with discussions of a few particular trills, then devotes a chapter to describing fingerings for the *battement* (mordent) and *flattement* (fingered vibrato). For the other ornaments, he refers the reader back to the appropriate chapters in his flute section, which covers the *port-de-voix* (ascending appoggiatura), *coulement* (descending appoggiatura), *accent*, and *double cadence* (trill with turn). Hotteterre provides additional instructions on ornaments in the preface to the second edition of his *Pièces pour la flûte traversière et autres instruments, avec la basse continue*, Op. 2 (Paris, 1715), introducing the *port-de-voix double* (slide), *demi cadence apuiée* (trill with very long appoggiatura), and two types of turn: *tour de gosier* and *tour de chant*. He also specifies that *flattements*, *tremblements*, and *battements* must be made 'slower or quicker according to the tempo and character of the piece'.[87] He observes candidly, 'These ornaments are not marked in all pieces of music – normally only in those that masters write for their students. . . . One can hardly give more certain rules about the distribution of these ornaments in playing: it is taste and practice rather than theory that can teach you to use them appropriately.'[88]

All of the French authors leave the rhythm, accentuation, and number of oscillations of their ornaments open to interpretation.

FRENCH ARTICULATION

Loulié, Freillon-Poncein, and Hotteterre employ only two tonguing syllables, *tu* and *ru*, in which the *t* is pronounced behind the upper front teeth and the *r* by the tip of the tongue curling back almost to the palate.[89] Patricia M. Ranum has argued that these syllables helped players mimic French song, which in turn was influenced by poetic structure.[90]

Loulié writes about articulation: 'All those who teach recorder playing use *tu* and *ru*, and you find that the mixture of these two syllables, pronounced in turn in certain places, renders the tongue strokes less harsh and the playing more flowing. But the way of placing them is not really constant, because [teachers] each have their own particular way. . . . All these ways can be good, but the student who has a good teacher must take the ways from him.'[91] Freillon-Poncein's practice is similar.

Hotteterre recommends *tu* for longer notes and most quavers; stepwise quavers and all semiquavers intermix *ru* in three ways: (1) *tu | ru* for *notes inégales*; (2) *tu ru | tu* for dotted notes and patterns of crotchet–quaver–quaver–crotchet or quaver–semiquaver–semiquaver–quaver; and (3) *tu ru tu | tu* to conclude a phrase

(Ranum's interpretation).[92] He considers slurring (*coulez*) an ornament; yet the preludes and *traits* in his *L'art de préluder* (1719), influenced by the Italian violin style, feature many slurs over long groups of smaller note values. He still says that the two-note termination of the trill could be tongued.

As the Italian violin style became the predominant influence on woodwind music, according to Quantz (1752), French flautists such as Michel Blavet and Pierre Gabriel Buffardin modified their articulation to *ti* and *tiri* or *di* and *diri*,[93] and before long *tu* and *ru* were dropped entirely. Michel Corrette's flute tutor (ca. 1739) reports that the virtuosi of his day considered them 'an absurdity that serves only to perplex the student'.[94]

<h2 style="text-align:center">ITALY</h2>

Bartolomeo Bismantova's 'Compendio musicale' (1677/1694) reiterates that all wind instruments should be played 'in imitation of one who sings'.[95] His tonguing syllables are still similar to the Renaissance models. Bismantova is the only writer to differentiate between syllables suitable for the cornetto (*te*) and the recorder (*de*). He uses what he calls the *lingua dritta* (*de*) for all note values from a semibreve to a quaver; the *lingua roverscia* (*de re le re*), for quavers, semiquavers and demisemiquavers. In this he differs from Ganassi, who employed *dritta* (direct) for the first of a pair of tonguing syllables and *roverscia* (reverse) for the second. Two other kinds of syllables (*de che* and *der ler*), unnamed, are declared 'not used, but at times sound beautiful to accompany in the *Stile cantabile*,'[96] perhaps advocating the use of a wider range of articulations to help the player imitate the nature of the words in vocal music – as in Ganassi.[97] The first of these kinds was Ganassi's first basic type of tonguing, and the second kind is similar to a combination of Ganassi's second and third basic types of tonguing, but at speed, when the second vowel disappears. Significantly new in Bismantova is the *lingua legata*, represented as slurred pairs of notes, with a change of syllable under every note: *de a de a de a* (even under a six-note slur). The development of slurring, even in this transitional form, presumably reflects the influence of violin technique.

Bismantova recommends trilling 'on every note, provided it is of half a bar, or a whole bar, or even a quarter of a bar, and also on all dotted notes'.[98] Dickey et al. remark: 'this rather unclear passage is probably intended to indicate that the execution of a *trillo* requires a certain amount of time and is therefore scarcely possible on very short notes.'[99] The other ornament mentioned is the *accento* – similar to the French *accent*. Seventy-five years before the well-known section in Quantz's *Versuch*, Bismantova gives basic advice on when to take a breath: 'in such a way that no one will be aware of it, and it must be done during rests the length of a half note or a whole note, or in dotted notes.'[100]

SPAIN

A treatise by the Spanish organist Pablo Nasarre, *Escuela de música según la práctica moderna* (Zaragoza, 1723–24), includes a short chapter on wind instruments 'such as curtals, shawms, and recorders', in which he derives all the intervals as proportions of the sounding length of the instrument.[101] He goes on to explain that, in addition to having a well-tuned instrument, the musician must learn how to adjust notes up or down one or two commas, so that they are in tune with the organ.

Pablo Minguet y Irol's *Reglas, y advertencias generates que enseñan el modo de tañer todos los instrumentos mejores, y mas usuales* (Madrid, 1754) has a section devoted to members of the flute family, including *flauta dulce*, which includes a fingering chart and some elementary guidance on holding the instrument. The chart includes alto fingerings chromatically up to c^4, the highest note shown in any chart for the Baroque-type recorder. Of special interest is the expansion of the principle already found in Loulié (1680s) for b^3 and c^4 of 'pinching', or partial venting, on holes other than the thumb-hole, now used for $g\sharp^3$ and $a\sharp^3$ as well.

SAMUEL PEPYS AND THE TRANSPORT OF THE SOUL

Samuel Pepys (1633–1703), an administrator for the English Navy and later a Member of Parliament, wrote about the flageolet from the beginning of his celebrated diary in 1660.[102] He played the instrument at a tavern, on a boat on the River Thames, in a grotto in St James's Park, in a cellar that had a good echo, at home, at his cabin in Kent, in an echoey vault under a house, in the garden, on a roof, at a dinner party, out of his bedroom window, and in his bedroom before going to bed, as well as many duets with his wife Elizabeth. He had bought a matched pair of instruments from the woodwind maker Samuel Drumbleby (1629–71 or later). Showing an easy familiarity with royal musicians, Pepys took a lesson from Thomas Blagrave in 1660; he and Elizabeth took lessons from Thomas

Greeting in 1667–68, despite impatience with Greeting's teaching methods; at a dinner party at his house, he listened to John Banister I play the flageolet and theorbo; he was promised 'some things' for two flageolets by Christopher Gibbons in 1668; and he tried further 'things' by Matthew Locke.

The consort of recorders that was used frequently in the London theatres before the Civil War may not have been revived for use there immediately after the Restoration. Recorders are not mentioned in the texts of any plays of the 1660s until Abraham Bailey's *The Spiteful Sister*, which was licensed for performance in 1667 but apparently never performed.[103] Flageolets, however, are mentioned in the texts of several plays, including two attended by Pepys.[104]

On 16 February 1661, Pepys went to a revival of Philip Massinger and Thomas Dekker's play *The Virgin Martyr* by the King's Company and found nothing to comment on in the music.[105] On 27 February 1668, in contrast, he attended another revival of the same play by the same company and was moved to write one of the most famous passages in recorder history:

> But that which did please me beyond anything in the whole world was the wind music when the angel comes down, which is so sweet that it ravished me; and indeed, in a word, did wrap up my soul so that it made me really sick, just as I have formerly been when in love with my wife; that neither then, nor all the evening going home and at home, I was able to think of anything, but remained all night transported, so as I could not believe that ever any music has that real command over the soul of a man as did this upon me; and makes me resolve to practice wind music, and to make my wife do the like.[106]

Three days later, on 2 March, he went again to the play, 'which does mightly please me, but above all the music at the coming down of the angel – which at this hearing the second time does so still command me as nothing ever did, and the other music is nothing to it'.[107] He also returned on 6 May, 'and heard the music that I like so well', and the next day.[108]

What were these ravishing instruments? On 8 April, he went to visit Drumbleby again, 'and there did talk a great deal about pipes; and did buy a recorder, which I do intend to play on, the sound of it being, of all sounds in the world, most pleasing to me. . . . So home to my chamber, to be fingering of my recorder and getting of the scale of music [gamut] without book.'[109] Eight days later, he wrote: 'Th. Greetings book. . . . Begin this day to learn the Recorder.'[110] No trace of a recorder tutor by Greeting exists, only a flageolet tutor. Why Pepys should have bought such a book when he wanted to learn the recorder has never been explained. Did he hope for some crossover between the techniques of the two instruments? Curiously, the surviving flageolet tutor that stemmed from Pepys' library is not Greeting's but an early edition of *Youth's Delight on the Flagelet*, dating from the late 1670s.[111]

Edgar Hunt asks about the theatre performance: 'What new sound could he have heard that had this strange effect on him? From the fact that . . . he bought a recorder, and his opinion of that instrument's tone quality, it is most reasonable to assume that it was a consort of recorders that he heard.'[112] He suggests that the recorders may have been the Baroque type, recently imported from France, 'which looked and sounded different from the earlier types'. But if Renaissance recorders had not yet been heard on the stage since the Restoration, they too would have been a novelty to Pepys, who was not old enough to have heard them in Caroline (pre-1642) productions. Moreover, Drumbleby was a native woodwind maker, part of a long line who had been working in London since at least the turn of the century,[113] and he is more likely to have been selling his own (Renaissance) instruments than the latest products imported from France. Only seven years earlier, Renaissance-style recorders were still being imported to England: customs duties imposed on merchandise commonly imported in 1660 included 'Recorders, the set or case, containing five recorders £1.'[114] Also, as we have seen, the Baroque recorder seems to have been invented in France around 1668 as more a soloistic than a consort instrument; and the French players who brought it to England in 1673 induced a change of name. On balance, the evidence suggests that Pepys heard Renaissance recorders, probably being played on the London stage for the first time since the Restoration.

Postscript: In the 1690s, Pepys was living in York Buildings, a street in London where a celebrated concert series was promoted by Gottfried Finger and Giovanni Battista Draghi. Of course, by this time Pepys would have owned the Baroque type of recorder. He clearly had some connection with Finger, as he bought two editions of the composer's recorder music: *A Collection of Choice Ayres for Two & Three Treble Flutes* (1691) and the only surviving copy of the first edition of *Six Sonates a 2 flustes et 2 Hautbois ou Violons et 1 Basse Continue* (1698): four sonatas by Finger and two by Gottfried Keller.[115] Since Pepys lent Draghi his own harpsichord for the York Buildings concerts, it seems highly likely that he attended them himself.[116]

REPERTOIRE THE ALTO

The extensive repertoire of solo sonatas and a smaller body of pieces for recorder and orchestra have naturally attracted particular attention among modern professional players and skilled amateurs. Even in their own day, these pieces seem to have been conceived to show off advanced skills, even when published for amateur use. Yet many of the finest and most idiomatic recorder parts of the period under consideration are in chamber or vocal music. This section concentrates on a selection of outstanding compositions featuring the alto; other sizes of recorder are considered separately in the next section.

FRANCE

From 1668 until his death in 1687, Jean-Baptiste Lully wrote no fewer than twenty-five ballets, operas, and other vocal works in which recorders are named in the scores or *livrets* (printed librettos) and the players generally appeared in costume on stage.[117] The associations of the recorder are similar to those of the Renaissance: the pastoral, sensuality, love, sleep, water, birds, magic, the gods, sacrifices, death, Mercury, the Muses, and conflict.[118] See the 'Symbolism and Associations' section in the previous chapter.

Recorders were involved in a delicate moment in Anglo-French diplomacy. Robert Cambert, the composer of the first French operas, was put out of business when Lully was granted monopoly control of all opera in France. Sent by Louis XIV to England in 1673 to work for Charles II's French mistress, who had received the title Duchess of Portsmouth, Cambert was accompanied by four French oboists and recorder players: [Jean?] Boutet, Maxant de Bresmes, Pierre Guiton, and the young James Paisible.[119] In 1676, concern arose that the duchess, who had been helping French interests in England, might be displaced in Charles's affections. Louis thereupon dispatched a mission of three French singers to influence Charles with music: Gillet (*haute-contre* = high tenor), La Forest (*taille* = low tenor), and Godonesche (*basse-taille* = baritone). The French ambassador, Honoré Courtin, wrote to Louis that Charles had attended a dinner party given by the duchess, 'taking the greatest pleasure' in hearing the French singers; 'furthermore, he wants them to repeat the *Sommeil* [from Lully's *Atys*] tomorrow, for the fourth time. Cambert accompanies the singers with his harpsichord, and recorders are added; there are two Frenchmen here who play them perfectly. The King of Great Britain always beats time, and admires the beauty of the voices and the precision of your musicians, as do all the court.'[120] A week later, 'the King of Great Britain has often heard Messieurs Gillet, La Forest, and Godonesche at her apartments; they have several times sung the *Sommeil*, and many other scenes from [Lully's] *Alceste*, *Cadmus*, *Thésée* and *Atys*. Monsieur Cambert accompanied them on his harpsichord [and] there are five or six men who play the recorder very well. Your Majesty's musicians have acquired a great reputation here and all the ladies have counted it an honour to have them visit them.'[121]

All the Lully operas mentioned in the ambassador's dispatch have recorder parts. Of particular interest are those in *Thésée* (1675) and the recent *Atys* (1676), which feature a pair of high soprano and low soprano voices – as we shall see in the next section, probably matched by alto recorder and voice flute.[122] The *livret* of *Atys* names six recorder players, including four members of the Hotteterre family, who appeared on stage dressed as *Songes* (Dreams) for the famous *Sommeil*, framed by a prelude for two (evidently tripled) recorders, five-part strings, and continuo, in which slurred pairs of crotchets, overlapping phrases, suspensions, and judicious use of the sighing ornament called *accent* invoke a sleepy mood. See illustration 3.6. The following vocal duet, 'Dormons, dormons' (Let us sleep), for Morphée and Le Sommeil, the god of Sleep, is accompanied by the recorders, and features word painting for murmuring streams, more overlapping and suspensions, and eventually a vocal trio for Morphée, Phantaste (sung in the original performance by La Forest), and Phobetor. Presumably Cambert arranged his rival's music for the limited forces available in these unique private performances, designed to win over a king.

Marc-Antoine Charpentier (1643–1704) studied in Rome with Giacomo Carissimi, developing a taste for Italian harmony, more dissonant than in the French music of the day.[123] Between 1670 and 1687, he primarily composed for the Guise Music, the ensemble at the Hôtel (urban palace) belonging to the devout Mademoiselle de Guise, a wealthy princess and duchess, where the recorder player Étienne Loulié worked from 1672 onwards. Between 1679 and about 1690, Charpentier also composed for the private chapel of Louis XIV's son, Louis, the Dauphin, whose musicians included the court *flûte* players Pierre II, Joseph, and

21. Opening of 'Le Sommeil' from *Atys* (1676) by Jean-Baptiste Lully.

Pierre-Antoine Pièche. Furthermore, between 1673 and 1685, Charpentier also wrote music for the theatre company led by Molière, and continued by Thomas Corneille and Jean Donneau de Visé. From 1671, Charpentier received commissions from the Jesuit Order, which employed him from 1688 until he was finally awarded a royal post, at the Sainte-Chapelle in 1698.

Charpentier scored for *flûtes* in no fewer than 120 works spread over his whole working life, from his first known composition in 1670 until his last surviving one of 1702. Another eighty unmarked works were probably intended for the *flûte*. In just four works, written between 1674 and 1687, does Charpentier differentiate between the recorder (*flûte à bec* or *flûte douce*) and transverse flute (*flûte d'allemand*), apparently in special circumstances, as he evidently otherwise relied on the musicians to know the appropriate instrument. The large majority of his *flûte* parts, especially before 1686, are within the range of the alto recorder. Probably he was retaining flexibility for any given performance, as revealed in his instruction '*s'il y en a*' (if there are any) for the *flûte* parts in two works entitled *Ouverture pour le sacre d'un évêque pour les violons, flûtes et hautbois*, H. 536 and H. 537 (ca. 1694). From 1687 onwards, roughly three out of four of his *flûte* parts still fit the alto recorder. Some may have been intended for the recorder, such as Jason's air in the opera *Médée*, H. 491 (1693), although other writing in the same work seems more suited to the transverse flute. Charpentier's works for other sizes of recorder are discussed in the next section.

In *Orphée descendant aux enfers*, H. 471 (1683) and '*Usquequo Domine*', H. 196 (1687), the first part is written for alto recorder, the second for transverse flute. Charpentier wrote nine more works between about 1683 and 1690 for which he seems to have intended such a pairing (H. 189, 201, 275–76, 346, 373–74, 409, 480), mostly for the Pièche family. Some of these compositions have bass recorder on the third line. I believe that Charpentier conceived of this pairing of recorder and flute to match the *haut-dessus* (high soprano) and *dessus* (soprano) voices of his female singers in the Dauphin's Music, perhaps earlier also in the Guise Music. He used the transverse flute, rather than the voice flute developed for Lully's music, probably because the flute had become sufficiently established in the hands of the players such as the Pièches by about 1679 that Charpentier had no need to call on the voice flute.

Whether Charpentier wrote abundantly for *flûtes* of both kinds because they were so readily available, or simply because he liked the sound and associations of the instruments, they were eminently suitable for what his biographer Catherine

Cessac has called the 'poignant introspection' of his music, which 'moves us so deeply today'.[124]

Little purely instrumental music was written solely for the recorder in France, although publishers from the 1690s to the 1750s often listed the instrument as an alternative to the flute, vielle, musette, etc. on title pages. But a fine *Sonate pour la flûte à bec* – appropriately, in a mixed French–Italian style – was composed by the woodwind player Anne Danican Philidor (Paris, 1712), presumably for himself to play at court. Jacques Hotteterre suggests that his suites, trio sonatas, preludes, and duets for flute in a mixed style (Paris, 1708–22) may be transposed a minor third higher for the alto recorder.

ENGLAND

Two small instrumental masterpieces by Henry Purcell (1659–95) call for recorders. His early *Three Parts upon a Ground* (ca. 1678) was written for three violins (in D major) or three recorders (in F major) on a ground bass also used by Christopher Simpson in his *Compendium of Practical Music* (London, 1667) to illustrate canonic writing over a ground. Peter Holman observes that *Three Parts* alternates three different types of writing: the French orchestral chaconne and passacaglia with dotted rhythms and sighing suspensions; imitative counterpoint and divisions in the style of John Jenkins; and strict canon.[125] He wonders whether Purcell 'was trying to develop a new style of court consort music, attuned to Charles II's musical tastes', since *Three Parts* also sounds superficially like dance music.[126] In contrast, Purcell's *Two in One upon a Ground, Chaconne for Flutes* from his semi-opera *Dioclesian* (1690), for two recorders and continuo in C minor over a six-bar ground, is a strict canon at the unison, written at an interval of two bars, over an elaboration of the passacaglia, the phrase lengths being varied skilfully to avoid any sense of predictability.

Purcell's vocal music – semi-operas, incidental music to plays, birthday and other odes, welcome songs, and 'symphony songs' – contains a wealth of obbligatos for two recorders that evoke love, peace, the pastoral, the supernatural, or birdsong, or bring to life textual references to 'flute' or 'pipes'.[127] 'Hark! Behold the Heavenly Quire!' (*Theodosius*, 1680) scores the descending angelic choir – an image which twelve years before had so beguiled Pepys in *The Virgin Martyr* – for bass voice, two recorders, and continuo. In the song 'In Vain the Am'rous Flute' from *Hail Bright Cecilia* (1692), the poet Nicholas Brady questions the recorder's ability 'to inspire wanton heat and loose desire', but Purcell's music leaves little doubt.

James Paisible (ca. 1658–1721), cited elsewhere as performer and teacher, was also an accomplished composer for the recorder. His most notable works are thirteen sonatas for recorder and continuo, probably written in the 1690s, that were never published but survive in several manuscripts. The style is a unique mixture of the Corellian sonata da camera and sonata da chiesa with the dance music of Lully, bearing some resemblance to the suites of Paisible's friend Francis Dieupart and displaying a French (and English) fondness for stepwise passage work.[128] They pose considerable technical demands for the time in the rapidity of some passage work and ornamental figuration.

The operas, oratorios, cantatas, and anthems by George Frideric Handel (1685–1759) contain a wealth of obbligato parts for recorder, notable for their broad range of associations. The careful scoring allows the instrument to be heard readily: muting the strings or having them play softly, reducing the size of the continuo group or having the continuo strings play pizzicato, using violas or even violins as

22. *Recorder Player* (ca. 1720) by the Bohemian painter Ján Kupecký (1667–1740), active in Hungary, Vienna, and Nuremberg. Playing the recorder with the right hand uppermost was common in the Middle Ages and Renaissance, but rare by the eighteenth century.

the lowest-sounding line, and having the recorders play unaccompanied or make soloistic forays into the high register for a few bars.[129] The recorder is mainly associated with love and the heart; also water (the sea, waves, zephyrs), death, sleep, the supernatural, and birdsong.[130] The main differences from Purcell are that Handel also uses the recorder in sacred music, and choses the traverso to illustrate textural references to 'flute'.

Handel's six recorder sonatas – G minor, HWV 360; A minor, HWV 362; C major, HWV 365; D minor, HWV 367a; F major, HWV 369; and B♭ major, HWV 377 – are generally considered the finest in the Baroque repertoire. Displaying great variety in the structure of the sonatas and the form of their movements, Handel combines inventive vocal writing – straight out of his operatic arias – with an instrumental idiom learned largely from Arcangelo Corelli, incorporating surprising leaps and turns of phrase, widely varied phrase lengths, and strong interplay between melody and bass line.[131] These works were composed around 1724–26, when Handel was at the height of his fame as an opera composer, writing such masterpieces as *Giulio Cesare* and preoccupied with the fortunes of his London opera company, the Royal Academy of Music. The recorder, having been the pre-eminent instrument for the gentleman amateur for over forty years, was now on the decline, losing ground rapidly to the transverse flute. Why would he have written solo works for the instrument at this time?

One partial answer may lie in the concert scene of the day. Members of the opera orchestra supplemented their income by taking part in concerts, either in special concert halls such as Hickford's Room or during the intervals of performances at the opera house or theatres. Newspaper advertisements for these concerts suggest that the woodwind players in the orchestra were particularly active. For example, Jean Christian Kytch, a Dutchman who had arrived in London around 1707 and was now the first oboist in the orchestra, performed instrumental arrangements of Handel's opera arias in concert on oboe, bassoon, and recorder. Kytch and his colleagues John Festing, Richard Neale, and Carl Friedrich Weidemann would have been called upon to play the recorder from time to time in the orchestra, when the mood of an aria represented love, death, or the supernatural. *Giulio Cesare* (1724), *Tamerlano* (1724), *Rodelinda* (1725), *Scipione* (1726), and *Alessandro* (1726) all included arias with recorder parts. The concerts thrived by presenting the newest music. It would have been natural for Kytch, in particular, to have asked Handel to write him some recorder sonatas (as well as oboe and flute sonatas) for his concert appearances.

Another motivation for writing the recorder sonatas might have been the figured bass lessons that Handel started giving to Princess Anne, daughter of George II, and to John Christopher Smith junior, the son of his amanuensis and principal copyist, in 1724–25. Probably to assist with these lessons, Handel made fair copies of four of the sonatas (A minor, C major, F major, and G minor) *a Flauto e Cembalo* (for recorder and harpsichord) with particularly rich figuring. Anne is known to have played the flute, and probably also the recorder. Siegbert Rampe points out that, besides keyboard instruments, in his youth Handel learned to play the violin, recorder, and oboe.[132] So composer and royal student would have been able to alternate playing the recorder part and realizing the continuo on the harpsichord. We can also presume that Anne's younger sisters Amelia and Caroline Elizabeth had a similar musical education, perhaps including recorder playing. The royal sisters could therefore have played the sonatas themselves. This educational and domestic context would account for the generally modest technical demands of the solo part compared with Handel's violin sonatas.

Handel's recorder sonatas have a curious publication history. Five of them were first issued between 1726 and 1732 by the leading London publisher of the day, John Walsh, in a collection entitled *Sonates pour un traversière, un violon ou hautbois con basso continuo* (Sonatas for a transverse flute, violin, or oboe with continuo). Perhaps because he had obtained copies of the sonatas without the composer's consent, Walsh pretended that the publication was the work of the Amsterdam music publisher Jeanne Roger (d. 1722), faking the title page to look like one of hers. In 1732 he republished the collection under his own imprint with an English title, *Solos for a German flute, a hoboy or violin with a thorough bass for the harpsicord or bass violin*, and the notoriously misspelt statement 'This is more Corect than the former Edition.' He later advertised this collection as Handel's Opus 1. Despite the instrumentation on the title page, four of the recorder sonatas call for *flauto solo* at the foot of their first page. The fifth recorder sonata, originally in D minor, appears in a transposed version in B minor for the flute. When the autograph manuscripts of all six sonatas finally became known in the late 1970s, the sonatas could now be viewed as a group; the manuscripts give a slightly different text that probably represents Handel's final thoughts.

Francesco Barsanti (ca. 1690–1775), an oboist, viola player, and music copyist born in Lucca and trained in Italy, self-published six solo sonatas, Op. 1, in London in 1724, about a year after he settled in England.[133] These imaginative works, like Handel's, are notable for a wide variety of types of movement (binary, ternary, fugal, through-composed, variations) as well as unusual phrasings and refined harmonies.

His contemporary, Giuseppe Sammartini (1695–1750), wrote no fewer than thirty-two sonatas for alto recorder and continuo, far less well known than his soprano recorder concerto; at the time of writing they have not even been published completely in modern editions. Whether they are in four movements or the more progressive three, these sonatas are surprisingly original: constantly unpredictable melodically, harmonically, rhythmically, and in phrase length. Sammartini, a fine oboist, emigrated to London in 1729, where he performed in the opera orchestra and in concerts. In 1736 he became music master to Augusta, the Princess of Wales, and her five children. Sammartini's probate inventory mentions 'four flutes', which could well have been both recorders and transverse flutes.[134]

ITALY

In Italy, the recorder repertoire of the late Baroque was primarily associated with the cities of Venice and Naples. Venetian masters included the Marcello brothers: Benedetto (1686–1739), who published a set of twelve recorder sonatas, Op. 2 (1712), and Alessandro (1669–1747), whose manuscript *Concerto di flauti* is mentioned in the next section; as well as the Benedictine monk Diogenio Bigaglia (1678–1745), who published a set of twelve sonatas, Op. 1 (Amsterdam, 1725). Notable works published in Venice included the twelve sonatas, Op. 1, by Paolo Benedetto Bellinzani (ca. 1690–1757); a set of twelve sonatas in manuscript by the Florentine composer Francesco Maria Veracini is dated Venice 1716 on its dedication to the Elector of Saxony.

The dominant composer in Venice, who wrote some of the finest recorder music in the entire repertoire, was Antonio Vivaldi (1678–1741). His C minor concerto for alto recorder and strings, RV 441 (early 1730s?), is described by Federico Maria Sardelli as 'the most profound, elaborate, and inspired work ever written by Vivaldi for either the recorder or the flute . . . [its] musical quality is comparable with that of mature, demanding violin concertos', and indeed it seems to have been derived from the violin concerto in the same key, RV 202 (published in *La cetra*, 1728).[135] Its rapid violinistic passage work, containing large leaps and idiomatic lyrical writing in all registers, showcases the Baroque instrument's expressive potential. So, too, do the eight delightful chamber concertos with combinations of oboe, violin, and bassoon (RV 87, 92, 94–95, 101, 103, 105, and

108), in which the solo instruments make their own ritornellos, and a remarkably athletic trio sonata in A minor with bassoon (RV 86, ca. 1730).[136]

Several of Vivaldi's instrumental works involving the recorder, from ca. 1708 up to the early 1720s, may have been intended for an alto in g^1. The newly discovered recorder sonata, RV 806, dating from around 1716, is in G major with lowest note g^1,[137] and the chamber concerto RV 101 (early 1720s) has the same features.[138] The chamber concertos RV 90a (1710s?), RV 92 (early 1720s), RV 94 (early 1720s), and RV 95 (1710s?) are all in D major, and the last three go up to $f\sharp^3$, a note difficult to produce in tune on *some* altos in f^1 and omitted from *some* Baroque fingering charts. Sardelli also remarks that the chamber concerto in A minor, RV 108 (early 1720s; lowest note g^1), 'which can be performed quite comfortably on [an alto] instrument in F, is more grateful to the player of a G instrument'.[139]

The collection of six sonatas *Il pastor fido*, published in Paris in 1737 ostensibly as Vivaldi's Op. 13, was in fact composed by the French musette player Nicolas Chédeville, partly based on themes by Vivaldi, Joseph Meck (Chédeville probably believed his music was by Vivaldi), and Giuseppe Matteo Alberti.[140] Vivaldi's *flautino* concertos are discussed in the next section.

Sardelli writes:

> Throughout his career as a composer of operas – from his first opera, *Ottone in villa*, RV 729 (1713), to the pasticcio *Rosmira fedele*, RV 731 (1738) – Vivaldi included parts for recorder or flute in the stage works that he composed alone or with contributions from others. . . . Even though the recorder and flute were, according to Baroque rhetoric, the pastoral instruments par excellence, used to evoke bucolic scenes, birdsong, and wafting breezes, Vivaldi, to his credit, did not confine them to this expressive register but employed them also to create atmospheres of a less conventional kind or to suggest pathos. In this way, the *flautino* came to represent on the stage both the peace of night and a roaring sea. . . .[141]

A substantial repertoire of recorder sonatas, concertos, sinfonias, and obbligato parts in arias, cantatas, operas, oratorios, serenatas, and sinfonias stems from Naples. Especially in the period 1715–30, celebrated opera composers, including Leonardo Leo, Francesco Mancini, Nicola Porpora, Domenico Sarro, Alessandro Scarlatti, and Leonardo Vinci, as well as lesser-known figures, featured the recorder in works that Inês d'Avena Braga describes as including:

theatrical elements such as contrasting fast/slow sections, abrupt pauses, surprising harmonic progressions; tempo indications such as Amoroso, Spiritoso, Comodo, etc.; musical material evenly distributed among all instruments; interesting bass lines; an abundance of works in minor keys; particularly vocal melodic lines; a style on the border of the Galant, lighter but still deeply rooted in a complex and well-studied manner; and fugal second (or third) movements.[142]

Part of the recorder music collection of Aloys Thomas Raimund, Count Harrach, the Austrian envoy in Naples 1728–33, is now housed in the New York Public Library. It includes a few technically demanding works – a sonata by the Neapolitan violinist Nicolo Fiorenza, and concertos by the Mainz Konzertmeister Matthäus Nikolaus Stulick and the Zerbst Kapellmeister Johann Friedrich Fasch – probably performed by musicians in the count's employment, and easier works, probably for him to play himself.[143]

GERMAN-SPEAKING LANDS

Reinhard Keiser (1674–1739), the foremost German opera composer of the day, was trained at the Thomasschule in Leipzig, long before J. S. Bach worked there. From 1696 or 97, on and off until about 1728, paralleling the fluctuating fortunes of his workplace, Keiser was the main house composer for the Hamburg Opera at the Gänsemarkt (Goosemarket) Theatre. He wrote at least sixty-six operas, of which complete scores of only nineteen survive, together with substantial portions of several others.

No fewer than twenty of Keiser's operas between *Adonis* (1697) and *Circe* (1734) feature the recorder: in total, fifty-nine arias and eight other movements.[144] The recorders are scored mostly in pairs, but also solo, in unison, in groups of three, four, and even five, and sometimes in unison or octaves with other instruments such as the violin, viola, cello, and *zuffolo* (perhaps bagpipe). Keiser employs recorders with the symbolism and associations familiar from other composers, representing nature (wind, flowers, forest), birds, sleep, and love fulfilled. He also puts recorders in what Lucia Carpena calls 'unusual contexts': unrequited love, suffering, or unhappiness; farewell, lament, or despair; irony; and magic.

Keiser creates haunting *affects* from the simplest of figures, as in the short *Le Sommeil* in *Masaniello furioso* (1706) – influenced by Lully's *Sommeil* from *Atys*

– mostly slurred pairs of quavers doubling the violins at the octave. In contrast, *Masaniello* includes an aria with recorder obbligato, 'Philomele, kräusle die Züge', in which the recorder sets up virtuoso figuration, more brilliant than anything before Vivaldi, subsequently taken up by the soprano voice.[145] A bird-imitation aria with three recorders, 'Seliger Stand!', reminiscent of Handel's 'Augelletti' from *Rinaldo*, but written five years earlier, is full of trills and rapid notes. Another bird aria, 'Du angenehme Nachtigal' from *Ulisses* (1722), has a top part for 'Violini con Flauto' (violins with recorder) and a second part marked 'Flauto d'Echo' (echo flute). Alas, it does not provide a clue about the famous *Fiauti d'echo* problem in Bach's Fourth Brandenburg Concerto – the echo-flute part merely echoes the top part, without any notated dynamics, implying that the instrument might have been played offstage. The aria 'Ihr fliegenden Sänger' from *Orpheus* (1709) is scored for tenor singer and an unprecedented combination of four alto and one tenor recorders and continuo; the recorders play at the same time, mostly in semiquavers and demisemiquavers, suggesting both the birds in the background and Orpheus's torments.[146] We could be forgiven for presuming that many of Keiser's recorder obbligatos were in the style of Handel, Bach, or Telemann, but these later masters were all indebted to him.

Few compositions for recorder have been welcomed into the modern canon of 'great music', but there has never been any doubt about the Brandenburg Concertos Nos 2 and 4, written by Johann Sebastian Bach (1685–1750) while he was working in Weimar in 1721.[147] No. 2 in F major, BWV 1047, treats a single alto recorder as an equal soloist with trumpet, oboe, and violin accompanied by strings; the trumpet and the ripieno strings drop out in the slow movement. No. 4 in G major, BWV 1049, matches two *fiauti d'echo* with a violin, although in the staff headings of the first movement he wrote only *Fiauto 1mo* and *Fiauto 2do*, perhaps taking the 'd'echo' appendage for granted, or else having alto recorders in mind. The concerto plays inventively with the identity of the soloists: does it have one (the solo violin) or three (violin plus echo flutes)? Bach later arranged this concerto clearly for two alto recorders (*Fiauti a bec*) with harpsichord in F major, BWV 1057 (ca. 1738).

The term *Fiauti d'echo* is unique to the Fourth Brandenburg Concerto, and scholars have spilled perhaps more ink over the identity of these instruments than any other issue in the recorder's repertoire, including Vivaldi's *flautino*. Several main schools of thought have developed.[148] (1) The instruments were regular alto recorders in F. (2) The instruments were alto recorders in G. (3) The first instrument was an alto recorder in G; the second, an alto recorder in F. (4) The instruments were sopranino recorders or flageolets sounding an octave higher than written. (5) The term *echo* referred to an echo, literal (even spatial), figurative, or symbolic, as well as perhaps the secondary function of the *Fiauti* in relation to the violin (which is reversed, however, in the slow movement). (6) To create a literal echo, at least in the second movement, the instruments were echo flutes made by joining two recorders together with a flange (such an instrument has survived).[149]

The slow movement of the Fourth Brandenburg Concerto contains some *f* and *p* markings, mostly in the *Fiauti*, some in the solo violin. There are three principal explanations: (1) they are genuine dynamic markings; (2) they indicate *tutti* and *soli* phrases; (3) they are both dynamic markings and indicators of *tutti* and *soli* phrases. But in any case, the markings are inconsistent, and such inconsistencies are commonly found in the works of Bach and other composers of the period. If they were indeed intended to be dynamic markings, we cannot assume that a special instrument was needed for them, not least because Bach wrote *p* markings in his recorder parts in three other works, including the Second Brandenburg Concerto. Furthermore, quite apart from the inherent dynamic contrast in Bach's orchestration between *solo* and *tutti*, countless performances and many recordings by skilled recorder players have demonstrated – with the aid of alternative fingerings, for example – their ability to produce the echo effect with great expressivity.

Despite the copious evidence now available, it seems impossible to provide a definitive answer to the identity of the *fiauti d'echo*, for at every turn alternative explanations are plausible. Since Siegbert Rampe and Michael Zapf suggested using flanged pairs of recorders in 1997–98 this has been tried several times – partly because of the authors' persuasiveness, surely also the striking visual impression produced by such novel instruments.[150] Nevertheless, alto recorders in F, the first with a good f♯[3], remain the generally accepted solution, although some players today prefer an alto in G for the upper part, partly for ease of tuning the unisons in the third movement.

Bach employed between one and three recorders – but mostly two – in nineteen cantatas. Those written for churches where the instruments played a minor third lower than the choir pitch, as in Mühlhausen (*Gottes Zeit ist die allerbeste Zeit*, BWV 106, 1707 or 1708) and Weimar (*Himmelskönig, sei willkommen*, BWV 182, 1714), present a challenge to modern performers: either the singers must transpose up uncomfortably high, or the recorder players find 'alto' instruments in E♭ (BWV

23. Brandenburg Concerto No. 4, BWV 1049 (1721), by Johann Sebastian Bach, second movement, opening.

106) or D (BWV 182). Indeed, Bach faced a similar problem in 1723 when he moved to Leipzig, where the difference between *Kammerton* and *Chorton* was only a major second: his compromise for a performance of BWV 182 in 1724 was to rewrite the solo recorder part, removing the lowest note at the price of altering many of the most expressive phrases.

Once these practical difficulties have been overcome, Bach's cantatas provide the recorder player with some of the most sublime music in the entire repertoire, in an exciting range of different instrumentations. The recorders are placed in the orchestral *tutti*, as in most of *Preise, Jerusalem, den Herrn*, BWV 119 (1723); as obbligato solo instruments, as in the opening alto aria 'Komm, du süße Todesstunde' from BWV 161 (1715); sometimes in very unusual instrumental settings, as in the opening Sinfonia from *Gleichwie der Regen und Schnee, vom Himmel fällt*, BWV 18 (by 1715), in which two recorders and four violas build chains of striking suspensions. Other priceless combinations include the opening sonatina from BWV 106, for two recorders, two viole da gamba, and continuo; the alto aria 'Doch Jesus' from *Schauet doch und sehet*, BWV 46 (1723), for two recorders and two unison oboi da caccia without continuo; and the soprano aria 'Die Seele ruht in Jesu Händen' from *Herr Jesu Christ, wahr'r Mensch und Gott*, BWV 127 (1725), in which two recorders play an accompaniment of continuous staccato quavers against a florid oboe obbligato.

Any solo sonatas and chamber music that Bach may have written for the recorder are now lost – like more than one hundred of his Leipzig cantatas. Pending unexpected archival discoveries, Michael Marissen has provided some encouragement by arguing that the Sonata in A major for flute and obbligato harpsichord, BWV 1032 (1736), originated as a trio sonata for alto recorder, violin, and continuo in C major.[151] Given the frequency with which Bach arranged his own music to fit the instruments and players available, it is hardly surprising that recorder players today have made their own transcriptions, many of which have been successfully performed, recorded, and published in commercial editions.

In his autobiography of 1740, Georg Philipp Telemann (1681–1767) tells us that he taught himself to play the recorder as well as the violin and zither before the age of 10, and continued to practise the recorder into his teens. This love and practical understanding of the instrument help to explain why he wrote so much music for it – dozens of duets, solo sonatas, trio sonatas, quartets, suites, concertos, and obbligatos in vocal music – and why the parts always sound well and lie gratefully under the hand. Not only was Telemann the most prolific composer of

24. Georg Philipp Telemann, second movement of duet from *Der getreue Music-Meister* (Hamburg, 1728), showing three alternative instrumentations: two alto recorders in B♭ major (French violin clef), two traversos in G major (treble clef), or two viole da gamba in A major (alto clef).

the Baroque period, with some 3,000 works to his name, he was also extremely active as a publisher of his own music.

Telemann's manuscripts are specific about requiring the recorder, but in his publications that he engraved himself he sometimes offered transpositions or alternative clefs, so that the recorder could play music written for other instruments, or vice versa. Of his nine solo sonatas, among the most popular Baroque recorder music today, an apparently early one survives in manuscript (TWV 41:f2), all the others being published: two from *Essercizii musici* (TWV 41:C5, d4, 1726); four in Telemann's musical periodical *Der getreue Music-Meister* (TWV 41:C2, F2, f1, B3, 1728), the one in F minor being conceived for the bassoon, alternatively played two octaves higher on the recorder; and the two distinctly galant *Neue Sonatinen* for recorder, bassoon, or cello (TWV 41:c2, a4, 1731). Equally idiomatic and challenging are Telemann's nineteen trio sonatas with recorder, written between 1713–14 and 1737–44, which add as partners obbligato harpsichord (TWV 42:B4), oboe (TWV 42:c2, c7, e6, F9, F15, a6), second recorder (TWV 42:C1, F7), treble viol (TWV 42:C2, d7, F6, g9), viola da gamba (TWV 42:F3), and violin (TWV 42:d10, F8, f2, a1, a4).

Telemann's sonatas incorporate formal and stylistic procedures from the operatic aria and concerto, and imaginatively exploit the new 'mixed' German style, which drew on elements of French and Italian music. Some movements are obviously inspired by Polish folk music, the 'true barbaric beauty' of which he had experienced first hand, with enormous enthusiasm, when he worked in Sorau (now Żary) in 1705–06. His quartet in G minor for recorder, violin, viola, and continuo, TWV 43:g4, written ca. 1710–15, is one of the earliest examples by any composer of the *Sonate auf Concertenart* (concerted sonata), in which at least one movement exhibits features of ritornello form; it has much in common with the chamber concerto developed by Vivaldi. Three other exceptionally fine quartets featuring the recorder (TWV 43:d1, G6, a3) and the concerto for recorder, horn, and continuo, TWV 42:F14, are also examples of the concerted sonata.

Among Telemann's works for recorder and orchestra, the *Ouverture* (Suite) in A minor, TWV 55:a2, for recorder, strings, and continuo is perhaps the most popular today, an excellent showcase for his skill at mixing French suite, Italian concerto, and Polish folk music. The concertos in C major, TWV 51:C1, and F major, TWV 51:F1, are less familiar, but the double concertos for recorder and flute, TWV 52:e1, and recorder and viola da gamba, TWV 52:a1, are deservedly well known for their thrilling Polish finales. Besides writing many outstanding compositions using recorders in large chamber or orchestral formations, Telemann employed the instrument in no fewer than ninety-three cantatas and vocal serenades, written between 1716 and 1762 (but concentrated in the years 1720–31). These include thirteen of his first published cycle of sacred cantatas, *Harmonischer Gottes-Dienst* (1725–27), for voice, recorder, and continuo, intended for home worship.

Many of Bach and Telemann's contemporaries, including Fasch, Johann Joseph Fux, Christoph Graupner, Johann David Heinichen, and Kusser, wrote for the recorder, notably the Darmstadt Kapellmeister Graupner (1683–1760), whose concerto and *Ouverture*, both in F major, are imaginative works for recorder, strings, and continuo.

SIZES AND THEIR REPERTOIRE: NOT JUST THE ALTO[152]

The Baroque-style alto in F became the standard solo size, and almost the only size for which music was offered in publication to amateurs. We can therefore easily gain the impression that the remaining sizes had virtually disappeared, although in fact there is abundant evidence of their use. As the tenor and bass tended to drop out of the repertoire after the 1730s and 1750s, respectively, sizes above the alto even increased in popularity in the second half of the century.

CONSORTS

A number of Baroque-style recorder consorts, cases, or sets, without named sizes are documented: sale catalogues in The Hague (four recorders, 1686), The Hague (1689), Leiden (four recorders, 1690), and London (1701); the requirements for the Anhalt-Zerbst Hofkapelle (1699); inventories of monasteries in Ossegg, Bohemia (1706) and Kremsmünster (1710); a letter from the Basel maker Christian Schlegel (1708); and four advertisements for instruments by Peter Bressan: 'a complete case' (1732), five recorders and another case with a flute, an oboe, twelve recorders, and a pitch pipe (1740); a 'fine set' (1743); and another set (1774). Two sales of doctors' belongings in the Dutch Republic show that amateurs might own recorder consorts, presumably for domestic playing. The wording of an advertisement for the London sale in 1701 of 'a Consort of Flutes, and Flagelets, all in one Box, that any Person may play a Tune in a Minute's time' suggests that the sellers were anticipating an amateur purchaser.

Other sources, describing instruments intended for the musicians of the establishments in question, spell out numbers and sizes: Richard Haka's invoice for the Swedish navy in 1685 names a sopranino, two sopranos, three altos, tenor, and bass; his larger consort in the Florence court inventory of 1700 comprised a sopranino, four sopranos, four altos, two tenors, and two basses; the consort with the 'fly' mark (apparently left over from the Bassano family in the sixteenth or early seventeenth century) in the same Florence inventory consisted of two sopranos, three altos, four tenors, and two basses. Jacob Denner's invoice for the Duke of Gronsfeld in 1710 mentions four altos, one tenor, and two basses; and Denner sent an estimate to Göttweig Abbey around 1720 for three altos, a tenor, and two basses.

Three sets comprising more than two sizes have survived. The famous 'Chester recorders' by Bressan consist of alto, voice flute, tenor, and bass. A set of two altos, tenor, and bass by Gahn was perhaps made for a German convent.[153] The Bavarian National Museum in Munich owns four ivory recorders made by Jean Jacques Rippert (two sopraninos, an alto, and a tenor), originally part of a seven-member consort that belonged to the Bavarian court; another alto, another tenor, and a bass were destroyed during the Second World War.[154]

Alessandro Marcello's manuscript *Concerto di flauti* for soprano, alto, tenor, and bass doubling strings (Venice, n.d.) was probably intended for amateurs to play in the Accademia degli Animosi in Venice, to which Marcello belonged. A concerto with a similar-sounding scoring by Marcello was among the possessions of another amateur, the Danish customs inspector Stephen Kenckel, in 1732. Kenckel owned several recorders (two small, fourth flute, four probably altos, and bass) that could have been used to play the concerto with the collegium musicum he seems to have run in Helsingør (Elsinore). (On fourth flute, see p. 189.)

Michel Pignolet de Montéclair's opera *Jephté* (Paris, 1732) is exceptional in calling for five sizes of recorder – sopraninos (*Petits dessus*), sopranos (*Hautes-contres*), altos (*Tailles*), tenors (*Quintes*), and basses (*Basses*) – including one air that employs all of them at the same time.

Tables 11 and 12 show statistics for reported surviving recorders of the period under consideration. Andrew Robinson points out that the mere fact of survival does not necessarily indicate historical significance; instruments had greater chances of survival in institutions than in homes, and some recorders were made for export. Nevertheless, 'the picture that is given of recorder use is extremely striking – in particular, the large proportion of [tenor and] bass recorders. . . . As with the documentary evidence, [this evidence] gives a completely different picture from the one given by [the surviving] recorder music of the period: it shows that recorders of all sizes were made, and played, across the whole of northern Europe.'[155]

BASS AND GREAT BASS

A total of seventy-nine Baroque bass recorders exist today (thirty-nine of them made by the Denner family), representing about 16 per cent of surviving recorders. The instrument is mentioned in treatises, encyclopaedias, advertisements, and catalogues from around 1692 to 1801. The early use and approximate demise of the bass are cited in Johann Samuel Petri's *Anleitung zur praktischen Musik* (2nd edn, Leipzig, 1782): 'In the trio . . . where there are two transverse flutes, it is preferable to have a bassoon played softly as the bass, rather than a violoncello, the tone of which does not resemble the flute's so closely. In the previous [seventeenth] century, more attention was given to this, because the weak recorders were accompanied with bass recorders, but which have now gone out of fashion because they require so much breath.'[156]

Table 11. Reported surviving seventeenth- and eighteenth-century recorders of the Baroque type by country of residence of maker

Country	Sopraninos	Sopranos	Altos	Tenors	Basses	Total
Germany and Switzerland	5 2%	6 3%	126 60%	25 12%	49 23%	211
England	0	7 6%	59 55%	35 32%	7 6%	108
Dutch Republic	8 9%	18 21%	45 52%	4 5%	12 14%	87
France	2 4%	4 9%	20 43%	11 23%	10 21%	47
Italy	5 19%	2 7%	14 52%	5 19%	1 4%	27
Totals	20 4%	37 8%	264 55%	80 17%	79 16%	480

Sources: Bouterse 2005, chapter 4; d'Avena Braga 2015, 30; Robinson 2003, 115; Young 1993. The 'soprano' category includes sixth flutes and fourth flutes; the 'tenor' category, voice flutes.

Table 12. Makers of reported surviving seventeenth- and eighteenth-century recorders of the Baroque type represented by the largest numbers of instruments

Maker	So	S	A	T	B	Total
Bressan, Peter Jaillard (1663–1731), London		1	38	27	9	75
Denner, Johann Christoph (1655–1707); Denner, Johann Carl (1660–p1702); Denner, Johann David (1704–64), Nuremberg, mark I. C. DENNER	2	2	21	1	39	65
Denner, Jacob (1681–1735), Nuremberg, mark I. DENNER			26	15		41
Oberlender, Johann Wilhelm I (bap. 1681; d. 1763); Oberlender, Johann Wilhelm II (bap. 1712; d. 1779); Oberlender, Wendelin (bap. 1714; d. 1751), Nuremberg	1		33		3	37
Gahn, Johann Benedikt (bap. 1674; d. 1711), Nuremberg	1	3	24	2	1	31
Rippert, Jean Jacques (fl. 1697–p1716), Paris	2		10	5	6	23
Stanesby, Thomas, Jr (bap. 1692; d. 1754), London		5	12	6		23
Schell, Johann (bap. 1660; d. 1732), Nuremberg			11	2	5	18
Boekhout, Thomas (1666–1715); Boekhout, Jan (bap. 1696; fl. 1718), Amsterdam	2	1	6		8	17
Heitz, Johann (1672–1737), Berlin		1	14		1	16
Haka, Richard (a1646–1705), Amsterdam	3	5	3	2	2	15 (plus 1 walking-stick)
Anciuti, Giovanni Maria (1674–1744), Milan	2	1	6			9 (plus 5 double)

Stanesby, Thomas, Sr (ca. 1668–1734), London		1	9	2	1	13
Walch, Lorenz I (1735–1809), Berchtesgaden	1		3			4 (plus 9 double)
Schlegel, Christian (ca. 1667–1746); Schlegel, Jeremias (bap. 1730; d. 1792), Basel	2		5	4		11 (plus 1 double)
Van Aardenberg, Abraham (1672–1717), Amsterdam	2	2	7			11
Beukers, Willem I (1666–1750); Beukers, Willem II (1703–1781), Amsterdam		4	3	2		9
Van Heerde, Jan Juriaensz (1638–1691); Van Heerde, Albertus (1674–ca. 1720); Van Heerde, Jan (1704–ca. 1750), Amsterdam	1		7		1	9
Steenbergen, Jan (1676–1752), Amsterdam		3	5		1	9
Walch, G. (? Georg Walch, b. 1690; fl. 1716), Berchtesgaden		1	3	4	1	9
Castel, N. (fl. 1720–50), Venice?	1		4 (plus 1 head piece)	3		8
Schuchart, John Just (ca. 1695–1758); Schuchart, Charles (1720–65), London		1	7			8
Terton, Engelbert (1676–1752), Amsterdam		1	7			8
Parent, Michiel (1663–1710), Amsterdam			1			1 (plus 7 double)
Totals	20 4%	32 7%	265 56%	71 15%	82 17%	470

Sources: Bouterse 2005; d'Avena Braga 2015; Recorder Home Page Databases; Young 1993.

In Lully's works from 1668 to his death in 1687, the bass recorder was specified occasionally for the bass line of his trios, or implied by the large number of *flûte* players mentioned in the *livret*, as in *Les amants magnifiques* (1670), *Psyché* (1671), *Alceste* (1674), *Atys* (1676), *Isis* (1677), *Proserpine* (1680), *Amadis* (1684), and *Acis et Galatée* (1686). The instrument was mostly notated in bass clef, sounding an octave higher, sometimes in a C clef at pitch.

Charpentier specified or implied the *basse de flûte* in fourteen works written between 1674 and 1693 (H. 189, 196, 326, 328, 336a, 409, 480, 491, 513, 523/329, 524, and 528–30), apparently when an instrument and performer were available: a uniquely extensive use in recorder history before the twentieth century. He employed the size partly on bass lines, partly on the third line, in C1, C2, C3, and F4 clefs. All the parts could have been played by the bass recorder in f^0, either at pitch or sounding an octave higher than notated, occasionally with a little adjustment of the notes to fit the range at cadences. The melody instruments involved were sometimes two alto recorders or sopraninos doubling altos, but more often paired alto recorder and traverso or two traversos, sometimes doubled by strings.

Trios and quartets for alto recorders and bass recorder with continuo, sometimes (also) voice flute or tenor recorder, are found in both secular and sacred vocal music, not only in France and Germany but in Austria and England from the 1670s, petering off in the 1720s. The bass recorder could take the third or middle part as well as the bass part. Using bass recorders in such situations may well have been a broadly established practice, as Petri's *Anleitung* implies.

In an ensemble concerto by Heinichen in G major from his Dresden period (1717–29) for two alto recorders, two oboes, two violins, strings and continuo, S. 215, bass recorders are sometimes allotted the bass part when the recorders enter. In the Dresden manuscript of a concerto by Telemann in B♭ major for two alto recorders, strings, and continuo, TWV 52:B1, Johann Georg Pisendel, Konzertmeister at the Dresden court, added *pour le Flût* as well as *soli* and *tutti* markings to the bass line. Both these instances suggest once more that when recorders took the top parts, the bass recorder may have been routinely used when an instrument was available.

Two isolated examples are found of the bass recorder taking a solo part in chamber music at the court of Frederick the Great, unique for their instrumentation and lateness: the trio sonata in F major for bass recorder, viola or bassoon, and continuo, H. 588/Wq 163, by Carl Philipp Emanuel Bach (Berlin, 1755) and the trio sonata in F major for violin, violoncello or bass recorder, and continuo by one of the Graun brothers (by 1763), which has been reconstructed by Klaus Hofmann.

Bass flute or *Fluto basso* are designated in six English collections of music for one or two alto recorders and continuo in the early eighteenth century: Arcangelo Corelli, Opus 5, part 1, arranged (London, 1702); John Christopher Pepusch, sonata (London, 1704); *A Collection of Severall Excellent Overtures* (London, 1706); Pepusch, *A Second Set of Solos* (London, 1709); *New Aires made on Purpose for two Flutes and a Bass* (London, 1712); and Corelli, Opus 2 and 4, arranged (London, 1724). The range of the bass parts tends to stray below the range of the bass recorder. So either *Fluto basso* really meant 'a bass part to the recorder', or else bass recorder players adjusted the range to fit their instrument.

The Amsterdam maker Thomas Boekhout (1666–1715) advertised that he sold 'bass recorders that have all the notes as on an ordinary recorder' in 1713.[157] Jan Bouterse suggests that these new instruments could be played with the same fingerings as the alto because of wider-spaced finger-hole placements, both the third and seventh holes being closed with a key.[158] A year later, Van Driel, first name unknown, advertised that he sold: 'all manner of excellent recorders . . . which do not get clogged up and never let the player down, as well as oboes, bassoons, flutes, and bass recorders, constructed in a new manner of his own invention which has never been seen before'.[159] Perhaps Van Driel's claim had something to do with Boekhout's new type of bass recorder.

Despite four bass recorders said to be either in need of repair or else old and unplayable at the Baden-Württemberg court in Stuttgart in 1718, its musicians included seven who played (alto) recorder and a bass-register specialist called Aegidius Mühlhäuser (d. 1714), who performed on the violone, bassoon, and bass recorder, replaced by Carl Gustav Radauer on the violin, viola, bass violin, bassoon, and bass recorder.

Two surviving Baroque great basses have been reported: one by the Denner family and the second by an otherwise unknown German maker, N. Pappe.[160] The manuscript about musical instruments by James Talbot (ca. 1692–95) mentions both *Pedal or Double Bass* and plain *Bass*. An auction catalogue in Amsterdam (1759) lists 'a long bass recorder' made by Bressan, which may well have been a great bass.[161] Otherwise, the only hints of this size after 1668 are the parts for bass recorder that sometimes go a little below f^0 (or F^0 played an octave higher).

TENOR

About eighty Baroque tenor recorders (and voice flutes) have survived, roughly 17 per cent of surviving instruments. The tenor was generally employed for secular and sacred vocal music in the middle or low recorder parts.

Only occasionally was it used as a melody instrument, in effect a lower version of the alto, as in four cantatas by Scarlatti, written in Rome between 1697 and 1709, and two cantatas by Porpora (Naples, date unknown), and we know of only one attempt to establish it in this unaccustomed role. The celebrated woodwind maker Thomas Stanesby Jr published a pamphlet entitled *A New System of the Flute a'bec, or Common English-Flute* (ca. 1732) in which he proposed 'to render' the recorder 'universally useful in concert, without the trouble of transposing the music for it'. He pointed out that, in going down only to f^1, the standard recorder (alto, 'concert flute') was different from the oboe (c^1) and flute (d^1, with attempts at the time to extend it to c^1), thus requiring transposition or the use of different sizes and causing the instrument to lose 'much of your esteem'. His solution was to make the tenor the standard size of recorder, becoming 'the true concert flute', although he conceded that amateurs might be reluctant to learn C fingering.

Not only did Stanesby's attempt fail to catch on, recorder history swung away from sizes larger than the alto. The terms 'all sizes' or 'all sorts' of recorder appearing in English and American advertisements from 1743 onwards are clarified in Philadelphia in 1762 as 'Common Flutes, from a Concert to an Octave', or an alto up to a sopranino.[162]

VOICE FLUTE

Documented throughout the late Baroque, a recorder in d^1, larger than the alto but smaller than the tenor, is first noted in a commonplace book (ca. 1674) that belonged to Thomas Britton (1644–1714), a prosperous charcoal merchant and alchemist who sponsored concerts: 'For my great flutes one note and [a] half lower than the treble common flute.'[163] 'Great' was not so large, only a minor third below his alto, as Talbot succinctly points out in his manuscript (ca. 1692–95): *Voice, Third lower.* The basic scale on an alto recorder is in F major; that on the voice flute, in D major. Britton helped himself to learn the new size with exercises, in which the same notes can be thought of as, say, in D major in G2 (treble) clef or in F major in G1 (French violin clef). If Britton had some music in D major, it would have gone too low for his alto recorder (bottom note f^1). But he could play it by thinking of the music as being notated in G1, then adding three sharps to or subtracting three flats from the key signature (or a mixture of the two processes). Later records include the purchase of some voice flutes by the court of George II in 1732, and an instrument by Bressan listed in the probate inventory of the music publisher Michel Charles Le Cène (Amsterdam, 1743) under the almost-translated name *sang fluyt*.

The voice flute probably originated in France. On eleven occasions between 1668 and 1685, Lully wrote second *flûte* parts notated in G1 (French violin clef) going down to e¹ or d¹. In seven of these, the two *flûtes* have the same musical material as vocal duets scored for what Lully would have called *haut-dessus* (high soprano, treble clef) and *dessus* (soprano, C1 clef). The second *flûte* therefore corresponds to the *dessus* voice part. I have proposed a theory that these *dessus flûtes* were in fact voice flutes, and that this size had been newly conceived by 1668 to play along with the *dessus* voice in contrast with the *haut-dessus*.[164] In *La grotte de Versailles* (1668) the instruments going down to d¹ are twice called *flûtes douces*, which establishes that they are recorders. The parts could also have been played on tenors (in c¹), but the lowest note is always d¹ or e¹, suggesting a slightly higher-pitched instrument. The intention to create a recorder to match the soprano voice would explain the name 'voice flute'.

Perhaps the most celebrated use of the voice flute comes in four of the six suites by François (Francis) Dieupart (1676–1751), the son of Nicolas Dieupart, *Fluste et Cromorne ordinaire de la Chambre du Roy* at the French court from 1667 until his death in 1700, and thus intimately acquainted with recorders.[165] Strong and tuneful examples of the French style, Dieupart's suites were copied out by Johann Sebastian Bach, who based the melody of the prelude in his English Suite in A major, BWV 806, on the gigue in Dieupart's suite in the same key. The Amsterdam music publisher Estienne Roger issued two different versions of the collection in 1701. The first, for harpsichord, contains rich ornamentation in the contemporary French style. The second, unornamented, is in two parts, 'arranged by Dieupart for a violin and recorder with a viola da gamba and an archlute',[166] probably meaning that the upper part was intended either for recorder *or* violin, rather than both instruments in unison. The first suite, notated in A major in G2, carries the instruction: 'This suite must be played in C major on a voice flute,'[167] meaning that we are to read the part as if it were written in G1, using alto fingerings; the transposition (up a minor third) is counteracted by the lower pitch of the voice flute (down a minor third). Three further suites in sharp keys – D major, B minor, and

E minor – are treated the same way; the fifth and sixth suites, in flat keys – F major and F minor – are to be played on the fourth flute. In 1702, a London newspaper advertised 'Mr Dieupart's Book of Lessons for the Harpsichord, made in consorts, as it was performed last Friday at the Consort at the Theatre in Little Lincoln's Inn Fields', and sold by Roger's London agent.[168] The recorder player in the 'consort' performance would almost certainly have been Dieupart's close family friend Paisible, who left two voice flutes in his will (1721).

Johann Hugo von Wilderer's opera *La monarchia stabilita* (Düsseldorf, 1703) has a couple of arias with parts for *Flauto di Voce humana* (G2, f^1–g^2) or *Flauto Humano* (G2, g^1–g^2), indicating that the voice flute was known in Germany at the time.[169]

The opera *Camilla* was first performed in London in 1706 with music by Giovanni Bononcini (1670–1747), in a version adapted by Nicola Francesco Haym from *Il trionfo di Camilla* (Naples, 1696). Between 1706 and 1728 it had no fewer than 111 advertised performances, second only to *The Beggar's Opera* in that era. Walsh and Hare published an arrangement between 1711 and 1725 under the title *The Opera of Camilla with the Overture Symphonyes and Accompanyments / [the Opera] to be Perform'd either Vocally or Instrumentally / When by Instruments The Vocall Parts by Hoboys or Violins, German Flutes, Voice Flutes or octaves to Voice Flutes* [sixth flutes] */ To be done by single hands or as Great Concertos by Doubling the Parts*. This is perhaps the only evidence that the voice flute could be seen as an alternative to the traverso, a practice that has become common today.

The use of various sizes of recorders to play music written for other instruments in its original key can be seen clearly in the anonymous arrangement of Corelli's Concerti grossi, Op. 6, published by John Walsh and John and Joseph Hare (1725). The title page reads: *Corelli's XII Concertos Transpos'd for Flutes, viz a Fifth a Sixth a Consort and Voice Flute, The proper Flute being nam'd to each Concerto and so adapted to the Parts that they perform in Consort with the Violins and other Instruments Throughout, the Whole being the first of this Kind yet Publish'd*. The arrangement replaces the concertino parts by two recorders and continuo, keeping the original keys so that the works can be played together with the strings of the concerto grosso. The first eight concertos are scored for two altos; the next three (in sharp keys) for two sixth flutes or voice flutes (both in D); and the last for two fifth flutes (sopranos in C).

The close association between the voice flute and musical arrangements is documented by the activities of the Rev. Edward Finch, who will be discussed in more detail below. A manuscript chart in Finch's hand (by 1738) indicates seventeen major and minor keys for the alto recorder ('Consort Pitch Flute') and transpositions for voice flute in d^1 ('Upper Voice Flute a lesser 3d Lower') and voice flute in c#^{1} ('Voice Flute a greater 3d Lower yn Consort Pitch'), among others. Peter Holman comments, 'If Finch was using the higher "consort pitch" of roughly A 415, established in England by about 1720, then the "Lower Voice Flute" would presumably have been a d^1 recorder at the French *Ton d'Opéra*, roughly A 392. . . . Finch seems to have used larger sizes of recorder . . . to enable him to play . . . violin music without having to arrange it.'[170]

A Quintet in B minor for two voice flutes (*Flute de Voix*), two transverse flutes (*Flute traversa*), and continuo was attributed 'Del Mr Loeillet' in a note added to the manuscript later and in another hand; a modern edition names its composer as Jacques Loeillet (1685–1748). Jacques is indeed recorded as having appeared at Versailles in 1727, where he performed on 'the bassoon, violin, flute, recorder (*Flute Douce*), [and] voice flute (*Flute à voix*), making two parts, and the oboe'.[171] But the Quintet's manuscript also attributes a concerto for *Flauto solo* to 'Loeillet' that is almost certainly by Robert Woodcock, so the Quintet's composer may have been someone else entirely.

SMALLER RECORDERS

In writings, advertisements, sales, and inventories, many recorders are identified merely as 'small' in various languages, or have a diminutive ending (*flautino*, *Fletl*, *fluitje*), showing only that the sizes in question were higher than the alto. At other times, the size can be deduced from the name or range.

Only about twenty Baroque sopraninos have survived: a mere 4 per cent of surviving recorders. This size is scored for in secular vocal music in England, France, Germany, Ireland, and Italy into the 1730s, then almost exclusively in England up to the end of the century. Thus we find works by Thomas Augustine Arne, Samuel Arnold, J. S. Bach, Thomas-Louis Bourgeois, André Campra, André-Cardinal Destouches, Matthew Dubourg, Joseph Paris Feckler, John Ernest Galliard, Francesco Gasparini, Christoph Willibald Gluck, Handel, Montéclair, Scarlatti, Georg Caspar Schürmann, William Shield, Telemann, Tomaso Traetta, Vinci, and Vivaldi. About half the instances are bird arias or airs; a couple represent whistling. Otherwise, some traditional general associations of the recorder are present: love, the divine, sleep, and the pastoral. Perhaps the most novel symbolism is that in Bach's cantata *Herr Christ, der einge Gottessohn*, BWV 96 (Leipzig, 1724), depicting Jesus as the morning star.

Antonio Vivaldi's three concertos for the *flautino*, RV 443–445, are highly popular today, especially the Concerto in C major, RV 443. A fourth concerto, RV 312, whose first movement was almost completed for *flautino* but subsequently transcribed for violin, has been reconstructed and published as RV 312r. These works celebrate the small recorder's ability to imitate the rapidity and ebullience of the violin in passage work in the fast movements, negotiate complicated ornamented lines in the slow movements, and be heard clearly above an orchestra. The *flautino* was almost certainly a sopranino recorder, although two of the concertos were indicated by the composer as transposable a fourth lower for the soprano recorder. Sardelli has dated the works to the late 1720s or early 1730s.[172] Vivaldi's earlier *flautino* part in the opera *Tito Manlio* (Mantua, 1719) was performed by the oboist Giorgio Ratzemberger, who wrote his own sopranino recorder concerto, the solo part of which is now tantalizingly lost. Perhaps Vivaldi's *flautino* concertos were also written for him.

After the piccolo (octave transverse flute) came on the scene in the late 1730s, we find fewer clear attributions to the sopranino recorder. This is certainly the case in France: the *petite flûte* parts in Jean-Philippe Rameau's output of opera and ballets from 1737 to 1764 all seem to have been written with the piccolo in mind. Yet it was not used consistently all over Europe until well into the nineteenth century, so small sizes of recorder often supplied the 'high flute' timbre until a resurgence of popularity of the flageolet around 1800. An advertisement by Vincent Panormo in 1772 claims that the sopranino recorder was unknown in France and used mostly in Italian orchestras (although no repertoire for it seems to have survived). It was still being made by Andrea Fornari in Venice in 1791. In London, it continued to be listed in the Astor, Goulding, and Clementi catalogues (1799–1823).

Wolfgang Amadeus Mozart (1756–91) wrote for the *flautino* or *flauto piccolo* in seventeen works between 1771 and his death. The context, keys, and range mostly suggest soprano or sopranino recorders. In any case, Mozart himself revealed that the choice of high member of the flute family depended on the performing ensemble: on the autograph manuscript of his *Sechs deutsche Tänze*, KV 509, first performed in Prague on 6 February 1787, he wrote: 'As I do not know what kind of *flauto piccolo* is here, I have set it in the *natural* key; it can always be transposed.'[173]

Some three dozen Baroque sopranos in B♭, C, and D have survived, or 8 per cent of surviving recorders, except in the Dutch Republic, where they make up about 21 per cent of surviving recorders from that country. Around 1692–95, Talbot reported only the soprano and sopranino sizes above the alto. But as we have seen, the fourth flute was known to Francis Dieupart in 1701; and the sixth flute – whose ancestor, the soprano in D, was already reported by Cardano in the mid-sixteenth century – had appeared by 1720. The first reference to an alto recorder a third above that in F comes from the monastery of Kremsmünster in 1739: *Flautten . . . 1 paar ex A* (recorders . . . a pair in A). William Tans'ur documented the third flute in 1746, and John Hoyle added the term 'second flute' in 1770 (although it was just a new name for the alto in G). All the sizes from alto to sixth flute plus sopranino turn up in Astor's catalogue of 1799. Finally, but not until 1823, in the Clementi firm's catalogue a seventh flute is mentioned for the only time. The little surviving repertoire for these extra sizes suggests that their principal function may have been in making music originally written for other instruments accessible without transposition – for professionals, perhaps not only those who mainly played other instruments, or amateurs seeking easy access to new literature.

The sixth flute (soprano in D) is documented primarily in England. The term is found in advertisements for the performances of John Baston (fl. 1708–39) and other players from 1720, discussed later, Baston's own published concertos (1729), an arrangement of Corelli's Concerti grossi (1725), and the published solo and double concertos of William Babell (ca. 1726) and Woodcock (ca. 1727). The English concertos show their difference from Italian ones in their inclination to stepwise passage work. The most notable other compositions for sixth flute are the possible original version of Handel's Concerto Grosso, Op. 3, No. 3 (Cannons, 1717–18) and an obbligato *flauto piccolo* part in Bach's cantata *Ihr werdet weinen und heulen*, BWV 103 (Leipzig, 1725).

For the fifth flute (soprano in C), again pride of place goes to concertos: by Baston (1729); Sammartini (London, 1729–35); Vivaldi (late 1720s–early 1730s, as indicated by the composer in two of the *flautino* concertos for transposition from the sopranino); and possibly the original scoring of Handel's Concerto Grosso, Op. 3, No. 3 (1717–18). Sammartini's Concerto in F major for soprano recorder and strings fully deserves its modern popularity. The fast movements, in *da capo* form rather than ritornello form, are so lyrical that even the passage work partakes of the same mood; and the slow movement, an impassioned siciliana in *empfindsam* style, is equally expressive.

The prefix 'Quart' or a reference to 'four' in several languages can designate a soprano recorder in C, a fourth above the old alto in G, as in the *Quartflöte* scored for in no fewer than nine late vocal works by Telemann (1744–61); or else a tenor recorder, a fourth below the alto in F. Some 'fourth flutes' are clearly high, but the term alone is not enough to determine the size. It may sometimes signify a soprano recorder in B♭, a fourth above the normal Baroque alto in F. This seems to be the instrument Dieupart calls *flute du quatre* in his fifth and sixth suites (1701; notated a major second higher, then fingered like a soprano) and William Boyce the *common 4th Flute* in *The Shepherd's Lottery* (1751); we also find instances in writings and catalogues up to 1823. Despite the name ('little tenor'), the *tenorino* (also *flauto tenorino* and *flauto dolce tenorino*) scored for in manuscripts at the Einsiedeln monastery from the 1770s and 1780s by the Italian composers Pasquale Anfossi, Andrea Favi, and Domenico Mancinelli was a soprano in B♭, experiencing a late blooming.

PERFORMERS ON SMALL RECORDERS

Performances of concertos for the 'little flute' or 'small flute' took place frequently during the intervals of plays in London in the 1710s–30s. Some of the soloists, who were accompanied by the theatre 'band' (small orchestra), are known to us by name. James Paisible was advertised in 1716–18. John Baston, whose concertos for the sixth flute and fifth flute were noted above, was billed on two dozen occasions between 1719 and 1733. Other composers are named twice: Dieupart and Woodcock. Baston's brother Thomas, a violinist, would have been the second recorder player in the double concertos.

Robert Woodcock (1690–1728), a civil servant, later marine painter, and amateur musician, may have played his concertos himself.[174] His friend, the art historian George Vertue, wrote of him: 'He was very skillful in music, had judgment and performed on the hautboy in a masterly manner, there being many pieces, some published, and much approved by skillful masters in that science.' Since Woodcock's twelve published concertos are for recorder (6), flute (3), and oboe (3), we may perhaps understand 'hautboy' in the broad sense of 'woodwind'.

Other performers of concertos for small recorders included Jean Christian Kytch (1721), the transverse flute player Lewis Granom (1722), and the otherwise unknown John Jones (1726) and Jacob Price (1730). Sammartini may well have written his fifth-flute concerto for himself to perform in London. Advertisements for such events stop in London in 1738. In Dublin, concertos were performed by the visiting London woodwind player Richard Neale in 1732 and in 1749–57 by the local musician Luke Heron, who later published a tutor for the transverse flute. Parts for Woodcock's concertos were bought by the Dublin Charity Concerts in 1754.

In Sweden, concertos by Babell, Ratzemberger, and Sammartini form part of the collection of Utili Dolce, a literary and musical society in Stockholm active between 1766 and 1795, so they were presumably played by amateurs. The collections of the Akademiska Kapellet (Academy Orchestra) of Lund University, founded in 1745, and the Akademiska Kapellet of Uppsala University, founded in 1627, both contain works for small recorders that were evidently played by students.

SOCIAL HISTORY

AMATEURS

It is well known that the recorder was the amateur instrument *par excellence* in England in the late seventeenth and early eighteenth centuries.[175] It requires no reeds or special embouchure, is not fatiguing to play, and is therefore easy to learn in the early stages, which is where most amateurs would have remained. Its adoption by amateurs during this period is intimately connected with the rise of the middle class, although the upper classes were just as enthusiastic. Those well-placed citizens who flocked to the theatres and concerts emulated the professionals performing there to an unprecedented extent. Professionals wrote music suited to amateurs, allowed some crumbs of technical information to fall from the table in the better tutors, and offered lessons to such laypersons as could afford them. Although during the 1720s and 1730s this large and eager amateur audience mostly transferred their allegiance to the transverse flute, we have evidence of continued activity in England, the Dutch Republic, and especially colonial North America and the early United States until the end of the century.

TEACHING

In 1695, 'by encouragement of His Majesty', an attempt was made to found a pair of Royal Academies in London to give public instruction in languages, mathematics, writing, music, dancing, and fencing.[176] Abraham de Moivre, later a celebrated statistician, was to have taught mathematics. His brother Daniel de Moivre (ca. 1669–1733)[177] was named as one of the recorder teachers along with James Paisible and John Banister II (who was also to teach the violin). Unfortunately, the attempt foundered, owing partly to the curious lottery method by which pupils were to be admitted to the academies: 40,000 tickets sold at £1 each, with only 2,000 winning tickets allowing students to attend. But presumably these men were already teaching privately. The Huguenot De Moivre brothers had fled to London after the Revocation of the Edict of Nantes in 1685. Banister was a court violinist, described by Roger North as an excellent singing teacher.[178]

Paisible's career demonstrates that celebrated teachers demanded high fees. In 1710 the London opera band, in which he played bass violin and occasionally the recorder, was singled out for praise by the German traveller Zacharias Conrad von Uffenbach. Two weeks later, Uffenbach reported attending a concert directed by Pepusch in which he played a 'concerto' with recorder and viola da gamba. 'The person who plays the recorder is a Frenchman called Paisible, whose equal is not to be found.'[179] Uffenbach added that a member of his party, 'Herr Gramm, who comes of a noble Luneburg family and frequents our society and is an amateur of the recorder, wished to take lessons from him, but he wanted three guineas for eighteen lessons, which frightened Herr Gramm off. . . .'[180] On Paisible's death in 1721, a bill was found in his possession 'under the hand of Sir Bowshire Wray for the sum of £33 to the . . . deceased for teaching him to play the recorder'.[181] This is a much larger sum, almost ten times what Uffenbach cited. Of course, Paisible had not collected it. . . . Given this, and that three guineas (£3 3s) was about what Paisible made for two nights' performance in the opera band, the fee quoted to Gramm may actually have been substantially higher, which would further explain the frightening effect.

Several recorder teachers advertised in London newspapers: 'James Piron living in Grafton Street, Soho . . . teaches the French tongue to young gentlemen, and others, and likewise to play upon the flute, at a very reasonable rate' (1698).[182] 'A gentleman, who through misfortunes is now reduced, is very desirous to be a tutor to any of the nobility's or gentry's children . . . with music on the violin and flute may be taught' (1707). 'A sober man that plays on several sorts of music, as the flute, violin, and can teach on the spinet or harpsichord, would be with a merchant, brewer, woodmonger or warehouse-keeper, to receive or pay money, or gather in book-debts, or any such business as does not require much writing; or if any gentleman has any children that would learn music, he would be in their house by the year, either in town or country' (1709). 'One who teaches French, the flute, harpsichord, and needlework would be a governess' (1717).

The would-be governess would have had to wait for five years to encounter the misogynistic opinion of the famous dancer and choreographer John Essex, who wrote in *The Young Ladies Conduct: or, Rules for Education* (London, 1722): 'There are some others [instruments] that really are unbecoming the fair sex; as the flute, violin and hautboy . . . the flute is very improper, as taking away too much of the juices which are otherwise more necessarily employed to promote the appetite and assist digestion.' Essex's admonishments probably did not affect demand, as the death notice for Daniel de Moivre from 1733 attests: 'died at his house in St Martin's Lane, Monsieur de Moinor, very famous for teaching young gentlemen and ladies on the flute and other instruments of music'.

A Mr Hart advertised in 1748 that he could teach 'the violin, German flute, common flute, French horn, clarinet, or any other instrument' at his home in Rotherhithe, four days a week, from 10 a.m. to 6 p.m. – those who learn more than twice a week, 'at 2s. 6d. the first lesson, 1s. each lesson after; and those gentlemen that choose to be taught at home may be waited on at a very reasonable rate'. Others offered their services as servants or assistants: 'Any person of quality that hath occasion for a butler that plays upon the flute and violin may hear of one' (1705). 'A sober man about 30 years of age that plays upon the flute and violin is willing to be a butler to a person of quality, or wait upon a young gentleman, where they will not oblige him to wear a livery' (1706).

In 1750, a new Academy was announced, 'where gentlemen are taught to play on the German or common flute, violin, French horns, etc. . . . an assembly weekly, where those that are not scholars are admitted on subscribing for a month. The expense is very moderate.' In 1768, the 'dancing and music-master' Mr Patence, advertised that he taught 'ladies and gentlemen the minuet, louvre, county and hornpipe dancing, in the most concise and expeditious manner, and defies any French or English master to teach more polite or better; as likewise the organ, harpsichord, and violin, German flute or common flute, on very reasonable terms'.

No fewer than twelve men and one woman advertised their ability to teach the recorder in five cities in colonial North America. In Boston, the school of the gentle George Brownell, later the schoolmaster of Benjamin Franklin (1713); the music and dancing school of the organist Edward Enstone and his partner Rivers Stanhope, who fought with the city fathers to authorize the school (1716); and the dancing master and schoolmaster Increase Gatchell (1729). In Philadelphia, the school for young ladies of Mrs Dickson from Scotland (1744); John Beals, 'music master from London', who taught 'the violin, hautboy, German flute, common flute, and dulcimer, by note' at his house or 'young ladies, or others, that may desire it, at their houses' (1749); and the school of the 'limner' (painter) William Williams, lately returned from the West Indies, 'for the instruction of polite youth, in different branches of drawing, and to sound the hautboy, German and common flutes' (1763). In New York, 'A gentleman lately arrived here', who made his pitch to 'young gentlemen, or others, inclinable to learn', at their lodgings, undertaking 'to teach the meanest capacity (on strict application) two tunes in the first fortnight, and so on in proportion' (1745); and the school of Charles Love, 'musician from London . . . teaching gentlemen music on . . . hautboy, German and common flutes, bassoon, French horn, tenor, and bass violin, if desired' (1753). In Charleston, Jacob Hood and Philip Hartunoz, teaching at their home and outside 'all musical instruments of every denomination whatsoever, particularly the violin, violoncello, harpsichord, hautboy, bassoon, German and English flute, French horn, etc.', also the Black slaves of 'any gentleman, a lover of music' (1772); and John William Beck, who taught 'clarinet, flauto traverso, flauto a bec, hautbois or oboe de Simon [*cimeau*?], bassoon, violin, tenor violin, and bass violin as perfectly as any master in America' – no false modesty here – on very reasonable terms at people's houses or his own (1773). Finally, the school of Francis Russworm for young gentlemen, 'the violin, German and common flutes' (Williamsburg, 1771). That the recorder was being taught as late as 1773 comes as no surprise, given the number of instruments that were still being advertised in the 1770s and beyond.

RISE AND FALL

The French woodwind maker Peter Bressan went to live in London around 1688. In 1721 he testified in a law suit that 'in making of musical instruments and particularly of flutes [i.e. recorders]' he had 'acquired a considerable reputation and by his great business he had in that way and by his own industry, frugality, and good management . . . considerably improved and advanced his fortune in the world'.[183] He went on to say that since about six years before, however, his trade had fallen off considerably. This suggests that the decline of the recorder as an amateur instrument in England may have started around 1715.

John Walsh – by far the most successful English music publisher of the Baroque era, leaving a fortune estimated at £20,000–£30,000 – was in business from the early 1690s until his son took over around 1730. To put Walsh's prosperity in context, the annual earnings of Paisible, the most successful recorder player of the era, were about £500. In the instrument's heyday, 1695–1720, recorder music made up one-sixth of Walsh's total output of instrumental music.[184] He published two types of recorder music: first, simple duets, arrangements, or other little pieces intended for the amusement or education of amateurs; second, music that professionals had written for themselves to play in concerts and theatre entertainments. In the first category, songs, and indeed whole operas, were also printed with the melodies transposed for solo alto recorder at the foot of the page. Perhaps surprisingly, the second category produced more titles. Initially, Walsh tended to publish recorder music by composers resident in London (for example, De Moivre, Johann Wolfgang Franck, Finger, and Daniel Purcell). When the Italian opera hit London in 1706, Walsh regularly published recorder arrangements of the arias, and sometimes also the instrumental music, occasionally offering an incentive to buy them by throwing in bonuses, such as recorder duets. Around 1710, Walsh began to rely more on imported music (Jean-Baptiste Loeillet, Johann Mattheson, Johann Christian Schickhardt).

By the 1720s, Walsh shrewdly offered mixed editions of recorder music with works for other instruments (flute, oboe, violin). His son, John Jr, followed a similar practice in issuing Handel's recorder sonatas in a collection marked for flute, oboe, and violin around 1732. Nevertheless, some of Walsh Sr's most important recorder editions date from the 1720s: for example, the sonatas and trio sonatas of John Loeillet and the concertos for small recorders by Babell, Baston, and Woodcock. The last advertised publication of Walsh Jr for the recorder not arranged from vocal music was Robert Valentine's sonatas, Op. 13 (1735); his last arranged music was a song collection called *The British Musical Miscellany*, 'set for the Violin, the German-Flute, Violin, the Common Flute, and Harpsichord' (1737). But other publishers announced recorder arrangements up until 1768–69.

DUDLEY RYDER[185]

In 1715, Sir Dudley Ryder (1691–1756), then a law student, began keeping a diary chronicling his daily activities. The surviving part covers only eighteen months but is full of priceless details of the social life and opinions of the age, the thoughts and feelings of a sensitive young man, and the musical life of a keen amateur musician and dancer. Ryder played the viola da gamba and recorder, sang a little, listened to singing more, attended the occasional concert and church performance, and danced a great deal. Although he seems to have spent precious little time studying, he eventually rose to become a Member of Parliament and Chief Justice of England.

Ryder reports playing the recorder far less than the gamba: only ten times in all. One day he played with a friend, John Emmett, 'immediately after rising' at 8 a.m. That and breakfast took two hours. Another day he played after breakfast and again one morning when he 'was not very much inclined to study'. Twice he played after dinner. Another evening he went to the coffee house, walked for an hour, musing on his lovelorn condition, then 'Came home. Played upon my recorder: that composed me a little.' At the house of another friend, George Smith, a Nonconformist minister, Ryder played 'two or three sonatas'. On another occasion he played unspecified music with Smith – probably recorder duets. Ryder also played recorder and gamba twice with his cousin Joseph Billio, another Nonconformist minister. Only once does Ryder identify the music that he played on the recorder: an air from Lully's ballet *Psyché*, with Smith on gamba.

Ryder makes frank comments on his friends' recorder playing. Smith 'plays much better than he did' before. Jackson 'has very little judgement and cannot play in time'. Emmett 'plays pretty well but a little confused, as persons that play by the ear only generally do'. Lastly, Hudson 'played some tunes upon the recorder, though but indifferently'.

Smith seems to have studied with Daniel de Moivre, whom Ryder depicts as making his living by teaching – we have seen that his death notice mentions 'young gentlemen and ladies' – and by performing in coffee houses, taverns, and concerts. Jackson may also have studied with De Moivre; he certainly visited the coffee house and played on an occasion when Smith and De Moivre were playing duets. Ryder also reports visiting an unidentified tavern to hear De Moivre play the recorder, perhaps including his own suites for alto recorder, the third collection of which was published by Walsh in 1715.

EDWARD FINCH

The Rev. Edward Finch (1663–1738) was a keen amateur performer, composer, arranger, and copyist who worked in church posts in York, Kirkby-in-Cleveland, Wigan, and Canterbury.[186] The instruments in his collection that were passed on to the Sharp family after his death included three flutes d'amour, a fife, a tenor recorder ('1 Large C Common Flute in the Oct.[ve] below'), two alto recorders ('2 Common Flutes concert Pitch'), and an oboe. His charts of transpositions for voice flutes were mentioned in the previous section; he apparently used these larger recorders to play violin music without having to transpose it.

The Armstrong–Finch manuscript at Spetchley Park, Worcestershire, begun for Finch by William Armstrong (d. 1717), a viola player and professional copyist, was completed by Finch himself.[187] The Armstrong section (from about 1705) includes recorder sonatas by Finger as well as a recorder sonata, a set of divisions on *La Folia*, and a suite for two recorders and continuo, all by Finch. The section copied by Finch (between about 1717 and 1720) does include another recorder sonata by Finger but, tellingly, mainly sonatas and divisions for the transverse flute. The latter include works by Finch and John Grano as well as Finch's arrangements of works by Corelli, Finger, Francesco Geminiani, Grano, Jean-Baptiste Loeillet, John Loeillet (who may have been his teacher), and Gasparo Visconti; a fingering chart for the flute is attached. Thus we see a keen recorder player learning the flute and creating his own repertoire for it, when music specifically for the instrument was just beginning to be published in England.[188]

CLAVER MORRIS[189]

Claver Morris (1659–1727) was a doctor in the West Country, whose private passion was clearly music. He danced, sang, played the harpsichord and organ, and had some facility on the violin, bassoon, oboe, and recorder. Two diaries of his have survived as well as most of his account books. In 1688, on a visit to London, he purchased 'a flute' (recorder) for 13s and 'a bassoon, or curtall' for £2 10s (about four times as much).[190] Morris's first diary, 1709–10, shows that he held his own private music-meetings, and also was the leading light in the Wells Music Club, which met weekly in the church hall. The climax of the club's year was a performance of Henry Purcell's 'Hail, Bright Cecilia' on St Cecilia's Day, 22 November 1709, although Morris does not tell us who played the two recorder parts. Morris rode around the area a great deal to visit patients. One day he recorded: 'We stayed all day at Major Prater of Froom. Colonel Berkeley, the Major, Mr Jesser, my servant, and I played recorder sonatas almost all the day.'

Morris bought recorder music by Francesco Antonio Bonporti, William Corbett, and Johann Christoph Pez. In 1719, Morris's Music Club 'had the first trial of Handel's pastoral'. This was no less a piece than *Acis and Galatea*, which had been composed only about eight months before, containing some beautiful airs for the recorder: 'Hush, ye pretty warbling quire', 'O, ruddier than the Cherry', and 'Heart, the seat of soft delight', symbolizing birdsong and love.

Later in 1719, Morris 'was at our music meeting, and Mr Ducket of Calne in Wiltshire played on a recorder one song with us. But Mr Hill's harpsichord being near a note below consort pitch, and no sure hand performing the trebles (being only young lads of Wells and Skepton), our music was very mean.'

JOHN LOEILLET'S CONCERT SERIES

Professional musicians organized music-meetings in their own homes, notably the oboist, recorder player, and harpsichordist John Loeillet, at his house near Covent Garden.[191] Although the repertoire was never advertised, it probably included his six sonatas for alto recorder and continuo, and six trio sonatas for recorder, oboe/ violin, and continuo, published by Walsh during the 1720s. Sir John Hawkins reported that Loeillet, 'dwelling in a house . . . in which was a large room, had a weekly concert there, which was frequented chiefly by gentlemen performers, who gratified him very handsomely for his assistance in conducting it'.[192] Loeillet's convivial, generous, and self-effacing character, as depicted in an anonymous poem 'The Session of Musicians' (1724), doubtless helped. Loeillet's Opus 2 was dedicated to the Duke of Rutland and Opus 3 to Charles Edwin, Esq., presumably two of the gentlemen who patronized his concerts. Not least through his concerts, Loeillet amassed a considerable fortune for a musician, estimated by Hawkins to be £16,000. His will shows that he had several domestic servants (Paisible had only one). A year after his death his possessions were auctioned off, including 'a very excellent drawing of the Last Supper by Raphael'.[193] It evidently paid to associate with wealthy amateurs. . . .

OTHER AMATEURS

Advertisements for estate auctions provide information about the professions or standing of several people who had owned recorders: Guy Vane, Esq., lawyer, 'four Flutes' (1730). An 'eminent virtuoso', 'several German and English flutes' (1745). James Hunter, scarlet-dyer, 'sundry Sorts of Flutes' (1757). William Popely, organist, 'several German and common Flutes' (1761). William Pocklington, jeweller, 'German and other Flutes' (1766). A blind gentleman, 'A set of Concert flutes' (1767). Thomas Pierce, organist, 'sundry German and other Flutes' (1777). A nobleman, 'English and German Flutes' (1784).

In colonial North America, recorders are mentioned in the estate inventories of two men in Boston: Walter Rosewell, sea captain, in 1717 (*1 Flute & book*); and James Scolley, shopkeeper, in 1721 (*1 fflut*). The word *flute* is also found in several inventories of Virginia gentlemen between 1736 and 1791. At least until the 1750s, these instruments are likely to have been recorders – explicitly so for Colonel Henry Fitzhugh, Esquire, plantation owner, Stafford County (1743): 'a case containing a German and an English flute'. Freedom-seeking slaves and servants are mentioned in advertisements for their capture: Thomas Dunfy, an Irish servant of William Montgomerie, aged about 21, in Burlington County, New Jersey (1737): 'He can play on the flute.' Cambridge, a Black slave of James Oliver, Boston (1743): 'plays well upon a flute, and not so well on a violin'. Jo, a Black slave of John Johnson, aged about 23, Boston (1748): 'He can play on the flute.' William Mangles, an English servant of John Leathes, aged about 27, Philadelphia (1753): 'He plays pretty well on the common flute.'

PROFESSIONALS

The *livrets* of Lully's ballets and operas mention no fewer than thirty-two players of *flutes* from the French court, and a few guests, in the performances of these works between 1657 and 1682, including seven members of the Hotteterre family, James Paisible and his father Louis, two Philidors, and five Pièches.[194] Other musicians noted among a group of *flutes et hautbois* in Lully's ballet *Le Triomphe de l'Amour* (1681) included Jean-Baptiste Hannès Desjardins, who taught, owned, and made recorders. Not even London in the era of the royal recorder consort or Amsterdam in the 1970s could boast so many recorder professionals who made most of their living from playing.

Virtually all the professional recorder players in England during the period 1670–1740 earned their living primarily on other instruments, and most also composed: John Banister II (violin), Francesco Barsanti (oboe, viola, and copying), John Baston (violoncello), John Ernest Galliard (oboe and bassoon), Robert King (violin), Jean Christian Kytch (oboe and bassoon), Peter La Tour (oboe), John Loeillet (oboe and harpsichord), Louis Mercy (oboe), James Paisible (oboe and bass violin), and Giuseppe Sammartini (oboe).[195]

The woodwind players at many German courts made use of the recorder. Perhaps the most virtuosic was Johann Michael Böhm, *capellmeister* at Darmstadt in 1711–29, who then moved on to the Baden-Württemberg court in Stuttgart. He impressed Telemann as an oboist (and became his son-in-law) and also played the recorder, probably giving the original performances of works that have survived in Darmstadt manuscripts such as the *Ouverture* in A minor.

In 1724, Claver Morris wrote that in Bath, 'we went to the Grove, and Mr Broad got Mr Grano to entertain me with his trumpet, German flute, and small flute in the new dining room at the Three Tuns. They dined with me.'

John Grano (ca. 1692–ca. 1748), who had previously been a trumpeter in Handel's opera orchestra, was imprisoned for debt in the Marshalsea prison, Southwark, in May 1728. During the next eighteen months, he and his family had enough money to allow him to benefit from the more comfortable accommodation on the Master's side of the prison – the Common side was squalid – as well as the curious arrangement whereby prisoners could purchase passes that allowed them to range around the town during the day, although they had to be back by curfew. His diaries detail his adventures, musical and otherwise, as he struggled in vain to earn enough money doing freelance work and giving benefit concerts to get himself released.[196] He was eventually freed by a general amnesty for debtors passed by parliament.

Grano makes a handful of tantalizing comments about the recorder. Francis Ryall, the son of a judge, 'made me a present of a very good sixth flute of Young Stanesby's making'.[197] One day Grano gave Thomas Benfield, a local blacksmith, 'a lesson on the common flute'.[198] A musician called Jacob promised to play 'the little flute' for one of Grano's benefit concerts.[199] Perhaps he may be identified with the Jacob Price 'who never performed in public before' and played 'a new concerto on the flute' on the stage at the Goodman's Fields Theatre, London, in 1730.[200] One afternoon Grano visited the governor of the prison and 'put a little flute into his pocket, which he pulled out and gave to his son' aged 4; while Grano fingered, the boy blew on it with alternating 'pleasure and surprise' showing on his face.[201] One night at the Devil Tavern, Grano 'entertained the company with a solo on the German flute, another on the little flute, a song and several airs on the trumpet'.[202] At the Oak Tavern 'in came Mr John Baston, belonging to the Old House' (presumably a reference to the Drury Lane Theatre, where Baston was a member of the band); and three days later, Grano wrote a letter 'to Jack Baston, the first flute in England'.[203]

TRAINING

Eight teaching or apprenticeship contracts that mention the recorder are known for woodwind musicians at the French court, all except one pertaining to the Hannès Desjardins family. See Table 13. The nature of the *flute* involved is spelled

Table 13. Apprenticeships involving the recorder in France, 1697–1717

Year	Teacher	Apprentice	To Learn	Period	Cost	Terms
1697	Jean-Baptiste Hannès Desjardins, hautbois in Chambre du Roi and first company of musketeers; instrument maker	François Gousset, son of Jean Gousset dit La Jeunesse, drummer in first company of musketeers	*flutte*, oboe, music	until can earn a living	300 livres in six instalments over 2½ years	Daily lessons at teacher's house at convenient hours
1700	same	Dominique Maréchal	*flûte*, oboe	same	250 livres	
1702	same	François Gilloteau, valet of Abbé Bouchard	oboe, *flutte*, instrumental music	same	185 livres in four instalments, last after teacher placed him 'in some regiment'	Daily lessons at teacher's house. No instruments to be supplied at end
1707	same	Pierre Pajot, footman of Princess of Conti	oboe, *flûte douce*, and bassoon, sight-read		300 livres: half down then 7 livres 10 sols per month	Provide own instruments and music books. Daily lessons at teacher's house at convenient hours
1709	same	Jean-Baptiste Perrin, valet of Madame Hennin	*flûte traversière*, bassoon, sight-read		250 livres over 2½ years	Daily lessons at teacher's house at convenient hours. Furnish own instruments
1700	Philippe Breteuil, member of Cromornes et Trompettes Marines at court; instrument maker	Thomas Buchot, aged 10, son of Laurent Buchot, musician in Académie Royale	oboe, *flûte*, flageolet			

Year	Teacher	Apprentice	To Learn	Period	Cost	Terms
1712	Philippe Hannès Desjardins	François Matreau, son of late Pierre, member of Joueurs de Fifres et Tambours at court; François succeeded him in 1714	oboe, *flûte*, bassoon, flageolet	as long as necessary	150 livres, half after mutually agreed apprentice has been fully taught	
1717	François Hannès Desjardins, court wind player in four ensembles	François Le Vasseur dit Fleury	bassoon, oboe, flute, recorder, flageolet, transpose	as long as teacher judges necessary	300 livres in 2 instalments	If Desjardins dies before student finishes, his brother Charles, oboist in first company of musketeers, to take over

Sources: https://francearchives.fr/fr/facomponent/fc6f4c180c29654db742592bda23f5ba4613ddfa; MC/ET/206; https://francearchives.fr/fr/facomponent/a66b017dcb9d5e79d150d6aa703fee14ebe 41f3c; https://francearchives.fr/fr/facomponent/6bc0e872b6d8e01fcff2628073a34747fd67349b; MC/ET/LXX/227; https://francearchives.fr/fr/facomponent/e2e73ea565cdb08cb11f852c004b 06d78086134d; https://francearchives.fr/fr/facomponent/1eac1dc08a3d8801784d2e933e0642 ddc1cd978f; Benoit and Dufourcq 1968, 198, 230, 245.

out three times. The contracts show that military musicians in France could play the recorder (and sometimes flageolet). Only one apprentice is clearly a child beginner; two seem to be completing the training they had begun with someone else; and the rest were adults apparently wishing to change professions.

EDUCATION

Apart from Hawkins's sarcastic report that from about the year 1710 'the practice of the flute à bec descended to young apprentices of tradesmen, and was the amusement of their winter evenings',[204] little information about children and the recorder has been unearthed. An otherwise unknown woman named Elizabeth

Henson left two childhood notebooks (ca. 1691) that include her notes on technique and tunes in staff notation for an alto recorder with the compass of only g^1–a^2.[205] Around 1696, the German portraitist John Closterman painted *The Children of John Taylor of Bifrons Park*. John was a Member of Parliament. His son Brook (1685–1731), who holds a fine Baroque recorder with ivory mounts, perhaps symbolizing family harmony, became a famous mathematician.

4

DUCT FLUTES IN THE NINETEENTH CENTURY
NIKOLAJ TARASOV

In 1809, after discussing the recorder (*common flute*, or *flute-a-bec*), *The British Encyclopedia* correctly observed that 'All the flageolet tribe, which are of various sorts and sizes, belong to this species.'[1] Duct-flute enthusiasts of the time could choose between four main types of instrument, some with specific national associations: the csakan in the Austro-Hungarian Empire; French flageolets; several kinds of English flageolet; and recorders similar to their eighteenth-century predecessors in Austria, England, France, and Germany.[2] These instruments produced sound identically, and were played in a similar manner, albeit with occasional major differences in fingering.

The csakan and the various flageolets ranged from simple, inexpensive models up to elaborate instruments modernised to meet the musical expectations of the day. Their repertoire was accordingly diverse, catering for amateurs and for the demands of virtuosos whose public performances were reported by the press. Recorders made along traditional lines had a shadowy existence: few efforts at modernisation were reported at the time, and no new repertoire has subsequently come to light.

THE CSAKAN

ORIGINS

New attention was drawn to the recorder by the travelling flute virtuoso Anton Heberle (fl. 1806–16) and his taste for presenting previously unfamiliar instruments. The earliest concert featuring the 'surprise' of an unnamed 'woodwind instrument unknown here with a special form and a very pleasant tone'[3] took place on 21 April 1806 in one of Vienna's leading music venues, the Kleiner Redoutensaal. In the following year, a poster displayed in the royal town theatre of Pest (later part of the Hungarian capital Budapest) announced a performance by Heberle on 18 February, playing the Hungarian *Tsákány*, 'an instrument that deserves special attention for its lovely tone'.[4] At a time when the recorder was considered old-fashioned, this *Tsákány* – or csakan – elicited a strong response, enabling the instrument to live on for another 50 years.

Christian Daniel Friedrich Schubart (1806), comparing woodwind instruments that had been modernised to produce a more powerful sound, observed that the 'all-too quiet tone and the narrow compass' of the recorder (*Flauto doulce*) 'have taken it almost out of fashion today. It is no longer to be heard, either in church or at concerts.'[5] Heberle's shrewd marketing, however, clearly attracted a new audience, leading to a temporary recorder revival, and transforming its perceived disadvantages into an attractive contrast to other instruments of the day.

Besides the new name, the tale of a mysterious provenance began to spread, as related in the first part of the tutor published in 1830 by Ernest Krähmer (1795–1837), the instrument's leading performer from the 1820s: 'The csakan is, from its origin and in the way [the name] is written and pronounced, a Hungarian instrument. A wandering musician found it at the beginning of the nineteenth century in a ruined hermitage in Hungary.'[6] The 'wandering musician' was presumably Heberle, who may have used this story of discovery in his presentations.

The word *Tsákány* (*Csákány, csakan, Czakan*, etc.), well known in the Austro-Hungarian Empire, implied a fascination with 'old times', originally describing a work tool, then a dreaded weapon used during the Ottoman invasion of the Balkan region. Primarily used by the *Heiducken* – cattle drovers, who become legendary mercenary soldiers fighting against the Turkish invaders – and thus called a *Heiduckenczakan*, it designated 'an axe for throwing and striking against the head'.[7] A definitive German book on the development of weapons defines it thus: 'The hammer: By the gipsy word *Czakan* in the Slavonic languages (Hungarian: *Czakany*) a sort of war hammer or pickaxe for miners is described. On a short handle is the hammer, and on the opposite side an axe-like or peaked end, both fixed with clamps. It was used at the end of the seventeenth century and beginning of the eighteenth by the imperial Heiduck-corps. A German Czakan was a pickaxe with a device for a gun. Such short hammer sticks, called also *Puzikan* and *Pusdogean* in Hungary and *Tschekan* in Russia, were formerly carried in Hungary and Poland by higher officers as a sign of their class.'[8] According to Marianne Betz, Czakan weapons were reported until 1818 among Hungarian units in the Austro-Hungarian army.[9]

As this weapon was replaced by more effective ones, it emerged as a symbol of national pride and self-confidence, even more so once it was equipped with its determining musical feature: finger-holes and the mouthpiece of a duct flute. This sort of csakan, described as a 'Slavonic stick-whistle', was retained as an instrument of war on the battlefield.[10] Nonetheless, as the striking weapon turned into a musical folk instrument, its function as an axe or hammer diminished, becoming increasingly stylized through rendition in wood.

This unusual combination of a traditional weapon with a folk instrument provided Heberle with a dramatic tool for the musical stage. The transformed csakan and its legend of origin communicated messages of freedom and national fortitude to a people whose liberation from the Ottoman invasion remained in vivid recent memory, finding echoes in such genres as 'Turkish music' and Oriental fashion in dress. Hungarian sentiment against the Austrian monarchy gained new force at the same time as the French invasion fostered solidarity between the peoples of Hungary and Austria. In this context, the csakan possessed symbolic power: its discovery by a travelling musician implied authenticity, a unique combination of the good 'old' with the exciting 'new': a heady Romantic mixture, which may have contributed to the instrument's success.

In 1810 Archduke Rudolph of Austria (1788–1831) returned with a csakan from Hungary, where the imperial family had lived in exile during the French invasion. Rudolph started composing works for the new instrument, which he discussed with his music teacher, Ludwig van Beethoven. Beethoven was subsequently asked to compose a sonata for the csakan depicting a pontoon bridge across the Danube constructed from boats in Bratislava (Pressburg), then part of Hungary – a musical project that obviously failed to come to fruition.[11] Another prominent nobleman, the charismatic and innovative Hungarian statesman, freedom fighter, and writer István Széchényi (1791–1860), enjoyed playing the csakan as a symbolic gesture of patriotic resistance to the French.[12]

Stockflöte (walking-stick flute) is the first word in the preface to the csakan tutor published in 1816 by Wilhelm Klingenbrunner (1782–1850). Although walking-stick transverse flutes were made at that time, the term *Stockflöte* (stick-flute) seems to have been reserved for the more characteristic csakan. Gustav Schilling's music encyclopaedia (1835) notes that the 'Stick-flute or Czakan . . . is, especially in Austria, very much in use and a newer invention very similar to the recorder' – a statement repeated by later dictionaries.[13] In 1878, Hermann Mendel's musical lexicon was one of the last sources associating the *Stockflöte* with the csakan, concluding by observing that the instrument 'is to be found less often now'.[14] Indeed, later sources describe the *Stockflöte* as a kind of simple walking-stick flute flageolet (which combines a duct-flute head with a transverse-flute body, like the seventeenth-century *Dolzflöte*).[15]

The csakan became a perfect 'folk' instrument: an object of identification associated with yearning for a better life, for independence and freedom, as well as a symbol for glorification of a supposed national past, expressed in a taste for naturalness and simplicity. For gentlemen enjoying travel, voyages, trips to the countryside – or at least, promenades in suburban or municipal parks – carrying a walking stick was *de rigueur* once they no longer had to wear a status sword or *épée*. The addition of a musical instrument to these sticks was merely another expression of personal freedom. For the rustic csakan, association with folk history had already achieved a similar mystical incorporation: the instrument became an ideal candidate for further improvement and 'civilization'. Once the csakan had been presented on stage by Heberle, this once folk-like instrument commenced its refinement for employment in art music.

Contemporary press announcements suggest nationwide sympathy for the instrument. Heberle published the first illustration of a walking-stick csakan together with a fingering chart in 1807, as a newspaper supplement in Pest. This was followed by a separate publication in Vienna by the imperial printing house: the *Scala für den ungarischen Csakán* or *Flûte douce*, depicting a recorder built into a walking stick. As the title implies, the csakan was identified as a recorder from the outset. Klingenbrunner observed in 1816: 'this currently very popular instrument, owing to its pleasing tone and the modest effort [needed to play it], bears the appropriate name *Flute douce*'.[16] The Viennese magazine *Der Sammler* noted in 1822 that Krähmer's 'playing of the *Flûte douce* or Czakan has aroused an even greater enthusiasm' (presumably than his normal oboe playing).[17] Although Krähmer performed only on a csakan, never an earlier type of recorder, his instrument was nevertheless understood as a contemporary recorder, as documented after his death by Leopold Sonnleithner (1862): 'for the flute: the late Ernest Krähmer (*Flûte douce*)'.[18]

The characteristic feature of this new recorder was its incorporation into a walking stick. Although such instruments were made as early as the 1690s and throughout the eighteenth century, Heberle's csakan created widespread public demand. The instrument was equipped with a mouthpiece fitted with a crook perforated with two small holes through which it was blown, and its prolonged body ended in the walking stick's spike, the function of which is perfectly illustrated in a section of the atmospheric verse *Das Schifflein* (The Little Boat) by the German poet Johann Ludwig Uhland (1787–1862). On a boat trip whose passengers are strangers at first, a huntsman starts to play the horn, and another passenger prepares his csakan: 'From his walking stick / he unscrews pin and cap / and mixes fluty tones / into the mellow roar of the horn. . . .'[19]

The notated compass of the csakan illustrated by Heberle in 1807 was two octaves, from c^1 to c^3. The holes are the same as on a recorder: a thumb-hole, pinched to produce the second octave, and seven finger-holes. The fingerings differ from those in late-Baroque recorder fingering charts when shifting between registers: $c\sharp^2$ works with only the thumb-hole closed, d^2 proves to be the first harmonic of d^1, b^2 works as the first harmonic of b^1, and the fingering for c^3 is new.[20]

Heberle's published csakan works, mostly unaccompanied solos, do not indicate the instrument's pitch. From the start, however, the csakan was evidently conceived as a transposing instrument. In his concert works, the csakan is pitched in ab^1, a tuning that remained the standard size. Krähmer explained this unusual pitch in the first part of his tutor (2nd edn, 1830) thus:

I have often been asked why the csakan is pitched in A flat. I could answer, because the first one had this pitch, or, isn't A-flat major one of the most beautiful keys? But a better explanation is that every duct flute pitched above A flat becomes too screaming and, particularly, too unpleasant in the high register. If an instrument is pitched lower, the high notes may well be more beautiful, but the low register becomes too weak and sometimes the notes completely fail to work. I would accept a tuning in G. But as all published music for the csakan is based on a pitch of A flat in relation to its accompaniment, I would consider it advisable to keep on using a csakan in A flat, except when somebody performs without an accompaniment or wishes to transpose the accompaniment a semitone lower.[21]

A practical aspect may have been just as important: the instrument's diameter fitted the ideal dimensions for a fashionable walking-stick instrument; a soprano size would have been too small; an alto, too large and heavy.

Most surviving Viennese csakans from the first half of the century are indeed pitched in ab^1; only a few are in g^1, a^1, or bb^1, and later on, solitary examples –

without a walking stick – are in f¹ and c². They were made only as solo instruments, not as a family of different sizes.

INSTRUMENT MAKERS AND THEIR IMPROVEMENTS

We do not know who first produced a csakan in a technically mature version based on Heberle's concept, although his publication in 1807 suggests he was involved in the initial series of instruments. A 'new and improved' scale for the instrument was published anonymously in 1810 with a brief commentary in German and French (*Neue verbesserte Scala für den Csakan = Nouvelle gamme pour la flûte douce*) – we may presume that Heberle was involved. The novelty is an expanded chromatic compass, notated c¹–g³, achieved by occasional operation of a new additional closed key for D♯, similar to that of the transverse flute.

Heberle the pioneer was soon joined by others wishing to profit from the new instrument, which, despite its 'folk' origins, could not escape the Industrial Revolution. The most celebrated woodwind makers of the Austro-Hungarian Empire started to produce their own models, and the csakan was copied and developed further in neighbouring countries, especially Germany and Russia. Inspired by the wishes of professional musicians, the original model was technically upgraded, incorporating features of other woodwinds so that it could hold its own with established orchestral instruments. The two types were differentiated by the names ordinary or simple csakan (*einfacher Csakan*) and complicated csakan (*complicierter Csakan*).[22]

Krähmer reflected on this development in 1830: 'The still very imperfect instrument came into the hands of the Pressburg instrument maker Franz Schöllnast, who first copied it and shortly afterwards brought several more successful ones to the public. . . . But it was soon found that many more improvements could be made to the csakan, and from the attempts that have been made so far, it has gained enormously in both outer shape and complexity.'[23]

The numerous new features deserve a closer look. To achieve a more respectable outer shape, the characteristic walking-stick parts became optional. Instead of the grip, a small, thin, hat-shaped embouchure cap could be screwed into the upper tenon. The former dual embouchure holes were given up, replaced by a slot that led directly to the windway entrance, without a hollow air chamber. In a further step, the new embouchure cap was superseded by a thin hull, so that the windway entrance and the flat block in front of the plug were in direct contact with the player's lips. The regained direct access to the windway entrance made articulation easier and faster, and the sound clearer. At the bottom end of the instrument, a small open bell shaped like that of the clarinet replaced the solid walking stick and spike. Krähmer states that the instrument maker Johann Ziegler (1792–1852) 'has taken most of the credit for the outer design and makes csakans on request in the pleasing shape of an oboe, only the mouthpiece excluded'.[24] In fact, this redesigned csakan, first illustrated along with a fingering chart in Krähmer's tutor, did look like a little oboe or clarinet: it became the new standard model for advanced players.

As in the Baroque recorder, the head piece was now separated from the instrument's body. On more expensive instruments, head and body could be fitted with a metal tuning slide. Its basic effect was an enhanced opportunity to adjust the pitch – implying a desire to play it with other instruments. By means of two accurately fitting metal cylinders, the pitch could be flattened up to almost a semitone, with fewer negative consequences for the instrument's internal tuning. Furthermore, the tuning slide made the inner surface of the instrument's head piece consist of about two-thirds metal, creating a more brilliant sound. In addition – and not only for strengthening – part of the labium was sometimes plated with metal, or the entire labium could consist of a solid metal plate, also permitting a sharper finish for the labium edge.[25]

Although the turnable head piece theoretically allowed the window at the back of the instrument to be moved to the upper side, surprisingly few instruments took advantage of that obvious possibility, perhaps because the back end of the block remained flat, making playing with the window in front less comfortable. A few instruments by Franz Harrach, Anton Kraus, Franz Carl Kruspe, Lange, Nielsen, August Rorarius, Wanscheid, and Ziegler display a recorder-like beak and were therefore almost certainly played with the labium on the top side.

The thumb-hole was often bushed with a bone or metal 'washer' that penetrated the inner bore up to 4 mm, preventing moisture from entering the hole. The bushing's main purpose was, however, to reduce the aperture to the size of a register hole. For this reason, the bushing was also designed like a miniature thimble inserted into the thumb-hole, and its rounded part looked into the bore. On the top of that rounded part, a small hole served as a register hole. By raising the thumb, the tone octaved automatically, and the old technique of pinching could be given up. 'Hence a not insignificant difficulty fell away by itself,' as Klingenbrunner commented in his tutor of 1816.[26] Functionally comparable to the

English patent flageolets, this system minimized the amount of practice needed for the csakan, thus further increasing its appeal to amateurs. Krähmer gives preference to this system in his tutor. The last mention of both techniques dates from fingering charts published by Krähmer in 1822, where traditionally built instruments are called Viennese csakans (*Wiener Csakans*), whereas those with bushed thumb-holes appear as Pressburg csakans.[27] Before long, the new system prevailed everywhere. As only Schöllnast was active in Pressburg, presumably he was its inventor.

A significant feature of the complicated csakan was the addition of new keys, modelled on other woodwind instruments of the day. Besides the above-mentioned standard closed D$\sharp$ key, a key permitting an extension of a semitone below the basic note is found among the first additions, as on some flutes of the era. To play this new note, the sound-holes were moved to an even lower position, and an open key-hole added, operated by a long lever for the left-hand little finger. Although arrangements by Anton Diabelli printed in 1813 exploit this semitone extension, as do other works published at the time, it was omitted from Krähmer's 1830 tutor, which may have been attempting to establish something like a standard model, and occurs later only as an optional extra on some deluxe models. The new model benefited from closed keys that enable tonally stable alternatives to notes otherwise produced by partly covering holes or cross-fingering, such as C$\sharp$, D$\sharp$, F, F$\sharp$, G$\sharp$, B$\flat$, and the octave C. Furthermore, Krähmer's seven-key custom model permitted all chromatic trills in the notated range c^1–d^3. As mentioned in the extra sections of his tutor published in 1833, some sophisticated models even offered more alternative keys for trills that otherwise required difficult fingering combinations, or for an acoustically better lower position of hole 7.[28] Several surviving deluxe csakans show different solutions for the fundamental and the first semitone, both operated by the little finger of the right hand, using either a paired combination with an open key for low C and a closed low C$\sharp$, or open keys coupling the two notes. These open keys not only stabilized the low notes but eased the attack and tuning of notes in the transition between the second and third registers.

Keys on cheaper instruments were made of brass or nickel silver, silver for the expensive ones. For padding, leather and cork were used, or, as a more durable system, relatively airtight keys using pewter or lead plugs over metal-lined finger-holes.

As Schöllnast's business books show, the choice of material, quality of fittings, and quantity of keys depended on the customer's budget.[29] Eventually, systems with more than ten additional keys were developed. The Boehm system, which never prevailed among Viennese woodwind instruments, was also never applied to the complicated csakan. Thus, the earlier basic fingering system remained unchanged, and cross-fingering continued to be used alongside alternative keys.

Finally, the brilliant sound produced by deluxe csakans made from tropical hardwood or ivory was augmented by replacement with a new dense and highly resistant synthetic material. A surviving complicated csakan, attributed to the Ziegler workshop, is made of dark hard rubber or ebonite (vulcanite), a patented material discovered in 1839 by Charles Goodyear Sr.

Mechanisms with seven or more keys can be found on instruments made by Sebastian Knechtl, Stephan Koch, Kraus, Franz Muss, Martin Schemmel, Schöllnast, Johann Stehle, Johann Tobias Uhlmann, and Ziegler. Krähmer, whose main occupation was playing principal oboe in an orchestra, may have transferred the improvements of his Viennese Koch–Sellner oboe to the csakan in collaboration with the makers Schöllnast and Ziegler. Certainly, his personal connection to this development is indicated by its decline in elaborate concert instruments produced after his death in 1837.[30]

The csakan, like other duct flutes, continued to be produced and sold – in mostly simplified versions – by manufacturers in the Vogtland, Germany. Around 1875, Ludwig Heberlein's musical instrument catalogue offered inexpensive '*Stockflöten*

25. Csakan in a♭[1] by Johann Ziegler (Vienna, ca. 1830s), ebony, horn, tuning-slide, 10 silver pewter-plug keys.

or *Czakans*' made as walking-stick instruments in pear and boxwood with only one key alongside a grenadilla version with four or six keys 'in clarinet form'. Another catalogue, from Paul Stark in Markneukirchen (after 1893), advertises various models of csakans 'by the dozen', fitted with one to eight keys. Although the illustration of one of Stark's instruments is still reminiscent of the Viennese design of a more or less complicated csakan (now uniformly beaked with the window on the top side), Julius Heinrich Zimmermann's catalogue from 1899 depicts instruments – promoted since Ernesto Köhler's tutor that supported the catalogue (Leipzig, 1886) – which suggest a cross between the *Flötuse*-recorder and the csakan. These 'Czakane' were soprano-size instruments with up to six keys, exclusively pitched in c^2 and thereby disconnected from their distinguished Viennese ancestors and their repertoire – mostly unbranded instruments of the lowest quality. As they subsequently lost their thumb-hole and seventh finger-hole during the following decades, they became hard to distinguish from simple flute flageolets.

AMATEURS, PROFESSIONALS, AND CONCERT LIFE

Although the Viennese csakan – a walking-stick recorder – seems designed for performance in the open air, in contrast to French flageolet culture there are no reports of outdoor public concerts. All csakan performances, including Heberle's, took place in closed rooms. The idea of going out for a stroll or making a journey to the countryside and pausing for a moment to play a sounding walking stick was restricted to the amateur of a certain prosperity, as illustrated in literature. In Adalbert Stifter's novella *Feldblumen* (1834), for example, a doctor plays his *Stockflöte* during a pause in an alpine hike.[31]

An urban citizen promenading with his csakan would not have sunk to playing on the streets, retreating instead to the salon. Some csakans were status symbols, boasting engraved silver monograms and ivory grips made sufficiently daintily to outfit a lady, as in the case of an instrument from the estate of Sophie Lindpaintner, wife of the bandmaster at the Stuttgart court. If the instrument's owner were able to play a tune in social circles, or even manage to execute a more demanding piece, emulating professional musicians such as Heberle, a social reputation could be won. The instrument's quiet and pleasant tone was ideal for home music-making, perhaps explaining the mass of arrangements surviving in manuscripts and print, most of which may be considered 'house music' – a term that came into circulation by the mid-nineteenth century.

The csakan, easy for every woodwind player to learn, became a supplementary instrument for many. Archduke Rudolph, for example, performed his own compositions at court at the piano, accompanying his chamberlain, Count Ferdinand de Troyer, who otherwise played the clarinet, on the csakan.

Professional musicians also used the csakan for recreation and technical studies. Adam Joseph Schott, son of Bernhard Schott (founder of the music publishing house that became B. Schott's Söhne of Mainz, Germany), asked his brothers in a letter from 1828 to send him 'a *Chakan*, which will serve to entertain me on the voyage and to keep my fingers moving'.[32] He was about to emigrate to North America, where he worked as a clarinettist and bandmaster.

As professional musicians were in the public eye, their csakan-related activities were better reported than those of amateurs. In 1810, the *AMZ* reported that a romance with variations on a theme from Luigi Cherubini's *opéra comique Faniska* for 'Hungarian *Csákány (Flûte douce)*' accompanied by a string ensemble was performed at the Augarten in Vienna by Joseph Gebauer (fl. 1804–18), a flute virtuoso and composer who contributed about a dozen pieces to the csakan repertoire: 'It pleases us to be able to speak of this modest artist with well-deserved praise; because his playing, on this instrument as well as on the flute, testifies to much feeling and a rare, expressive delivery.'[33] Such musical programmes were pot-pourris, combining single movements or excerpts from larger works – symphonic, choral, and solo – that provided a platform for various soloists who shone on one or more instruments, and guaranteed entertainment for all. Whether in Vienna or the provinces, they generally included a single piece for the csakan.

Krähmer became the instrument's most important figure. By 1814, he was teaching the csakan at the age of 19 in his native city of Dresden, and ordering instruments made by Schöllnast for his students.[34] In 1815, Krähmer was appointed first oboist at the k. k. Hoftheater in Vienna, followed in 1822 by a post in the k. k. Hof- und Kammermusik. Together with his wife Caroline Schleicher, a noted clarinettist, he undertook a series of acclaimed concert tours through German-speaking countries.

Although Krähmer's job as an oboist guaranteed a regular income, he grasped the freelance opportunities opened up by his incomparable virtuosity on the csakan. The *AMZO* reported in 1821 that his performance in the k. k. Kleiner Redoutensaal 'satisfied the demands of the concert organizer in all respects, because [the hall] was full. That may have been because the great number of Czakan players and admirers filled the hall, or because Krähmer organized the concert with more care than many concert organizers do.'[35] In another concert a year later 'before a large audience' at the Landständischer Saal, he 'played very difficult variations on the csakan, giving much pleasure, above all with the imitation of Drouet-like passages. It would not be easy to hear anything comparable on this instrument.'[36] Evidently Krähmer was able to emulate the virtuosity of the flautist Louis Drouet (1792–1873), celebrated as the Paganini of his instrument for his fast double tonguing. Although Krähmer was frequently accompanied by his wife on the guitar and the piano, several announcements suggest that, like Heberle, he preferred the 'accompaniment of the whole orchestra' and not a small group of players.[37]

Krähmer generally performed his own pieces, putting little effort into convincing other composers to write for the instrument. Indeed, in a prolific collaboration with the publisher Anton Diabelli (1781–1858), he contributed both didactic and concert works to the repertoire, writing in his tutor (1830): 'The most brilliant concert pieces were written for the csakan, and as soon as they were well performed by trained players, they were met with decided approval by larger audiences as well as in smaller circles.'[38] One measure of the commercial success of their partnership is that Diabelli placed an advertisement for his newest csakan music in the capital's daily newspaper, the *Wiener-Zeitung*, on 14 January 1822.

26. Title page of sheet music for Ernest Krähmer, *Introduction und Variationen . . . für den Csakan* (1827).

After Krähmer's early death in 1837, Diabelli continued to publish his works, along with a complete catalogue of them. The csakan had, however, lost its guiding star. The instrument's status rapidly faded, its symbolic power was forgotten, and its development ground to a halt while that of other woodwind instruments continued. Simplified by musical instrument makers in eastern Germany, it lost its significant walking stick towards the end of the nineteenth century; cheap csakans were used in schools for class instruction, heralding the invention of the *Volksblockflöte* in the 1930s. The German recorder maker Joachim Paetzold recalls his experiences at a school in Liegnitz (Lower Silesia) in 1931: 'In the fourth, fifth, and sixth grade, we played on these csakan-flutes without a thumb-hole, on which you had to produce the octave by blowing harder. You can imagine that when around 60 or 70 students played monophonic chorales, it was more than horrible.'[39] These instruments, pitched in d^2 (like an octave flageolet flute) and equipped with two additional keys, were bought by parents for their children at a price of RM 2.10.[40]

TUTORS AND PLAYING TECHNIQUE

Relatively few fingering charts and tutors for the csakan were published compared with those for flageolets. Perhaps the instrument was considered so straightforward and easy to learn that even Heberle himself never produced a tutor to supplement his fingering charts.

Klingenbrunner was a taxman who devoted his spare time to music, using various pseudonyms for his activities as instrumentalist, singer, and playwright. In 1816, he published the first tutor for the csakan in Vienna; in 1822, an abridged version, without his name and probably pirated, was published by Schott's for the German market.[41] The work begins with a chromatic scale from c^1 to g^3, giving up to three alternative fingerings for several notes, and stating that notes above d^3 must be forced. A short introduction to the instrument and a few practical hints lead on to nine pages about elementary musical theory. All the dynamic marks are listed, but without any indication of how to produce them on a csakan. The appendix contains forty progressive two-part exercises in appropriate keys.

Heberle's scales, as well as the fingering charts in Klingenbrunner and in *Krähmer's Neueste theoretisch-praktische Csakan-Schule nebst 30 fortschreitenden Übungsstücken und einer Triller Tabelle für alle Töne*, Op. 1 (Vienna: Diabelli, 1822), call for manual octave pinching. Klingenbrunner and Krähmer also consider the new octaving device, which finally prevailed after Krähmer's reworked second edition of his Op. 1, *Neueste . . . 40 fortschreitenden Übungsstücken und Tabellen auf dem einfachen und dem complicirten Csakan*, published by Diabelli in 1830. That tutor features a scale and a trill fingering chart for the single-keyed simple csakan (compass notated c^1–$f\sharp^3$) and the complicated csakan with a standard of seven alternative keys (compass notated c^1–f^3).

Krähmer clearly aspired to produce stable, reliable, and good-sounding notes with the aid of the new keys, showing no interest in expanding the compass to further screaming high notes. His systematic approach to fingering is certainly oriented to the registering principle of the oboe, in which an upper hole partly covered by the index finger helps to achieve a stable d^3 or $d\sharp^3$, a technique expanded during the first decades of the nineteenth century to provide all notes between d^3 and f^3. The idea is already evident for two notes in the anonymously printed csakan fingering scale of 1810, and may indeed be traced back to a tradition documented in two advanced alto recorder fingering charts of the eighteenth century, Pablo Minguet y Irol's *Reglas* (1754) and the *Principes pour la flute* by Father Ferdinand von Everard (1770).

Krähmer's tutor offers advice on posture, finger position, and musical timing. The chapter on 'basic rules on the fingering'[42] includes a comprehensive explanation of the choice between using keywork or cross-fingering, illustrated with musical examples. He concedes: 'Although keys were invented for the proper tuning of the instrument, and to make playing much easier, one often finds passages of one or more bars that would be very difficult and imperfect to perform without the aid of cross-fingering.'[43] As the Boehm system was never adapted to the complicated csakan, the instrument's repertoire favours keys close to the fundamental scale. Indeed, the alternation of cross- and normal fingering, typical for recorder technique, remained typical for the instrument, producing tonal irregularities despite its additional keywork. Nevertheless, in 1833, Krähmer added second and third parts to his tutor, introducing musical exercises in all major and minor keys, extending into the third register, 'written only for all those who would like to play around with it and whose instruments produce these notes well and in tune'.[44]

The correct execution of double tonguing is dealt with in remarkable detail. Possibly because of his musical training in Dresden and the conservative Boys Military Education Institute in Annaburg, Krähmer recommends using the syllables 'dadd'll', similar to Johann George Tromlitz's flute treatise (1791) and a descendant of Quantz's 'did'll' (1752).[45] 'The csakan is perfectly suited to it, because it is not as difficult to perform on it as many assume, but easier, rounder, and faster to execute than on any other suitable instrument.'[46] Fast and brilliant playing was the signature feature of the csakan, best represented by Krähmer, as the press reported in 1821: 'The ease of the embouchure naturally enables performance of the fastest passages, and if somebody could play comparably on the oboe, he would be called a magician.'[47]

Although Krähmer's complete tutor offers many elements of a complex approach to the instrument, it omits several basic aspects, probably deliberately, as the book seems primarily intended not for self-study but in lessons with a 'master'.[48] Perhaps the handling of such sophisticated techniques as dynamics belonged to the 'secrets' Krähmer demonstrated in a concert in Lemberg in 1823, where 'his swelling and diminishing of tones down to a barely hearable level astonishes and produces admiration'.[49]

A later tutor, the *Schule für Flageolet, Czakan für den Selbstunterricht geeignet = Self Instructor for Flageolet, Czakan and Stickflute* by the flute virtuoso Ernesto Köhler (1849–1907) (Leipzig: Wilhelm Zimmermann, ca. 1886), marks the decline of artistic csakan playing. Reduced to the most basic of instructions and an appendix of easy melodies, this popular tutor – in German, English, and Russian – clearly treats the school csakan as an introduction to other woodwind instruments. The true Viennese csakan had faded into obscurity.

REPERTOIRE

Although Heberle's story about the discovery of the csakan may be read as an account of an 'old' instrument's rebirth at a time of rapid change around 1800, it is hardly comparable to the recorder revival a century later. The allusion to the csakan's past was essentially a legend, one strong enough to inspire the development of a new, complex musical instrument, but unconnected with efforts to play the music of the past: its repertoire was exclusively contemporary.

That Heberle published six exercise booklets 'for the beginner' in the same year he presented the csakan in concert can be seen as commencing a marketing strategy successfully continued by the production of more advanced pieces, such as dances, variations, a fantasia, sonatas, and a solo concerto. In this respect, the csakan was treated like other popular instruments: most Viennese publishing houses hired amateur or professional players to arrange appropriate music, and commissioned new works. This repertoire consisted mainly of lighter music, 'little pieces, rondos, variations, polonaises, potpourris, etc.', as Johann Georg Albrechtsberger and Ritter von Seyfried noted in 1837.[50]

The large repertoire for csakan solo is dominated by arrangements of popular pieces of the day. The prominent Viennese publishing houses of Diabelli and Haslinger each produced a periodical series of arrangements. Orchestral works were rendered as piano reductions, but also reduced to a single melodic line for an unaccompanied solo instrument, for example as 'flute scores'. Such arrangements were transposed to appropriate keys and adapted to lie comfortably within the range of the instruments, including the csakan. Amateur csakan players were therefore able to play the latest music at home.

Reductions of operas for a single csakan were a speciality of Diabelli, who produced the subscription series *Mon Plaisir, Ouvrage périodique pour csakan*. Between 1821 and 1844, forty-one items were printed, each devoted to a specific subject, such as imitations of characteristic variations performed by famous singers, Lieder by Heinrich Proch and Franz Schubert, or – mostly – operas by Auber, Bellini, Donizetti, Rossini, Verdi, and others. Meanwhile, popular ballroom music was made available in the form of solo arrangements of dances by Joseph Lanner (1801–43) and Michael Pamer (1782–1827). Haslinger produced sets of waltzes as well as many marches and quadrilles by Johann Strauss Sr (1804–49) in the series *Lieblings-Walzer für Csakan*. Indeed, no fewer than 140 of Strauss's approximately 250 original works were published between 1830 and 1849 in csakan arrangements, a clear indicator of the instrument's popularity.

Duets were published, notably by Diabelli, Gebauer, Anton Kargl (fl. 1808–19), Klingenbrunner (arrangements of two Mozart operas), Krähmer, and Karol (Charles) Scholl. More demanding pieces, such as Stefan Franz's *Grand Duo* in sonata form, remained in manuscript.

Besides csakan solos or duets, a favoured genre was the duet with guitar, such as Diabelli's own *Grande Serenade* in A major, Op. 67, written in sonata form, and published in 1813/14. Diabelli, probably the central figure in the csakan's musical development, understood how to handle the instrument advantageously. As with other attempts to raise the instrument to a higher musical level, however, he faced the csakan's obvious handicap: its home key of A flat, uncomfortable for most accompanying instruments, and restricting the potential of its music for the adventurous modulations so popular in the Romantic era. Thus his *Grande Serenade* has parts for flute and guitar in A, but a transposed csakan part notated in C; as the csakan was pitched in A flat, the guitar would have had to be tuned down a semitone. Another example of Diabelli's writing for flute or csakan is his two-volume *Abendunterhaltungen* ('Nocturnal Entertainments') from 1820 to 1824, arrangements of popular pieces by several composers for solo instrument and guitar, published with two solo parts, one for flute or violin, another – with an appropriately reduced compass – for csakan.

Diabelli's *Thèmes favoris de l'opéra Zelmira de Rossini*, Op. 128, for csakan and guitar ad lib. (1822) expressly calls for a *Terzgitarre* (third-guitar), to match the (rare) csakan in c^2. For other pieces, he published the accompaniment in separate versions for guitar or piano, or reduced it for a second csakan. Sometimes the accompaniment was wholly dispensable, as in his arrangement of Weber's opera *Der Freischütz* for csakan alone, two csakans, csakan and guitar, or csakan and piano (1822). For this reason, the guitar parts of pieces written in combination with the csakan mostly supply a simple accompaniment of broken chords. Only a few works, by Diabelli and Franz Bathioli (d. 1861), for example, treat the guitar as an equal partner. The same applies to most works with piano accompaniment by Diabelli, Joseph Fahrbach, Gebauer, Jean Baptiste de Hunyadi, Krähmer, Jean Ruckgaber, Johann Baptist Vanhal, etc., although some more ambitious settings survive, mostly in manuscript, by Archduke Rudolph, Valentin Czeyka (Czeika) (1769–ca. 1835), and Jean Ruckgaber (1799–1876), as well as in print by Krähmer and Abbé Joseph Gelinek (1758–1825).

The csakan's chamber music repertoire is small, featuring such works as Scholl's *Quartett* for csakan, violin, viola, and violoncello (ca. 1813); the *Potpourri*, Op. 13 (1816) for csakan, viola, violoncello, and guitar by Stefan (Etienne, Istvan) Franz (1785–1855); and Wenzeslaus Thomas Matiegka's *Notturno*, Op. 25, for csakan or flute, viola, and guitar. A few pieces combining csakan and voice, by Diabelli, Mathias Durst, and Henrik Rung, survive in manuscript.

Because the csakan was used by several composing virtuosos – Gebauer, Heberle, Hunyadi, and Krähmer – as a flashy solo instrument, some concert pieces with orchestra were published, also in piano reduction. All surviving pieces start with a slow introduction followed by variations or polonaises in rondo style. Only in two compositions by Hans Christian Lumbye (1810–74) does the csakan appear as an orchestral instrument, evoking a special alpine atmosphere. It is, however, conceivable that the csakan was employed more frequently in ensemble settings: Antonio Tosoroni's *Trattato pratico di strumentazione* (Florence, 1850) states that the sound of the csakan 'is very frail and seems suited for use in the chamber. But we note that in Germany it is also used with success in the orchestra.'[51]

FRENCH FLAGEOLETS

The French flageolet, as we have seen, emerged in the Baroque era as a duct flute with four holes on the top and two thumb-holes on the bottom of the instrument, the upper thumb being used for playing octaves, as on a recorder. The additional thumb-hole resulted from the impossibility of playing an instrument smaller than c^3-size using seven fingers in a row. Their high pitch in the 2′ register, combined with a gentle tone, predestined these flageolets for the imitation of birdsong, not to mention the contemporary practice of training caged singing birds. A German *Conversations-Lexikon* published in Amsterdam (1809–11) states that the flageolet 'would not be worth a mention among other woodwind instruments, if it were not, surprisingly, imitated on the violin by certain virtuosos',[52] referring to the high 'flageolet tones' familiar in string technique.

From 1800, however, the cooperation of ambitious players and instrument makers resulted in the development of a new, larger type of French flageolet with increased volume. This created another market beyond replicating birdsong, as pointed out by Schubart (1806): 'The bigger [flageolet] is used at respectable places, as in operas, where these instruments sound extraordinarily well.'[53] French flageolets in the 4′ register could indeed play louder than any comparable recorder of the *flautino* or *flauto piccolo* category, simply because of their larger proportions. This advantage established the French flageolet as the most successful instrument with a high recorder-like tone throughout the nineteenth century. In consequence, it was the only duct flute that underwent a significant development comparable to that of other woodwinds at a time of profound innovation in musical instrument making. Standardised as a non-transposing instrument in a^2, it acquired additional keys, and its most elaborate version, made from the 1840s to the 1930s, boasted a key mechanism comparable to that of the modern Boehm flute. A characteristic feature was a windcap containing a sea sponge intended to dehumidify the player's breath, to prevent clogging and improve tone quality. Although efforts to establish this instrument in the regular orchestra were unsuccessful, it became popular in dance orchestras.

Professional soloists who pioneered the flageolet as a concert instrument included J. Bellay, Edme Collinet (1765–1841), C. Eugène Roy (ca. 1790–1827), and Jean Carnaud aîné (1781–1861). Their attempts to establish it in solo concertos, chamber music, and concertante duos were, however, soon overshadowed by the instrument's success in popular square-dance music, as reported by François-Joseph

Fétis (1866): 'Julien Clarchies [1769–1814], celebrated for a long time for his talent as a director of the dance orchestra, engaged Collinet to devote his instrument to this kind of genre; the latter appreciated his advice, and soon the exhilarating vogue became so strong that everybody in Paris wanted to dance to nothing but Collinet's flageolet.'[54]

Collinet inspired many imitators, and in 1822, *flageoletiste* became an official professional title in Gardeton's annual listing.[55] No fewer than 60 of the 538 'artists for balls and soirées' listed in Planque's *Agenda musical* (1836) for Paris played the flageolet. Nineteen offered their services exclusively as flageolettists; the rest doubled on clarinet, cornet, flute, or violin. Of 339 teachers of wind instruments, 55 offered instruction on the flageolet.[56] In 1819, Roy is mentioned as 'the flageolet soloist at parties in the Tivoli and Prado pleasure gardens of Paris'.[57] Hubert Collinet (1796–1867), Edme's son, was a steady soloist in the renowned dance orchestra of Philippe Musard (1793–1859), which performed every evening in 1836.[58] Of seven dance-orchestra conductors mentioned in the *Agenda musical* (1836), six composed extensively for the instrument, and three were well-known flageolet soloists and teachers (Hubert Collinet, J.-M. Weber, and Rubner aîné).[59]

Hubert Collinet, whose activities were acknowledged by English and American newspapers, seems to have been the first flageolettist to tour abroad. His regular appearances in London inspired many imitators, his brilliant execution of contradances and quadrilles leading the French flageolet to displace the English flageolet in its home nation. In his English tutor, Collinet affirms: 'The Quadrille Flageolet is a very modern Instrument – so much so that there are not enough performers upon it to meet the demands of the London Season.'[60] Collinet became a star soloist in the famous travelling orchestra of Louis Antoine Jullien (1812–60). The *Musical World* reported in 1850 on an appearance in Glasgow: 'We have had the pleasure of a visit from M. Jullien, accompanied by his excellent orchestra. . . . The variations were played by . . . Collinet (flageolet). . . . The Concert Hall was crowded in every part. . . .'[61]

Before Collinet's visit to the United States in 1853 with Jullien's orchestra, the *New York Daily Times* announced: 'M. JULLIEN will have the pleasure of introducing several new and eminent Solo Performers in the course of the forthcoming series of Concerts at Metropolitan Hall, among them . . . M. COLLINET, Conductor and Flageolet solo of the Court Balls of Napoleon the First, in 1812, who will appear, this being his last engagement prior to his retirement from public life, after forty years' continued success, as the only recognized artistic performer on the Flageolet. . . .'[62]

Flageolet soloists not yet mentioned included Narcisse Bousquet (1820–69), Hippolyte Bonnisseau (d. 1882), and Louis A. Saint-Jacome (1830–98), all also renowned performers on the cornet, as well as Ribeault and Baton, mentioned in the music company Millerau's catalogue in 1890.[63] Less virtuosic flageolettists continued to be engaged to perform in French dance ensembles and orchestras at home and abroad until the end of the century, as reported in a catalogue of the London branch of J. R. Lafleur & Sons around 1891–99: 'Every Flute-player should use this instrument. It is a most agreeable one with a small or large Ball-room Band, very easy to learn, and much less fatiguing than the Flute; more powerful, showy, and preferred to the Flute in all dancing rooms and private parties on account of its brilliant and pleasing tone, it makes the same part as the Flute, Violin, or treble of the Piano.'[64]

ENGLISH FLAGEOLETS

In the 1790s, some English recorders, equipped with a similar windcap to the French flageolet, were consequently renamed 'English flageolets'. In 1802, William Bainbridge (d. 1831?) transformed the recorder's fingering into a pattern similar to that of the transverse flute, with only six finger-holes, and usually featuring a narrowed first upper fingerhole to facilitate octaving. Several patented models remained in use until the mid-nineteenth century. One important variant was the English patent flute flageolet which, as we have mentioned, combined a duct-flute head with a transverse-flute body. The same principle persisted under various names until the 1930s for inexpensive piccolo-sized instruments, probably intended for educational purposes.

'Duo' and 'Trio' flageolets, whose double or triple bodies were attached to one mouthpiece blown by a single player, echoed the double recorder of the past. Such variants developed a small repertoire, mostly for the amateur. The few professional performances recorded include 'a young Frenchman' (probably Hubert Collinet) playing the duo flageolet in 1818, 'with such pleasantness, precision in the double scales, and above all improvised fantasies with such artistic perfection, that the effect throughout was charming, even truly pathbreaking. The young man especially knew how to execute little fugue-like pieces with true mastery.'[65]

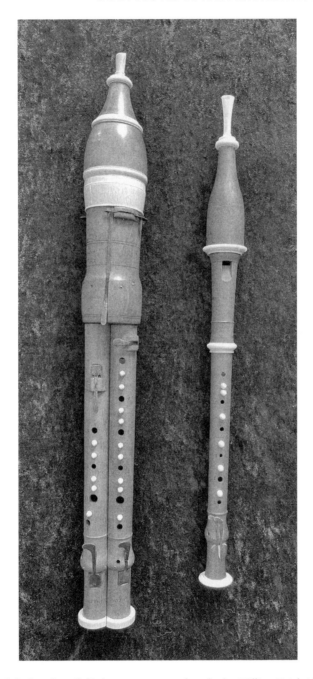

27. Two English flageolets: (left) duo patent octave flageolet by William Bainbridge (London, ca. 1810), boxwood, ivory, five brass keys, and two wind-cutter keys; (right) English patent octave flageolet by Bainbridge, boxwood, ivory, two silver keys.

TRADITIONAL RECORDERS

Modifications made to surviving recorders by Baroque masters, including Johann Christoph Denner, Johann Benedikt Gahn, and Nikolaus Staub – the addition of closed chromatic keys in the foot piece and insertion of a narrowed thumb-hole bushing for ease of octaving – suggest that such instruments remained in use at least in the first decades of the nineteenth century.[66] Later German makers such as Johann Friedrich Boie (1762–1809) and Heinrich Grenser (1764–1813) made recorders with features characteristic of flageolets and csakans: a closed universal key in the head piece that raised every note by a semitone, a windcap, and an open extension key of a semitone to low E (sopranino in F by Boie); two closed keys for steps I and II and again an open extension key for a semitone below the fundamental note (alto by Grenser).

More generally, recorders continued to be made without keywork, a sign that they were being manufactured cheaply. In the second half of the century, the French musical instrument-making dynasty of Thibouville distributed recorders – *flûtes douces à bec* – in three sizes: *haute-contre* (c²), *tierce* (a¹), and *taille* (f¹). Made of boxwood with optional horn mounts, they were offered as catalogue items by the dozen. It is still unclear for what kind of music these instruments were used.

5

THE RECORDER IN THE TWENTIETH CENTURY
ROBERT EHRLICH

The recorder was added relatively late to the small family of historical musical instruments that were rediscovered towards the end of the nineteenth century. Only in the 1920s did a small number of expensive hand-made recorders become commercially available. Within the following fifty years, however, the physical instrument itself and its players, repertoire, and technique were to experience two remarkable transformations. First, mass production of an inexpensive *Volksblockflöte*, or 'people's recorder', introduced in Germany in the early 1930s, served after the Second World War as a model for the widespread international use of soprano recorders in elementary music education. A second paradigm shift originated in the Netherlands in the mid-1960s. Inspired by Frans Brüggen, an unprecedented number of professional musicians chose the recorder as their principal or even sole instrument. By the end of the twentieth century more people were playing a wider diversity of recorders in a greater variety of ways than ever before.

SCHOLARS, GENTLEMEN, AND PLAYERS

As we have seen in the previous chapter, contemporary music was played on duct flutes throughout the nineteenth century, and even the recorder itself survived in some nooks and crannies of musical activity. But although the physical instrument was preserved in often excellent condition in museums, private antiquarian collections, and attics, its playing technique was remembered less well with each passing generation. In the absence of a continuing tradition, on those occasions when historical recorders were dusted off and played in order to understand the past, the results were often unappealing. The first attempts at reconstructing the instrument were similarly hindered by lost skills.

A significant moment in the modern revival took place in Brussels, where Victor-Charles Mahillon (1841–1924), curator of the Conservatory's Instrumental

Museum and a distinguished wind-instrument maker and acoustician, copied a set of eight recorders[1] after instruments dating from ca. 1670 by Hieronymus Franciscus Kynseker: a bass in g^0, two tenors in d^1, two altos in g^1, and two sopranos in d^2 preserved in Nuremberg.[2] Mahillon added a sopranino in g^2 to his set, stating that it had been copied after an ivory recorder, possibly the Kynseker garklein in c^3, from the Nuremberg collection.[3] These instruments were played at concerts in Brussels and elsewhere, their best-documented public airing being at three performances organized and directed by Mahillon in 1885 at the International Inventions Exhibition in the Albert Hall, London. The concert by 'members and professors of the Brussels Conservatoire' was described in the London *Musical Times* thus: 'Some of the effects were beautiful as well as curious, while others were only curious. In the latter category must be placed the sounds produced by the eight *flauti dolci* in a Sinfonia Pastorale from "Eurydice", by Jacopo Peri. . . . The pupils of M. Dumon's class handled them well, but the effect resembled a description of a street organ now happily but rarely heard.'[4] Jean Dumon (1829–89) was professor of flute at the Brussels Conservatory from 1857; at the London concerts he also performed music by Bach, Handel, Quantz, and Rameau on a one-keyed flute.[5] Perhaps the most famous witness was the Irish dramatist George Bernard Shaw (1856–1950), who in a review compared the sound of the recorders 'to the cooing of an old and very melancholy piping crow', summarizing thus: 'The effect of the *flauti dolci* music was, on the whole, quaintly execrable.'[6]

Mahillon was not working alone. Towards the end of the nineteenth century, a number of antiquarians in England showed an interest in the recorder. The Reverend Canon Francis W. Galpin (1858–1945), a passionate collector of early instruments who organized diverse musical activities within his parish, had several Renaissance-style recorders made to his own design, finishing at least two of them himself, drilling the finger-holes, fitting the blocks, and setting up the voicing.[7] Joseph Cox Bridge (1853–1929) reached a wider audience – for example, with three lectures at Chester Cathedral on 'Music of the Past' in 1892, soon repeated in Liverpool. The first was the earliest occasion in the modern revival on which the celebrated 'Chester Recorders' made by Peter Bressan were played in public.[8] Bridge believed that recorder music had been 'of a very simple character and confined, more or less, to an octave of notes', demonstrating this by performing 'Cheshire Rounds', 'The Blue Bells of Scotland', and 'Cheshire Waits'. Accompanying Bridge's second lecture, Arnold Dolmetsch (1858–1940) and his daughter Hélène (1878–1924) played music by composers including Henry and

William Lawes, John Jenkins, and Christopher Simpson on viols, lute, and spinet.[9] The dramatic contrast between the simple tunes chosen for the recorders and works by some of the greatest English composers of the seventeenth century played on the stringed instruments illustrates how far the recorder revival initially lagged behind that of other early instruments.

Bridge's presentation of the Chester Recorders at the august Musical Association in London on 12 February 1901 included a performance of his own *Andante* for recorder quartet, almost certainly the first recorder composition of the twentieth century. In keeping with his convictions about the recorder's limitations, Bridge restricted the tessitura to the bottom octave, requiring only the first (alto) part to play up to g^2.[10] The story (first related in print by Edgar Hunt in 1962) that Bridge and his colleagues did not understand the function of the thumb-holes and therefore covered them with stamp paper is probably apocryphal, not least because of the difficulty of producing the note g^2 in tune with a closed thumb-hole.[11]

A more scholarly approach was adopted by Christopher Welch (1832–1915), whose lectures to the Musical Association on 'Literature Relating to the Recorder' (1898) and 'Hamlet and the Recorder' (1902) were published in 1911 as part of his *Six Lectures*.[12] Welch displayed formidable knowledge of the instrument's history, gained primarily through reading at the British Museum library. He provided a wealth of practical detail, not least in his overview of the recorder's repertoire in early eighteenth-century London, which included a serious attempt to establish which of Handel's compositions were written for the flute and which for the recorder, and pointed to original recorder music by Barsanti, Babell, Baston, and Woodcock. Furthermore, he discussed a substantial number of historical methods and sources, ranging from Virdung and Praetorius to eighteenth-century English tutors.

It would take time for Welch's discoveries to be assimilated by performers. Meanwhile, in 1904, John Finn (b. 1853 [or 1856]–after 1935)[13] gave a modest address to the Worshipful Company of Musicians in London entitled 'The Recorder, Flute, Fife and Piccolo'. Finn, a flautist who had played in Bridge's quartet three years before, paid tribute to Welch's 'two admirable papers' and recycled a diluted part of their erudition before proceeding to discuss the transverse flute, upon which subject he was better informed. Although the tunes he played included the overblown note f^3, it seems unlikely he had mastered the thumb-hole ('The recorder has only a short scale of two octaves, the second of which is not easy of production'). His choice of musical examples further indicates the primitive state of recorder playing in England at this time: a modest selection of anonymous tunes from Salter's *Genteel Companion* of 1683 (e.g. 'Hey! Boyes up goe we') on the recorder, and one tune apiece on the flageolet and double flageolet, led on to works of much greater difficulty and musical complexity by Quantz, Kuhlau, and Doppler on a variety of transverse flutes.[14]

A higher degree of accomplishment was displayed by the Bogenhauser Künstlerkapelle, a group of professional and amateur musicians who met for regular playing sessions in Bogenhausen, a wealthy suburb of Munich. Their remarkable instrument collection included original recorders by Jacob and Johann Christoph Denner, Bressan, and Oberlender, as well as an alto recorder by the Munich wind-instrument maker Gottlieb Gerlach (1856–1909), copied after one of their original Jacob Denner instruments, probably the first attempt in the modern revival to make a recorder based on a Baroque model. Martin Kirnbauer, describing Gerlach's Denner copy as barely playable and certainly not comparable to the originals in the Bogenhauser collection, points out that his craftsmanship reveals how little he *understood* about what he was copying.[15]

The ensemble's repertoire included arrangements of popular classics such as the Andante from Joseph Haydn's 'Drumroll' Symphony (No. 103) and the 'Funeral March' from Frédéric Chopin's Piano Sonata in B♭ minor, Op. 35; marches and folk songs; transcriptions of organ and lute music from the sixteenth and seventeenth centuries; as well as arrangements of Johann Sebastian Bach, Handel, and Telemann.[16] Although some of this music was technically demanding, the manner and context of its performance reflected its players' recreational ambitions. The Bogenhausers played mainly sitting at home around a communal table upon which their part-books were laid out in true Renaissance manner, the players refreshing themselves from steins of beer clearly visible in photographs. One delightfully bucolic picture of an *al fresco* session even shows two members playing Baroque alto recorders while lying on their stomachs amid wine bottles.[17]

Public performances by the Bogenhausers are documented over a forty-year period from 1899, in which they presented some historical instruments and pre-Classical music principally as charming light entertainment.[18] A notable exception was their contribution to a concert on 20 September 1925 at the Munich Bach Festival: the Sonatina from Bach's Cantata *Actus Tragicus*, BWV 106, for two alto recorders, two viola da gambas, and continuo. The recorders, original instruments by Johann Christoph Denner, were played by Heinrich Düll (1867–1956) and Georg Petzold (1865–1943). This solitary, if historically important, event in the ensemble's career was reported in several newspapers, which emphasized the rarity and novelty of the recorders' sound.[19]

ARNOLD DOLMETSCH

Arnold Dolmetsch, the celebrated French-born pioneer of historical instruments and performance practice, started making recorders around 1920. Given that he had been playing and building a variety of early bowed, plucked, and keyboard instruments since the early 1890s, he displayed remarkably little interest in the recorder during the three subsequent decades. His first encounter with the instrument was perhaps inauspicious enough to have discouraged him. While studying at the Brussels Conservatory in the early 1880s, he is reported to have attended a lecture on early wind instruments in which soprano, alto, tenor, and bass recorders – presumably the instruments made by Mahillon – were demonstrated by piccolo, flute, clarinet, and bassoon students, respectively. Their efforts met with 'derisive laughter'.[20]

In 1905, at an auction in London, Dolmetsch purchased a boxwood and ivory alto recorder by Bressan, describing it in his diary as being in a state of 'perfect preservation' and having a 'sweet tone'.[21] He left England shortly thereafter and was kept busy during the following decade balancing his family life and concert career with his day jobs, first in Boston and then in Paris, making historical stringed and keyboard instruments for the firms of Chickering and Gaveau, respectively. Researching his monumental book *The Interpretation of the Music of the Seventeenth and Eighteenth Centuries Revealed by Contemporary Evidence*[22] must have been a considerable extra drain on his time until it was published in 1915, one year after he returned to England.

It is indicative of Dolmetsch's priorities during this period that he accorded the recorder scant attention in his book compared with the lute, viols, and keyboard instruments. Nonetheless, he taught himself to play a limited repertoire of mainly sixteenth- and seventeenth-century tunes on the instrument, probably using his copy of *The Compleat Flute-Master*, a tutor published in London in 1695, from which he would have been able to learn the basic fingerings.[23] A contemporary witness to the unfamiliarity of the recorder was the American poet Ezra Pound (1885–1972), who wrote of his first encounter with Dolmetsch, probably in 1914:

I have seen the God Pan and it was in this manner: I heard a bewildering and pervasive music moving from precision to precision within itself. Then I heard a different music hollow and laughing. Then I looked up and saw two eyes like the eyes of a wood-creature peering at me over a brown tube of wood . . . when I picked up the brown tube of wood I found that it had ivory rings upon it. And no proper reed has ivory rings on it, by nature. Also, they told me it was a 'recorder', whatever that is.[24]

It took the temporary loss of the Bressan alto, famously left on a platform of Waterloo Station after a concert in London on 30 April 1919 by his youngest son Carl (1911–97), to focus Dolmetsch's full attention upon the recorder.[25] His efforts to make a playable instrument by trial and error were, paradoxically, more successful than those of many others before or since who had direct reference to a physical model. Perhaps the practical necessity of questioning and testing the influence of every element of design upon the instrument helped him to achieve better results than those attempting to copy or modify a barely understood historical model. And perhaps Dolmetsch's lack of experience as a woodwind maker enabled him to approach recorder making from first principles, without being prejudiced by a prior knowledge of flute or organ acoustics. His craftsmanship and musicality undoubtedly helped. The breakthrough came in August 1919 when, according to Dolmetsch family legend, he rushed into the kitchen shouting 'Eureka! Eureka! I've got it!'[26]

When Dolmetsch started making recorders at the age of 61, they were a sideline to his prodigious activity as a musician and craftsman. Nonetheless, the family workshop was able to finish approximately fifty instruments per year starting in 1920, a rate of production maintained until 1933, when it doubled.[27] Among his more prominent customers in the early years was Shaw, who had evidently changed his mind about the recorder. Dolmetsch gradually expanded and consolidated his activities in Haslemere, Surrey, founding an annual music festival in 1925. The first Haslemere Festival constituted a major event in the Early Music revival, and although the recorder initially played a small role compared with that of the viols, for example, its appearance was a landmark in the instrument's return to public attention. On 4 September 1925, Dolmetsch's oldest son Rudolph (1906–42) and Miles Tomalin (1903–83) played the solo recorder parts in a performance of the Concerto in F major for harpsichord, two alto recorders, and strings, BWV 1057, by Bach, using two instruments from the Dolmetsch workshop. For the first time in the modern revival a masterpiece from the recorder's original repertoire had been performed on newly constructed instruments before an international audience.[28]

At the second Haslemere Festival in 1926, Dolmetsch demonstrated that his family was now taking the recorder very seriously indeed, presenting a consort of recorders in f^0 (bass), c^1 (tenor), f^1 (alto), and c^2 (soprano), which could be ordered from his workshop. The opening concert, broadcast live on BBC radio, included a performance of Bach's Fourth Brandenburg Concerto, BWV 1049, using two Dolmetsch alto recorders in g^1 played by Rudolph and Carl.[29]

Despite this public exposure, and the respect Dolmetsch commanded within a literary and artistic elite, he was largely ignored by the British musical establishment of his time. Perhaps the irascible pioneer was destined to be an outsider: he retained his French nationality until 1931 and his French accent for life. His performances in period costumes, during which he spoke freely to his audience between pieces, were so untypical for the day that few practical musicians took them seriously. His sharp criticism of '*les musicologues*' (musicologists) inevitably estranged him from academic circles.[30] The pugnacious English music critic John F. Runciman (1866–1916) complained, as early as 1898, that in Germany Dolmetsch would 'long ere now have been appointed as a professor or lecturer in one of the big music schools'.[31] This remark was remarkably prescient of the next important stage in the revival of Early Music in general and the recorder in particular.

THE COLLEGIUM MUSICUM

In stark contrast to the British revival, music-making on historical instruments in Germany began at the very heart of the musical establishment, in the Musikhochschulen (practical music colleges) and universities. The Staatliche Akademische Hochschule für Musik in Berlin, for example, invited Wanda Landowska (1878–1959) to set up a harpsichord class as early as 1913; the cellist Christian Döbereiner (1874–1961) taught a course in historical instruments at the Königliche Akademie der Tonkunst in Munich in 1922; and Paul Grümmer (1879–1965), a member of the Busch Quartet, founded a viola da gamba class at the Staatliche Hochschule für Musik in Cologne in 1926. Each of these celebrated artists made profound concessions to contemporary performance practice, which, although they would have been anathema to Dolmetsch, undoubtedly helped to win acceptance for their cause.[32]

In university departments of musicology throughout the German-speaking world, the Collegium Musicum movement, initiated in 1908 by Hugo Riemann (1849–1919) in Leipzig, became an important part of scholarly and artistic life.

The list of directors of Collegia founded over the following two decades reads like an honour roll of German musicology, including Friedrich Blume, Werner Danckert, Wilibald Gurlitt, Curt Sachs, and Max Schneider. In several towns, the Collegium came to play a major role in the musical life of the wider community.[33] Initially, modern instruments were used for performances of the historical music being studied and published in scholarly editions by German musicologists. In the early 1920s, however, tentative moves towards historical performance practice within the Orgelbewegung, the German Organ Reform Movement, although evidently lacking the insight and focus of Dolmetsch's work, stimulated many a Collegium Musicum to reconsider its instrumentarium.[34]

Of particular importance to the history of the recorder was the inspiring work of Riemann's student Gurlitt (1889–1963). Following his appointment to a lectureship at Freiburg University in 1919, he founded a Collegium Musicum with the intention of performing a far greater variety of Early Music than the German Baroque masters favoured by Riemann, on appropriate historical instruments.[35] To this end he commissioned a 'Praetorius organ', loosely based on information in Michael Praetorius's treatise *Syntagma musicum* (1619), from the workshop of Oscar Walcker in Ludwigsburg. This instrument, delivered in 1921, caused excitement far beyond its home town and inspired a wealth of legends, imitations, and newly invented traditions.[36] At about the same time, Gurlitt borrowed the celebrated Kynseker recorders from Nuremberg and commissioned Walcker to copy five instruments, which were played from 1922 onwards in the Freiburg Collegium's concerts.[37]

Gurlitt's example was swiftly followed by Werner Danckert (1900–70), who in 1922 commissioned the Nuremberg woodwind maker Georg Graessel to make a consort based on the Kynseker recorders for the newly founded musicological seminar at the University of Erlangen. Four of these, a great bass in c^0, a bass in g^0, and two altos in g^1, are preserved in the museum of the Institut für Musikwissenschaft in Erlangen.[38] Graessel's recorders then served as models for a further set ordered by Danckert from Max Hüller, director of the Kruspe factory in Erfurt, known for its clarinets and flutes.[39] Both the Graessel and Hüller consorts were used regularly for concerts of music from the Middle Ages and Renaissance. In 1925–26, Hüller also made copies of Baroque recorders by Jacob Denner and Johann Heitz.[40] Danckert founded a recorder quartet with musicology students after his appointment at Jena University in 1926, and initiated a collection of instruments and a concert series in the city in 1933.[41]

The experience of playing and hearing the recorder consort in Gurlitt's Freiburg Collegium inspired many pioneers of the German recorder revival, among them the colourful musical all-rounder, businessman, and visionary Peter Harlan (1898–1966), virtuoso performers such as Gustav Scheck (1901–84), and outstanding pedagogues such as Erich Katz (1900–73). Each of these remarkable men was to have a profound influence on the recorder's history.

PETER HARLAN

If Dolmetsch and Gurlitt were the primary instigators of the recorder revival, Peter Harlan was its first flamboyant impresario, born into a prominent Berlin literary and artistic family – his father Walter was a successful playwright, and his younger brother Veit (1899–1964) later achieved international notoriety as the director of the anti-Semitic film *Jud Süß* (1940). Harlan's grandson remembers him as a 'free spirit' and bon vivant who 'exercised an irresistible, hypnotic effect on others'.[42] His ebullient personality was intrinsic to his success as a businessman,

28. Peter Harlan (ca. 1960).

and helps to explain the many contradictory and sometimes misleading accounts of his life and work, originating from himself or others. Detail interested Harlan less than the big idea, and his frequent embellishments of the truth were evidently infectious.

Although untangling his career awaits further research,[43] the broad pattern has been established. At the age of 10, he joined the Wandervogel, an ideal environment in which to develop his strongly independent opinions. In 1915, Harlan's father apprenticed him for three years to Ernst Kunze, master guitar maker in Markneukirchen (Vogtland), at that time the most important centre of musical instrument making in Germany. His training was interrupted by military service in the First World War, following which he left his apprenticeship, preferring to work for another Markneukirchen craftsman, Oskar Zimmer. In 1920, Harlan's father contributed 15,000 Marks registered capital to his son's first business enterprise, supplying 'Wandervogel and other friends of music' with instruments and sheet music.[44] This sum was equivalent to approximately US$150 in February 1920; a conservative estimate of the current (2021) earnings equivalent might fall in the range US$7,500–11,500.[45]

'Organic' music: The Wandervogel and the Jugendmusikbewegung

Officially founded in Berlin in 1901, the Wandervogel ('wandering bird') movement provided adolescent boys opportunities to visit the countryside, combining the attractions of independence from adult supervision and the camaraderie associated with physical exercise, camping, folk music, and dance. Initially largely attracting middle- and upper-class boys, it had expanded by 1913 into a national association with 25,000 members of mixed gender and social background. After the First World War, in which many leaders of the movement died, the divisions within the Wandervogel reflected those within the German Jugendbewegung (Youth Movement) and German society as a whole: in 1922 the national association broke up into a plethora of local groups, ranging from socialist associations to those with a nationalistic, proto-fascist ideology. Despite these divisions, the Wandervogel retained common romantic ideals (escape from the city to an idealized and romanticized nature; togetherness in the great outdoors), ethical values (abstinence from alcohol and nicotine), and a critical stance towards official institutions such as schools. Its fundamentally anti-authoritarian principles did not, of course, survive the movement's forced integration into the Hitler Youth after 1933.

The musical practice of the Wandervogel was typical of the wider Jugendmusikbewegung, which revolutionized musical activity in Germany and beyond in the first half of the twentieth century. Passive consumption of high culture was criticised, active music-making encouraged. The 'decadent' traditions of the orchestra, opera house, or theatre; the technology and commercialization of the nascent sound recording and film industries; the strict training towards virtuosity offered by the colleges of art and music – all were rejected in favour of such songs and dances as could easily be produced within an untrained group. The recorder was revived too late and was then initially too expensive to be used by the Wandervogel, whose musical instruments were the guitar, referred to with typical irreverence as the *Zupfgeige* ('plucked violin'), and the 'lute', a guitar with a bulbous belly. Once the recorder finally arrived, however, it fit the Youth Music Movement's requirements: 'on the one hand, for an amateur "community music culture" in which a very large number of people should participate, one need[ed] simple, easily playable, instruments as cheap as possible. On the other hand, one sought alternatives to the instruments of bourgeois concerts.'[46]

The recorder, hitherto unknown, or seen as a 'historical instrument', was thus reinvented as a *Volksinstrument* ('folk', or 'people's instrument'). In the terminology of the Youth Music Movement it was perceived as being ideally 'organic': unencumbered by traditions of repertoire or performance practice and by connections to professional concert life. Apparently simple, easy to play, and hand-made, the recorder was seen as the antithesis to, say, a Steinway piano (obviously complicated, hard to play, manufactured with advanced technology, and therefore not 'organic').[47] The consequences of this definition for the physical instrument, its repertoire, and performance practice were to be profound and long-lasting.

In 1921, Harlan founded another firm, this time bearing his own name, employing master craftsman Max Fischer to direct the six to eight instrument makers in his workshop.[48] Meanwhile, he continued his education on his own terms, attending Gurlitt's seminar in Freiburg, where he probably first encountered the recorder in the Collegium Musicum in 1921–22. A further important experience was his journey to England in 1925 to visit the first Haslemere Festival in the company of the musicologist Max Seiffert (1868–1948).[49] Because Harlan was later to describe Walcker's Kynseker copies in Freiburg as 'unusable', it may well have been the experience of hearing the Dolmetsch ensemble's performance of the Bach Concerto, BWV 1057, that inspired him to have his first recorder made in Markneukirchen.[50]

Accounts differ as to exactly when the first 'Harlan' recorder was made. Harlan later claimed to have constructed one himself in 1921, but this is certainly false. At some time between 1922 and 1926, he borrowed a Baroque alto from the collection of the Staatliche Musikinstrumentensammlung in Berlin and commissioned a copy from the woodwind maker Kurt Jacob (1896–1973).[51] Jacob's daughter, writing shortly after the end of the Second World War, stated that her father made his first instrument for Harlan in 1923, but some recent writers have dated this as late as 1926.[52] The earliest Harlan–Jacob instruments display the typical features of a late Baroque design: elegant wood turning, inverse conical bore for the body, and significantly, as will be seen, hole placements requiring the historical forked fingering for bb[1].[53] The development work took nearly a year. Harlan's son Klaus later quoted his mother as saying that Jacob's extended weekly visits included discussions which 'were often terrible, and they both often nearly despaired. They [wished] they could have cut the recorder up and put it back together again.'[54]

Although the challenges faced by Harlan and Jacob ostensibly resembled those overcome by Dolmetsch some six years earlier, there were important differences of intent and methodology. Dolmetsch always understood his craftsmanship to be in the service of the (Early) music he was playing. His modernisation of the harpsichord, for example, was relatively modest compared with the radical transformations carried out by many of his peers.[55] The design of Dolmetsch recorders did subsequently emerge as distinct from historical models, largely due to the innovations of his son Carl, who was put in charge of the recorder workshop in 1926. As his repertoire expanded after 1939 to include contemporary works in which the recorder was combined with modern piano, other wind instruments, and strings, equal temperament and modern pitch became obligatory; he introduced modern standard 'English' fingering; straight-bored finger-holes with little or no undercutting; and a voicing characterized by a wide, straight windway, large chamfers, and a broad labium with strongly outward-facing side walls. Nonetheless, despite his many contributions to what he called the recorder's 'evolution' – including a range of patented gadgets such as thumb rests, bell keys, echo keys, and tone projectors, all intended to increase the instrument's expressive range or ease of playing – Carl remained convinced that 'the recorder itself remains *basically unchanged . . .*'.[56]

Unlike Arnold Dolmetsch, Harlan was clearly motivated from the outset by his desire to produce commercially viable recorders for public sale: when commercial production of alto recorders – in the workshop of Martin Kehr (1884–1960) in Zwota near Markneukirchen – commenced in summer 1926, he had already secured approximately 100 orders, equivalent to two years' production in the Dolmetsch workshop.[57] Harlan felt he had discovered in the recorder an ideally 'organic' musical instrument for the German Youth Music Movement, a vision enabled by his 'instrument maker's desire to make up stories'. The unwieldy German word he coined to describe this, *Instrumentenbauerfabulierbedürfnis*, displays the rough humour of the Wandervogel and was in no way intended as self-deprecating.[58] Driven by a creative urge unbound by Dolmetsch's concern to serve the music of a bygone age, he evidently regarded 'making up stories' as part of his contribution to the lively contemporary musical culture that he and many others in the Youth Music Movement envisaged. Seen in this light, it is not surprising that Harlan quickly abandoned any attempt to produce recorders based on historical models. Within a year of the first commercially available Harlan–Jacob alto recorders, he introduced a set of four instruments made to an entirely new design. Their wide bore gave them a mellower sound and rather stronger low notes than the narrow Baroque bore adopted by Dolmetsch. In the words of one present-day commentator: 'the intended sound, the bore and fingering differ so greatly from the historical models that, from today's perspective, one must speak of a new creation'.[59]

Harlan never made a recorder himself but marketed instruments made under his brand name, initially by Jacob, later mainly in the workshop of Kehr. This remained a fundamental difference between German and English recorder making until after the Second World War: the recorders sold by Harlan's competitors – for example, the publishing houses of Bärenreiter (Kassel) and Moeck (Celle) – were also branded products made mainly by workshops in Markneukirchen or nearby villages in the Vogtland.

HARLAN'S LEGACY I: 'ENGLISH' AND 'GERMAN' FINGERING

Harlan's most notorious contribution to the recorder's modern history was undoubtedly 'German' fingering. The majority of recorders made before the twentieth century require the forked fingering 0 123 4 6 for the fourth diatonic step (b♭^{1} for the alto). Carl Dolmetsch's 'English' system modified this only slightly to

0 123 4 67. The exact circumstances under which Harlan introduced the simplified fingering 0 123 4 are obscured, like so many details of his career, by contradictory accounts. Hunt's claim that the 'German' system stemmed from Harlan's ignorance of historical recorder fingerings is almost certainly incorrect.[60] Not only were the first Harlan–Jacob recorders evidently designed to be played with historical fingerings, but Harlan enclosed a copy of a fingering chart from Ganassi's *Fontegara* (1535) with the first instruments he sold in 1926, adding that his recorders were 'easy to play, almost completely chromatically, with the help of cross-fingerings'.[61] After the Second World War, Harlan took pains to distance himself from the 'new' system, claiming it was the result of a mistake by a novice recorder tuner in his workshop. His further explanation seems perhaps too over-eager to be entirely true: '[people] simply didn't want the forked fingering, although really from the very start I always pointed out that it was correct'.[62]

The most immediately obvious weakness of 'German' fingering is the increased difficulty of playing the sharpened fourth degree of the scale in tune (b^1 and especially b^2 for the alto) – essential for any music straying outside the diatonic scale of the recorder's home key. This note, easily produced on all instruments derived from historical models using some variation on the basic forked fingering 0 123 56 for b^1, is usually too high in the 'German' system, requiring the partial shading of hole 4 to bring it down to pitch. Many comparatively simple works in the recorder's original Baroque repertoire, let alone any with chromatic figures, are thus harder to play in tune. The apparent absurdity of introducing a simplified fingering for IV that renders IV♯ more difficult can be perhaps best understood in the context of the notion of the recorder as an 'organic' musical instrument, whose simplicity and restrictions were its essential assets. For the majority of Harlan's customers, chromatic notes were probably irrelevant. A leading protagonist of the Youth Music Movement, Wilhelm Twittenhoff (1904–69), wrote in 1937: 'Since chromaticism is not appropriate for the recorder, one should not . . . try to prove the opposite, but just see in this the pleasant opportunity to [cultivate] simple diatonicism, which today is generally starting to replace exaggerated chromaticism.'[63]

Although the quality of the best recorders made with 'German' fingering improved during the 1930s,[64] those German players who had the opportunity to try a Dolmetsch instrument generally acknowledged its superiority. For example, Manfred Ruëtz (1907–44), at the start of his short career as Germany's leading recorder virtuoso, published a series of frank consumer reports in the early 1930s in which he consistently found Dolmetsch recorders to be the best available.[65] Ruëtz stopped short

29. Gofferje–Merzdorf alto recorder in f¹ by König (Zwota, after 1932), maple, one key, German fingering.

of directly criticising 'German' fingering, but in response to readers' queries, he twice addressed the difficulty of playing IV♯ and IV♯´ in tune, giving hints for the partial venting/shading of finger-holes that clearly reflected his own practical experience as a player and teacher.[66]

The first instruments with 'German' fingering that Ruëtz considered worthy of direct comparison to Dolmetsch's recorders were designed by Karl Gofferje (1893–1966), a dentist who turned his hand to music and played an important role in the German recorder movement for several years. The instruments bearing his name were made in the workshop of Max König & Söhne in Zwota and marketed by the firm of Walter Merzdorf (1896–1975) from 1932.[67] Ruëtz explained that: 'Gofferje . . . did not stick slavishly to ancient models, but went new ways, principally out of pedagogical considerations, in order to produce a flawless yet cheap instrument. Material (maple), external form, bore [design], cut-up, labium, and windway – and therefore *last not least* [sic: in English] the tone character – show the deliberate deviation from museum instruments.' Summing up, Ruëtz noted:

The Dolmetsch recorders are almost unaffordable for us in Germany, but the price is justified in view of the precision of every last detail of their construction. The purity of intonation of every instrument within itself as well as the perfect tuning within a consort, the ease of playing into the highest registers with a quite balanced strength of tone, and finally the faultless workmanship satisfy every legitimate demand. It is clear that such precision work cannot be offered for the price of a sandwich.[68]

The first instruments to be manufactured in Germany with 'English' fingering, made by König and marketed by the Markneukirchen firm of Wilhelm Herwig under the Herwiga Rex brand from 1934, were initially developed for export to England (at the instigation of Hunt).[69] In Germany they sold at nearly three times the price of the Gofferje recorders, naturally attracting the attention of Ruëtz. His report praised their tuning and tonal balance between registers, but found tone quality and ease of playing no better than those of cheaper German instruments. Observing that Dolmetsch's design was not protected by a German patent, Ruëtz listed features that had evidently been directly copied from Dolmetsch: the bore design (but not the exterior form) and the shape of the windway, block, and labium. He concluded with a sharply critical analysis of the division of labour in Germany: 'The Dolmetsch recorders have character: they demand great mastery from the player if they are to sound good, but offer him in return the necessary prerequisites. These will, however, never materialise unless the instrument maker is at once a craftsman and an excellent player; that is the secret of the Dolmetsches and all great instrument makers and, besides the compulsion to keep prices low, the reason the hitherto so unsatisfactory results in German recorder-making.'[70] Harlan offered his customers the option of forked fingering for IV in the same year with his *Barock* model, which Ruëtz damned with faint praise.[71] Other familiar brands followed suit, including Bärenreiter, whose *Meisterflöte* was designed by Ruëtz himself around 1935,[72] and by the end of the decade, Moeck[73] and Merzdorf.[74]

'German' fingering remained the accepted standard system for recorders in central Europe until well after the end of the Second World War. It is still common at the time of writing among cheaper instruments, especially those imported from East Asia. An indication of continued demand is that Moeck's *Schulflöte* (school recorder), advertised in their 2003 catalogue as offering 'the serious entry into the world of music', is still available at the time of writing in a version with 'German' fingering.[75]

HARLAN'S LEGACY II: TUNING CONFUSIONS

The prevailing standard pitch in France and Germany between the wars was the *diapason normal* of $a^1 = 435$ Hz (A 435); in Britain it was generally slightly higher at A 440. In the 1890s, however, Arnold Dolmetsch had chosen A 415 (approximately an equal-tempered semitone lower than A 440) for his recitals. He maintained this pitch in his workshop and at the Haslemere Festival until 1937, when Carl Dolmetsch took over as director and initiated the use of A 440.[76] The pitch of most Dolmetsch recorders made before this time was, therefore, A 415. Although the first alto recorders produced by both Dolmetsch and Harlan sounded at nearly the same pitch, Dolmetsch referred to his as being in f^1 (at A 415) and Harlan to his as being in e^1 (at A 435). It has been suggested that Harlan was unaware that the instrument from the Berlin collection he took as a model for his recorders had been made at a lower pitch. Given his typical lack of concern for accuracy of historical detail and his background as a guitar maker, perhaps he simply regarded E major as a natural home key for a musical instrument.[77]

Harlan's designation of the principal member of the recorder family as an 'alto in E' was to cause much confusion in Germany over the following decade. In addition to intractable problems of notation and transposition, recorder players wishing to play together were often frustrated by the simultaneous availability of no fewer than three sets of instruments made in mutually incompatible sizes. In chronological order of development, these were:

(1) The consort presented by Dolmetsch at the 1926 Haslemere Festival, consisting of instruments in f^0 (bass)–c^1 (tenor)–f^1 (alto)–c^2 (soprano), pitched at A 415.

(2) A set of recorders sold under the Harlan brand name from 1927, consisting of instruments in e^0 (bass)–a (tenor)–e^1 (alto)–a^1 (soprano), pitched at A 435.[78] Having invented the alto recorder in e^1, it was only natural to pitch the bass an octave lower (in e^0 at A 435, roughly equivalent to Dolmetsch's bass in f^0 at A 415). Harlan's introduction of tenor and soprano instruments in a and a^1, however, altered the historical interval of a fifth between the bass and tenor to a fourth, causing widespread confusion. Perhaps he drew on his guitar maker's intuition to invent the tenor in a, the pitch of the guitar's second string. Indeed, one of his early customers recalled that Harlan explained his system 'offered favourable opportunities for playing together with lutes and gambas'.[79]

(3) A quartet in d^0 (bass)–a^0 (tenor)–d^1 (alto)–a^1 (soprano) at A 435, sold, for example, under the Bärenreiter brand name from 1930.[80] This set had the advantage of restoring the interval of a fifth between the bass and tenor, but further compounded Harlan's initial error by taking his instruments in a^0 and a^1 as the starting point for the ensemble.

It is worth noting in this context that the less common sizes of recorder made in the Dolmetsch workshop in Haslemere at the time were historically justifiable and expressly designed to enable the performance of specific compositions.[81] The plethora of recorder sizes manufactured in Germany, however, originated solely as a consequence of Harlan's invention of the alto in e^1.

By 1933, Harlan offered the following instruments for sale: d^0, e^0, f^0 (bass), a^0, c^1 (tenor), d^1, e^1, f^1 (alto), a^1 and c^2 (soprano) at A 435, and *Barockflöten* in f^0, c^1, f^1, and c^2 at A 415.[82] Other manufacturers offered their own selection, including some not available from Harlan, such as altos in g^1, sopranos in d^2, and sopraninos in g^2. It was evidently confusing for the novice to be confronted with such a wide choice of recorders, and frustrating to discover that your instruments were incompatible with others in an ensemble. The movement's leading authorities, however, not only failed to agree on which tuning system to recommend, they were evidently led by commercial interests. From its inception in 1931, for example, writers in Moeck's journal *Der Blockflötenspiegel* (*BS*) advocated instruments in F and C. Nonetheless, Moeck continued to offer every size of recorder that might find a buyer: thus an advertising brochure from 1932 pragmatically offered instruments in d^0, f^0, a^0, c^1, d^1, f^1, g^1, a^1, c^2, d^2, and g^2, as well as in e^0, g^0, e^1, and b^1 by special order.[83] As Gofferje, himself an advocate of the D–A consort, joked in 1931: 'You'd need to have [all] the various "necessary" recorders carried behind you in a bag, like a golfer!'[84] More practically, champions of the alto in e^1, such as Waldemar Woehl, advocated *Griffschrift*, or transposing notation, in which a notated C always represented the bottom note of a given recorder.[85]

A survey of German recorder teachers published by the magazine *Collegium Musicum* in 1932 showed a clear majority in favour of a standardized F–C consort, whether at A 435 or the lower pitch of A 415, at which the f^1 altos, above all, were described as sounding better.[86] The D–A consort was recommended only for accompanying singers, playing simple tunes in at most two parts, and youth groups. It would, however, be wrong to attribute the persistence of recorders in D and A solely to ignorance or commercial exploitation. The sound and playing characteristics of the D–A and the F–C sets displayed clear differences in character. Harlan wrote in 1933 that the former sounded mellower and the latter brighter, comparing the difference to that between a viola and a violin.[87] Quite apart from the vested interests of manufacturers and publishers, some important works written specifically for recorders in D and A, notably Helmut Bornefeld's suites (1930) and Paul Hindemith's Trio for the *Plöner Musiktag* (1932), helped to maintain awareness of the special qualities of these instruments.

In 1937, Manfred Ruëtz wrote that recorders in F and C had become much more common than those in D and A, citing the instrumentation of most original recorder music and the relative ease of playing together with other instruments, but also noting the clearer and more penetrating sound of F–C instruments, which he described as 'more up to date' and appropriate for playing in large rooms. Nonetheless, he added: 'it is beyond doubt that a quartet of A and D recorders sounds much more unified and rounder than a C–F quartet. Whenever the same piece is played in turn on recorders [made in the two different tuning systems] for a larger circle of listeners, this has always resulted in a unanimous preference for the D–A quartet.'[88] The intractability of this question and the sheer degree of confusion it caused are indicated by the fact that the Nazi educational authorities attempted to settle it by decree in 1937. An order initially circulated to Hitler Youth leaders and later summarized in the journal *Musik in Jugend und Volk* stipulated that the F–C tuning would henceforth be used in both general music-making and schools, supplemented by the D–A tuning, 'if at all . . . in chamber music'.[89] The D–A consort, despite its positive tonal qualities, had evidently come to be seen as an unnecessary complication. After the end of the Second World War, recorders in F and C were internationally accepted as standard. Indeed, the original version of Hindemith's Trio was replaced by its publishers in 1952 with a transposed edition for soprano recorder in c^2 and two alto recorders in f^1.[90]

HARLAN'S LEGACY III: THE *VOLKSBLOCKFLÖTE*

Peter Harlan assiduously promoted the recorders sold under his name in the late 1920s, providing many later enthusiasts with their first experience of the instrument. An audience member at one of his concerts in Hamburg wrote some three decades after the event: 'I can still remember clearly the impression that the recorder music left on us and our pupils. We bought recorders and tried them out in small groups. . . .'[91] Nevertheless, the recorder remained unfamiliar in Germany until the end of the decade. Dietz Degen (1910–89), for example, who played in an Early Music group as a student in Leipzig in the late 1920s, noted in his doctoral dissertation on the recorder (1939) that he had still not heard of the instrument in 1929.[92]

At the turn of the 1930s, however, several commentators described the 'outbreak' of a 'recorder epidemic',[93] in which 'recorders popped up in so many music circles, school classes, and indeed families, as if they had been awakened all of a sudden from their centuries-long sleep by a mysterious call'.[94] In 1931,

Gofferje wrote about 'the great fashion' for the instrument: 'it does not seem as if a wave is ebbing away; on the contrary, one feels apprehensive, because the flood is still rising'. Sharply critical both of the gullibility of those who, 'led astray by untrue claims, believe the recorder is a kind of toy, which can be learned in a week', and of the cynicism of craftsmen who 'do not know how the instrument is played or how it must sound', Gofferje wished the recorder 'the good fortune to find instrument makers who don't make it [just] because they sense a commercial boom, because it is "in demand".'[95]

In 1932, the lutenist Hans Neeman (1901–43) wrote of the 'Recorder Circus': 'the fashion for the recorder has reached dimensions of which Arnold Dolmetsch . . . could surely not have dreamed'.[96] Warning of the increasingly obvious nationalistic political tendencies of the *Führer* (leaders) of the Youth Music Movement,[97] Neeman described the extent to which the recorder itself and those who sought to play it were being exploited:

> Nearly monopolistic traders deliver the instruments, government authorities give their support, and now methods and editions of mostly unsuitable music for recorder . . . appear. There has to be a recorder magazine (!), and other like-minded periodicals set up recorder corners, instrument agencies, and advice centres. Courses and lectures . . . conferences and meetings . . . are set up so that the pious flock will follow its false prophets. Promotional concerts and radio programmes with recorders do the rest.
>
> By no means are . . . old original works given preference and a correspondingly perfect presentation. Rather, one somehow 'arranges' [everything] possible and impossible. The undiscriminating followers generally notice too late that this is an artificially promoted fashion and that the *serious* mastery of the keyless recorder, which is supposed to be 'so easy' to play 'after a few minutes', is harder than that of the modern flute.[98]

The 'hothouse atmosphere'[99] in which the recorder boom flourished was the product of several complementary factors. As we have seen, the recorder appealed both to antiquarians in search of the past and revolutionaries seeking to distance themselves from it. In particular, it appeared to be an ideal instrument for the German Youth Music Movement. Ideology aside, inflation and unemployment had cut off large parts of the German population from participation in cultural life. To many people, young and old, the recorder seemed to offer a cheap and easy

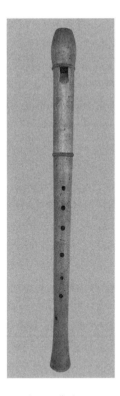

30. Peter Harlan 'Volksflöte' (alto recorder in f¹) by Martin Kehr (Zwota, after 1933), maple, German fingering.

ticket back to musical and social experience. A further boost was provided by the comprehensive reforms of music education initiated in the mid-1920s by the Prussian Ministry of Education under the guidance of Leo Kestenberg (1882– 1962), which included the extension of school music teaching to include instrumental tuition.[100] Last but not least, the musical instrument-making industry, already weakened by the general economic depression and the destruction of middle-class savings, and hit again by the international economic crisis of 1929, had enormous idle capacity.[101]

Harlan, with his acute sense for marketing, called the cheapest instrument in his catalogue a *Volksblockflöte* or *Volksflöte*, 'people's recorder'.[102] The idea of making a previously unaffordable luxury item widely available was in the air: the most familiar example today being the *Volkswagen* ('people's car').[103] Adolf Hitler first called for the German automobile industry to develop a *Volkswagen* on 11 February 1933, in the second week of his rule. Despite opposition from within the industry, the engineer Ferdinand Porsche presented the first prototype of the Beetle at the Berlin Automobile Exhibition in 1934. Although the comparison between the obviously expensive and complicated new technology of personal transportation and the apparently cheap and straightforwardly familiar recorder may seem far-fetched today, it withstands closer examination.

Hitler envisaged an economical car costing less than RM 1,000. From 1937 it was possible to buy savings stamps towards the advertised price of RM 990 in the denomination of RM 5, bringing the dream – if not the reality – of a *Volkswagen* within reach of almost everyone. In 1932, a Dolmetsch alto recorder cost RM 110–120 and a soprano approximately RM 80 in Germany, making them prohibitively expensive.[104] Even the best domestic instruments were much cheaper. Harlan, in common with other manufacturers, offered instruments in three price categories. His first '*Blockflöten (flauto dolce)*' in the summer of 1927 cost RM 20,[105] a price-level that was roughly maintained for most brands of mid-range alto recorders over the following two decades.[106] By 1936, Harlan also offered more expensive models, a *Luxusflöte* ('luxury recorder') for RM 40, and a *Bachflöte*, advertised as being played by Scheck, for RM 35.[107] The most expensive German recorders in regular production at this time were the Herwiga Rex recorders (with 'English' fingering); an alto cost RM 45.[108] Harlan's *Volksblockflöte* was much cheaper: an alto cost RM 11, and a soprano RM 4.80,[109] almost exactly the same price as a thrift stamp for a *Volkswagen*. Even less expensive instruments were available from Merzdorf,[110] Bärenreiter,[111] and Herwig.[112] The cheapest branded recorders were probably those of Johannes Adler, which cost as little as RM 2.80 and were advertised as guaranteeing that 'children's bright eyes will thank you'.[113]

Even allowing for the profound differences between the division of labour practised in Germany and the artisanal craftsmanship in Haslemere, the sheer volume of recorders produced in the Vogtland was remarkable. The Dolmetsch workshop, the only commercially significant manufacturer in England before the Second World War, made fewer than 1,800 recorders in its first quarter-century of production, from 1919 until 1945.[114] By way of comparison, Hermann Moeck Sr (1896–1982), one of perhaps two dozen businessmen selling German-made instruments in the domestic and export markets at the time, estimated that 150,000 recorders had 'gone through his hands' by 1941.[115] Substantial numbers of instruments were sold at all price levels. Merzdorf, for example, advertised in summer 1935 that he had sold 8,800 relatively expensive 'Gofferje' recorders in the previous two-and-a-half years, and 'several thousand *Chorflöten* within a few months'.[116] It is worth noting that both Moeck and Merzdorf belonged to the more quality-conscious brands: in a 1934 consumer report comparing thirteen different soprano recorders, Ruëtz remarked that many others that failed to meet his basic quality criteria had been excluded from the survey, including a large number of instruments without a manufacturer's stamp.[117] Such inferior recorders were widely available in department stores and by mail order for prices as low as RM 2.40.[118] Total annual production in Germany must have exceeded a million recorders by the late 1930s.

The market for self-instruction books and sheet music was proportionately substantial and lucrative. Nagel advertised having sold 11,000 copies of Waldemar Woehl's recorder method, 'which is also suitable for teaching oneself, and is therefore the *best* recorder method', in the two years preceding March 1932, at RM 3 a copy. The number of 'instructions for the school recorder' (mentioned in the same advertisement as being 'sufficient for children') sold at RM 0.60 was not disclosed.[119] From the mid-1930s the number of publications of all kinds for recorder increased sharply, including historical and modern repertoire in excellent practical editions, some of which can still be found in the catalogues of Bärenreiter, Moeck, and Schott today, but also vast quantities of ephemeral or meretricious *Spielmusik*, or 'recreational music'.

The early career of Hermann Moeck Sr shows what could be achieved in this expanding market with hard work, good products, and astute marketing. From a modest start in 1930, he energetically developed a profitable business selling branded recorders and publishing sheet music and methods, which he promoted in part through his (loss-leading) periodicals *Der Blockflötenspiegel* (1931–34) and *Zeitschrift für Spielmusik* (*ZfS*; 1932–2006).[120] His commercial success is documented in his application to the British occupying authorities in December 1945 for a licence to resume business after the war, in which he declared his increasingly substantial personal income over the previous decade, peaking at over RM 23,000 in 1940. Moeck registered his firm's capital at the end of the war as RM 100,000, and reported his intent to employ twenty-four persons at a total weekly payroll of RM 1,000: a realistic ambition in light of his continued success after the war.[121]

THE RECORDER IN BRITAIN DURING THE 1930S

The contrast between the German recorder boom of the 1930s and the nascent British scene could hardly have been more extreme. Those developing an interest in the recorder in Britain had in Haslemere a single authoritative source for tuition, fine instruments, and artistic inspiration, and were thus protected from the pitch confusions, fingering uncertainties, and personal rivalries of the German scene. As noted, however, Dolmetsch recorders were made in small quantities and expensive: 5 guineas for a soprano and 6 guineas for an alto. Many people who might have wished to start playing the recorder could not obtain an instrument, even if they could have afforded one.[122] The instrument remained largely unfamiliar within British professional and amateur musical life, in education, and in the music trade. As late as February 1939, *The Recorder News* reported that 'the recorder was entirely unknown' to most of the audience at a concert in central London.[123]

Wider popularisation of the recorder in England was initiated by Edgar Hunt (1909–2006), who first heard about the instrument in 1927 from Bridge, his Director of Studies at Trinity College of Music, London.[124] Hunt obtained Welch's *Six Lectures* in the same year and finally heard recorders being played by a visiting German group in Bristol in 1928. In 1930 he attended the Haslemere Festival and bought an alto recorder made by Oskar Dawson, a former Dolmetsch employee, to play on the genteel semi-professional fringe of English musical life. At the Bristol Madrigal Society's 'Ladies Night' in 1931, one member of the audience was so impressed that he lent (and later gave) Hunt four original eighteenth-century recorders 'which had been in his Yorkshire family for many years and he had never heard played', including a particularly fine Bressan alto in f', now part of the Bate Collection in Oxford.[125]

Hunt was invited to play the traverso in the 1931 Haslemere Festival, on which occasion he first met Carl Dolmetsch and was 'very impressed by his craftsmanship' in the recorder workshop,[126] but he was never a Dolmetsch insider. Well aware that there was much to learn about the instrument outside Haslemere, he ordered an alto recorder from Bärenreiter in Kassel (with 'German' fingering) and studied both *Directions for Playing on the Flute* (1731) and Robert Götz's *Schule des Blockflötenspiels* (1930). Noting the lack of a contemporary tutor for the instrument in English, Hunt wrote *A Practical Method for the Recorder*, the manuscript of which he submitted to Oxford University Press in 1931. The ensuing dispute illustrates both the Dolmetsch family's unique position of authority at the time, and its tendency to regard with suspicion anyone holding ideas that did not conform to what Hunt memorably described as the 'Use of Haslemere'.[127] Hunt's editor at OUP showed his work to Arnold Dolmetsch, whereupon there was 'a huge explosion', the patriarch insisting that it could only be published after revision by the musicologist Robert Donington (1907–90), then secretary of the Dolmetsch Foundation. The resulting book, which Hunt no longer felt conveyed 'the sort of things that I had originally hoped', finally appeared in 1935.[128] In the meantime, annoyed by the alterations he was obliged to make and 'fed up with waiting', he wrote *A Concise Tutor for Use in Schools*, which was published in the same year by the rival firm of Boosey & Hawkes.[129]

The title of Hunt's second recorder method indicates one of his major preoccupations at this stage: the future role of the recorder in Britain in light of its enormous popularity in Germany. Having become aware of the success of the *Volksblockflöte*, he 'was determined . . . to make similar instruments available in England but with English fingering'.[130] Given Arnold Dolmetsch's negative reaction to his *Practical Method*, it was clear that Hunt could expect little help or sympathy for this project in Haslemere: he went instead to Germany, visiting the Kasseler Musiktage in 1934, where he heard Scheck perform and met many of the leading German recorder manufacturers. Furthermore, he persuaded Wilhelm Herwig to start producing recorders with 'English fingering' and secured the sole agency for Britain. The fine Herwiga Rex instruments have been mentioned earlier in the context of the German market. In Britain the cheaper Herwiga Solist and Herwiga Chor models were perhaps more important, as they were the first truly inexpensive recorders available. Shortly afterwards, Hunt passed his agency on to the Liverpool firm of Rushworth and Dreaper, who had the expertise and financial resources to import large quantities of instruments, including the English-fingered answer to the *Volksblockflöte*, the Herwiga Hamlin, which sold for four shillings and sixpence, less than 5 per cent of the price of a Dolmetsch soprano recorder.[131]

In the mid-1930s, Hunt's work came to the attention of Cyril Winn, His Majesty's Staff Inspector of Music at the Board of Education, who was responsible for overseeing music education at all publicly funded elementary schools in the country. Winn invited him to travel extensively, demonstrating the recorder in schools and at teacher-training courses. An important breakthrough was his July 1937 workshop for school teachers in Bradford, attended by Frederick Fowler and Edmund Priestley, whose *School Recorder Book*, first published in the same year and still in print at the time of writing, was to introduce millions of children to the soprano recorder.[132] Hunt's reputation as the leading authority on the instrument outside the Dolmetsch family was enhanced by his classes at Trinity College in London. Initially these were aimed at amateur musicians; in his inaugural winter term of 1935/36 he had no fewer than nineteen students, mainly in groups. Although a diploma-course syllabus was approved by the college authorities in 1939, the first examination was not to take place until after the end of the Second World War.[133] Perhaps most importantly, Hunt started working at the London office of the music publisher B. Schott's Söhne in 1936, where he secured the British Empire agencies for other German publishers of recorder music and worked to make the company's London showroom at 48 Great Marlborough Street (in the words of a later advertising slogan) 'The Centre for Recorder Players'.[134]

Meanwhile, Carl Dolmetsch gradually consolidated his position as his family's recorder specialist. From the mid-1930s he appeared independently of his brother Rudolph, who died in 1942. He played the *flauto* part in a recording of the Handel F-major sonata, HWV 369, for the encyclopaedic *Columbia History of Music by Eye and Ear*, and undertook the first of many extensive concert tours as a recorder virtuoso, notably in the USA in 1935 and 1936, playing Bach, Handel, and Telemann together with his former student Suzanne Bloch (1907–2002).[135] In February 1939, he gave the first of his solo recitals at the Wigmore Hall in London, which became an annual tradition after the Second World War.[136] Writing shortly after his father's death in 1940, Carl was able to look back on performances of music by 'Bach, Handel, Purcell, Telemann, Loeillet and many an Elizabethan' at Haslemere since the first festival in 1925.[137]

The foundation of the Society of Recorder Players (SRP) in 1937 brought Carl Dolmetsch and Edgar Hunt together as joint musical directors under the presidency of Arnold Dolmetsch. Their reconciliation was brokered by mutual friends, Max and Stephanie Champion; by all accounts it managed to avert the establishment of two rival societies. The extensive diplomacy this must have involved can be deduced from the four pre-war and wartime issues of the SRP's journal *The Recorder News*, in which the musical directors wrote separate editorials that clearly reflected their own priorities and interests – Dolmetsch emphasizing his concert life, Hunt his work in schools and with amateurs. An important point of agreement was, however, stated by Max Champion at the inaugural meeting on 7 October 1937: 'Instruments . . . made according to the German system could not properly be regarded as recorders by the Society owing to the bore and the placing of the holes; although this allowed for a greater ease of playing in certain keys, it did not allow for modulation, and it was not possible for all the literature of the recorder to be played on such instruments.' This meeting was attended by some seventy people, 'nearly all [of whom] were strangers to each other'. Within one year approximately two hundred SRP members were attending regular branch meetings across the country.[138] Early editions of *The Recorder News* give a vivid impression of the society's activities, especially of the 'combined' or 'massed' playing sessions in which all those present at a meeting took part (and which remain the principal form of musical activity within the SRP to the present day). The standard of playing must have been generally poor. Hunt's editorials criticised 'the amateurishness of many of [the recorder movement's] keenest supporters' and warned that 'musicians in general will not accept the recorder seriously until recorder players behave as normal musicians'. At the end of the decade, he complained that 'it is not enough that there should be a handful of reliable players; the movement needs hundreds'. Some thirty years later he reflected that 'at these early meetings . . . we spent most of the time getting in tune'.[139]

In 1938, one of Hunt's students, Manuel Jacobs (1910–93), wrote a substantial article for *The Musical Times* entitled 'The Recorders', clearly intended to introduce an unfamiliar instrument to an otherwise well-informed readership. Jacobs, who wrote under the pseudonym Terpander, was familiar to readers of *The Recorder News* as an ambitious amateur player who rehearsed weekly with his recorder trio and hoped 'one day to make some interesting gramophone discs'.[140] In his *Musical Times* article, he wrote of the SRP: 'There is no reason, should England follow the example of Germany, where the recorder flourishes exceedingly, why the Society should not come to count its members in the thousands rather than hundreds. . . .'[141] He also remarked: 'if the recorders are to establish themselves permanently in England as they have already done in Germany, and similarly enrich our musical life, modern composers must be made to realize their potentialities (if not their existence!) and to write regularly for them'. This was far from being an idle invocation. Jacobs was remarkably successful in approaching contemporary composers to write for the recorder, resulting in seven substantial works that have come to occupy a place in the instrument's standard repertoire. The most celebrated of these, the Sonatina, Op. 13, by Lennox Berkeley (1903–89), was given its first performance on 17 June 1939 by Carl Dolmetsch at a joint concert with Hunt at the London Contemporary Music Centre, in a programme that included three further works commissioned by Jacobs, the Hindemith trio, and a *Sinfonia* for three recorders by Jacobs himself.[142]

THE RECORDER IN NAZI GERMANY

PROFESSIONALS AND PROFITEERS

Following Hitler's rise to power in January 1933, the Nazi authorities moved rapidly to integrate previously diverse aspects of German economic, social, and cultural life into the 'total' state. Professional musicians were licensed and regulated in the *Reichsmusikkammer* (RMK), or Reich Music Chamber, which set wages, implemented procedures for professional certification, and brought musicians into the social security system. Only card-carrying RMK members were allowed to perform, teach, publish, or otherwise profit from music; even petty infringements were energetically prosecuted. For 'Aryan' musicians the grim economic conditions of the Weimar Republic gradually improved, not least owing to opportunities arising from the progressive exclusion of Jews from RMK membership.[143] By 1940 *The Times* of London cited a speech on German radio reporting a shortage of 'racially pure' musicians.[144]

Within this framework, the German recorder boom of the 1930s provided employment for a remarkable number of musicians, ranging from dedicated professionals to opportunists and profiteers. Scheck's ensemble, the Kammermusikkreis Scheck–Wenzinger, was so successful that it employed a secretary from 1937 until 1944 at a commission-based salary averaging RM 300 per month.[145] Scheck taught at the Berlin Musikhochschule from 1934,[146] and published a substantial chapter on the recorder in a book on woodwind instruments in the prestigious *Hohe Schule der Musik* series in 1938.[147] His student Dorothea ('Thea') Gräfin von Sparr (1915–88) found a secure basis for her other activities, including first performances of works by Johann Nepomuk David (1895–1977), by teaching at the Berlin Hochschule for church music.[148] Ruëtz toured extensively throughout Europe, notably with his highly dedicated Berlin Recorder Quartet,[149] taught at the Berlin Konservatorium, commissioned new music,[150] and published editions of standard works from the instrument's repertoire (several of which are still in print at the time of writing), essays, reviews, consumer reports, and a recorder method.[151] After his death on the Eastern Front in 1944, his status as 'the leading virtuoso recorder player of recent years' was confirmed by a special grant of RM 300 to his widow by Goebbels' *Künstlerdank* foundation.[152]

There is no evidence that Scheck, von Sparr, or Ruëtz profited from the hardship of others. Other recorder players, however, had fewer scruples. Ferdinand Enke (1903–82), another member of the Berlin Recorder Quartet, was particularly adept

31. Berlin Recorder Quartet, 1939: Manfred Ruëtz, Ferdinand Enke, Alfons Zimmermann, Erich Mönkemeyer.

at exploiting the commercial opportunities offered by the Nazi music bureaucracy. In doing so, he left a paper trail that reveals much about how the recorder fitted into the planned musical economy. Enke played concerts, made radio broadcasts, and taught at several Berlin musical institutions. He also acted as a consultant to *Kraft durch Freude* ('Strength through Joy': the most important Nazi cultural and tourism organization) and volunteered at the RMK in Berlin, ostensibly without payment, conducting the examinations for certifying recorder teachers. At the same time, however, he taught courses at the Berlin Arbeitsamt (Labour Exchange), retraining unemployed musicians of all kinds as recorder teachers, directed the Working Group of Berlin Recorder Teachers in the RMK,[153] and offered to supply the very teachers he was training and examining with students in exchange for a percentage of their fees. This created a lucrative conflict of interest. On 4 March 1938, for example, Enke was sent 531 draft contracts by the RMK, using which he was able to assign 101 small groups of students to his own students. A subsequent audit found that his commission for arranging this batch of contracts alone, at 10 per cent of all fees paid, amounted to a handsome RM 1,212 per year.[154]

Other recorder enthusiasts sought to advance their careers by belonging to notorious paramilitary organizations, or aiding and abetting the organized looting of countries under German occupation. Twittenhoff joined the brownshirts (SA) in 1933, taught recorder at the Weimar Musikhochschule in the new department of Hitler Youth music from 1937, and became its director in 1943.[155] Gofferje, who rose to the rank of *Oberscharführer* in the SS,[156] repeatedly claimed to have joined the Nazi Party as early as 1925, although his membership number, 2512347, identified him as having applied several months after Hitler had seized power in 1933. The rejection of his formal application for a lower party membership number in 1936 did not damage his career, however: he was appointed professor of music education at the teacher-training college in Frankfurt (Oder) in 1938.[157] Degen, whose *Zur Geschichte der Blockflöte in den germanischen Ländern* (1939) stands beside Welch's *Six Lectures* as a landmark in scholarly writing about the instrument,[158] was considered by his teachers to be 'politically reliable beyond question'.[159] On 18 February 1943, supervising Nazi plundering in occupied France, he reported the transport of fifty expropriated pianos to Germany.[160]

PERSECUTION AND EXILE

The principal line of division in Nazi Germany was race. 'Aryans' enjoyed privileges within the constraints of the 'total state'. 'Aryans' married to Jews were sanctioned, including Gurlitt, dismissed from his Chair in Freiburg in 1937. As a 'half-Jew', Alfred Mann (1917–2006) was allowed to teach at the Berlin Musikhochschule as late as 1937, before escaping via Italy to the United States in 1939. Jews faced systematic persecution. Cornelia Schröder-Auerbach (1900–97), who performed regularly with Peter Harlan until she was expelled from the RMK in 1934, first became fully aware of the personal danger she faced after being praised, tragicomically, as a 'gothic madonna with a recorder' in the Nazi Party newspaper *Völkischer Beobachter*. Despite being listed in the directories *The Jews and Music* (1938) and *Dictionary of Jews in Music* (1941), she survived in hiding.[161]

Erich Katz (1900–73) studied musicology in Berlin and Freiburg, where he encountered the recorder in the Collegium Musicum, became Gurlitt's assistant in 1924, and received his doctorate in 1926. Prodigiously active as a teacher, scholar, and practical musician until April 1933, he was dismissed from Freiburg University, denounced in the *Völkischer Beobachter* ('Dr. Erich Katz, Jude'), and fired as music correspondent of the local newspaper. Katz continued to publish under

32. Erich Katz teaching at New York Music College in the 1950s.

pseudonyms, and found work as organist at the Freiburg synagogue until it was burned down during the *Kristallnacht* pogrom in November 1938. Following several months in Dachau concentration camp he was able to leave for England in 1939, separated from his son and his (Protestant) first wife, but reunited with his daughter and his fiancé. The family immigrated to the United States in 1943 where, as we will see, he transformed the emerging recorder movement.[162]

Katz and Mann were by no means the only musicians fleeing from Nazi persecution who carried their knowledge of the recorder into the wider world. Among the many exiled Europeans who placed advertisements in the journal of the World Centre for Jewish Music in Palestine, *Musica Hebraica*, was one Werner Fries, who offered 'Lessons in FLUTE and RECORDER (Blockflöte)' in Jerusalem.[163] Perhaps the most profound impact of any German emigrant upon the development of the recorder after the Second World War, however, came from Walter Bergmann (1902–88), who had studied the flute at the Leipzig Conservatory in the early 1920s before training as a lawyer. He bravely continued to represent Jewish clients until his own Jewish ancestry and a scandal over his marital infidelity

33. Alfred Mann (recorder) and his wife Edith Weiss-Mann (harpsichord), New York, after 1939.

led to imprisonment in 1938 and exile in 1939. Bergmann reached England 'with ten marks and two suitcases, one filled with clothes, the other with music, including the Fantasias of Purcell, a recorder and a flute'.[164]

AMATEURS AND CHILDREN

Although the Nazi authorities ostensibly controlled amateur music-making, in practice the *Hausmusik* movement (and its many recorder players) remained relatively free of political interference. Amateur players met at weekend courses and summer camps such as those led by Gofferje, Ruëtz, and Woehl, finding spaces for private 'inner emigration' and discourse with others.[165] Supervision of children's education was much closer, however, and forced integration of the diverse German Youth Movements into the Hitler Youth ended the spontaneous, anti-authoritarian musical practice of groups such as the Wandervogel.

Carl Orff's *Olympische Reigen*, or Olympic round dances, written for the opening ceremony of the 1936 Berlin Olympic Games, provided a very public

34. Walter Bergmann (left) and Rudolf Barthel, Berlin, 1955.

demonstration of the propagandistic use of youth music in the 'Third Reich'. An orchestra of thirty children, half of whom played recorders, directed by Orff Schulwerk's primary originator, Gunild Keetman (1904–90), accompanied nearly 6,000 children dancing.[166] After the war, Orff claimed that he had accepted this commission on the assurance that the Olympics would permit 'no political accents',[167] an extraordinarily disingenuous statement given the comprehensive propagandistic exploitation of the games long before they started. Certainly, others were quick to understand the true ideological message. Twittenhoff, for example, described *Olympische Reigen* as a demonstration of gender-specific training for later obedience (girls) and armed combat (boys), literally a prelude to dances of war, death, and mourning, set to music by Orff's colleague Werner Egk and played by the Berlin Philharmonic Orchestra: 'childish round dances lead to happy ball games for the girls. The boys romp around in rougher and untamed games and contests – in which they steel themselves for the highest service to their people, the deployment of their body and life in war – here symbolically represented by a "weapons dance". A dance of "lamentation for the dead" by the women bewails the fallen. . . .'[168]

On 1 December 1936, all German children were declared members of the Hitler Youth, henceforth to play as important a role in their upbringing as their parents and schools, and specifically ensuring their 'physical, spiritual, and moral education in the spirit of National Socialism'.[169] The portrait *Hitler Youth* (1936) by Konstantin Gerhardinger (1888–1970), showing a boy in uniform complete with swastika armband holding an alto recorder, suggests that the instrument had found a 'firm home' in the organization, as an article in the journal *Völkische Musikerziehung* claimed.[170]

The recorder had hitherto been regarded in Germany as particularly appropriate for boys, specifically for those whose voices were breaking and were therefore temporarily unable to sing in choirs; the exertion of playing a wind instrument was, furthermore, considered an appropriate physical activity for growing boys, whereas girls were expected to concentrate on needlework or dancing.[171] As the Hitler Youth (for boys) and its girls' wing, the *Bund Deutscher Mädel* (BDM, or Federation of German Girls), expanded, music was increasingly used for indoctrination, a spiritual counterpart to the strict sports training by which children's bodies were 'steeled' in preparation for military service. The recorder became strongly gendered for the first time in its history: whereas boys were encouraged to bang drums and blow trumpets, Nazi propaganda reframed the recorder as a 'girls' instrument'. As a Nazi functionary stated in late 1936: 'It is unimaginable that the Hitler Youth would take recorders with them on the march, although it is conceivable that they might occasionally be used at a *Heimabend*. They are more useful in the *Bund Deutscher Mädel* for accompanying folk songs.'[172]

After 1937, it is rare to find a published picture of a boy playing the recorder, whereas the recorder-playing girl in a *BDM* uniform became an icon of Nazi propaganda. Two uniformed girls thus adorned the cover of the December 1937 issue of *Das Deutsche Mädel*, in which an article urged the paper's readers to 'say "yes" to the recorder', while warning against trying to play chromatic notes, or into the second octave, which would require 'intensive work'.[173] Similar illustrations in the October 1938 issue of the venerable *Zeitschrift für Musik*, dedicated to music in the Hitler Youth, were captioned: 'Recorder music is particularly popular among the girls' and 'The popular recorder'.[174] To celebrate Hitler's fiftieth birthday in 1939, the Reich Postal Service even offered pictorial telegrams featuring a uniformed *BDM* recorder quartet.[175] The recorder – only recently reinvented as an 'organic' instrument ostensibly free of traditions of technique, repertoire, or playing style – had been appropriated once again, but for a very different purpose: as a symbol of the gender-specific indoctrination central to education in the 'Third Reich'.

'THE TRIUMPHANT PROGRESS OF THE RECORDER'

Nazi Germany forced its more independent-minded citizens to make painful choices between resistance and conformity. As a successful publisher who never joined the Nazi Party, and continued to express his opinions in public, Hermann Moeck Sr faced particularly close scrutiny. The story of his balancing act between apparent conformity and private dissidence illustrates how even a wounded 'Aryan' veteran of the First World War could find himself in constant danger of denunciation and persecution.

As late as August 1933, six months after the Nazis' rise to power, Moeck still wrote critically about the new regime. In the final issue of *BS* to appear as a separate journal he complained about 'the current rise of "truncheon" music', and reported hearing daily from recorder groups that 'can no longer work because their members are required for other purposes due to the political revolution and have no time for music'.[176] One month later, however, *ZfS* struck a different note: 'Six National Songs' arranged for recorders, included '*Deutschland, Deutschland über alles*', 'I want to fight with the enemy in the wide [battle]field', and 'Awake, awake, Germany, you have slept long enough'. Moeck offered to take recorders in E, D, or A in part exchange for instruments in F and C, describing this as '*Gleichschaltung*', the contemporary term for forced integration into a Nazi monopoly.[177] In the accompanying *BS* supplement, an advertisement for the magazine *Deutsche Musik* boasted two prominent swastikas.[178] From 1934, the joint *ZfS/BS* regularly printed vituperative tirades by Nazi functionaries.[179] Particularly unsettling are ten issues of *ZfS* from 1940–43 that ostensibly reprinted previous numbers in 'fully revised editions'. In August 1940, for example, Franz Bibl's 'New Bavarian Dances' for two recorders was published as a 'second fully revised edition' of *ZfS* 26 (1934); and in March 1941, Alfred von Beckerath's trios for three soprano recorders ('sent from the [battle]field'), as a 'second fully revised edition' of *ZfS* 57 (1937).[180] Nowhere was it mentioned that both issues had originally contained music by Alfred Mann, forced into exile because of his Jewish origins.

Moeck's apparent conversion to 'National Socialism' reached its apotheosis in a promotional text dating from ca. 1940: 'An event such as the triumphant progress of the recorder has only one parallel in our time, namely the coming into existence of the New State itself.'[181] This comparison, for the modern reader absurdly strained, surely reflects the intense pressure Moeck had been under for several years. Following repeated denunciations by his neighbours, who reported gossip gleaned from their own observations and conversations with his children, he was investigated in 1936, 1937, and 1940 by Nazi Party functionaries working together with the Gestapo and the local branch of the Reich Propaganda Department. Moeck was accused of criticising his maidservant for greeting him with the Hitler Salute, which he allegedly refused to use himself, even in public. Moeck must have realized that both he and his family were in grave danger; by professing his loyalty in print, he was probably trying to save his life. The superficiality of his allegiance was noted during the 1940 investigations: 'His attitude towards the National Socialist State was initially negative, [but is] now outwardly affirmative, although it remains doubtful that he inwardly agrees ... his years-old open rejection of National Socialism, demonstrated for example by his refusal to give the Hitler Salute, has only recently – perhaps under the influence of his children – been replaced by a position that outwardly does not allow recognition of any opposition to National Socialism.'[182] A further denunciation in 1943 led to renewed investigations, which concluded that Moeck appeared to live withdrawn and occupy himself entirely with his business and with collecting early musical instruments.[183] In June 1944, however, he was summoned to the Nazi Party office in Celle following reports that he had made defeatist remarks about the war during visits to the local savings bank and a concert ticket office. Harangued as a 'traitor to the Fatherland and a rogue' but spared immediate arrest, he was sent to work in a salt mine shortly afterwards, where he was fortunate enough to survive the few remaining months of the war.[184]

WARTIME ENGLAND AND AMERICA

The outbreak of the Second World War in September 1939 stopped imports of inexpensive German recorders and sheet music, the staple of the British movement. Severed from its parent company in Mainz, Schott's London office initiated its own series of publications, including several of the new works commissioned by Jacobs, and started producing recorders. The first Schott plastic sopranos, designed by Hunt, had several deficiencies: they were not voiced individually unless returned by a customer for adjustment, the initial plastic formula of cellulose acetate melted in the sun, and the subsequent Bakelite model produced a crude sound. Nonetheless, they sold well: 362 sopranos in November 1941 alone, at four shillings and sixpence each, the same price the wooden Herwig Hamlin soprano recorders had gone for before the war.[185] Carl Dolmetsch, writing in 1941, acknowledged commercial mass production as 'one great service . . . rendered to the recorder by the Germans', but he would not be able to produce plastic instruments himself until after the end of the war, as his workshops had been requisitioned for the manufacture of aircraft parts.[186]

As the war increasingly disrupted civilian life, the SRP suspended its activities. Katz and Bergmann were interned in 1940; following their release the following year Katz worked as music master at Bunce Court School for German refugees,[187] and Bergmann filled the gap left at Schott's by Hunt, who had been called up for military service. Besides testing and packing recorders and preparing the first of his many publications, Bergmann contributed to London musical life, maintaining his concerts and recorder evening classes at Morley College throughout the war.[188] Hunt's London flat was bombed early in 1941, but his recorders were 'miraculously rescued from the debris'. Writing as 'Gunner' Edgar Hunt shortly afterwards, he described how 'Schott's wooden treble and tenor recorder were designed in our shelter during heavy raids.'[189]

Long before the United States entered the war in December 1941, a number of firms saw the domestic market's potential, including the Dushkin Recorder Co. in Winnetka, Illinois (from 1934), whose plastic soprano with a wooden mouthpiece was described as 'especially good' in a wartime edition of *The Recorder News*,[190] and the Lewis & Scott Mfg. Co. in Plantsville, Connecticut, makers of the plastic 'Scotty Piccolo Recorder' (from 1939).[191] The American Recorder Society (ARS) was founded in New York City in 1939 by Carl Dolmetsch's student Suzanne Bloch, Margaret Bradford (a school music teacher), and Irmgard Lehrer, who had been director of 'the department of old instruments' at Greenwich House Music School in New York City since 1935.[192] It soon benefited from the arrival of German exiles, notably Mann in 1939 and Katz in 1943.[193] In 1946, *The Recorder News* reported a concert in which Mann performed works by Bach, Handel, Loeillet, Marais, Scarlatti, and Telemann in New York with a large ensemble.[194]

His fine LP record of four Handel sonatas was released in 1952.[195] The celebrated Boston woodwind maker Friedrich von Huene (1929–2016), who emigrated from Germany in 1948, stated that hearing Mann's playing in Cambridge, Massachusetts inspired him to make his first recorder.[196] Although Bloch 'never got along' with Katz, whom she thought 'dull musically', she was wise enough to make way for him; as she later admitted, 'the day I left, [the ARS] flourished'.[197] As director from 1947, Katz became 'the true father of the recorder movement' in the United States,[198] 'responsible for turning a floundering New York Recorder Society into a prominent national organization'.[199]

NEW BEGINNINGS

After the Allied victory in 1945, Germany was divided into four areas of occupation. The Vogtland recorder manufacturers were in the Soviet Zone, later to become the German Democratic Republic, and therefore inaccessible for West German firms. By the early 1950s, however, companies such as Moeck in Celle and Mollenhauer in Fulda had started local production and were again selling large quantities of inexpensive soprano recorders in c^2 and alto recorders in f^1 in both domestic and export markets.[200] Few East German manufacturers were able to resist pressure to join a large collective firm, notably the 'Publicly Owned Enterprise for Musical Instrument Making', VEB Musikinstrumentenbau Markneukirchen, which continued to produce 'Adler' and 'Heinrich' recorders, as well as to introduce new brands, including 'Musima', 'Venus', 'Jupiter', and 'Saturn'.[201] A notable exception was the Schneider family's workshop in Zwota, which never lost its independence. Schneider's alto recorders in particular were highly regarded in the GDR.[202] Throughout Germany, ardent Nazis faced obstacles to continuing their careers in the manner and places they might have wished. Twittenhoff, barred by the Soviet authorities from his post at the Weimar Musikhochschule, made his way to the West, where he continued his career in music education. Gofferje remained in East Germany until retiring to the West. Degen died in Sweden in 1989.[203]

In West Germany, despite Ruëtz's death, the recorder had persuasive advocates. Some leading figures reattained positions of influence, notably Gurlitt and Scheck, who together founded the Freiburg Musikhochschule in 1946. A new generation emerged: Ferdinand Conrad (1912–92) and Günther Höller (1937–2016), former students of Scheck, were appointed to tenured professorships at the

Musikhochschulen in Hannover (1962) and Cologne (1972), respectively;[204] Gerhard Braun (1932–2016) received his chair in Karlsruhe in 1971. In West Berlin, Linde Höffer-von Winterfeld (1919–93) established herself as an authoritative voice on recorder technique, completing and publishing the third volume of Ruëtz's recorder method in 1956 as the *Hohe Schule des Blockflötenspiels*; her own analysis of finger technique, the 'Position Method', remained controversial long after its publication in 1965.[205]

Hildemarie Peter (1921–2012), a former student of Enke, ended her doctoral dissertation in 1951 with an analysis of the recorder's status in German musical life. Seeing its tasks as lying 'mainly in the educational field', she praised the efforts of those teaching beginners and youth groups, but warned against 'groups of 50 or more pupils' playing 'masses of cheap factory-made recorders'.[206] Meanwhile, the director of the Volksmusikschule in the working-class suburb of Berlin– Neukölln, Rudolf Barthel (1908–78), was developing a more positive vision of large ensembles. By 1955 his Neukölln Recorder Choir consisted of 1 sopranino, 8 sopranos, 8 altos, 7 tenors, 5 basses, and 4 great basses in C; by 1963, renamed the Neukölln Recorder Orchestra and following much disciplined rehearsal, it had fifty members.[207]

In Austria, the country most closely linked to Nazi Germany as a result of the *Anschluss* of 1938, the recorder was temporarily regarded as an embarrassment. The state recorder examination instituted in 1939 was abolished shortly after the end of the war, and recorder tuition removed from the syllabus at the Staatsakademie and the Konservatorium in Vienna. Hans Ulrich Staeps (1909–88), the teacher at both institutions, protested, but was told that 'the *Führer*'s favourite instrument' was to be actively discouraged. It took four years of lobbying by Staeps to achieve its reinstatement in the curriculum.[208] In other European nations, the recorder was less familiar and perhaps also less encumbered by recent association with Nazi Germany. Even in the fledgling state of Israel, where the school recorder's origins as a *Volksblockflöte* were presumably known to refugees from German-speaking countries, they appear not to have been seen as a problem. On a visit to England in 1950, Ziporah Jochsberger, a Governor of the New Jerusalem Conservatory and Academy of Music, reported that the recorder was an obligatory part of teacher training for the 800 students at her institution. Her Tel Aviv recorder orchestra consisted of 'a hundred children' playing instruments with 'German' fingering.[209]

In Britain, the almost complete exclusion of recorders with 'German' fingering from the market may have helped to prevent the impression arising that the recorder was anything other than '*our own* English flute', as Hunt wrote during the war: 'we have left the Germans still piping their folksongs, while pseudo recorders with "German" fingering are locked up with the rest of the Fifth Column'.[210] Indeed, a member of the British Military Commission processing Moeck's application for a publisher's licence in 1946 noted: 'something like the Dolmetsches of Haslemere. Strongly recommended.'[211] The SRP resumed its activities in 1946, Bergmann joining Carl Dolmetsch and Hunt as a Musical Director in 1948. Bergmann's position at Schott's, his good contacts in continental Europe, and his association with such prominent musicians as Michael Tippett and Alfred Deller helped him promote the recorder in post-war Britain, his legacy including many editions of standard works from the Baroque repertoire and several original compositions.[212]

Carl Dolmetsch's first post-war Wigmore Hall recital in 1947 featured the premiere of the Sonatina by York Bowen; this fine work and his subsequent commissions have deservedly received renewed attention in recent years.[213] The Dolmetsch workshop had resumed production of approximately 400 wooden recorders per year in 1946, increasing gradually to an annual peak of 1,000 in the late 1970s, but still not sufficient to meet demand: as late as 1975, the waiting list for a Dolmetsch wooden recorder was around eighteen months.[214] Inexpensive plastic school instruments were, however, rapidly made available. In 1950, Dolmetsch reported production of 'thousands of trebles' as well as 'an initial order of 25,000 descants'.[215]

Acceptance of the recorder in schools continued to grow after the war, as documented in the 'New Series' of *The Recorder News* (from 1950) and its successor, *The Recorder and Music Magazine* (from 1963, various titles). In 1950, a contributor to the *Sussex Recorder News* looked back at 'five years' experience of the use of the recorder in a boys' grammar [high] school', in which 'recorder playing has been regarded as an entirely voluntary activity', attracting 75 students out of a total of 600.[216] The subsequent issue reported on the growth of recorder teaching in both state and privately run schools: 'In every Rudolf Steiner [Waldorf] school the children start learning the recorder as soon as they enter the first class.'[217]

A particularly thorough approach to the school recorder was adopted in the Netherlands, where compulsory recorder lessons were introduced as part of general teacher training as early as 1946, to replace the violin lessons previously required. After this project failed because of a shortage of qualified instructors, the Dutch Ministry of Education, Science, and Culture formed an official commission on recorder teaching in 1949, also charged with establishing objective quality criteria for 'school', 'ensemble', and 'solo' recorders, in order to forbid the import of instruments deemed inferior.[218]

Indeed, it was in the Netherlands that the next major development in the recorder's modern history was to take place: a second paradigm shift within less than fifty years in the nature of the physical instrument itself and its players, repertoire, and technique. Although it is generally credited to one remarkable musician, Frans Brüggen, his story is inseparable from the cultural and social history of his native land.

FRANS BRÜGGEN

FRANS BRÜGGEN I: EDUCATION AND EARLY CAREER

Born in Amsterdam, the youngest of nine children in a middle-class Roman Catholic family, Franciscus ('Frans') Jozef Brüggen (1934–2014) was introduced to the recorder by his eldest brother Hans, a talented oboist, during the first winter of the German occupation of the Netherlands (1940–45). Brüggen subsequently described how the privations and boredom of a wartime childhood focused his interest on recorder playing: the German authorities had confiscated most of the coal supplies, so there was no heating, and schools were often closed. He practised hard ('I spent the whole war playing the recorder')[219] and found encouragement in his family's lively music-making at home ('I remember that with the help of some uncles and aunts we could play the complete Brandenburg Concertos').[220] Even as a teenager Brüggen's stated ambition was to become a professional recorder player, doubtless a surprise for his father, who had hoped he would join the family cotton-trading firm.

The recorder was not yet taught at any of the state music conservatories, so Brüggen began his studies in 1949 at the Muzieklyceum in Amsterdam, a private institution independent of state educational policy. His teacher, Kees Otten (1924–2008), had introduced the recorder into the curriculum as a principal study only two years previously. Otten divided his time between the clarinet and the recorder, playing both instruments in jazz concerts and cabaret shows as well as more traditional formations, a diversity of musical practice that may well have inspired subsequent generations of Dutch recorder players.[221] Brüggen's father, having been warned that in the absence of orchestral positions the recorder offered few opportunities for steady employment, insisted that his son also learn the Boehm flute, which he studied with two members of the Concertgebouw Orchestra, Hubert Barwahser and Johan Feltkamp.[222] Following his graduation in 1953, as the second Muzieklyceum student to be awarded a recorder diploma, Brüggen was appointed to the institution's staff. He continued his education for three years, studying musicology at the University of Amsterdam without gaining a formal qualification.[223]

Brüggen started his career at a turning point in the recorder's modern history. The Dutch recorder commission had been negotiating the introduction of recorder diploma courses at the state music conservatories, a goal finally achieved in 1955.[224] Among the first recorder teachers appointed were Otten (Rotterdam), Joannes Collette (1918–95) (Utrecht), and Brüggen (The Hague).[225] The principal aim of the educational authorities in establishing a state diploma examination had undoubtedly been to improve the standard of recorder teaching in schools. Indeed, Collette and Otten dedicated themselves initially to the education of specialists to be employed in teacher-training colleges,[226] an occupation that provided financial security 'at the expense, he [Otten] believes, of his artistic survival', as the editor of *American Recorder* noted in 1961.[227] In contrast, within a decade of his appointment, Brüggen was to transform his class in The Hague into the leading international centre for a new generation of recorder virtuosi.

The recorder emerged in the 1960s as a debutante in the high society of professional musical performance, as Brüggen succeeded in wresting it briefly into a position of unprecedented glamour. Why should this have happened in the Netherlands and not in Britain or Germany, the two countries at the forefront of the rediscovery and reinvention of the recorder, or indeed the United States, the new home of Katz and Mann? Although the most important answers to these questions undoubtedly lie in the artistry, musicianship, and sheer personal magnetism of Brüggen himself, phenomena that will be examined in detail below, the proudly lavish state patronage of the arts in the Netherlands provided an ideal environment.

Once the institutional door had been opened, recorder students gained access to a publicly funded education. Study grants became freely available to Dutch nationals, and also, on a more restricted basis, to foreigners.[228] Excellent teaching, the possibility of financial assistance, and not least the renowned openness of Dutch society in the 1960s and 1970s encouraged aspiring recorder players from all over the world to study in the Netherlands. Furthermore, the new state diploma provided access to a comprehensive system of patronage: qualified recorder players received the same generous support as other professionally qualified artists.[229] The least successful were eligible for comprehensive welfare benefits, although few would initially have needed them, as demand for qualified recorder teachers remained strong until at least the mid-1970s.[230] In this golden age of musical opportunity, musicians and composers of all kinds were supported by state-funded institutions such as the Nederlands Impresariaat, a national concert agency, and Donemus, a national publishing house that printed and promoted the work of modern Dutch composers, including the recorder music they were encouraged to write, often 'by commission of the State'. Brüggen estimated the number of broadcasts of recorder solo or chamber music on Radio Hilversum in 1961 at 'about 60 a year by Dutch players alone'.[231] In Britain or the United States the very idea of a 'state recorder commission' would have seemed odd or even comical. In the Netherlands, it was as unsurprising as the existence of a publicly funded concert agency or music publishing house. Brüggen was the right person, in the right place, at the right time.

RECORDER REPERTOIRE, 'VIRTUOSITY', AND PLAYING STYLE CA. 1962

Frans Brüggen's first LPs – a recital entitled *The Virtuoso Recorder*[232] and his first recording of Handel sonatas[233] – were released in 1962. Together with contemporary recordings of the same repertoire by Carl Dolmetsch, Conrad, and another German former student of Scheck, Hans-Martin Linde (b. 1930),[234] these discs document many typical features of recorder performance before the profound changes in repertoire, playing style, and instrument type initiated by Brüggen during the following decade. That all four players should have chosen to record Handel is hardly surprising, given the canonical status of these works in the recorder's repertoire throughout the modern revival. *The Virtuoso Recorder* contains many less obvious selections, however, including notably undemanding pieces by Willem de Fesch, Jean-Baptiste Loeillet, and Veracini, as well as the partita in E minor, TWV 41:e1, from Telemann's *Die kleine Kammermusik* (1728), a collection recommended by Hunt in 1962 as providing 'some comfort . . . for the novice appalled at the difficulty of much of Telemann's music'.[235] It evidently fitted the contemporary view of the recorder's repertoire, however, as the discography and concert repertoire of Conrad[236] and Dolmetsch[237] testify.

During the 1950s, Conrad had published a series of essays characterizing the recorder's sound as 'objective', 'clear', 'undifferentiated', and 'poor in affect'.[238]

Similar terms, reminiscent of the 'organic' aesthetic ideals of the German Youth Music Movement, were used approvingly both before and after the Second World War by advocates of the recorder to explain their affinity for the instrument.[239] The equation of the recorder with a narrow range of expression was a paradigm of the age, rarely questioned by friend or foe, and trenchantly addressed in Theodor W. Adorno's polemic against the Youth Music Movement, 'Kritik des Musikanten' (1956), which decried the recorder as exemplifying a musical aesthetic relishing 'the exhumed colours for their very lack of colour and sensuousness, their brittleness. One only has to hear the sober, ridiculous sound of a recorder and then that of a real [flute]; of all the deaths constantly suffered by the great [god] Pan, the recorder is the most shameful.'[240]

Brüggen's playing style in his 1962 recordings, like that of Conrad, Dolmetsch, and Linde, demonstrates 'objective' and 'sober' features that both contemporary advocates and detractors of the recorder would probably have regarded as appropriate to the instrument. A continuous, fast vibrato is intrinsic to his basic sound, an obvious borrowing from contemporary Boehm flute technique, but less expressive when separated from that instrument's overtone-rich timbre and wide dynamic range. Brüggen's execution of fast passages, notably the semiquaver runs in the *Aria 3* (Vivace) from the Telemann Partita, demonstrates his excellent finger–tongue coordination (a particularly weak point in the recordings by Conrad and Dolmetsch), but also the absence of the subtle details of articulation, rubato across phrases, or agogic variation within small structural units that were to become so characteristic of his mature playing style. This general lack of flexibility makes the very notion of a 'Virtuoso Recorder' appear an oxymoron, confirming the recorder's status in 1962 as a marginal instrument of limited expressive potential.

INSTRUMENT DESIGN, 1965–80

Although the differences between 'modern' and 'historical' recorders may not be as immediately evident as those between the iron-framed harpsichords of the mid-twentieth century and those based on historical models, they are equally relevant to the instrument's musical properties. In *The Virtuoso Recorder*, Brüggen played recorders from the Dolmetsch workshop; for his Handel recording he chose an instrument by the Dutch maker Hans Coolsma (1919–91).[241] The celebrated Australian craftsman Frederick Morgan (1940–99) described how typical Baroque recorders differed from 'modern' instruments, exemplified by those made by

Coolsma and Dolmetsch, 'in almost every aspect of [their] design. The finger-holes are smaller and undercut, the outside form is different, the windway is shallower and curved from side to side, the pitch is different, the tuning is different, even the finish has a different feel to it.' 'Apart from the ingenuity of the bore design, the most impressive feature of these instruments is their voicing, and thus the quality of sound of all three registers. But d³, e³ and f³ are particularly fine: these notes sound clear and full, with a flexibility of tone and minimum change in pitch that is a revelation when first experienced, and a continuing source of wonder with further acquaintance.'[242]

Brüggen started to play antique recorders in 1964 and was particularly impressed by Hunt's Bressan alto, which he borrowed in 1965–66.[243] Readers of Hunt's survey of 'The Recorder Today' had been told about that instrument's 'quality and ease of tone production, with its full and easy low notes' as early as 1962.[244] Until the end of the decade, however, the dominant trend in recorder making remained one of modernisation. Dolmetsch declared in 1968: 'In all my experience I have yet to meet an antique recorder that was expertly voiced originally, or that has not shown an immediate improvement . . . after the most modest re-voicing.' He had proudly altered 'the tuning and pitch of the famous Chester recorders made by Bressan' when he 'revoiced them in 1939 and again in 1963', declaring 'who but a bigoted antiquarian could prefer the wheezy, ill-voiced and out-of-tune performance of most early recorders?'[245] Although by 1968 this attitude represented the spirit of an age that was coming to an end, it had already led to the mutilation of some of the finest historical recorders to have survived into the twentieth century.

Once Brüggen started to make recordings using original instruments, the quality and flexibility of their sound was widely acknowledged. A review of *Frans Brüggen spielt 17 Blockflöten* (Plays 17 Recorders, 1972)[246] noted: 'Words simply cannot describe the fascination emanating in equal parts from his immensely differentiated playing (not to mention his stupendous virtuosity) and from the unimagined shades of tone colour of the original instruments he uses. . . . [These recordings] are capable of converting the most stubborn sceptic, transforming his prejudices against the allegedly restricted expressive possibilities of the recorder into bright enthusiasm.'[247] In 1965–66, Brüggen commissioned copies of Hunt's Bressan from Coolsma and Martin Skowroneck (1926–2014). All his subsequent recordings of Early Music were made either on antique recorders or on copies, notably from the workshops of Von Huene[248] and Morgan.[249]

After Coolsma initiated commercial production of his Bressan copy with a series of 100 instruments in 1968,[250] the notion of 'copying' started to gain importance as a marketing tool. Within a few years both individual craftsmen and large factories advertised recorders named after historical models. Coolsma and Skowroneck's first Bressan copies had indeed been fairly exact replicas, their principal modification being a relatively small adjustment to the recorder's sounding length in order to raise its pitch from ca. A 404 to A 415, the pragmatic international modern standard for 'Baroque pitch'. (The interval of an equal-tempered semitone between A 415 and A 440 is historically arbitrary but practical, because a harpsichord with a moveable keyboard can be played at both pitches.) Many later 'copies', however, derived only superficial elements of their external shape from a historical model, being modified internally to play in equal temperament with modern 'English' fingering, at A 440 or above, and perhaps most importantly, to facilitate mechanized mass production.[251]

Moeck, for example, produced 700,000 'Rottenburgh' recorders between 1968 and 1998, based on a design by Von Huene. Their collaboration was marked by differences in opinion over essential design features, such as whether the windway should be made curved, as intended by Von Huene, or straight, to make mass production easier.[252] Tuned at modern pitch – an alto at A 415 was produced only in limited quantities between 1975 and 1982 – the resulting product was essentially a good, reliable, inexpensive modern recorder. In 1979 Moeck admitted that Von Huene had compared his own craftsmanship to that of the luxury automobile maker Ferrari, and the Moeck factory to General Motors.[253]

By 1977, the marketing revolution was complete. A Japanese producer advertised 'The Schott Zen-On "Bressan" recorders . . . the first modern plastic version of one of the finest Baroque examples. . . . It is tuned to British Standard Pitch and has modern English fingering with double holes, but this "Bressan" model [has] faithfully reproduced the tonal characteristics and design of the original.'[254] Once again, the design work was undertaken by Von Huene, using Hunt's Bressan alto as the model. Hunt wrote: 'I have tried countless other treble recorders by different makers over the years, hoping one day to find something approaching the original, but in modern pitch. At last this "copy" of my original Bressan appears to be the answer.'[255] This ringing endorsement seems implausible given the true nature of the product. Zen-On had undoubtedly produced a good plastic recorder, but its 'Bressan' was historical only in name, its limits defined not least by ABS plastic injection technology, with all its associated problems of aesthetics, quality control, and non-reparability.[256]

FRANS BRÜGGEN II: REPERTOIRE

Within a decade following his first recordings in 1962, Brüggen documented a substantial part of the instrument's major historical repertoire, on over 30 LPs for Telefunken.[257] Some works, such as those by Italian masters (Barsanti, Benedetto Marcello, and Veracini) and English music from Anthony Holborne to Henry Purcell, were perhaps familiar to recorder enthusiasts at the time. Others, notably French suites and sonatas by Anne Danican Philidor, Dieupart, and Hotteterre, Vivaldi solo and chamber concertos, and what Brüggen later referred to as the 'rock-hard, glorious Italian canzonas'[258] of Girolamo Frescobaldi, Giovanni Battista Riccio, and their contemporaries were all but unknown – and a revelation.

Brüggen acknowledged 'the real lack of solo repertoire for the recorder',[259] but never accepted this as an immutable fact. He emphasized the significance of interpretation in musical performance: 'I cannot fill my life with Dieupart, Couperin, Bach, Telemann, and the others. But I can fill my life by *playing* them.'[260] Increasingly, he enriched his recital programmes with arrangements, at first choosing works that required little modification, such as the partita by J. S. Bach for unaccompanied flute, BWV 1030, part of Brüggen's concert repertoire as early as 1966.[261] In 1973, however, Brüggen published transcriptions of the first three Bach suites for unaccompanied cello, BWV 1007–1009,[262] recording them a year later for EMI.[263] Challenged to justify these arrangements, Brüggen evoked his understanding of Baroque aesthetics: 'The art of the seventeenth and eighteenth centuries is also the art of simulation. . . . You should have read the reviews in Germany. . . . That's completely impossible, imitating a cello on a recorder. As if I didn't know that for myself. The intention was: imitation by forgery. Artificial ivory.'[264]

In 1953, Brüggen's final examination recital at the Amsterdam Muzieklyceum had included two important works from the contemporary British repertoire, the Partita by Franz Reizenstein (1939), written for Dolmetsch, and the Sonatina by Walter Leigh (published 1944), commissioned by Jacobs.[265] In 1961 he was clearly still interested enough in traditional, tonal music to have entertained the editor of *American Recorder* by playing tapes of his radio performances of the Concerto (1956) by Arnold Cooke, written for Philip Rodgers, and Lennox Berkeley's Sonatina (1939).[266] By the middle of the decade, however, Brüggen was approaching a wide range of composers – from minor Dutch figures to Igor Stravinsky – with his own commissions for new works. Stravinsky's response (in April 1966) indicates the difficulty Brüggen faced in promoting accurate knowledge of his instrument at the time: 'I know you*rr* instrument. It is a kind of cl*aa*rinet.'[267] Among those who accepted the challenge, Louis Andriessen (*Sweet*, 1964), Luciano Berio (*Gesti*, 1965), and Makoto Shinohara (*Fragmente*, 1969) established avant-garde idioms that have since been widely imitated.[268] Although insiders consider other recorder players, notably Linde, Braun, and especially Michael Vetter (1943–2013),[269] to have been equally influential in promoting extended techniques, Brüggen's popularity undeniably enabled him to bring avant-garde recorder music to the attention of audiences who might otherwise have chosen to ignore it.

In retrospect, Brüggen was to describe the works by Leigh and Reizenstein that he had chosen to play in his examination recital three decades earlier, as 'repugnant, so-called modern piece[s]',[270] a remark characteristic of his activism in the Dutch contemporary and Early Music scenes – speaking, for example, in defence of the *Notenkraker* action that disrupted a concert by the Concertgebouw Orchestra in Amsterdam on 17 November 1969.[271] By the late 1960s, his focus had clearly shifted to the avant-garde, in both composition and performance. His recorder trio Sour Cream, in which he was joined by his former students Kees Boeke (b. 1950) and Walter van Hauwe (b. 1948), took particular delight in pushing boundaries; for example, in their composition *Sourcream 1971*, described by one listener as a 'convincing imitation of a nightmare founded on a TV police drama'.[272] Reports on the ensemble's concerts emphasized the shock of informal dress (flared jeans and leather jackets in Oberlin, Ohio),[273] provocative stagecraft (in Boston, 'while Kees and Walter played Telemann duos, Brüggen wandered onto the Jordan Hall stage, donned a pair of dark sunglasses, stretched himself on a chaise longue, and nonchalantly began reading a copy of the local paper'),[274] and sheer loudness (in Bruges, Belgium, this 'hurt the ears and became so unbearable that many listeners left the hall. A majority of those who remained were shocked, depressed, or annoyed').[275]

FRANS BRÜGGEN III: MATURE PLAYING STYLE

Contemporary observers reported dramatic changes in Brüggen's playing style in the mid-1960s, which can be traced in retrospect with a high degree of objectivity thanks to the ready availability of sound recordings. Since particular attention was paid at the time to his use of vibrato, wide dynamic contrasts, and the so-called 'Brüggen bulge', these will be discussed in detail here, rather than his equally original use of rhythmic alteration and subtle variations in articulation.

As already noted, Brüggen's early playing featured a fast, constant vibrato. In his interpretation of the Sonata in G major by Veracini (1716, no. 2) from *The Virtuoso Recorder* (1962), for example, its frequency in the opening phrase of the first movement, Largo, is approximately 7 pulses per second. Six years later, in his second recording of the work, the same passage is played completely without vibrato on the short notes, vibrato being applied only to certain long notes, beginning approximately 0.5 seconds after the initial articulation, with a frequency of approximately 5 pulses per second.[276] This selective, ornamental use of a slow breath vibrato against a background of notes played without vibrato is one of the most characteristic features of Brüggen's mature playing style, which he described in 1974 thus: 'vibrato should [be played on] notes which are either particularly interesting harmonically or melodically, or high points which are, in some way, just too long in duration to be without any colouring . . .'.[277]

This technique allowed Brüggen to suggest wide dynamic contrasts: for example, between a *forte* played with a strong standard fingering and a slow, wide breath vibrato, and a *piano* played without vibrato, using a weaker, alternative fingering. This can be heard in the second Veracini recording, notably in mm. 18–22 of the first movement, in which he plays a *crescendo* from *piano* (alternative fingerings, no vibrato) to *forte* (standard fingerings, vibrato). As anyone who has heard children blowing into a recorder before learning to control their airstream will be painfully aware, blowing harder into the instrument's fixed windway raises the pitch of a given note, while blowing more gently lowers it. In theory, there are a number of ways to maintain pitch when altering breath pressure to achieve dynamic contrasts, including the use of alternative fingerings, leaking air through holes that are normally fully covered, and varying the speed (as opposed to the volume) of the airstream by altering the shape or position of the tongue. These techniques can be traced back to Ganassi and Cardano, and have been described in our time in books by Edward Kottick, Anthony Rowland-Jones, Van Hauwe, and Johannes Fischer.[278] Furthermore, many advanced recorder players are aware of the profound differences in dynamic range and tone quality associated with changes in posture and the meditative exploration of the body's natural resonance cavities. In practice, however, pitch is notoriously difficult to control. Although Brüggen by no means invented these techniques, he was the first recorder player in the modern revival to master them.

Contemporary concert reviews document the strong impression his mature playing style made: for example, in *The Times* of London from 1966: 'a fine artist, able to transcend all the instrument's legendary limitations'; 'draws more expressiveness from the recorder than one would have thought it capable of '.[279] Yet critical reactions were not uniformly positive. Amateur recorder players in particular found aspects of his technique disturbing, particularly once Brüggen's students started appearing on the international stage more frequently and talk of a 'Dutch School' of recorder playing became more widespread. The two characteristics most frequently criticised were the 'Brüggen bulge' and his distinctive stooping posture. In 1971, Theo Wyatt, contributing to a symposium in *Recorder and Music Magazine* entitled 'Frans Brueggen and the New Mannerism', defined the 'bulge' as 'the habit of blowing a steep crescendo into the middle of every note long enough to take one'. Like other contemporary writers, Wyatt was disturbed by what he perceived as uncorrected fluctuations of pitch accompanying variations in breath pressure intended to create dynamic contrasts: '[the bulge] . . . disturbs the pitch, which can distinctly be heard wandering up and down. . . . The violin or oboe can make a crescendo without going sharp. We expect consistent intonation from them as of right. How are we to condition ourselves to something different from the recorder alone?'[280]

From the mid-1970s, however, references to the 'bulge' became less common. Some writers even noted that they no longer heard it: 'Brüggen appears to have abandoned the mannerism which excited so much criticism a few years ago.'[281] In 1982 Van Hauwe was quoted as stating that 'the so-called Dutch "wow-wow" or "bulge" is now very much a thing of the past, although fashionable less than 10 years ago'.[282] Did Brüggen and his students indeed alter their playing style, or had listeners' perceptions of it merely changed? Wyatt's definition of the 'bulge' was clear enough. Where exactly he and others heard it, is more obscure. It seems to have been regarded as such a distinctive feature of Brüggen's technique that its use did not require analysis beyond the mere indication of its presence, let alone differentiation from the use of breath or finger vibrato, dynamic or tone-colour changes not causing an alteration of pitch, or indeed a listener's subjective reaction to unfamiliar unequal temperaments or the lower pitch of Brüggen's antique instruments and copies.

Perhaps some listeners' first experiences of hearing a recorder played in tune, but in an unequal temperament, at low pitch, and with a slow, selectively applied vibrato were so startling that they focused acutely on small variations in pitch which, in another context, they might have considered insignificant. After all, vibrato itself is nothing other than a constant undulation of pitch around a median perceived by the listener as the 'note' itself, a phenomenon tolerated by fans of operatic singing without demur, even though a note with vibrato is only genuinely 'in tune' for the fractions of a second in which its varying pitch meets the perceived median frequency. Furthermore, it is widely accepted that different instruments are played 'in tune' in different ways, a phenomenon that may be observed by comparing commercial recordings of piano concertos from about 1950 until the present day. In some earlier recordings the piano, tuned in equal temperament and often with octaves 'stretched' to enhance the instrument's brilliance in extreme registers, is objectively out of tune to the woodwinds playing in unison with it. The contrast between this poor but culturally accepted intonation[283] and the more accurately synchronized tuning in later recordings[284] is striking: what we prefer is evidently strongly influenced by what we are accustomed to hearing.

Amateur recorder players, conditioned to expect a narrow dynamic range, may initially have been unable to hear true dynamic contrasts on the recorder without imagining pitch fluctuations. As one correspondent to *Recorder and Music Magazine* in 1971 pointed out: 'When we first heard FB play we were all astounded at his technique and at the fact that he managed to suggest dynamics. Then we listened with twitching ears to detect how he did it; and the "Brüggen bulge" was given full publicity.'[285] Listening to recordings made by Brüggen and his students in the late 1960s, it is indeed possible to identify a swelling, *messa di voce* effect on some notes. Despite close study of over thirty commercial or radio recordings by Brüggen and his students, however, I have yet to find a single instance of a phrase in which a 'bulge' is blown 'into the middle of every note long enough to take one'. Even when a specific instance of an audience being disturbed by the 'bulge' was reported, it is hard to establish today exactly what they heard and where they heard it. In May 1971, for example, Brüggen 'found himself in a hornet's nest', having aroused tempers at a meeting of the Music Club of London 'by playing a recording of a Hotteterre suite for 2 recorders with . . . fluctuating intonation'.[286] It seems likely that this was either the 1970 Telefunken recording of Jacques Hotteterre's *Première Suitte de Pièces*, Op. 4 (1712) by Brüggen and Boeke,[287] or a private tape made about the same time. Listening to the Telefunken version today, I hear fluctuations in pitch most clearly in the sometimes very wide finger vibrato (*flattement*). There is, however, no mention of *flattement* in the extensive report on the Music Club of London meeting. Otherwise, the recording is, to my ears, not merely full of expressive contrast, but consistently well 'in tune'.[288]

Recorder & Music

35. Cover of *Recorder & Music* 4, no. 8 (December 1973), showing Frans Brüggen's slouching posture with legs crossed (right), contrasted with an eighteenth-century oboist, upright despite his crossed legs. 'Recorder Player' by Ruth C. Loretto.

Unlike the 'bulge', Brüggen's posture is unequivocally identifiable from contemporary evidence. A tall man playing a quiet instrument, he explained his refusal to play standing up thus: 'The recorder . . . makes such a small sound, that if one stands, the audience is already expecting a greater sound . . . with string orchestras. I always sit, *always*. I tell all my pupils to do this as well.'[289] It was less his sitting that attracted attention, however, than the manner of it. Slumped forward in his chair, legs crossed, shoulders hunched, and neck bent forward, Brüggen held the recorder almost vertically. In order to avoid hitting the bell against his right thigh, he twisted his upper torso and arms to the side. Some of Brüggen's students copied his posture exactly, at times with unintentionally comic effect, as for example in a photograph of Sour Cream from 1970.[290] Caricature was perhaps inevitable. The December 1973 issue of *Recorder & Music* carried a memorable cover picture of a sculpture described as 'capturing the typical Dutch playing position – started, of course, by Frans Brueggen', juxtaposed with a silhouette of a pristine, erect, eighteenth-century oboist.[291] Much of the force of this illustration stems from the almost decaying scruffiness implied by the sculpture's flaking metal, suggesting an association between Brüggen's stoop and slovenliness, even physical degeneracy.

Undoubtedly, Brüggen's deportment offended orthodox teaching on posture in woodwind playing and contravened contemporary norms of concert performance.[292] An important additional factor, however, may have been the appearance and demeanour of Brüggen and his students off the concert podium, which reflected prevailing standards of dress and behaviour among a wider artistic and progressive community in post-1960s Amsterdam. Fashions were extravagant: men, for example, tended to wear their hair long and their trousers flared. Brüggen's love for Dutch gin, *oude genever*, was commented on by outsiders, and he was not above joining his favourite students for drinking bouts.[293] As has been noted in discussing the performance style of Sour Cream, this raffish image was not toned down in public. Or on camera: in the film *Sour Cream* by Alan Howlett (1981) the trio is physically ejected from an art gallery after dancing, smoking, and sleeping inside.[294] In this context, widespread imitation of Brüggen's posture seems a relatively minor aspect of the colourful visual picture of Dutch recorder students for the writers and readers of *Recorder & Music* to have identified. Perhaps, in trying to describe and explain the flamboyant appearance and radically new sound of Brüggen and his students, a concentration on disturbing superficialities – or even the construction of a phenomenon referred to as 'the bulge' – was unavoidable.

FRANS BRÜGGEN IV: STARDOM AND LEGACY

The critical reception of Brüggen's playing is well documented in print. Whereas specialist recorder magazines tended throughout the 1960s towards understatement, typically preferring terms such as 'purity' and 'transparency' to more outspoken praise, by 1969 the astonishing expressiveness of his personal style was commented upon by the music critics of major daily newspapers such as *The Times* of London. An Adagio 'sang with a heart-stopping, pathetic eloquence'.[295] Brüggen was acclaimed 'the doyen of recorder players'.[296] In 1973 his reputation among a specialist readership was secure enough for the musicologist Howard Mayer Brown to entitle a concert review in *Recorder & Music* 'What makes Brüggen great?'[297] When J. M. Thomson resigned the editorship of that journal in 1974 to found *Early Music*, he wrote: 'I [have] tried to extend the influence of Frans Brueggen, the greatest living player of the instrument and a virtuoso and artist of unique stature. . . . It may be an aeon before we have such a commanding figure to raise the instrument to such heights.'[298]

Brüggen's recording career carried his artistry far beyond the narrow borders of the Netherlands. Around 1965, three years after his first recording for Telefunken, a decision appears to have been taken to build Brüggen's image as an international star. Pictures constituted a particularly important element in Telefunken's marketing strategy, making a fetish out of three images by their frequent repetition: Brüggen's physical appearance; his association with unusually rare, beautiful, or simply large recorders; and his name itself. The design of the 1972 boxed set *Frans Brüggen spielt 17 Blockflöten* is typical. In the picture on its front cover, Brüggen is artificially elevated against a Dutch skyline, carefully lit to suggest masterly authority offset by a sporty cheerfulness. His left hand grasps an antique recorder, its suggestion of phallic symbolism echoed by the out-of-focus church bell tower behind. Suspended above his head, in glowing pink, are the only two words apart from the name of the record company: 'Frans Brüggen'. Some photographs were probably intended, and undoubtedly widely used, as pin-ups, notably a 60 × 60 cm poster (four times the size of an LP sleeve) included with this box, and reprinted at least three times.[299]

As a case history in marketing, none of this is unusual or surprising, since many artists of comparable stature were being promoted by their record companies in similar ways at the time. Wolfgang Mohr, who worked on the marketing side of Telefunken before advancing to become A&R director of the company in the late 1980s, remarked that Brüggen did not receive unusually strong promotion for a

Telefunken solo artist of the day.[300] Unprecedentedly, however, the artist being marketed was a recorder player. The novelty of this was acknowledged in Telefunken's promotional texts, even as they drew extravagant comparisons between his own lifestyle and instruments and those of a star violinist: 'a recorder virtuoso is by no means overshadowed by more popular soloists like violinists, pianists or cellists. "Financially certainly not. I earn more money than I can spend."' '. . . from his writing-desk he produces an ebony instrument about a metre long with ivory rings on it every ten centimetres. "Stainsby [sic], London, 1730, the best of the best, the Stradivari of recorders" is his brief but pithy comment.'[301] Such texts promoted the idea that a successful, even glamorous, career could be made playing the recorder. They offered concerned parents of subsequent generations of aspiring recorder players an answer to the questions raised by their children's ambition – one not available to Brüggen's father in the 1940s. By the time of his first recording for RCA in 1979, Brüggen's image was evidently secure enough for that company to include his picture next to those of Plácido Domingo, James Galway, Vladimir Horowitz, and Artur Rubinstein in their *Label der Stars* [label of the stars] advertisement.[302]

Brüggen stopped teaching in 1974: 'I noticed . . . a deterioration in my own playing. Teaching . . . makes you tired and uncreative.'[303] 'It was driving me crazy . . . no, listen, not because they imitated me. I'd had enough of ordinary students: I just wanted to deal with masters. I also avoid all conversations with former students, apart from Walter [van Hauwe] and Kees [Boeke].'[304] Despite such critical remarks, and his rapidly developing career as a conductor, he continued to give occasional recorder masterclasses and to play actively for at least another fifteen years, gradually reducing the number of recorder concerts he gave from approximately ninety a year in 1978 to 'at least' fifty in 1989.[305] A television recording from the mid-1980s shows him in full possession of his expressive powers.[306]

Brüggen's legacy continued to inspire until at least the end of the century. In 1989, I asked nearly thirty recorder students and teachers at Dutch conservatories for their thoughts about him. I believe their replies to be both genuine and typical for several generations of musicians: 'a genius' (male, age 40); 'my idol' (male, age 32); 'an incredibly great musician' (male, age 29); 'he's the reason I play the recorder' (female, age 27); 'I used to have his posters on my wall' (female, age 26); 'my God, if only I could have twenty minutes with him to talk' (male, age 25); 'I think he is the most beautiful man' (female, age 23). Others told me at length how they felt spiritually close to Brüggen through his recordings, or that particular ornaments or timbres had become 'the only way to hear' a particular phrase: 'I could imitate his recordings very well.'[307] Even scholars have been moved to pay tribute, notably Richard Griscom and David Lasocki, who in 1994 chose to dedicate their recorder bibliography 'To Frans Brüggen, without whose existence we would never have bothered.'[308]

A 'DUTCH SCHOOL' OF RECORDER PLAYING?

By the late 1960s, the recorder had come to be seen as an astute career choice, as one first-study pianist discovered when she was advised by her teacher to concentrate instead on the recorder: here was an instrument with a bright future.[309] This transformation in the recorder's vocational status, initially led by the demand for teachers to fill positions in Dutch conservatories and music schools, was consolidated as a generation of outstanding students emulated Brüggen's glamorous career. Among the most successful were Boeke and Van Hauwe, who both graduated in 1969, Marion Verbruggen (b. 1950), and the Brazilian Ricardo Kanji (b. 1948). *The Times* of London noted: 'Many excellent players either come from Holland or have studied there. For several years Dutch conservatories have accepted the recorder as a performing instrument with its own rights. . . .'[310] As international recognition increased, Brüggen's class became oversubscribed. By 1973, when the number of recorder students at the conservatory reached fifty,[311] even gifted applicants were unable to secure a place in his class. Michael Barker (b. 1951), who later taught at The Hague himself, recalled being surprised on his arrival from the United States to find that 'There was Frans. And if you couldn't study with Frans you studied with Walter or Kees. That was for a few years second best but OK: it was sort of a way to work up. And . . . if you couldn't study with Walter or Kees, then you studied with Ricardo, Jeanette van Wingerden, or Bruce Haynes.'[312]

By the time Brüggen retired from teaching in 1974 there were several recorder classes of international repute in the Netherlands, notably those of Boeke and Van Hauwe in Amsterdam, Kanji in The Hague, and Verbruggen in Utrecht. Significant differences of approach emerged. In some Dutch conservatories, the recorder came to be categorized primarily as an 'Early' instrument, whether explicitly, as in the Early Music department in The Hague, or implicitly, through the musical practice of an individual class. In such cases, particular attention was paid to notions of 'authenticity', specifically the justification of a technique or type of instrument by reference to historical source material. The other extreme was represented by Van Hauwe's elaboration of a systematic method of recorder playing from first principles, documented in his three-volume method, *The Modern Recorder Player*.[313] His understanding of instrumental technique as an essentially functional, logical craft accorded with his belief in the recorder as a 'modern' instrument, not primarily defined by its pre-Classical repertoire or historical evidence: 'If it works, do it.'

A further point of difference among Brüggen's former students lay in the extent to which each sought to develop the essentially inspiring style in which they were taught into a more structured methodology. Although Brüggen did give technical advice to his students – suggesting, for example, that the best recorder tone could be achieved by opening the mouth cavity as if holding a small orange behind the teeth[314] – written accounts of his lessons, interviews, and my own experience of playing in a masterclass[315] confirm that his guidance was aimed more often at helping the student to 'know yourself and what you can do'[316] than at establishing firm technical rules. He disliked spelling out details methodically; became tired of 'students as a species', who, he later complained, 'asked far too many questions, questions, as if I had to know the answers to all of them'.[317] Only Boeke and Van Hauwe pleased him in this respect; they 'asked nothing and practised a lot'. It is hardly surprising that Brüggen never wrote a recorder method; his early *Five Studies for Finger Control* (1959) was his sole published contribution to the literature on recorder technique. In this respect, Verbruggen might be considered 'conservative', having taught, like Brüggen, with undeniable success but without having elaborated a systematic method, while Van Hauwe could be seen as more 'radical' in his methodical thoroughness.

According to Van Hauwe, Brüggen 'was not interested [in the first instance] in recorder technique . . . he was an artist, an educator'. He founded 'not so much a recorder school as a mentality . . . you learned to love the instrument so much it became part of yourself, your *raison d'être*'.[318] Indeed the 'physical connection with the instrument'[319] was vital to Brüggen.[320] He considered absolute devotion to the instrument the essential prerequisite for his students: 'tone doesn't matter, technique doesn't matter, style doesn't matter . . . all these things will come in six months if the other thing is right . . .'.[321] Barker defined a 'recorder mentality' as 'a more or less subservient role of the player to the instrument, much more one of exploration: what does this thing "want" to do, before the question "How can I get this or that out of it?" '[322] Studying initially under Kanji, Barker began to 'fall in love with . . . the idea of feeling the instrument out, finding what it can do . . . through a long process of growth with the instrument, really eating and sleeping with it . . .'.

Given these differences in approach among Brüggen's students, which have become even more pronounced in the performing and teaching practice of subsequent generations, it is hardly surprising that virtually every Dutch-trained recorder player I have asked rejects the notion of a 'Dutch School'. The common denominator among players who have studied in the Netherlands seems more likely to be the 'mentality' described by Barker and Van Hauwe: an intense dedication to the instrument, perhaps to the exclusion of worldly concerns, whether temporarily or as a lifetime passion. This suspension of belief in the paradigm of the recorder as an amateur's instrument or *Volksblockflöte* / school recorder is perhaps the most precious contribution of the Dutch recorder revolution to the instrument's history – a defining moment against which the intentions and achievements of subsequent professional players in all countries may be measured.

***

'Modernising' the recorder

'Modern' harpsichords, such as those made by Pleyel, Neupert, or de Blaise, were once ubiquitous, defining the sound of Early Music until well into the 1960s. But by the time the most important modernising makers and their innovations were chronicled in Wolfgang Zuckermann's *The Modern Harpsichord* (1970), massive, piano-like frames and multiple pedals were already becoming a rare sight. Today, it is hard to find an appropriate instrument in good playing order to perform the works written, for example, for Wanda Landowska by Manuel de Falla or Francis Poulenc.

Attempts to 'modernise' the recorder have generally been even shorter-lived. The most persistent inventions – Dolmetsch's 'English' fingering, Peter Harlan's 'German' fingering, the cheap school soprano recorder, and ABS-moulded plastic instruments – are discussed at length in this chapter. Other innovations have rarely been adopted outside a small circle of players, usually for too short a period to attract the attention of more than a handful of composers.

One important exception is the 'Ganassi' recorder design by Frederick Morgan. See chapter 2. Originally intended for playing sixteenth-century music, it has been adopted for performing transcriptions of virtuosic works from early seventeenth-century Italy, and for contemporary music, including fine works by Calliope Tsoupaki and Isang Yun. Original 'Ganassi' instruments from Morgan's workshop are highly valued for their exquisite workmanship, outstanding sound quality, and dynamic flexibility, and his design has been widely copied.

Another invention that has withstood the test of time is the square-bore plywood bass recorder design patented in 1975 by Joachim and Herbert Paetzold, currently available in the sizes: bass in f^0, great bass in c^0, contrabass in F^0, and subgreatbass in C^0. These distinctive instruments have large wooden keys and a surprisingly powerful sound, often enhanced by amplification or digital technology for performances of contemporary music. The repertoire of new music for such Paetzold bass models includes several virtuosic works commissioned by Antonio Politano from Emanuele Casale, Gabriele Manca, and Fausto Romitelli.

Although many patents have been registered for added keywork, no system has yet gained wide acceptance. This is true even for the simple bell key to close the end of the recorder, championed at various times by persuasive advocates, but only rarely seen today either in professional or amateur circles. More elaborate systems, whether drawing on the Boehm flute (Edward Verne Powell's OrKon or Chromette, 1941) or the saxophone (Arnfred Strathmann, 1984), have proved even less successful.

A number of innovative instruments develop the design – with a wider, less conical ('long') bore – of some recorders made in Germany in the 1930s. Friedrich von Huene's Modern Tenor recorder with five keys is such an instrument, as are several models based on Nikolaj Tarasov's 'Modern Harmonic Recorder' bore, including those by Maarten Helder (Harmonic alto and tenor recorders, from 1995) and Adriana Breukink in collaboration with Geri Bollinger ('Eagle' recorder, 2013). The latter two models, both featuring additional gadgets designed to increase dynamic range through moveable parts operated by the player's lips or chin, have attracted the attention of celebrated professional players, including Van Hauwe (Helder), and Michala Petri and Karel van Steenhoven (Eagle).

THE RECORDER AT THE MILLENNIUM

COMMUNITIES

Literary references to the recorder in the years immediately following the Second World War tended to characterize its players as colourful, even eccentric people. Gerhart Pohl's *Die Blockflöte* (1948), for example, describes a young traveller on a sea voyage from Tahiti, entranced by the recorder playing of first officer Captain Rugard.[323] In Kingsley Amis's bestselling satire on British academic life *Lucky Jim* (1954), much fun is made of Welch, a pompous history professor who pontificates in the very first paragraph about the differences between flutes *à bec* and *traverso*.[324] As the instrument became more familiar, however, some authors had become players themselves. John Updike ended his 1963 poem 'Vow' thus: 'With holy din / Recorder angels will tune us in / When we have run our mortal race / From sopranino to contrabass';[325] and he later drew on his experience as a member of a recorder ensemble in his short story 'The Man Who Became a Soprano' (1988).[326] Similar affection for the instrument was displayed by Umberto Eco, a member of the Società Italiana del Flauto Dolce and regular visitor to its summer school in Urbino. In his essay 'How Not to Talk about Soccer' (1990), he imagines annoying a fellow rail passenger by chatting to him as only a true fan could, not about sport, but Frans Brüggen, Baroque recorder repertoire, and 'German' fingering.[327]

Periodicals such as *American Recorder*, *Recorder Magazine*, *Tibia*, and *Windkanal* attest that the enthusiasm and sense of belonging to a community invoked by Updike and Eco are real experiences, not mere literary techniques. Nowhere is this more evident than when people come together to play, whether informally, for example at an ARS or SRP branch meeting, or in ensembles with more ambitious schedules, such as one of the amateur recorder orchestras worldwide, from Japan's Meguro Recorder Orchestra or the Scottish Recorder Orchestra (not to mention four National Youth Recorder Orchestras in Britain) to the eleven US Recorder Orchestras affiliated with the ARS. In Germany, the original Neukölln Recorder Orchestra, renamed Berliner Blockflötenorchester in 2012 and rejuvenated under the leadership of Simon Borutzki, has achieved a standard of performance of which Barthel would undoubtedly have been proud.[328]

The relationship between amateur players and professionals working with them has been widely discussed, notably in a joint interview with Brüggen, Linde, and Staeps, published in *American Recorder* in 1966. The relative ease with which a beginner can 'take a recorder, blow into it, and get a tone out of it' compared with other instruments makes it particularly attractive to adult beginners. This low threshold can, however, lead to the perception 'that [playing well] doesn't matter because it's not worth taking seriously' – indeed, to 'unbridled amateurism and dilettantism'. For the professional, it can indeed be frustrating to realize that many amateur recorder enthusiasts feel 'that the really important thing is to make music together, not to learn to play the instrument'.[329] When lines become blurred, and amateurs change roles – seeking employment teaching the recorder without having previously gained more than a rudimentary grasp of its technique, repertoire, history, or performance practice – more serious conflicts of interest can occur.

Important questions, not least: 'What is a professional recorder teacher?', remained unresolved at the millennium. The bad example set by Ferdinand Enke's recorder training programme for unemployed musicians in 1930s Berlin has been followed, albeit in less overtly corrupt forms, ever since. For example, the Recorder in Education Summer School, established by the SRP in 1948 'to help raise the standard of teaching', still advertised 'credit-bearing courses' for candidates taking external diplomas in Music Education at Trinity College of Music, London, in the early 1990s.[330] Should former participants at these workshops be considered 'professional' colleagues of graduates holding a teaching qualification from a university-level institution, or are they in fact still 'amateurs', trespassing on the territory of professionals?

Given how many recorder students in Europe had achieved formal qualifications by the millennium, it is hardly surprising that attempts have been made to form professional alliances, notably the European Recorder Teachers Association (ERTA), whose German (1992), Austrian (1995), and Swiss (2004) chapters are particularly active.[331] The challenges facing such organizations are particularly well documented in Switzerland.[332] The city of Zurich first introduced class recorder lessons to the school curriculum in 1947, creating a substantial demand for 'recorder teachers', most of whom were, however, unqualified. In an attempt to raise standards, the SAJM,[333] an independent body founded in 1956, offered basic certificate courses in recorder teaching. After a national association of Swiss music schools was founded in 1975, attempts to place the recorder on an equal footing with other instruments were again hindered by the difficulty of finding sufficient qualified teachers to meet demand. Many holders of the relatively easily obtainable SAJM certificates were employed, contributing further to a perception of recorder teaching as a low-skilled occupation. In 2005, over sixty years after the nation's first recorder diploma was awarded at the Schola Cantorum in Basel,[334] only 8 per cent of Swiss recorder teachers held a relevant professional qualification (compared with an average of 84 per cent of teachers of other instruments), the rest being either holders of an SAJM certificate or unqualified.

'SQUEEEEEEEEEEEEAAAAAAAAAK!'

Public attitudes towards the recorder since the Second World War have been shaped primarily by the school soprano recorder in c^2, probably the most common tool for basic musical instruction within the sphere of influence of Western art music at the millennium. The soprano's role as the principal size of recorder for educational use may appear to be a logical one, since it is small enough to be played by young children. Yet before the modern revival, except in the Netherlands in the seventeenth century, it was just one of an array of sizes played by professionals, and amateurs generally favoured the alto. The soprano's present-day ubiquity is therefore a modern phenomenon.

Ever since Harlan first marketed his *Volksblockflöte* in 1933, the principal merit of the school soprano recorder has been its low price. Today, owing to producers' economies of scale, the ease of distributing resilient small instruments, and high retail turnover, a plastic school soprano recorder can be bought virtually anywhere in the developed world for approximately the same cost as a hamburger meal in a fast-food restaurant.[335] An important secondary virtue is its ready availability in large numbers for class use. In the first decades of the post-Second World War era, a remarkable expansion of production occurred as manufacturers tooled up to meet growing demand. Even during the 1960s several hundred thousand plastic sopranos were being sold every year under the Dolmetsch brand name alone. In 1970, however, Dolmetsch's considerable investment in a new model made from ABS plastic, advertised as 'the £25,000 recorder for 17s 3d', meant that annual production could be expanded to millions of instruments.[336] Seventeen shillings and 3 pence was equivalent to approximately US$2.10 at the time; a conservative estimate of the current (2020) earnings equivalent might fall in the range US$17–21.[337]

Despite the best efforts of regulatory bodies such as the state recorder commission in the Netherlands and the British Standards Institution, which published recommendations for recorder quality in 1964,[338] the generally poor quality noted by Ruëtz in his 1934 consumer report remained characteristic of school recorders for several decades. Given that school recorders are often played together in groups or classes, a high degree of uniformity of response and tuning is clearly of great importance. Poor design and lax quality control long undermined such consistency, however, even among instruments from the same factory – a problem exacerbated by the proliferation of makers and different models. The arrival of high-quality imports from Japan in the early 1970s challenged Western manufacturers, as documented in a 1984 report by the German Consumers' Association *Stiftung Warentest*. This condemned several relatively expensive domestic wooden school recorders, including instruments by Hohner and Moeck, and the majority of German plastic models, as 'defective' (*mangelhaft*) or even 'very defective', whereas the Japanese plastic instruments tested were mainly judged 'good'. Clearly, these findings were humiliating and potentially commercially damaging to the German recorder industry, both at home (where the market penetration of foreign imports was still relatively modest, at about 23 per cent of all instruments sold), and in its export markets (two-thirds of its yearly production of over a million recorders).[339]

The school recorder's inherent limitations as a physical instrument have been aggravated by the class environment into which it has usually been introduced, and the methods by which it is taught. As has been noted, even in affluent countries like Switzerland, many 'recorder teachers' lack professional qualifications. Consequently, the generally unattractive noises inevitably produced by groups of beginners on most instruments are, in the case of the school recorder, rarely placed in the context of skilled playing by their teacher. Fingering technique is often taught without more than passing reference to bodily posture or to the hand and finger positions necessary to hold the instrument comfortably, leading regularly to the development of intractable problems, sadly familiar to the professionally trained teacher.[340] Such early experience can act as a disincentive to further study, as a 1983 study of approximately 1,400 schoolchildren with an average age of 14 in the German city of Hannover suggested: although 41 per cent 'played the recorder' (the next most widely played instrument was the guitar, with 27 per cent), fewer than a third of them 'had a teacher'. The gender stereotyping first evidenced during the Nazi era in 1937 appeared unbroken, as 90 per cent of the 'recorder players' were female. Only 3 per cent of the 'recorder players' said they did not want to play any other instrument (compared with 45 per cent of other woodwind players).[341]

The cultural status of the instrument, its players, and its advocates has suffered immense damage. Regularly described in mainstream German newspapers from across the political spectrum as an 'instrument of torture',[342] the recorder has even jokingly been compared to a lethal weapon, 'the Kalashnikov of musical instruments',[343] deployed 'without mercy, regardless of the consequences'.[344] Recorder-playing children are compared to sadistic inquisitors: 'With brutal energy they pull out their perforated squeaky tools and start the torture';[345] 'Squeeeeeeeeeeeeaaaaaaaaak!!!';[346] 'you ask yourself where Amnesty International is, when you urgently need the organization's help. In short: the recorder is known as the instrument of horror.'[347] Given this negative image, it is hardly surprising that demand for professional recorder teaching in Germany has declined. The number of children learning the recorder at music schools fell dramatically from 100,000 in 1995 to 50,000 in 2013, before stabilizing at around 60,000 in the years to 2019. During the same period, demand for lessons on other instruments increased steadily, leaving the recorder – in 1980 the most popular instrument of all – in fourth place behind the piano, guitar, and violin by the millennium.[348] These statistics were widely reported in the national and regional press, with headlines such as 'Swan song of the recorder: Fiep Fuuup Pffft'[349] and 'Children give recorder the cold shoulder – alternatives are more hip.'[350]

A three-year study of the musical activity of 1,209 schoolchildren aged between 10 and 12 years conducted by researchers at Keele University for the British Economic and Social Research Council concluded in 2001:

> The majority of children in both Year 6 and Year 7 [equivalent to the 5th and 6th grades] reported playing the recorder. This certainly affords opportunities since it is a small, light, inexpensive and relatively durable instrument that most children can learn to play and there[by] gain experience of active music-making. However, children do not associate playing the recorder with their musical role models in the adult world. [Rather], they view the recorder as 'not a real instrument' or a 'child's instrument' which is limited in its ability to express the music young people are most interested in playing.[351]

Widely reported in the British news media ('The recorder is annoying and boring and puts people off music'),[352] the Keele University report gives a clear picture of the damage done to the cultural status of the recorder since the end of the Second World War. Almost universal familiarity has bred widespread contempt: the belief of many children that the school recorder is 'not a real instrument' now appears firmly rooted in the popular imagination.

PROFESSIONAL ARTISTRY

As we have seen, the recorder's new post-war role as a virtuoso solo instrument was initially firmly rooted in the Netherlands. As the Dutch recorder revolution gained momentum, it cross-pollinated and enriched other traditions, leading to a widening diversity of training, outlook, and performance practice. Conservatories throughout Western Europe, and to a lesser extent in the Americas, Australasia, and Japan, opened their doors to recorder students in the 1970s. Career prospects for graduates, however, inevitably depended on reliable patronage. In countries where state support for the arts and music education was modest, such as the USA and Britain, the recorder remained essentially an instrument for children and amateurs. Elsewhere, however, more comprehensive public finance provided greater opportunities.[353]

The Netherlands remained unchallenged as the leading international centre of recorder teaching until well into the 1980s. As noted above, many of Brüggen's students became successful teachers in their own right. Boeke, Van Hauwe, Kanji, and Verbruggen in particular trained several generations of excellent musicians, far too numerous to be covered in detail here. A small selection might include the original members of the Amsterdam Loeki Stardust Recorder Quartet (Daniel Brüggen, Bertho Driever, Paul Leenhouts, and Karel van Steenhoven), Erik Bosgraaf, Carin van Heerden, Peter Holtslag, Lucie Horsch, Gerd Lünenbürger, Pedro Memelsdorff, Dorothee Oberlinger, Antonio Politano, Heiko ter Schegget, and Han Tol. At peak capacity, for example in the academic year 1988–89, approximately 200 recorder students were enrolled at Dutch conservatories – 24 in Amsterdam and 54 in Utrecht alone.[354] Even allowing for a substantial proportion of foreign nationals, this was clearly out of proportion to any possible demand for graduates. Unsurprisingly, since the 1990s the number of recorder classes has been substantially reduced as part of ongoing general reform of arts funding and tertiary-level music education.[355]

In Germany, despite some setbacks around the millennium, several Musikhochschulen maintain salaried faculty positions for the recorder. Furthermore, nationwide provision of professional music teaching for children at publicly funded Musikschulen continues to ensure relatively good employment prospects for college graduates. By contrast, the number of recorder students enrolled at British music colleges has rarely matched those at comparable institutions on the Continent. Whether this is the result of the low honorariums and lack of job security for their teachers, the high fees demanded, especially from foreign students, poor vocational prospects, or the absence of a 'recorder mentality' has been a matter for (sometimes heated) debate.[356]

A comprehensive survey of professional recorder playing at the turn of the century would require far more space than is available here. Besides mentioning virtuosi from countries far from Western Europe, such as Mexico (Horatio Franco, b. 1963), Venezuela (Aldo Abreu, b. 1962), or Australia (Genevieve Lacey, b. 1972), it would include many excellent chamber ensembles that have followed the outstanding examples of the Amsterdam Loeki Stardust Quartet (1978–2007) and Flanders Recorder Quartet (1987–2018). Three European musicians from outside the Dutch tradition may, however, serve to illustrate the diversity of background, training, and performance practice of professional recorder players as the millennium approached:

Hans Maria Kneihs (b. 1943), professor emeritus of recorder at the University of Music and Performing Arts in Vienna, started his career as a cellist in the Austrian Radio Symphony Orchestra (1964–69), before switching to the recorder as the principal focus of his activity. His Wiener Blockflötenensemble (Vienna Recorder Ensemble, 1972–85), made a vital contribution to the re-emergence of the professional recorder consort, documented in a series of LPs. The ensemble was particularly noteworthy for its mastery of large recorders, notably the first of many outstanding consorts made by Bob Marvin (1941–2018).

Michael Schneider (b. 1953), a student of Höller at the Cologne Musikhochschule who acknowledges the influence of additional lessons taken with Walter van Hauwe, shared the highest prize awarded for recorder at the prestigious international music competition of the German Broadcasting Union (ARD) in Munich in 1976.[357] His subsequent busy concert and recording career, notably with the ensembles Musica Antiqua Köln, Camerata Köln, and La Stagione Frankfurt, established new standards of excellence in chamber and orchestral recorder playing.[358] As professor of recorder at the Musikhochschulen in Berlin (1980–83) and Frankfurt (1983–2019), Schneider has had a profound influence on several generations of professional recorder players.

Michala Petri (b. 1958), the first child prodigy recorder player to attract wide international attention, was admitted by special dispensation to study with Conrad at the Musikhochschule in Hannover at the age of 11, commuting there with her mother from her native Denmark. Initially, she performed mainly with her mother Hanne (harpsichord) and brother David (cello), as reflected in a brilliant recital programme including music by Van Eyck, Castello, Handel, Heberle, Telemann, Vivaldi, and Berio (*Gesti*), released as an LP by the British Broadcasting Corporation in 1977.[359] Her subsequent discography documents her career as the world's best-known and longest-serving recorder virtuoso, sought after for collaborations by celebrated artists in the music profession, ranging from the

36. Michala Petri, 2013.

classical violinist Pinchas Zukerman (no friend of early instruments) to the jazz pianist Keith Jarrett. She has made a substantial contribution to the recorder repertoire through her commissions of new music, notably recorder concertos with symphony orchestra.

Petri's performance practice differs from that of any other comparably eminent recorder player of her generation. She plays the Baroque repertoire at modern pitch (A 440–444) and in equal temperament, on 'modern' instruments claiming no close resemblance to historical models. Her vibrato is faster than that of, for example, Brüggen's mature playing style, and is used as an essential element of the basic sound – in keeping with her characteristic style of phrasing, which favours a dramatic onward flow of the musical line over the highlighting of motivic detail. Her career, too, is perhaps unique among modern professional recorder players: Petri is best known neither as a teacher, nor for her work in chamber ensembles, but for bringing the recorder into the world's leading concert halls as a fully-fledged solo instrument, on an equal footing – and billing – with its peers.

EPILOGUE
MICHALA PETRI

The development of the recorder – its playing technique, repertoire, and construction – has been rapid since its revival in the twentieth century. Other instruments such as the violin have had an uninterrupted history, each generation building on its predecessors. But the recorder started anew a few generations ago, and it has been my fate to grow up along with it.

In my childhood, the recorder was considered a toy instrument, and I was often asked why I played it at a serious level. From the very beginning, this led me to wonder where exactly its charm and attraction lay. Clearly, there was more to it – for both me and many others – than just 'liking the sound' of the instrument, or it being apparently easy to play and transport.

Today I feel better able to put into words the sensation of being in touch with an inner or spiritual world in which things can be put right through the tools that any musician has: a free body, steady airflow and energy-flow, and a positive and creative way of thinking. On the recorder this sensation was always evident to me, and on a clearer level than with instruments that required more physical strength. I recall the feeling of my instrument reacting to the slightest change in breath pressure, of being physically in touch with it, not merely by carrying or touching it, but through the recorder's resistance against the airstream flowing from my diaphragm. When this feeling was right, the sound would be right as well, and I felt intertwined with the instrument. My body adjusted intuitively, and I had a palpable feeling of being shaped by both the instrument and the music I was playing.

So many aspects of the recorder have developed, and so fast. The quality of the physical instrument has improved, new modern designs have been invented, and diverse models from various historical periods have been revived. When I started, only a few recorders based on a specific Baroque instrument were available; today it is commonplace to have access to instruments appropriate for any music being played.

The notorious gap in repertoire between Baroque and modern has partly been filled through the rediscovery of nineteenth-century csakan music, and this once-forgotten instrument has re-entered production. I remember my excitement when, in the 1970s, the oboist and composer Heinz Holliger told me about a concerto he had seen in a library by an unknown composer, Anton Heberle, which he thought might interest me, after which I ordered it and performed it many times. Thereafter, knowing that there was something called a csakan, and having a composer's name, it was easier to search in the old card catalogues in various libraries for music from this period, leading to discovering Ernest Krähmer, for example.

The repertoire has been brought up to date by composers writing new works. Encouraging them to do that has been one of my principal aims throughout my career. The first time I played a new composition I was 6 years old. It was not just a new work, but also a piece written especially for me by a composer friend of my parents. I still recall the feeling of the piece speaking to me as something significant, and of the composer listening carefully as I played it, accompanied by my mother on the piano. I was aware of the music sounding strangely odd in my own mind, compared with what I had previously known, but I also felt that there was a silent understanding between the composer's mind and mine through his music.

Since then, I have premiered more than 150 works, often in close collaboration with their composers, and always with the same feeling of trust in the composer's intention. This work has enhanced my feeling of 'playing music' rather than playing a particular instrument and has naturally led me to push the instrument's boundaries. Often, after thinking that a new work was impossible to play, I practised hard, comparing the challenges with those of a more 'advanced' instrument, and telling myself that, logically, it had to be easier to solve them on the recorder, until suddenly that became true and the piece was, if not easy, then at least playable. It pleases me that younger generations of players will start out unaware that these compositions were ever considered difficult!

The recorder's growing reputation among the public is also something I have followed, not only over time but geographically when travelling. In my youth, in England and Japan it was an instrument that every child had to play in school. I still think that the recorder is one of the best instruments to give everybody an impression of what music-making is and feels like, and also, thanks to the great discipline and precision it requires, a fine base for continuing to other instruments. The degree to which concert audiences were familiar with the recorder as a suitable instrument for professional music-making, however, differed greatly from country to country. I still recall feeling like the odd one out when I saw my own concerts announced between those of famous string quartets and violin recitals, or when I was engaged by distinguished symphony orchestras playing in large venues, such as Avery Fisher Hall in New York or Orchestra Hall in Chicago.

The biggest practical problem in my youth, and the one I suffered from the most, was the recorder's relative quietness and its restricted dynamic range – which, on the other hand, taught me to create another kind of strength by playing very precisely, slowly learning by experience that precision in rhythm and intonation attracted the listener's attention and co-created the musical experience. Today we have modern recorders with greater dynamic potential.

Also today, the recorder is taught at many music academies, new repertoire is being discovered and composed, and the instrument has found a natural place in all kinds of music, including jazz, pop, folk, and rock. Thanks to the Internet and the opportunities it provides for reaching out among people, the instrument's potential is greater than ever. The recorder community is linked as never before, and all new developments can be accessed literally anywhere.

Paradoxically, in this time of overwhelming amounts of information, I think that the recorder is an ideal instrument for today: its 'simplicity' and its direct connection with the breath are perhaps more needed now than in the past, and it fulfils our need to express the human soul so well and in such a direct way.

NOTES

ABBREVIATIONS

AMZ	*Allgemeine musikalische Zeitung*
AMZO	*Allgemeine musikalische Zeitung mit besonderer Rücksicht auf den österreichischen Kaiserstaat*
AR	*(The) American Recorder*
BArch	*Bundesarchiv*
BJhM	*Basler Jahrbuch für historische Musikpraxis*
BS	*Der Blockflötenspiegel*
CM	*Collegium Musicum*
EM	*Early Music*
EMH	*Early Music History*
EMP	*Early Music Performer*
FoMRHI	*Fellowship of Makers and Researchers of Historical Instruments*
GDMI	*Grove Dictionary of Musical Instruments*, 2nd edn
GMO	*Grove Music Online*
GSJ	*Galpin Society Journal*
HBSJ	*Historic Brass Society Journal*
JAMIS	*Journal of the American Musical Instrument Society*
JAMS	*Journal of the American Musicological Society*
LMR	*Lexique musicale de la Renaissance*
M&M	*Music and Musicians*
MGG	*Die Musik in Geschichte und Gegenwart*
MQ	*Musical Quarterly*
NM	*Neues Musikblatt*
NRCH	*NRC Handelsblad*
NRD	*Nachrichtendienst der Beratungsstelle für Blockflötenspiel*
PSH	*Paisajes Sonoros Históricos*
R&M	*Recorder & Music*
RHPI	Recorder Home Page: Iconography
RM	*The Recorder Magazine*
RMFC	*'Recherches' sur la musique française classique*
RMM	*Recorder and Music Magazine*
RN	*The Recorder News*
SAJMZ	*SAJM Zeitschrift*
SRN	*Sussex Recorder News*
VN	*Vrij Nederland*
ZfH	*Zeitschrift für Hausmusik*
ZfM	*Zeitschrift für Musik*
ZfS	*Zeitschrift für Spielmusik*

INTRODUCTION

1. Hornbostel and Sachs 1961, 24–25.
2. Ibid., 26; *GMO*, s.v. 'Duct Flute', by Jeremy Montagu.
3. Brade 1975; Crane 1972, 29–42; Moeck 1967; *RHPI*.
4. *GMO*, s.v. 'Pipe and Tabor', by Anthony C. Baines and Hélène La Rue.
5. A shout-out to János Bali (2007a), whose fine book on the instrument is available only in Hungarian.
6. Ehrlich 2021.
7. Lasocki 2004, 2010, 2018b, 2018c, 2019, 2020; Brown and Lasocki 2006; Lasocki et al. 2022.
8. Lasocki 2018a.
9. Griscom and Lasocki 2012.
10. See www.davidlasocki.com/store.

1 THE ERA OF MEDIEVAL RECORDERS, 1300–1500

1. 'septem ante ac unum aliud retro instar fistule'. Weinmann 1917, 36; Woodley 1985, 245.
2. *GMO*, s.v. 'Aulos', by Annie Bélis.
3. *GMO*, s.v. 'Fistula', by James W. McKinnon, and 'Tibia', by McKinnon and Robert Anderson.
4. Palsgrave 1530, f. lviiiᵛ.
5. Another possible early recorder in a museum in Rhodes (Greece), made of bone, has not yet been studied in detail. Rowland-Jones 2006a, 14.
6. Tvauri and Utt 2007.
7. Inv. no. TM A 141:170. Taavi-Mats Utt, email message to DL, 25 June 2013.
8. Utt notes that the previous report of a compass of a ninth, 'Mittelalter-Blockflöte' 2006, 7, was incorrect; email message to DL, 3 December 2012.
9. Inv. no. 544045.
10. Weber 1976.
11. Inv. no. 50779.
12. Weber 1976; Hakelberg 1995, 11, n. 7; Kunkel 1953, 306–7, Abb. 4.
13. Weber 1976, 239.
14. Adrian Brown, email message to DL, 2 October 2016.
15. Hakelberg 1994; 1995, 3–12.
16. Hakelberg 1995, 5.
17. Reiners 1997, 31.
18. Ibid., 33.
19. Ibid.
20. Doht 2006, 105–7.
21. Hakelberg 2002, 30–31; and communication with Nicholas Lander, 2003.
22. Inv. no. MNa/A/182/6. Mateusz Łącki, email message to Lander, 22 July 2011.
23. Martin Kirnbauer, email message to DL, 21 August 2013; message from Krzysztof Dobrzański to Ture Bergstrøm, 9 January 2018.
24. Popławska and Lachowicz 2014, 75.
25. Inv. no. 4891. Naumann 1999; Kirnbauer and Young 2001; Kirnbauer 2002, 54–55; Popławska 2004; 2008; Popławska and Lachowicz 2014, 76.
26. Kirnbauer, email message.
27. Eugene Ilarionov, email message to DL, 14 October 2016.
28. Tarasov 2014.
29. Inv. no. MMP/Dep/991/17. Popławska and Lachowicz 2014, 75–76.
30. Pierre Boragno, email message to DL, citing Catherine Homo-Lechner, 14 March 2017.
31. Homan 1964, 74.
32. Crane 1972, 45.
33. Tarasov 2014.
34. Ibid.

35. Crane 1972; Brade 1975; a few additional instruments catalogued in Müller 1972.
36. Kulturhistorisk Museum Randers, catalogue no. 5816; see Brade 1975, DK 5; Müller 1972, no. 62.
37. Homo-Lechner 1993, 260–61; 1996, 100.
38. Crane 1972, 45.
39. Aleo Nero 2013, 228.
40. Brade 1975, 26.
41. Reichenthal 1976.
42. Adrian Brown, email message to DL, 19 January 2008.
43. Rowland-Jones 2005, 557.
44. Ibid., 561.
45. Sub-section based on Lasocki 2018b.
46. Montagu 1997; Boragno 1998.
47. 'une flute d'yvoire'. Lasocki 2018b, 13.
48. Page 1982.
49. 'est qui in minori fistula canit. Et voco minores fistulas, quas vulgariter flatillas nominamus, eoquod minuta flatillacione spiritus oris sonum reddant, sed debilem et remissum. Unde fidulis quandoque proporcionantur in concinendo.' Ibid., 193.
50. Lasocki 2018b, 13.
51. 'autem fistule amorosos animos excitant seu irritant et ad dulcorem devocionis quodammodo movent. Quapropter organa ex ipsarum varietate ac multitudine consistencia templis ubi divina peraguntur sollemnia, congrue deputantur.' Page 1982, 194–95.
52. 'Je n'ay mie si mal en l'ongle / Que je n'aie aprins a jouer / A l'eschequier et flaioler.' Lasocki 2018b, 24.
53. Earp 1995, 38.
54. 'sans doute du même atelier'. Grodecki 1968, 62.
55. Rowland-Jones 2006a, 20; 2006b, 11.
56. 'Tabours et muses et flaios / Y a assez, grelles et gros.' Adenès Li Rois 1865, 226.
57. 'Au chant dou flagol s'endormi.' Lasocki 2018b, 15.
58. 'flaios plus de x. paires, / C'est à dire de xx. manieres, / Tant des fortes com des legieres.' Machaut 1877, 35. Dating from Earp 1995, 191.
59. Machaut 1911, 145–46. Dating from Earp 1995, 190–91.
60. 'Les doulz flajolez ressonans / Que des selves des boys faisons.' Lasocki 2018b, 23.
61. 'Quivi Tedeschi / Latini e Franceschi / Fiamenghi e Ingheleschi insieme parlare; / e fanno un trombombe / che par che rimbombe / a guisa di trombe / che pian vol sonare. / Chitarre e lïuti / vïole e flaùti / voci alt'ed acute, qui s'odon cantare. / Stututù ifiù / stututù ifiù / stututù ifiù / *tamburar, suffolare*.' Ibid., 31.
62. Wegman 2002; Gómez Muntané 1990.
63. Wegman 2002, 11.
64. Gómez Muntané 1979, I, 36.
65. Peters 2012.
66. Gómez Muntané 1979, I, 74, 134.
67. Wegman 2002, 18–24.
68. Ibid., 15.
69. Ibid., 13.
70. Section based on Lasocki 2018b, 25–30.
71. 'Certificam vos que Matheu, tragitador nostre, va de licencia nostra a la ciutat de Valencia, e com ell s fort be en fer arpes, volum e us manam que digats a Ponç qui fa los lahuts, que ab consell e acort del dit Matheu nos faça una arp doble, e provehits que sien tots dies ensemps sus aço entro que la dita arpa sie acabada, e bestrets hi vos ço que mester faça, e fets la luirar al dit Matheu que la ns aport, e trametet nos los lahuts e los flahutes al pus breu que porets.' Gómez Muntané 1979, 182; Ballester 2000, 11. This document was originally discovered by Anglès 1936, I, 619, without commenting on the *flahutes*, although he does immediately note that, because the suffering Juan's minstrels had not yet returned from the schools, he 'wanted to hear songs and new music'. This suggestion might have given Jordi Ballester the idea that the *flautes* played chansons.

72. Receipt of 10 August 1378: 'Vostra letra havem reebuda e los lahuts e les flahutes que tremeses nos havets de que.ns tenim per servits.' Archivo de la Corona de Aragón, reg. 1745, f. 145; Gómez Muntané, email message to DL, 4 February 2008.
73. Lasocki 2018b, 25.
74. Ibid., 29.
75. *GMO*, s.v. 'Spain, §1, 1: Art music: Early history', and 'Shabbāba'; Torralba 1997.
76. 'Era tot françes.' Gómez Muntané 1984, 71.
77. First suggested in Ballester 2000, 11.
78. 'ad partes Francie et aliarum terrarum'; Anglès 1936, I, 613.
79. 'E tenia en la sua cort moltes cobles de ministres de totes maneras per haver plaer de dançare e cantar.' Tomich 1970, 109.
80. 'La maiorancia que en ell era si era en fer cercar perlo mon los pus abtes ministres que trobar se poguessen axi destruments de corda com de boca e xantres per que li sonassen e cantassen davant tres vegades al dia ço es una demati: e altra a migdia: e altra a vespre: e aquesta regla volia que fos servada cascun dia de la setmana: e ans ques gitas en lo lit voli efaea los donzells: e donzelles davant si dançar e solacar exceptats los divendres.' Carbonell 1546, f. CCVI.
81. 'entrevenents alcuns dels nostres xantres, fahem I rondell notat ab sa tenor e contratenor e ab son cant . . .'. Gómez Muntané 1979, 200.
82. Ibid., 92, 204.
83. 'Entes havem per letra de Johani, nostre ministrer . . . e car poch fa ell sie vengut de les escoles, volem que el mostre als vostres ministrers de les cançons novelles que ell sap.' Ibid., 138.
84. 'Los nostres ministrers han mostrades de nostre manament sis cançons novelles als vostres, e quant los dits nostres ministrers qui van ara a las escoles seran tornats, vos nos enviats los vostres e nos los farem moltes mostrar dels nostres esturments. Car cosi, vos trametem per los dits vostres ministrers dues xalamies, dues cornamuses, una museta gran e altra poca, una xalamia poca e una bombarda.' Ibid., 141.
85. 'Car los esturments dels ministrers de la Duquessa qui ara son aci dementre que ls toquen nos tabutxen lo cap, per ço vos pregam que per I hom vostre nos trametats les musetes vostres que Tibaut, ministrer vostre, vos aporta de Fflandres enguany. . . .' Ibid., 141.
86. 'los havem tramesses en Fflandres per esturments de novella guise . . .', 'ls havem enviats en Fflandes per portar esturments novells . . .'. Ibid., 160.
87. 'E vollem que aporten tot lo cant de la missa notat en un llibre on haia molts motets e rondells e ballades e virelays, pero guardat vos que no n haia alcun que haia servit al Duch d Anjou. E fet nos saber si alcun d ells sab d esturments e de quins com nos de havem de moltes maneres. . . .' Ibid., 198.
88. Ibid., 89–91.
89. Ibid., 77.
90. *GMO*, s.v. 'Trebor', by Yolanda Plumley; Upton 2013, 84, 86; Gómez Muntané 1979, 95, 99, 101.
91. Ibid., 77.
92. 'som certs que la vostres ministrers, qui son de novell tornats de les escoles, han aduyts molts esturments grans e petits, e car nos siam cas vides que oir sonar esturments grans nos ns fos agradable ni profitos, per tant, frare car, vos pregam affectuosament que ns trametats los dits vostres ministrers especialment ab los dits esturments petits, be que amem mes que tots los aporten.' Ibid., 142–43.
93. The suggestion that the recorder was developed in Avignon, whence it would have made its way to Aragón, has not borne fruit. Rowland-Jones, his footnote in Brown 1995, 22, n. 8; 1996, 16. One piece of evidence in favour of Avignon would have been Gómez Muntané's report in the liner notes to the CD *Medée fu*, performed by Tritonius XIV (Verso, VRS 2005, 2001), that a man named Pere Palau made both stringed instruments and recorders in that city in the late fourteenth century. But she was just speculating that Palau made recorders, based on the supposed model of Ponç in Valencia (email message, to DL, 14 July 2013).
94. Rowland-Jones 2006b, 27.
95. 'be sens alcun ministrer de xalamia e a ades sie lo plus plasent so . . .'. Gómez Muntané 1979, 147.

96. 'tres flautes, dues grosses e una negra petita ... dues flautes, una negra petita e 1 altra travessada'. Lasocki 2018b, 28.
97. Ballester 2000, 11; Rowland-Jones 2006a, 21; 2016b, 80–81.
98. Myers 2001, 380.
99. 'Sed certe difficilissimum fit diu vel pro cantilena una costantes quantitate sua voces continere.' Giorgio Anselmi, *De Musica* (1434); McGee 1998, 168, 114; Rowland-Jones 2006b, 80. In contrast, Page 1992a, 447, discussing a late fifteenth-century painting but apparently extending his remarks back through the fourteenth century, observes that 'The recorder, like the portative, might have doubled a part at the octave, but the inherent octave ambiguity of its sound might have made performers reluctant to entrust a tenor or contratenor part to it alone in company with singers.'
100. 'A Villaige, chantre, ledit jour, une canne et demye dudit [drap] gris, à ledite raison, que le roy lui a donné pour avoir monstré des chansons aux menestrelz dudit seigneur. . . .' Lasocki 2018b, 29.
101. 'Si vous suppli que vous le daingniez oir, et savoir la chose einsi comme elle est faite sans mettre ne oster. . . . Et qui la porroit mettre sus les orgues, sus cornemuses, ou autres instrumens, cest sa droite nature. . . .' Machaut 1998, 73.
102. Earp 2011, 367.
103. Brewer 2000, 200; Page 1992b.
104. 'tornerius sive flahuterius, civis Barchinone'. Lasocki 2018b, 29.
105. García Herrero 1984, 384.
106. 'salaris de sonadors d'estruments de corda, de flauta e cornamuses e altres'. Lasocki 2018b, 29.
107. Knighton 2016, 108.
108. Kreitner 1995, 191.
109. McGee 1989.
110. Rowland-Jones 2005, 561 suggests that soft high notes plus accidentals 'were an absolute necessity for imitating vocal music instrumentally'.
111. Bergstrøm 2020.
112. Musikmuseet (Music Museum), Inv. no. D 9745.
113. Bergstrøm 2020, 220.
114. 'Item ter selver tijt [4 April 1387] des hertoghen Dulfs vedelaer van Beyeren ende des bisschops floyter van Mens gheg. te gader . . . 2 dordr. gulden.' Lingbeek-Schalekamp 1984, 169.
115. 'spilluthe mit den floyten'. Müller-Blattau 1968, 13.
116. 'A Haquin Regnault, faiseur d'instrumens, pour l'achat de 8 grans fleustes, 54 s. . . . A Jehannin Culet, gainnier, pour un grand estuy de cuir bouly, ferré et fermant à clé, pour mettre et porter 5 grans fleustes dont ils jouent devant lad. dame.' Lasocki 2018b, 27.
117. Waterhouse 1993, 281 reports the unpublished research of Jindřich Keller that a man called only Nicolaus is documented as a 'flute maker' in Prague in 1397.
118. 'Bergier qui a pennetiere / bien clouant, ferme et entiere, / c'est ung petit roy. / Bergier qui ha pennetiere / a bons clouans par derriere, / fermant par bonne maniere, / que lui faut il, quoy? / Il a son chappeau d'osiere, / son poinsson, son aleniere, / son croq, sa houllecte chiere, / sa boiste au terquoy / beau gippon sur soy, / et, pour l'esbonoy, / sa grosse flute pleniere, / souliers de courroy / a beaulx tasseaulx par derriere. / Face feste et bonne chiere: c'est ung petit roy!' Ibid., 17–18.
119. 'des flajollès deux ou trois, / tabours et fleutes de chois'. Ibid., 28.
120. 'doulx accords et sons melodieux'. Ibid., 18.
121. '1er avril, le duc mandate 3 fr. à "Loyset, barbier de Jehan mons., pour avoir une musote et des fleutes pour led. Jehan mons." ' Ibid.
122. '1 fr. "pour un flajolet de cuivre ovvré et paint que Mgr donna au roy," le 1er aôut'. Ibid., 8–29.
123. 'molt brafs cantres et flusteurs musicals qui molt bien canterent'. Wright 1979, 37.
124. Myers 2001, 380.
125. Planchart 2001, 96.
126. Rowland-Jones 2005, 565; dating from Prochno 2002, 59, 293, 304, 308.
127. '3 ghesellen mit pipen ende luten'. Meyer 1971, 117.

128. '2 vedelen ende eene vloyte'. Polk 2005, 28.
129. 'quatre grans instrumens de menestrelz, quatre douchaines et quatre fleutes, tous garniz d'estuiz de cuir et de coffres'. Lasocki 2018b, 18.
130. David Fallows, email message to DL, 17 November 2010.
131. '4 flûtes d'ivoire, l'une garnie d'or et de pierreries et les autres non garnies'. Lasocki 2018b, 18.
132. 'trois custodes de cuir, paintes d'or, où a en chascune custode flutes d'ivoire, que grandes, que petites, dont l'une des deux grosses flutes est garnie au sifflet d'or, et par embas garnie de deux sercles d'or et semées de petites perles d'émeraudes, grenas et rubis, et n'y fault riens'. Ibid., 3.
133. 'Jamais on n'a compassé / N'en doulchaine, n'en flaiolet / Ce q'ung nagueres trespassé / Faisoit, appelé Verdellet.' Marix 1939, 106.
134. Ibid., 50, 82, 96, 106, 115–16, 182, 268.
135. Brown and Polk 2001, 106.
136. Marix 1939, 269–70.
137. Most scholars now agree that *trompette des ménestrels* was some kind of slide trumpet; *GMO*, s.v. 'Slide Trumpet', by Edward H. Tarr; Polk 1987; 1992, 58–60.
138. 'juèrent quatre menestreux de fleutres moult melodieusement'. Lasocki 2018b, 19.
139. Coelho and Polk 2016, 175–76.
140. Strohm 1990, 98.
141. A group of Venetian musicians visiting the court two months earlier, on 4 May, played *fleutes*. Fiala 2002, 64.
142. 'quatre loups ayans flustes en leurs pattes, et commencerent lesdits loups à jouer une chanson'. Lasocki 2018b, 19.
143. 'ung tabourin et ung flajol'. Ibid., 19.
144. 'iiij flautj novi'. Ibid.; Lasocki 2018a, 2.
145. 'gli fu sonato d'arpa, viola, flauti et de cithara excelentemente'. Muratori 1900–75, xx/2, App., 55.
146. 'Da puoi fecer venire un menacordo / Che avia sí alta voce, che un liuto / Apresso a quello gli parebbe sordo; / Con esso vi sonaro um buon fiauto / Et un saltero, se ben me ricordo: / Piú bel suon di quel mai non fo veduto.' Nádas 1998.
147. Ibid., 29.
148. 'Quattro zufoli fiaminghi / Tre zufoli nostrali / Tre zufoli forniti d'ariento.' Lasocki 2018a, 3.
149. 'Uno giuocho di zufoli grossi in una guaina. . . . Uno giocho di zufoli a uso di pifferi cholle ghiere nere e bianche, sono zufoli cinque. . . . Tre zufoli chon ghiere d'argento in una guaina guernita d'argento. . . .' Ibid., 4–5.
150. McGee 2009, 172.
151. 'In una cassa cinque flauti con la sua cassa tra li quali è uno pizzolo de avolio con sue pezze di tella verde.' Lasocki 2018a, 28.
152. '5 zufoli buoni in una sacchetto'. Ibid., 5.
153. 'La piva . . . ballo è da villa, origine di tutti gli altri è l' suon suo controuato ne l'avena per gli pastori. Dall' avena a le canne pallustri. Da quella, assottigliati gl'ingieni, si transferì ne gli fiautti e in altri instrumenti facti e usati hoggi di presso di noi. . . .' Libro 1915, 14.
154. 'certains compaignons venitiens qui ont joué de la fleute devant mondit seigneur'. Fiala 2002, 64.
155. '1 di leiuto, 1 di ribechino e l di fiuto'. D'Accone 1997, 689, 709.
156. 'liuti, cembali, arpe, staffeti, flauti, e diversi strumenti che facevano suavissima armonia'. Kinkeldey 1910, 166.
157. 'piffari, trombeti, fiauti, arpe, lauti, organo, e canto'. Paganuzzi et al. 1976, 80.
158. 'sona zentilmente de trumbone ed anche di fiauto e di chorneto'. Prizer 1981, 160.
159. 'Piedro, nostro trombono, sarà apparechiato insegnare Bartholomeo suo trombeta el modo et l'arte del sonare el trombono.' Ibid., 160–61, n. 36.
160. Section based on Lasocki 2018b, 71–82.
161. Trowell 1957, 83–84; Rowland-Jones 1999, 2000a, 2001.
162. See also Rowland-Jones 2001, 10.
163. Partridge 1983, 555.
164. *Tobler–Lommatzsch* 1954, 466.

165. Trowell was misled by its original transcriber (Wylie 1898, IV, 158; see also III [1896], 325, n. 3) into understanding that the term was 'Ricordo'. He therefore speculated that it was derived from the Italian verb *ricordare*, 'to remember', and thus meant a memento, keepsake, or souvenir; also that the instrument may have been 'given to the young Earl . . . by some Italian noble, merchant, or ecclesiastic'. This mistranscribed term and speculation were the source of further speculation by researchers that the recorder itself had an Italian origin, which is untenable now.

166. Mancinus 1518.

167. Palsgrave 1530, f. cccxxiv verso. More than two centuries later, Sir John Hawkins noted this usage in his second section on the recorder: 'Among bird-fanciers the word record is used as a verb to signify the first essays of a bird in singing.' Hawkins 1776, I, 479.

168. Drayton 1595, B2.

169. Holland 1613, [I].

170. Chaucer 1961, 293.

171. Hunt 1962, 19–20 commented: 'remembering that one of the French names for the recorder was *la flûte douce*, there is the possibility that the "Doucet" might be the fourteenth-century name for the recorder.' This seems unlikely in this loud context, and John Lydgate (1407) even explicitly puts the doucet in such a context, contrasted with flutes, in Pleasure's garden: 'And for folkys that lyst daunce / Ther wer trumpes and trumpetes, / Lowde shallys and doucetes, / Passyng of gret melodye, / And floutys ful of armonye, / Eke Instrumentys high and lowe / Wel mo than I koude knowe. . . .' *Lydgate's* 1901, I, 146–47. Although the outdoor dancing suggests loud instruments, this passage clearly mentions the English equivalent of the French terms *haut* and *bas* (loud and soft). *Flûte douce* is not documented in French until 1607.

172. Chaucer, *Canterbury Tales*, Prologue, lines 79, 91, 95.

173. 'Seignurs, Dames, bien viengez vus!'; http://www.anglo-norman.net/dissem/data/intro.htm.

174. *Lydgate's* 1923, I, 266, 270.

175. 'Pan primus instituit conjungere plures calamos cerâ.' Virgil 1882, Eclogue II, 8.

176. *Lydgate's* 1901, I, 47–48.

177. Ibid., I, 64.

178. 'fait sonner tuiaus / Et fleutes et chalemiaus'. Lasocki 2018b, 48.

179. Deguileville 1893, 386–87; glossary in Part III; Green 1978, 105–6.

180. 'Quar touz les decoif au flajol.'

181. Lasocki 2018b, 135.

182. Betscher 1995–96, 447–49 counters the earlier view by Fowler 1961 that the play was written in the third quarter of the fourteenth century.

183. *Cornish Ordinalia* 1969, 52.

184. 'wethong menstrels ha tabours / trey-hans harpes ha trompours / cythol crowd fylh / ha savtry / psalmus gyttrens ha nakrys / organs in weth cymbalys / recordys ha symphony'. *Ancient Cornish* 1968, I, 150–51.

185. *Lydgate's* 1891, 64.

186. 'tribus de villa Glascinensis pulsatis cum fleutis et citara'. Bradley 1992, 435.

187. Griffiths 1894, 44.

188. Hunter 1966.

189. *Records of English Court Music* 1993, 151.

190. Suggested by Herbert W. Myers.

191. Pearsall 1986, II, 38.

192. *Records* 1993, 159, 162–63.

193. 'In Ulm kamen abends Stadtpfeifer und spielten vortrefflich, auch Flöte. . . . Der Wirt hat eine sehr schöne Tochter, die dann auch anfing mit den Pfeifern Flöten zu blasen, und hernach mit anderen Sängern, die hinzukamen, sang. Dieselbe ist tugendsam und hübsch, spielt Flöte und Laute, tanzt auch und ist sehr ausgelassen.' Moser 1966, 12, 14.

194. 'vier knaben, so vor ku[niglicher] M[ajestät] auff den fleyten gepfiffen haben'. Wessely 1956, 130.

195. 'En su cámara avía un claviórgano, que fue el primero que en España se vido, e lo hizo un gran maestro moro de Çaragoça de Aragón, llamado Moferrez, que yo conosçí, e avía órganos, de clavicordios, e vihuelas de mano e de arco e flautas, e en todos estos instrumentos sabía el prínçipe tañer e poner las manos.' Fernández 1535, 166.
196. Polk 2005, 24.
197. *GMO*, s.v. 'Paumann, Conrad', by Christoph Wolff. Coelho and Polk 2016, 150–54 have a more extended 'case study' of Paumann.
198. Epitaph reproduced with article in *GMO*.
199. 'cieco miracoloso . . . in organis, lutina, cythera, fidella, ac fistula Tibiis ac Buccina et in omnibus Instrumentis Musicalibus'. Krautwurst 1977, 145n. 'E con l'ondia sonare uno verso overo uno chanto luy lo savia sonare ho in organo o piva overo in chitarrij o in arpa o in pittaro [piffaro].' Andrea Schivenoglia, *Famiglie mantovane e cronaca di Mantova* (Mantua, Biblioteca Comunale, Ms. 1019, f. 65v); Prizer 1986, 13.
200. 'Appointie entre Jeromene de Strossy, una, et Guillaume de Wilde, altera, que ledit Jeromene ou son procureur fera venir icy a la chambre sur demain Adrien la trompette de la ville, qui lui a vendu la couple des fleutes dont est question, sans commandement dudit Guillaume.' Gilliodts-Van Severen 1904–06, I, 203. On the Strozzi family in Bruges, see Strohm 1990, 64, 138.
201. 'eenen coker met fleuten'. Gilliodts-Van Severen 1904–06, 50.
202. 'jongheskins'. Vander Straeten 1885, IV, 100; Gilliodts-Van Severen 1912, 52, 54–56.
203. Ibid., 89.
204. Strohm 1990, 39.
205. Ibid., 86.
206. Ibid., 86.
207. Ibid., 144.
208. Ibid., 144.
209. 'Janne ende Willem van Welsens . . . ghebroeders, zyn commen voor scepenen [ende] sculdich zynde Joose Zoetink, de somme van 28 £. gr. . . . en dat over kenis moeite ende leringhe hemlieden by den zelven Josse ghedaen ende noch daghelicx doende in de conste van scalmeienne, fleutene ende andersins . . .'. Ghent, Stadarchief, Jaarregister van de Keuren Series 301, Number 62, f. 70v.
210. Polk 2005, 92.
211. For all works of art see *RHPI*.
212. Barcelona, Museu Nacional d'Art de Catalunya, Inv. 003950-000, Rowland-Jones 2006b, 25–26, n. 52.
213. Loretto 1995.
214. Marjanović 1995.
215. *RHPI*.
216. Rowland-Jones 1996; 1997b; 2006b, 25; Ballester 1990; 2000.
217. Rowland-Jones 2006b, 17.
218. Rowland-Jones 1996; 2005, 564; 2006b, 18–19.
219. Cèsar Favà Monllau, curator of medieval art, Museu Nacional d'Art de Catalunya, email message to DL, 13 October 2016; Ruiz y Quesada 2005.
220. Barcelona, Museu Diocesà. Rowland-Jones 1996, 19–20.
221. Barcelona, Museu Nacional d'Art de Catalunya, Inv. 003950-000; dating from museum's website; ibid., 20; Favà 2011.
222. Rowland-Jones 2005, 564.
223. Rowland-Jones on *RHPI*. When DL visited the monastery in 2016, the doors had been replaced by modern replicas.
224. Barcelona, Museu Nacional d'Art de Catalunya, Inv. 064025-000; Rowland-Jones 2005, 19–20; 2006a, 21–22.
225. Rowland-Jones 2006b, 27.
226. Ibid., 20.
227. Barcelona, Museu Nacional d'Art de Catalunya, reserve collection, 064035-000; Rowland-Jones 1997b, 11; 2006a, 20.

228. Rowland-Jones 2006b, 27, n. 69,
229. Miquel Nadal, Polyptych: *Retablo de los Santos Cosme y Damián con la Virgen*; Barcelona, Basilica del Santo Antonio de Padua. Rowland-Jones 1997b, 13.
230. Coelho and Polk 2016, 154.
231. Rowland-Jones 1997a, 13 calls them 'hybrid instruments, part recorder, part shawm, imagined by the silversmith . . .'.
232. Rowland-Jones 1996, pt 3, 10; Post 1958, 681.
233. Trottein 1993.
234. *Compost et kalendrier des bergiers* (Paris: Guy Marchant, 1493); Zurich, Zentralbibliothek, MS C 101, f. 12v (long-term loan from St Gallen Stiftsbibliothek); and USA, private collection, formerly Ulm, Schermarsche Bibliothek, Med. 8.
235. Ferrara, Palazzo Schifanoia, Salone dei Mesi.
236. Trottein 1993, 131.
237. Ibid. Rowland-Jones 1997a argues that, in the sixteenth century, a pair of recorders became a symbol of shared harmony, including marriage.
238. Lander 2021.

2 THE ERA OF RENAISSANCE RECORDERS, 1501–1667

1. Köhler 1987; Van Heyghen 2009; Brown 2018, 491.
2. Unless otherwise stated, references to inventories and purchases in this chapter are taken from Lasocki 2018a, which is arranged chronologically.
3. Lasocki with Prior 1995, 143–72.
4. Smith 2005.
5. 'una cassa o sia coppia di Flauti alemani che si sonano a mezo el flauto, e non in testa, come si fanno li nostri'. Lasocki 2018a, 8.
6. d'Alvarenga 2015, 10; Brásio 1954, 302.
7. Lasocki 2005b, 370.
8. Maaler 1971, 138, 316.
9. López Suero 2021b.
10. López Suero 2016.
11. Motolinía 2014, 84, 86.
12. Lasocki et al. 2022.
13. 'la delectation qu'a prins . . . les Italiens à iouer de celle qui est droite laquelle ilz nomment, Flauto, & me semble soubz correction qu'il ny auroit nul mal ny danger de la nommer fleute d'Italien, ou Flauto, comme eux; car ce nom de neuf trouz est vn peu sot selon mon iugement'. Jambe de Fer 1556, 54.
14. López-Calo 1996, 87.
15. Prizer 1981, 182–83.
16. 'litui Anglicani (vulgo recorders)'. McCabe 1938, 314; Edwards 1974, I, 60.
17. Du Val 1607.
18. 'Ces Flustes sont appellées douces, à raison de la douceur de leurs sons, qui representent le charme & la douceur des voix.' Mersenne 1636, II, 237.
19. 'le son de ces Flustes est jugé si doux par quelques-uns, qu'il merite le nom de charmant & de ravissant'. Ibid., 240.
20. Section based on Brown and Lasocki 2006.
21. Praetorius 1619, II, 21.
22. Jambe de Fer 1556, 52.
23. Van Heyghen 2005, 293–94.
24. Praetorius 1619, II, 34.
25. 'Tri flauti grandi, novi, da contrabasso.' Lasocki 2018a, 7.
26. 'une pour le contrebas de longueur d'un homme'. Ibid., 9.
27. 'Y cargan se le mas quatro flautas, la una muy grande, de tres baras poco mas o menos de largo.' Ibid., 24.

28. Vleeshuis Museum, Antwerp, Inv. No. 134(VH2111).
29. Museum Carolino Augusteum, Salzburg, Inv. No. M244.
30. 'Un bajon muy grande. . . . Es contravajo de flauta.' 'Otro bajon grande. . . . Es tenor de las flautas grandes.' Lasocki 2018a, 57.
31. Ibid., 16–18, 28.
32. Praetorius 1619, II, 37.
33. 'wenn der Gesang sonderlich darnach gerichtet'. Ibid.
34. Ibid., 42.
35. Ibid., 62, 64.
36. Van Heyghen 1995, 27.
37. Ibid.
38. 'Wenn man nun ein FlöttenChor, unter und neben andern unterschiedenen, mit andern Instrumenten besetzen Choren anstellen will: So erachte ich besser seyn, das zu dem Baß eine QuartPosaun, oder, welches noch bequemer ein Fagott; so wol auch zu dem Tenor eine Posaun oder Tenorgeig, an stadt der Flötten geordnet werden: Sintemal die Tenor und bevorab die Baßflötten in der tieffen gar zu gelinde, also das man sie vor den kleinen Discant- und Altflötten, auch vor den andern Instrumenten in den beygefügten Choren nicht wol und gar wenig hören kan. Wenn man aber sonsten die Flötten gar alleine, ohn zuthun anderer Instrumenten, in einer Canzon, Motet, oder auch in eim Concert per Chorus gebrauchen will: So kan man das ganze Accort und Stimmwerck der Flötten, sonderlich die Fünff Sorten von de gröbsten anzurechnen, und gibt eine sehr anmütige stille. Lieblliche harmoniam vonsich, sonderlich in Stuben und Gemächern; Sintemal in der Kirchen die grobe Bassett- und Baßflötten nicht wol gehört werden können. Darumb den auch die andern Chor, so etwa von Violen de gamba, odern Menschenstimmen darbey geordnet werden, gar submissa voce, still und sanfft ihre sachen herfürbringen und intoniren müssen; sofern anders ein Chor und eine Stimmen neben der andern eigentlich angehört und observiert werden solle.' Praetorius 1619, III, 158; translation, 162.
39. 'darumb dass man allzeit . . . drey und drey zusammen, also eine Art zum Bass, die ander zum Tenor und Alt . . . die dritte aber zum Cantu, gebrauchen kan'. Praetorius 1619, II, 37; translation, 47.
40. 'unas flautas, que tienen tres mixturas: flautones grandes y flautas medianas y otras pequeñas'. López-Calo 1963, I, 225.
41. Haynes 2002, 57–65, 78–82; 'dem gemeinem Tonum der Orgel'; 'Ain grosse flaut per concert von Venedig erkhauft'; '2 Fleutl di Cornedthöch'; Lasocki 2018a, 34, 54, 60.
42. 'In Engellandt haben sie vorzeiten, und in den Niederlanden noch anjtzo ihre meiste blasende Instrumenta umb eine tertiam minorem tieffer, als jtzo unser Cammerthon, intoniret und gestimbt. . . . Wie denn auch die Flötten und andere Instrumenta in solchem niedern Thon lieblicher, als im rechten Thon lauten, und fast gar eine andere art im gehör (sintemahl sie in der tieffe nicht so hart schreyen) mit sich bringen.' Praetorius 1619, II, 16. The term *coristi* (*corista*), which may refer to a pitch standard or else a common pitch for playing with other instruments, is mentioned in a letter from the composer Alessandro Orologio to Landgrave Maurice of Hesse-Kassel in 1594, in which he observes that a set of small recorders at this pitch (*Una coppia di flauti grossi. Et una di piccoli coristi*) can be bought in Venice. Lasocki with Brown 2023.
43. Brown with Lasocki 2023.
44. Ibid., 76.
45. Bali 2007b, 421.
46. Myers et al. 2005.
47. Lasocki 2018a, 11.
48. Ibid., 86.
49. 'La Basse de ce petit ieu . . . sert de Dessus au grand ieu, qui commence où l'autre finit.' Mersenne 1636, II, 239.
50. Lasocki 1995a, 119.
51. Basel, Universitätsbibliothek, Ms. F. X. 38. Ehlich and Fiedler 2003. *GMO*, 'Amerbach, Bonifacius', by John Kmetz.
52. 'und alles . . . zu lernen Kurtzlich gemacht . . .'.

53. 'So müst du auch die zungen lernen, die auch zü der flöte gebraulich, mit sampt den fingern applicirn gleich mit eynander zü lauffen. . . .'
54. Fernández Sanz 2018, 90.
55. 'Hab aber das aus sonderlicher ursach ynn deudsche Reymen und Rithmos verfasset, auff das die iugent und andere, so ynn dieser kunst studieren wöllen, deste leichtlicher begreiffen, und lenger behalten mügen.' Agricola 1529.
56. Hettrick 1980, 112.
57. 'für unser Schulkinder und andere gmeine Senger . . .'. Agricola 1545, t.p.
58. Ibid., f. 26.
59. Ibid., ff. 32–33v.
60. Ibid., ff. 33v–34v.
61. Rowland-Jones 2000b.
62. Quantz 1752.
63. Section from Lasocki 1995a, updated from Titan 2019 and correspondence with Pedro Sousa Silva and Giulia Tettamanti.
64. *Opera intitulata Fontegara / La quale insegna a sonare di flauto chon tutta l'arte opportuna a esso instrumento massime il diminuire il quale sara utile ad ogni instrumento di fiato et chorde: et anchora a chi si dileta di canto.* In the quotations from *Fontegara* in the following endnotes, typographical instances of *u* meaning *v* have all been changed to *v*.
65. Biography based on Pasquale 2019.
66. Baroncini 2022.
67. 'aggiontovi appresso che essa è stata mio discepolo, il che dico con molta mia laude'.
68. 'col dignarvi di havere gia maestro'.
69. 'un mio scolaro il qual e di boni sonatori che siano in tuta la Italia'. Pasquale 2019, 68, 90.
70. Tettamanti 2020.
71. Titan 2019, chapter 2.
72. Tettamanti 2010; 2016.
73. Titan 2019, 193ff, 256ff.
74. '& si il dipintore imita li effetti da natura con varii colori lo instrumento immitera il proferir della humana voce con la proportion del fiato & offuscation della lingua con lo agiuto de deti & di questo ne o fatto esperientia & audito da altri sonatori farsi intendere con il suo sonar le parole di essa cosa che si poteva ben dire a quello instrumento non mancarli altro che la forma dil corpo humano si come si dice ala pintura ben fatta non mancarli solum il fiato: si che haveti a essere certi del suo termine per dite rason de poter imitar il parlar.' *Fontegara*, Capitulo 1. This section follows the text of Titan 2019 and her translation, with adjustments.
75. 'el suficiente & perito cantore'. Capitulo 25.
76. Titan 2019, 78.
77. Tettamanti 2016.
78. Sousa Silva 2018, 5; Tettamanti 2023.
79. 'la voce humana come magistra ne insegna dover essere proceduto mediocralmente perche quando il cantor canta alcuna composition con parole placabile lui fa la pronuncia placabile se gioconda & lui con il modo giocondo pero volendo imitar simile effetto si prociedera il fiato mediocro accio si possa crescere e minuir ali sui tempi.' *Fontegara*, Capitulo 2.
80. Capitulo 5.
81. Titan 2019, 76–77.
82. 'per sillabe che causano effetto crudo & aspro'. *Fontegara*, Capitulo 5.
83. 'la drita sie quella che piu proferisse le silabe como e la prima delle originale'. Capitulo 6.
84. 'come tutti li effetti de lingua sia una sillaba dreta e laltra riversa la dretta sie la prima sillaba la contraria sie la seconda'. Capitulo 7.
85. 'tutti li effetti che fa la lingua dritta si adimanda lingua di testa perche la occupa il fiato disoto il palato & apresso i denti. & la lingua riversa sara lingua di gorza per la occupazione del fiato che la fa apresso la gorza'. Capitulo 8.
86. 'sillabe piacevole over plane'. Capitulo 5.
87. 'la roversa sera quella che mancho proferira le silabe . . .'. Capitulo 6.

88. 'sia moto mediocre . . . pero viene havere il temperamento di questi dui estremi cioe de dureza e tenereza'. Capitulo 5.

89. Capitulo 6 and 7.

90. 'accioche possi invistichar quala silaba over litera la natura ti habia dotato di esprimere tal che con piu velocita'. Capitulo 7.

91. 'dela sillaba de de ge che over da de di do du pero intenderai poter mutar la prima litera in ogni altra'. Capitulo 6. 'il terzo moto dele originale non produse altro effetto si non che serve la media de una sillaba come ditto inanti'. 'Procedendo con questo ordine deponendoti li tre moti originali e poi a moto per moto io distendero li sui varii effetti da essi derivati. . . . Dacha deche dichi docho duchu [second column] . . . chara chare chari charo charu.' Capitulo 7.

92. 'chel sia la verita doperandose con la sua velocita perde il suo proferire. . . .' Capitulo 6.

93. Capitulo 7.

94. '& trovasi unaltra lingua laquale non proferisse sillaba niuna & il moto suo sie da uno labro a laltro & per occupar il fiato arente i lapri la si domanda lingua di testa'. Capitulo 8.

95. Couto Soares 2021.

96. 'Sapi lettor mio dignissimo che molti anni ho esperimentado el modo de sonar & diletatomi di vedere & praticare con tutti li primi sonatori che a mio tempo sono stati onde che mai ho trovato homo degno in tale arte che piu dele voce ordinarie habi essercitato dil che protrebono havere agionto una de piu o due voce onde havendo io essaminato tal modo ho trovato quello che altri non ha saputo non che in loro sia ignorato tal via ma per fatica lasciato cioe sette voce de piu de lordinario detto dele quali ti daro tutta la cognitione: . . . le sette voce da me trovate con le comune .13. sono .20. le quale partiremo in tre parte cioe .9. grave .7. acute e .4. sopra acute: & cosi . . . le noue grave si pronuncia con fiato grave & le .7. con fiato acuto & le .4. ultime con fiato acutissimo.' *Fontegara*, Capitulo 4.

97. Reiners 1997, 39.

98. Sousa Silva 2018, 8.

99. '& prima advertisse che li flauti quali sono formadi da varii maestri sono differenti luno dalaltro non solo del foro ma nel compassar le voce & anchora nel vento & tali maestri alcuni di loro son differenti nel cordare esso instrumento per causa del suo sonar variado luno da laltro anchora lorechio: & per tal differentia nasce uno variado modo di sonar quello de uno maestro e quello de unaltro & cosi ti mostrero la via de piu maestri per le segni quelli hanno differenti liquali segni saranno dimostrati ne la figura di flauti.' *Fontegara*, Capitulo 4.

100. '& se non te reuscisce in tal modo e tu haverai da investigar di coprir e scoprir una e due voce de piu e manco anchora con proportionar il fiato'. Capitulo 4

101. 'tali si copriranno la mita e piu e manco secondo che seranno le sustentatione necessarie ala vera harmonia'. Capitulo 3.

102. 'So lassen die Römer die Pusaunen, flöiten, Vnnd krummbHörner Vast durchauß Von Nurnberg Herein Bringen.' Boetticher 1963, 89.

103. *Fontegara*, Capitulo 23. 'Artificial' because, as he says in *Regola Rubertina*, Capitulo X, 'la voce humana per essere istromento natural è piu degna che l'istromento accidentale over artificioso' (the human voice as a natural instrument is more worthy than the accidental or artificial instrument). Tettamanti 2023.

104. 'Sapi che la imitatione deriva da lartificio . . . la imitatione adunque debbe imitare la voce humana. . . .' *Fontegara*, Capitulo 24.

105. Titan 2019, 287–89.

106. '& primamente questa spetie di galanteria deriva e nasce dal tremulo del dito in su la voce di esso flauto'. *Fontegara*, Capitulo 24.

107. Titan 2019, 289.

108. '& sapi & ben nota che tale ordine & modo sara da me inteso per flauti de uno maestro solo. Pertanto se con altri non potesti in questo essercitarti bisogna industriarti con coprire & discoprire una o due voce o piu o manco . . .'. *Fontegara*, Capitulo 25.

109. 'che sono dui effetti che causeno el far della mano uno lo effetto & pratica di far la lingua laltro e il modo de diminuire'. Capitulo 9.

110. He uses the term *passaggi* in *Regola Rubertina* and *Lettione seconda*. Titan 2019, 89. Nevertheless, in *Regola Rubertina*, p. III, he describes *Fontegara* as a work 'laqual insegna a sonar di flauto & a diminuire' (that teaches to play the recorder and to make diminutions).
111. 'tu intenderai che altro non e diminuire che variare la cosa over processo che di natura se dimostra soda: e simplice'. *Fontegara*, Capitulo 9.
112. 'fatica intolerabile'. Capitulo 22. On his diminutions, see Titan 2019, 62–66, 80–134; Sela 2020.
113. 'Alquanto laboriosa. Et incommoda.' Capitulo 16.
114. Ibid., 100–05, 252–54.
115. Titan 2019, chapter 5; Siekiera 2000, 32–37.
116. Titan 2019, 213.
117. Ibid., 205.
118. Ibid., 214–15.
119. Ibid., 208, 217–20.
120. Ibid., 222–36.
121. Ibid., 85, 247–52.
122. Herzog August Bibliothek, Wolfenbüttel; Pasquale 2019, 80–81. In *Lettione seconda*, Capitolo 16, Ganassi promised a book on the lira. In *Regola Rubertina*, Capitolo 19, he also promised a book on counterpoint, 'se Iddio me imprestera vita habile' (if God gives me useful life).
123. Stevenson 1985, 72.
124. 'glosar juntos es disonança ynsufrible'.
125. 'Que Juan de Medina taña de hordinario el contralto y de lugar a los tiples no turbandolos con exceder de la glosa que debe a contralto y que quando el dicho Juan de Medina tañere solo el contralto por tiple con los sacabuches se le dexa el campo abierto para hacer las galas y glosas que quisiere que en este ynstrumento las sabe bien hacer.'
126. Tettamanti, email message to DL, 21 September 2021.
127. 'm'ho messo in cuore come gia feci l'altra opera detta Fontegara . . . accio che il talento datomi da Dio, si da me communicato . . . & agevolata la strada a chi si diletta di questa virtu'. *Regola Rubertina*, dedication letter.
128. Prizer 1981, 182–83; Baroncini 2002, 86.
129. 'sí de trombe e piffari, come de fiauti et corneti'; Glixon 2003, 131; 1979, I, 94–95; II, 33–34; Lasocki with Prior 1995, 4, 6.
130. 'sono . . . diversi ridotti. Dove concorrendo i virtuosi in questa professione, si fanno concerti singolari in ogni tempo, essendo chiarissima & vera cosa, che la Musica ha la sua propria sede in questa città.' Sansovino 1581, f. 139.
131. Baroncini 2018, 190–202.
132. 'Flauti grossi n° sei per musica da camera. . . . Una nuova sorte de flauti grossi con molto spirito fatti, col Privilegio dell'Eccellentissimo Senato, che imitano la voce humana.' Ferrari 1993, 16.
133. Vio and Toffolo 1987; Lasocki 2018a, 22–23.
134. 'magistérque meus & ipse vir probus ac praestans, & octuagenario iam nunc longè maior'. Cardan 1663, II, 177–78.
135. 'Exercebar multis diebus à summo mane ad vesperam usque armatus, sudorésque madidus operam dabam musicis instrumentis, nocte tota sæpe ad diem usque vagabar.' Ibid., I, 6; 1930, 27.
136. 'In Musica ineptus usui fui, contemplationi non impar.' Ibid., I, 31.
137. 'Instrumentorum nobilitas ex novem habetur conditionibus. . . . Quarta conditio est ut cum humana voce & aliis instrumentis facilè conveniant. Hanc ob causam elymae minimè laudantur, vix enim ullum aliud instrumentum minus convenit.' Ibid., X, 110–11; Miller 1971, 55.
138. 'Propria est imitatio humanae vocis non simplicter, nam hoc ut ostendetur commune est omnibus instrumentis, sed exactè imitare huic proprium. Id autem fit in flebilibus remissa voce, in incitatis aucta, in gravibus continuata, atque ita de alii affectibus. . . .' Cardan 1663, X, 115–16; Miller 1971, 69.
139. 'Prolatione, haec autem triplex lenis, quae per liquidas fit ut lere, aspera quae per mutuas aspiratas ut theche, mediocris quae mixta est ut there vel thara.' Cardan 1663, X, 113; Miller 1971, 61.

140. 'Spiritu primò dum minuit reflexa ad palatum vel extensa auget obstruendo meatum & aperiendo ut in cornibus: motu & hoc bifariam vel recto vel reflexo, mirum quantum iuvet voces ac variet mutétque.' Cardan 1663, X, 113; Miller 1971, 61.

141. 'At spiritus duae sunt differentiae generales, altera quidem à magnitudine sumpta altera ab impetu; ab impetu tres sumuntur differentiae remissus qui & gravis incitatus & medius inter hos: à magnitudine tres, rursus plenus vacuus ac mediocris. Gravi seu remisso utimur in instrumentis maioribus & quae facilè inflantur ut Elymis & in gravioribus vocibus, nam si intento utatis, maiora instrumenta stridebunt, & voces graves proferre non poteris. . . . Inani in paruis instrumentis acutis vocibus, sed instrumentis, quae facilè inflantur: plenissimo igitur & incitato utemur in cornibus maximis, plenissimo & remisso in maioribus elymis, inani & incitato in paruis elymis . . . pereat, nisi forsan in paruis elymis in gravioribus vocibus inani atque remisso utamur.' Cardan 1663, X, 112; Miller 1971, 60–61.

142. 'Est praeter id observandum ut spiritus nitidus non confusus aut inconstans sed stabilis reddatur, utque varietatem suam debito tempore nec procrastinando recipiat, atque haec observatio promptitudo appellatur.' Cardan 1663, X, 116; Miller 1971, 69.

143. 'Quia construuntur in diapente omnes elymae invicem cum succedentibus.' Cardan 1663, X, 114; Miller 1971, 65.

144. 'in optimis enim elymis multum est discrimen'. Cardan 1663, X, 114.

145. 'D apertum omnes voces ad diapason deducit, acutius intento spiritu, ex dimidio autem conclusum ac magis intento spiritu facit bis diapason.' Cardan 1663, X, 113; Miller 1971, 62.

146. 'Postquam verò ascendere per schilos volumus eadem ratio est quae in aliis, sed Sylvester Ganasus septem praeter alias addit voces: ultima enim vocum est in E la & est ultima seu acutissima vocum manus Guidonis.' Cardan 1663, X, 115; Miller 1971, 67.

147. 'Ego verò tam in his vocibus quàm in aliis, quae per primos fiunt altiore elyma utor. . . . Sed pro schilis est valde aperta, quia primus schilus ascendit extra manum & ultimus schilus ad G sol re ut extra manum. Et ita non desunt nisi duae voces ad inventionem perficiendam Sylvestri Genasi Veneti.' Cardan 1663, X, 115.

148. 'Fit autem hoc Elyma sensim applicata cruri & remisso spiritu, vocatúrque vox addita. Quòd si solù quarta pars claudatur, fiet semitonio gravior solum, & hanc vocem me docuit Leo Oglonus magister meus in Musica.' Ibid., X, 114; Miller 1971, 64.

149. Agricola 1529, ff. XV–XVv.

150. 'diesis quae est quarta pars toni, & dimidium minoris semitonij, & consistit in proportione 35 ad 34 & est minimum intervallum, quod cani possit ut demonstrabo sunt de genere utilum'. Cardan 1663, X, 107; Miller 1971, 45.

151. '& etiam cum seipsa bis ea utendo scilicet concludendo quartam partem foraminis tantum. . . . Fiunt & dieses repercussione sola linguae . . . lingua cohibetur spiritus, igitur vox fit gravior paulò, & hoc discrimen attingit diesim'. Cardan 1663, X, 114; Miller 1971, 63–64.

152. 'Auxilio huius praecedentis regulae voces omnes ad semitonia ac dieses deduci possunt, nam si ex dimidio concludatur B foramen toni semitonio fient graviores. Semitonia autem ad dieses, obstructo autem B ex quarta parte integri toni diesi fient graviores.' Cardan 1663, X, 114; Miller 1971, 64.

153. 'Inde considerandum est ut vox tremula persaepe diesi vel semitonio redditur acutior remissiórve: dupliciter autem tremula spiritu quidem ac motu tremulo digitorum. Hic si fiat foraminibus pluribus quandoque ditonum, quandoque trisemitonium consurgit plerúmque autem dimidio eius quod fit plenè aperto foramine; vel igitur semitonio tremente, vel etiam tono levissimè aperto fit discursus per dieses, quibus nihil melius nihil suavius nihil iucundius esse potest.' Cardan 1663, X, 116; Miller 1971, 69–70.

154. 'Vivaces igitur voces sunt cum digiti vel constant occludendo vel aperiendo, suaves cum tremunt: ut autem fiant voces suavissimae, tribus opus est observationibus. Prima ut gravioires non acutiores voces tremant, secunda ut leuiter digiti aperiantur ac valde parum: tertia ut reflexio non quiescat sed tremat velut vibratus vehementer ensis saepius in se rediens. Voces mediae fiunt accutioribus tremebundo motu digitorum variatis.' Cardan 1663, X, 116; Miller 1971, 69–70 (70, slightly modified).

155. 'meliores ex pruno albis. Quae ex albo ligno levi magis raucae, quae ex solido veluti buxo eò graviores ac magis incommodae quò suaviores.' Cardan 1663, X, 113; Miller 1971, 62.
156. 'quod imperitiam ostendunt artificis, qui quod ratione debuit assequi, quasi coecus manu ductus, dilatando foramina ad metam reduxit'. Cardan 1663, X, 113.
157. 'Cum vero haec duo praeter vocem sint propria instrumentis non quiescere in una voce nec tacere, sed perpetuò ipsas voces variare.' Ibid., X, 116; Miller 1971, 70.
158. 'Septimus modus est ut quinque iaequalia spatia septenis dividantur intervallis, atque hoc perficere difficillimum est. Praeter haec non est via alia utilis, nam quatuor in quinque si dividas discrimen exiguum valde maximam difficultatem parit, sed harmoniae expertem. Demonstratum est enim quod quae non percipiuntur ab aure, non delectant.' Cardan 1663, X, 116; Miller 1971, 71.
159. Cardan 1663, X, 190.
160. 'Il medesmo auuiene ne gli strumenti da fiato, come Flauti diritti, e trauersi, Cornetti diritti, & torti, & simili benche habbino la sua stabilità mediante i loro buchi, nondimeno il diligente sonatore si più accommodare con un poco più, un poco meno fiato: & anchora con aprire un poco più, ò un poco meno i fiori di quello; & accostarsi al buono accordo, quanto più pottrà: e questo fanno i diligente sonatori di tali strumenti.' Bottrigari 1962, 15.
161. 'A talche i Cornetti, i Fifari, i Flauti, i Fagotti, le Cornamuse, & gl'altri che sonano mediante i forami & buchi . . . in quel caso col coprire & discoprire alquanto, quei buchi & forami, che si doueriano discoprire, & coprire; si aiutano in tal maniera, che s'accomodano al meglio che possano.' Zacconi 1596, f. 217.
162. '& si à Vn ton en bas plus que la traverse, mais en haut, elle en à moins de trois ou quatre; car ses tons sont en nombre de quinze pour le plus, & la traverse en à bien dix neuf. En outre la partie du dessus ne se joue sus les tailles & haute contre comme en lautre, ainsi se joue à part, & descend ledit jusqu'en G sol re ut, le second puis remonte en haut jusqu'au quatriesme.' Jambe de Fer 1556, 53.
163. Virgiliano ca. 1600.
164. Bacon 1627, Century III, 170; Rusu and Lüthy 2017.
165. 'Or l'on fait quatre ou cinq parties differentes de ces Flustes pour un concert entier . . . qu'il imite davantage le concert des voix, car il ne luy manque que la seule prononciation, dont on approche de bien pres avec ces Flustes.' Mersenne 1636, II, 230.
166. 'sa tablature que je mets icy en deux manieres, à sçavoir par les notes ordinaires de la Musique, & par les marques dont usent ceux que ne cognoissent pas la valeur, & l'usage des notes ordinaires'. Ibid.
167. 'le trou que se bouche avec le pouce de la main gauche . . . doit estre à demy ouvert, & non pas tout debouché, comme il est dans la tablature, pour faire les tons qui passent l'Octave, parce que les tons en sont meilleurs & plus naturel'. Ibid., II, 236.
168. 'Encore que quelques-uns ne luy donnent qu'une Treziesme d'estenuë.' Ibid., II, 239.
169. 'celle-là est pratiquée par les villageois & par les apprentifs, & celle-cy par les Maitres'. Ibid., III, 235.
170. '& qu'elle imite la voix & la plus excellente methode de bien chanter'. Ibid., II, 275.
171. Wind 2011, 136–37.
172. 'Deze beschrijvinge om de Hant-fluyt heel zuyver te konnen bespelen, hebbe ick ten verzoecke van P. Matthysz., ende ten dienste van alle Lief-hebbers van he Handt-fluyt aldus gestelt' (f. [*6]b).
173. *Onderwyzinge hoemen alle de Toonen en halve Toonen, die meest gebruyckelyck zyn, op de handt-fluyt zal konnen t'eenemael zuyver Blaezen, en hoe men op yeder 't gemackelyckst een Trammelant zal konnen maken, heel dienstigh voor de Lief-hebbers.*
174. Griffioen 1991, 381.
175. 'zoo dient men op twee dingen wel te letten, als, te weten: dat men de vingers net stopt, ende het ander is, dat men niet te hart ofte te zacht en blaest, alzoo men daer deur de toonen te hoogh ofte te laegh maeckt'.
176. Section based on Brown and Lasocki 2006.
177. Brown 2018, 244.

178. Brown 2006; Griscom and Lasocki 2012, 260–65.
179. Marvin 1978.
180. Morgan 1982, 20.
181. Lyndon-Jones 1998.
182. Section based on Lasocki with Prior 1995.
183. For biographies, see Ashbee and Lasocki 1998.
184. 'Mastro Gieronymo, detto il Piva, inventore di un nuovo instromento di basso à fiato, Pifaro eccellentissimo, & salariato dalla Illustriss. Sig. di Venetia; il quale hebbe tre figliuoli Musici, disciplinati da lui, che con il padre insieme furono poi condotti dalla Serenissima Regina d'Inghilterra con gran stipendio, & molto suo honore; & fù la eccellenza di questi grande ancora nel far di sua mano flauti, onde li segnati del suo segno, sono tenuti in gran venerazione appresso Musici, & vengono ben pagati dove si trovano.' Marucini quoted in Ruffatti 1998, 351.
185. 'fraternae Compagniae'. Ongaro 1992, 413.
186. Lasocki 2018a, 34–35.
187. 'ont esté envoyées d'Angleterre à l'un de nos Rois'. Mersenne 1636, II, 239.
188. Lasocki et al. 2022.
189. 'Una caja de flautas que tiene ocho pieças que se labraron en Ynglaterra y son de la marca de ala de mosca. Esta caja tiene dos tiples y quatro tenores y dos contrabajos.' Reynaud 1996, 208; Miller 2018, 343.
190. Ruiz Jiménez 2021.
191. 'ain groß Fueter darin 27 Fletten. groß vnd klain Im Engelandt gemacht worden'. Lasocki 2018a, 29–30.
192. 'gemeinem Tonum der Orgel'.
193. Haynes 2002, 57–58.
194. Lasocki 1983, 560–70.
195. Lasocki 2021.
196. Lyndon-Jones 1999.
197. Brown and Lasocki 2006, 28–29, updated by Brown, email message to DL, 17 September 2021.
198. Brown with Lasocki 2023.
199. Prizer 1981, 182–83.
200. 'Sus, gallans qui avez l'usaige / De harper ou instrumenter, / Trop longuement faictes du saige: / Une chançon convient fleuter.' La Chesnaye 1991, 117–19.
201. Van Heyghen 2005, 230.
202. Smith 1978.
203. 'auff allerley Instrumenten zubrauchen, ausserlesen . . .'.
204. Van Heyghen 2005, 231.
205. Rowland-Jones 1997a, 2, 48–49.
206. 'espinetes, violons & fleustes'.
207. Van Heyghen 2005, 232.
208. 'Item nah der auendt maltidt sollen seh spellen IIII dubbelde dentze gelevet idt en szo mogen sze eynen dubblenden dantz mith flouten off krum hornern spelen.' Moser 1918, 139.
209. 'Es verlief bei herrlicher Musik und nachfolgendem Tanz, bei welchem jetzt mehr Personen als die Nacht zuvor auf einmal tanzten; es wurden auch nicht mehr die Trompeten, sonder Violen, Zwerchpfeifen, Flöten als stillere Instrumente gebraucht. Dasselbe war der Fall beim Nachtessen und dem selben.' Pietzsch 1960, 55.
210. 'Ein stimmwerckh flötten seind 12. als ein grosser bass. 3 tenor. 3 alt. 3 discant und 1 hoher discant. der ander hohe discant manglet. Fünf flötten als 2 tenor und 3 tenor.' Lasocki 2018a, 62.
211. 'lyres, luths, harpes, flustes et autres instrumens, avec les voix meslées'. Lacroix 1868–70, I, 39.
212. 'Ce nouveau intermede estoit composé de huict Satyres, sept desquels jouoyent des flustes, et un seul chantoit, qui estoit le sieur de Sainct-Laurens, chantre de la Chambre du Roy.' Ibid., I, 53.
213. The collection has not survived but is summarized in a manuscript written by the Duke of La Vallière around 1733 (Bibliothèque Nationale, Ms. fr. 24357) and described in Lesure 1956. The dated ballets range from 1597 to 1618.

214. '1587. TABLE / Des Ballets à 3. 4. et 5. parties qui se trouvent dans un Recueil fait en 1600 [sic] par Michel Henry l'un des 24. Violons, copié sur l'original dudit Michel Henry. . . . 1587 Sept Airs sonnez la nuit de St Julien en 1587 par nous Chevalier Lore, Henry l'ainé, la Motte, Richaine et autres et furent sonnez sur Luts Epinettes, Mandores, Violons, flutes à neuf trous, Tambour à main, avec la flute à trois trous, Tambours de Biscaye, Larigaux, le tout bien d'accord et sonnant et allant parmi la ville, ce fut en l'année 1587.' Bibliothèque Nationale, Ms. fr. 24357, f. 310.

215. 'Ce n'est pas que des particuliers quelquefois ne s'assemblassent auparavant pour chanter des Chansons, & où les flutes étoient bien venues. . . .' Sauval 1724, II, 493.

216. 'incontanente si pongono à cantare, & con flauti, cornetti, cornamuse, & altri tai loro stromenti cominciano sonare madrigali, sonetti, & canzoni amorose, & tutte lascive, & dishonestissime'. Zuccollo 1549, f. 23r.

217. Wienpahl 1979, 102.

218. 'une Espinette, un dessus de viole, un dessus de flute, un Bourdon'. McGowan 1994, 181.

219. 'á mesa houve dois musicos, com suas guitarras castelhanas, cantaram muito bem, os quaes hião em nossa companhia, avia frautas'. Vieira 1900, 6.

220. Munich, Bayerische Staatsbibliothek. Mus. Ms. A I, ff. 191, 204, 187.

221. Cambridge University Library, Ms. Dd.5.21.

222. 'Capellam Fidicini . . . nach art der Engelländer mit einem ganzen Consort.' Praetorius 1619, III, 117.

223. Section based on Lasocki et al. 2022, unless otherwise stated.

224. Kirk 1993, 3.

225. 'Por nueve flautas en una caja cubierta de cuero prieto.' Miller 2018, 343; Reynaud 1996, 208.

226. 'Joan gllz charamela tem de mãtin[to] cadano seis mil rs~ .ss. quatro mil de ordenado e dous mil por fazer as frautas e charamelas.' Estudante 2007, 80, 195.

227. 'charamela e "oficial de fazer as frautas e charamelas"'. d'Alvarenga 2002, 37.

228. López Suero 2021a, 136–38.

229. 'Que el motete que cantan después de haber alzado lo "digan con las flautas" los minístriles.' Jiménez Caballé 1998, 11.

230. 'Sabado sancto a la misa. Y a las conpletas con las flautas de fabordon el primo psalmo postrero y nunc dimitis.' Kreitner 2003, 49, 53.

231. *GMO*, s.v. 'Falsobordone', by Murray C. Bradshaw.

232. d'Alvarenga 2015, 10, 20, n. 45.

233. Ibid., 20, n. 50; Estudante 2007, 214.

234. 'Que en las fiestas del choro aya siempre un berso de flautas. que en las salves los tres versos que tañen el un sea con chirimias y el otro con cornetas y el otro con flautas porque siempre un instrumento enfada y ansi lo proveyeron.' Stevenson 1985, 72.

235. 'Lobo . . . puso singular diligencia, en que se aventajase toda fuerte de canturía, assí en los Psalmos, con varios instrumentos de Ministriles, Bajones, Cornetas, Flautas y dos organos, como en la composicion de tonos a las chançonetas, que se compusieron a proposito del Santo, que adelante veremos. . . . Prosiguiose la Misa con la mesma variedad, de musicas, y los de mas instrumentos della. que diximos en las vísperas, acompañada de Motetes, Villancicos, y otras composiciones del arte, en que el maestro quiso estremarse.' Borgerding 1997, 99.

236. 'Al tiempo que se acaban de cantar aquellas palabras Nativitas Domini nostri Iesus Christi segundum carnem, tañen los ministriles un verso vreve y devoto con los instrumentos que les parecieren mas a proposito, flautas, o Musas.' Miller 2018, 349; *LMR*; Jambou 1983, 284.

237. 'se añada mucha solemnidad y musica en las dichas fesetividades de Navidad y de los Reyes, eligiendo un verso en cada salmo, el que pareciere mas a proposito a la festividad, y que dichos versos se compongan por el maestro de capilla a canto de organo, usando en ellas de mucha variedad: unas veces con voces sencillas, otras con voces y flautas . . .'. Miller 2018, 349; Calahorra Martínez 1978, II, 137–38.

238. 'los dichos músicos se juntasen en la capilla y se pusiese en ella un organillo y cantasen a él y los ministriles tañesen las chirimías, flautas y violones . . .'. López-Calo 1981, II, 594.

239. 'y comenzarán los ministriles con las chimimías, y luego con las flautas y demás instrumenteos . . .'. Ibid., II, 599.

240. 'en todos los Iueues del año, quando se hiziere el Oficio del Santissimo Sacramento, la Missa se dira como en fiesta de primera classe, y las Completas de dichos Iueues con la mayor solemnidad que se pudieren dezir; diziendose vn verso con vna voz al organo, otro verso con fabordon de quatro, y otro verso con flautas, y vna voz; y juntãdose todos, y algún Menestril cõ ellos, quãdo dixerë Gloria Patri, etc.' Olson 2002, 60, n. 36.

241. Kirk 1993, 31.

242. Section based on Lasocki et al. 2022.

243. 'porque creo que si en ella se hallaran el Papa y Emperador con sus cortes, holgaran mucho de vella. . . . Iba en la procesión, capilla de canto de órgano de muchos cantores y su música de flautas que concertaban con los cantores, trompetas y atabales, campanas chicas y grandes, y esto todo sonó junto a la entrada y salida de la iglesia, que parecía que se venía el cielo abajo.' Motolinía 2014, 84, 86.

244. 'Han estos tlaxcaltecas regocijado mucho los divinos oficios con cantos y músicas. De canto de órgano tenían dos capillas, cada una de más de veinte cantores, y otras dos de flautas, con las cuales también tañían rabel y jabebas, y muy buenos maestros de atabales concordados con campanas pequeñas que sonaban sabotorosamente.' Ibid., 90.

245. 'caxa de flautas grandes'. Stevenson 1964, 343–44.

246. 'Además de enseñar a los niños indios a leer y escribir, fray Jodoco les enseñó a tañer todos los instrumentos de música, tecla y cuerdas y también el sacabuche y cherimías, flautas, trompetas y cornetas y la ciencia del canto de órgano y el canto llano.' Ruiz Jiménez 2020b.

247. 'Sumamente ingeniosos, aprenden fácilmente las letras, el canto, a tocar las flautas y otros instrumentos semejantes.' Ibid.

248. Ibid.

249. 'han mostrado y enseñado en el dicho colegio a tañer músicas de órganos, trompetas, flautas, chirimías de donde han salido muchos naturales mostrado donde ansí la iglesia catedral desta ciudad como de muchas iglesias e monasterios de esta tierra se han proveído de cantores y músicos e tañedores de que se ha seguido y sigue gran bien'. Ibid.

250. 'Conocí en este colegio a un muchacho indio llamado Juan, y por bermejo de su nacimiento llamaban Juan Bermejo, que podía ser tiple de la capilla del Sumo Pontífice, este muchacho salió tan diestro en el canto de órgano, flauta y tecla, que ya hombre le sacaron para la iglesia mayor, donde sirve de maestro de capilla y organista.' Lizárraga 2015.

251. Baker 2003, 18, 37; 2008, 143.

252. 'teniendo entre ellos escuela de los hijos de los naturales a quien les vestía y acariçiaba y enseñaba a leer y escribir y tañer instrumentos de flautas y chirimías y canto llano y de órgano . . .'. Ruiz Jiménez 2020c.

253. Stevenson 1952, 63; Barwick 1993, 352–53.

254. Stevenson 1952, 65.

255. Barwick 1993, 353.

256. Baker 2008, 155.

257. 'se hazen y celebran los oficios divinos con la decencia y aseo que se pudiera en la mas cuydadosa de Españoles asisten de ordinario muy buen numero de cantores tan diestros en canto de órgano y variedad de instrumentos de chirimías, flautas, bajones, cornetas, fagotes, órgano, arpas biguelas, discantes, rabeles, bigolones, clave y otros instrumentos que pueden competir con lo bueno o mejor del Reino'. Zuluaga 1988, 73.

258. 'cuatro flautas para el tiempo de cuaresma'. Lasocki 2018a, 92.

259. 'unas flautas y chirimías'. Ruiz Jiménez 2020a.

260. 'Hacen flautas bien entonadas, de todas voces, según se requiere para oficiar y cantar con ellas canto de órgano.' Knighton 2016, 336.

261. *GMO*, s.v. 'Morelia', by Robert Stevenson.

262. 'Los primeros Instrumentos de Musica, que hicieron y usaron, fueron Flautas: luego, Chirimias: despues, Orlos; y trás ellas, Cornetas, y Baxones. . . . Una cosa puedo afirmar con verdad, que en todos los Reinos de la Christiandad (fuera de las Indias) no ai tanta copia de Flautas,

Chirimias, Sacabuches, Trompetas, Orlos, Atabales, como en solo este Reino de la Nueva España.' Stevenson 1952, 68; Watkins 2009, 54. The last sentence was borrowed from Father Gerónimo de Mendieta, *Historia eclesiastica indiana* (Mexico, 1870), written in Mexico between 1571 and 1596; Guzmán-Bravo 1978, 355.

263. Holler 2006, I, 42.
264. Ibid., I, 51.
265. 'a qual foy com toda a muziqua de canto d'orguão e frautas, como se lá podera fazer'. Ibid., II, 70.
266. Ibid., I, 42.
267. 'Parézeme, según ellos son amigos de cossas músicas, que nosotros tañendo y cantando entre ellos los ganaríamos, pues differencia ay de lo que ellos hazen a lo que nosotros hazemos y haríamos si V. R.a nos hiziesse proveer de algunos instrumentos para que acá tañamos (imbiando algunos niños que sepan tañer), como son flautas, y gaitas, y nésperas, y unas vergas de yerro con unas argollicas dentro, las quales tañen da[n]do con un yerro en la verga; y un par de panderos y sonajas.' Ibid., II, 79.
268. 'En esta casa tienen los niños sus exercícios bien ordenados, aprenden a leer y escrevir y van muy avante, otros a cantar y tañer frautas, y otros mamalucos mas diestros aprenden grammática.' Ibid., II, 89.
269. Ibid., I, 42.
270. 'Houve nestas vésperas três coros diversos: um de canto de órgão, outro de um cravo e outro de flautas de modo que, acabando um, começava o outro, e todos, certo, com muita ordem quando vinha a sua vez. E dado que o canto do órgão deleitava ouvindo-se e a suavidade do cravo detivesse os ânimos com a doçura da sua harmonia, todavia quando se tocavam as flautas se alegravam e se regosijavam muito mais os circumstantes, porque, além de o fazer mediocremente, os que as tangiam eram os meninos Brasis, a quem já de tempo o padre António Rodrigues tem ensinado. Foi para o povo tão alegre este espectáculo que não sei como o possa encarecer . . . que não se fallava então na cidade em outra cousa sinão na boa criação e ensinamento destes meninos.' Ibid., II, 140.
271. Freitas da Silva 2011, 68–70.
272. 'Erat enim non solum Brasilicae linguae, sed etiam musicae, necnon tibicinij bene peritus; quibus plurimos Brasiles instruxit pueros; atque ex eo veluti seminario ad caeteros in Brasilia Indorum Christianorum pagos uscibus, tibiisqß canendi scientia permanavit. Quarum rerum suauitate deliniti Barbarorum animi plurimum ad deuotionis sensum, digne´qß de diuinis concipiendum rebus profi[erunt, erint]. Itaqß propterea Pater Antonius Rodericus in magno à Brasilibus Indis pretio habebatur.' Michelini Aguilar 2017, 242.
273. 'Um mercador tinha um terno de flautas muito bom, o qual vendo os Brasílicos tangerem, lh'o mandou, dizendo que muito melhor empregado seria nelles do que nelle.' Holler 2006, II, 141.
274. 'viola, flautas 7 juntas, cravo e órgãos'. Michelini Aguilar 2017, 222.
275. 'Havia flautas dispostas em harmonia de vozes, a que de quando em quando acompanhavam os tamborezinhos. . . .' Holler 2006, II, 489.
276. 'e apos isto se recolhem os meninos, para a escola cada hu a sua instancia hus a ler outros a cantar cantocham e canto dorgão, e outros a tanger frautas e charamelas para oficiarem as missas em dias de festas, e ornarem as prosições, na aldea e na cidade, e em outros autos pubricos, como quando se examínão na sala, os estudantes do curso para bachareis, e lesençeados, e quando tomão os gráos'. Ibid., II, 528.
277. Ibid., II, 381, 156.
278. 'trombetas e frautas'. Lopes Monteiro 2010, 79–80, 132.
279. 'Leva o Senhor Viso-Rei cantores mui escolhidos que officiam as missas e vesporas mui bem, e frautas e charamelas que alegrão hum pouco os navegantes.' Wicki 1962, 508.
280. 'En prego aqui, nesta casa da Madre de Deos, na qual he tanta a devoção desta gente de Cochim que, sem custar nada, ho mais do tempo do anno, todolos domingos e dias santos do anno, vem aqui a solenisar as nossas missas com canto de orgão, frautas e charamelas.' Silva Rego 1952, 464–65.
281. Frutuoso 1998, IV, 380.

282. 'Cõ as frautas folguey em estremo, Vieraõ a muyto bom tempo. Os negros caõtaõ toda a missa pequena de Morales e o motete de Saõto André a simco e huã Pamge limgua de Guereyro e a tangem nas frautas cõ outras cousas ordinarias [co]m braua abilidade e muyto afynados.' Brásio 1954, 302.
283. Lasocki 2018a, 8–9.
284. Bouckaert and Schreurs 2005, 115.
285. Lasocki 2022.
286. Lasocki 2018a, 32.
287. Paragraph based on Lasocki 1983, 221–26.
288. British Library, Add. Ms 31,390, f. 30v and f. 31r; Tenbury, Ms 389, 200.
289. Lasocki 1983, 228–41; 2018a, 43.
290. Lasocki 1984a.
291. López Suero 2021a, 80–82, 108–12.
292. Reynaud 1996, 355, 395.
293. López Suero 2021a, 140, 171–72.
294. 'una caxa de flautas'. Roa Alonso 2015, 21.
295. '1 Futter mit 3 gar kleinen Flöten.' Lasocki 2018a, 39.
296. 'blokpijpen'. Wind 2011, 45.
297. Williamson 1997, 239.
298. Boyd 1973, 15.
299. McCabe 1938, 314.
300. Wind 2011, 48.
301. Ibid., 48–49, 53.
302. 'Voce et fidibus canendo tum fistula et monorchia memet intra privatos parietes exerceo, tum praecipue cum studendo defessus sum, aliquando etiam rus exeo dambu latum.' Burgers 2016, 108.
303. Hall 1809, 515.
304. Unless otherwise stated, rest of section based on Lasocki 2018a.
305. Ibid.
306. Waterhouse 1993, 174.
307. 'Ein groß fueteral mit fünnffzehen stuckh fläthen, khlein und groß. . . . Mehr ein concert fläthen, mit aylff stuckhen unnd messinen beschlägen.' Ibid., 44–47.
308. 'frauti tra grande et piccoli'. Ibid., 50–51.
309. On the academies, see *GMO*, s.v. 'Academy', by Howard Mayer Brown, rev. Iain Fenlon.
310. Lasocki 2018a, 14.
311. 'Cioe il Madrigale Donna vra belta, l'altra a voce Mutate fece per li tromboni qual mi penso sara buona per le vostre flauti grosse se non almeno per le viole grande, et potrete sonare il motetto, a 7, di flautj. . . .' Ibid., 232–33.
312. Ibid., 27.
313. Inventory of the ridotto, 6 August 1593: 'Una coppia de Flautoni nº 7 . . . Flauti tra grandi e piccoli nº 9. . . .' Paganuzzi 1970, 145–46, 150.
314. 'zum lehrnen . . .'.
315. Waterhouse 1993, 419.
316. Wackernagel 2003, 12–13.
317. Based on *GMO*, 'Recorder', by David Lasocki.
318. Van Heyghen 1995, 7–9.
319. 'suene música de flautas tristes'. After line 482.
320. 'música de flautas o chirimías'. After line 639.
321. '(Tocan flautas y vase la Virgen.) Qué instrumentos concertados son éstos que escucho agora?'
322. Lasocki 1983, I, 272–78; 1984.
323. Rowland-Jones 1997a, 15.
324. Castiglione 1968, 95.
325. Lasocki 1983, I, 278–82.

326. 'En suitte de quoy on couchera la Mariée, où toutes les ruses et les galanteries que l'on a de coustume de pratiquer en semblables rencontres ne seront point oubliées. Pendant cela on oyra un concert de flûtes qui feront advoüer à l'assistance que toutes les merveilles que les histoires rapportent de cet ancien joüeur de flûte Ismenias, ne sont rien que l'ombre de ce qu'ils entendront.' Lacroix 1868–70, IV, 198.
327. 'Well lustich fluyterken wilt mijnen lust coelen, / fluyt met u luytken dat ickt mach voelen.' Koldeweij 1993, 59.
328. Ibid.
329. 'Hij stack 't aerdigh fluytjen / Bij mijn borsjens in. / Wech, wech, zeyd ick, guytjen, / Wat beduyt de min? / Wijl op 't fluytje speelen / Speelt soo dat behoort! / 't sal mij niet verveelen: / 't is genoegh geboort!' Ibid., 59.
330. 'Maar alle heylige daeghs gaet hier de Veel met de Fluyt an boort, / 't Gaet so ondeughdelycke moy, jy wilt wild worden dat gy 't hoort.' Wind 2006, 32.
331. Wind 2011, 39.
332. Ibid., 39–41.
333. 'six Satyres sonnans des fleutes . . .'. Lacroix 1868–70, II, 172.
334. 'sinfonia di flauti, storte, over di piffari'. Ibid.
335. 'Deux Bergers & deux Bergeres reuiennent des champs joüans de leurs flustes & leurs musettes, & conduisans chacun leurs trouppeaux au village à cause de la Nuict.' Canova-Green 1997, I, 106.
336. Stewart 1989; text only in English and unreadable in the reproduction.
337. Legêne 2005, 327.
338. Sub-section based on Van Heyghen 1995.
339. Lasocki 2020, 98–100.
340. Section based on Wind 2011.
341. The carillon also had an option for automatic play, operated by a rotating barrel with pegs to notate the pieces.
342. Directeur van de Klok-werken tot Uitrecht.
343. 'mits dat hij d' wandelende luijden opt kerckhoff somwijlen savons mit het geluijt van sijn fluijtien vermaecke'. Wind 2011, 60, n. 5.
344. 'Daer begindt hy op zijn fluydtje; / Dat was't! O! wat liever tuytje! / (Wech nu loome lompery!) / Of ick inden hemel sy? / O! vergoode Palmer-gaedtjes, / O! wat boven-menschte maedtjes / Vloeyen uyt u konstich rondt / Van een rappen aessem-mondt.' Ibid., 60.
345. 'Beminners vande konst van Maatgezang, en Fluyt, / Wiens lieflijk, tooverzoet, zieltrckende geluyt / Weet herten van metaal en klipp' en steen te dwingen . . . / So staak uw' vreugd.' Ibid., 702–3.
346. 'Die Fluyt en Klocken zulken zoeten taal déen spreken / Die aard en Hemel trok; en lokten yders oor / Soo kragtig, dat de ziel haar zelven gans verloor; De druk en rouw van 't hert als water afgestreken.' Ibid.
347. 'Nut en dienstigh, voor alle Konst-lievende Lief-hebbers tot de Fluit, Blaes- en allerley Speel-tuygh.'
348. 'zoo wel voor de Viool als Fluit, of eenigh Blaas-tuygh te gebruycken'.
349. 'op nieuws overhoort, verbetert en vermeerdert, door den Autheur'. The three compositions from *Euterpe* omitted in *Der Fluyten Lust-hof I* were 'Sarabande', 'Stemme nova [I]', and 'Stemme nova [II]'. Ibid., 133, 398–99.
350. Ibid., 440–51.
351. Ibid., 170.
352. Griffioen 1991.
353. Wind 2011, 384.
354. Ibid., 205.
355. 'dat ghy de hand-fluyt heel in u gewelt had . . . dezer edeler konste u E . . .'.
356. Wind 2021.
357. Ibid.
358. 'Om met 2. en 3. Fiolen, of ander Speel-tuigh te gebruiken.'

359. 'Komt dan Kunst-lievers, koopt, elkx gaangh is hier te haalen, 't Is voor de Fluyt, Fiool en alderley gespeel. . . .'
360. 'Zoo helder klonk in dien tydt Uw E. Fluit . . . de zoete snaaren van Uw E. Fiool de Gamba door haar zuiver geluid. . . .'
361. Wind 2011, 46.
362. 'met een korte onderwyzinge op de Hand-fluit'.
363. Amsterdam: XYZ, 1958.
364. Legêne 1995, 111–14.
365. Praetorius 1619, 16, 32; Wind 2011, 580–1, 584–85.
366. Wind, email message to DL, 3 October 2021.
367. Bouterse 2005, 71–72.
368. 'alle houtwaren, daeronder alle gedrayde houtwaren van essen, hechten ende dies meer aengaende, oock al wat van ivore off hooren gedrayt wert'. Wind 2024.
369. Adrian Brown, email message to DL, 10 October 2021.
370. Wind 2011, 577.
371. 'Ce fut comme un essai d'Opéra, qui eut l'agrément de la Nouveauté; mais ce qu'il eût de meilleur encore, c'est qu'on y entendit des Concerts de Flûtes; ce que l'on n'avoit pas entendu sur aucun Théâtre depuis les Grecs & les Romains.' Saint-Évremond 1709, XLV.
372. 'Trois Bergers, & autant de Bergeres de cette heureuse Contrée, que la douceur de la Solitude & l'amour ont reduits à cette vie Champestre, font avec plusieurs autres un Concert Rustique, auquel un Choeur de Flustes & de plusieurs autres instrumens respondent. . . .' Canova-Green 1997, I, 410.
373. 'Quatorze Concertans de Pan & de Diane précedoient ces deux Divinitez, avec une agréable Harmonie de Flûtes & de Musettes.'
374. 'avec un concert le plus agréable du monde'.
375. Lasocki 2020, 108–11.
376. Van Heyghen 1995, 45.

3 THE ERA OF THE BAROQUE RECORDER, 1668–1800

1. Unless otherwise stated, the data come from Lasocki 1983 and 2018a.
2. Section partly based on Lasocki 2012b and 2020.
3. Rowland-Jones 2002.
4. Lasocki 2019.
5. Lasocki 2018c.
6. Archives nationales, Paris, MC/ET/LIII/140, 15 April 1709.
7. Wind 2011, 589–92.
8. 't Nieuwe Hoornse speel-werck (1672), 77–78; Oprechte Haerlemse Dingsdaegse Courant, 16 July 1686, 2.
9. Two anonymous collections: Minueti e Ariete da Batelo per Flauto dolce, which once belonged to the Venetian Carminati family; and Sei Duetti Sonabili, e Cantabili Primo Secondo e Basso Per il Flauto Dolce o Traversier, Conservatorio 'Benedetto Marcello', Fondo Correr B 119.011. d'Avena Braga 2015, 21 and private communication.
10. Flauto e voce II 1998, 25.
11. Prinz 2005, 206–7.
12. 'Flöten, (sie seynd nun à bec oder Traversieri) . . .' Schriftstücke 1963, 60–61.
13. Kenyon de Pascual 1995, 71–72.
14. Kenyon de Pascual 1982, 311; Bermúdez 2020, 252.
15. Martín 1985.
16. Kenyon de Pascual 1982, 311.
17. Russell 2009, 385, n. 42.
18. Bluteau 1713; Costa 1768; Vieyra 1773; Cabral 1787. From a video lecture by Fernando Duarte de Oliveira.
19. Michelini Aguilar 2017, 248.

20. Kilbey 2002, 146.
21. Brown 2018, 243.
22. Lerch 1996.
23. Praetorius 1619, II, 37.
24. Inv. no. X/4266.
25. 'Daher mir dann dieses Mittel eingefallen, daß ich die Flötten, oben zwischen den Mund- und Fingerlöchern, mitten zertheilen, und das oberste Stück auff zweyer Finger breit lenger machen lassen, also daß man dasselb in das Untertheil, so weit man wil, oder von Noten ist, hinnein flecken, die Pfeiffen lenger, oder kürzer machen, und also einer solchen Flötten, daß sie jünger oder gröber werde, so bald alltmal helffen kan. Und ob gleich auch etliche berühmte Instrumentmacher vermeynen, daß die Flötten dadurch in etlichen Löchern falsch werden möchten. So haben sie doch hernacher sebsten daran kein mangel, außgenommen diesen, daß etliche in dem höchsten Clave nicht wo gar wol sprechen wollen, befunden. Imgleichen ist solches in den Bassanelli . . . auch versucht und just befunden worden.' Praetorius 1619, II, 34–35; 1986, 46; Foster 1992.
26. *Nieuw Nederlandsch Biografisch Woordenboek*, III, 826.
27. Lairesse 1712.
28. Lasocki 2019.
29. Haynes 2001, 57, 60, 124–25.
30. 'der französischen Musicalischen Instrumenta, so mainsten in Hautbois und Flaudadois bestehen . . . die ohngefehr von 12 Jahren in Franckreich erfunden worden . . .'. Nickel 1971, 204.
31. 'son elevation fit la chute totale de tous les entiens istrumens, a l'exception du haubois, grace aux Filidor et Hautteterre, lesquels ont tant gâté de bois et soutenus de la musique, qu'ils sont en fin parvenus a le rendre propre pour les concerts. De ces tems la, on laissa la musette au bergers, les violons, les flutes douces, les theorbes et les violes prirent leur place, car la flute traverssiere n'est venue qu'apres.' Benoit 1971, 455.
32. *GMO*, s.v. 'Philidor [Filidor]', by Rebecca Harris-Warrick.
33. http://www.rimab.ch/content/documents-dimage/GE/philidor-michel-ii-danican-1610-1679-lettre-de-retenue-de-michel-ii-danican-pour-la-charge-de-cromorne-et-trompette-marine-de-la-grande-ecurie-paris-1651.
34. Dupont-Danican Philidor 1997, 12.
35. Robin 2004, 23–36; email message to DL, 30 August 2021.
36. Haynes 2001, 30, n. 54. A recent discovery by Michel Quagliozzi that Louis Paisible, a member of the Cromornes et Trompettes Marines, was described in documents as 'joueur de hautbois et cromorne ordinaire du Roy' strengthens Robin's hypothesis. Email message to DL, 12 October 2021.
37. 'un homme unique pour la construction de toutes sortes d'instruments de bois, d'yvoire et d'ebéine, comme sont les musettes, flûtes, flageolets, haubois, cromornes; et mesme pour faire des accords parfaits de tous ces mesmes instruments. Ses fils ne luy cèdent en rien pour la pratique de cet art, à laquelle ils ont joint une entiere connoissance, & une execution encore plus admirable du jeu de la Musette en particulier.' Borjon de Scellery 1672, 38.
38. 'Les hautbois & les cromornes font aussi un agréable effet avec les Musettes assemblées.' Ibid., 33.
39. 'plusieurs ont esté ravis . . . de la Flute douce de la Pierre, & du Flageolet d'Osteterre'. Marolles 1657, 262.
40. Hotteterre 1738, 64–65.
41. *GDMI*, s.v. 'Hotteterre', by Tula Giannini.
42. Giannini 1993, 381.
43. Lasocki 2003.
44. 'les hautbois et autres instruments . . . fournis aux joueurs de hautbois des deux compagnies de mousquetaires du Roi'. La Gorce 2002, 134–35.
45. 'pour le paiement de plusieurs instruments'. Ibid., 211.
46. 'a Martin Hotteterre, haultbois et musette du Roy, la somme de 200 l., à luy ordonnée pour les instruments qu'il a fournis pour ledit ballet du Psyché.' Bougenot 1891, 79.

47. *GDMI*, s.v. 'Lissieu', by Denis Watel.
48. Hotteterre 1738, 64.
49. Haynes 2002, 99.
50. Lasocki 2018a, 106; James Kopp, private communication, points out that Jacques and his brother André both played the quart-contra bassoon and may therefore have made this instrument (see *États de la France (1644–1789)* for 1712).
51. Baines 1967, 276–77.
52. 'Lorsque la flute a certains trous doubles, cette meme ronde marque qu'il n'en faut boucher qu'un.' Loulié 1680s, XX, f. 194r.
53. Hotteterre 1707, 38, 40.
54. d'Avena Braga 2015, 62.
55. Ferrara, Biblioteca Municipale di Reggio Emilia, Ms. Reggiani E. 41.
56. 'Non si diede alla Stampa, per la Morte del soprad° Sig^r. Essendovi aggiunto di più le Regole del Violoncello da Spalla, del Contrabasso èdel Oboè.'
57. 'Si per le Mani, e Dite, come per il Fiato, e Lingue Dritta, e Roverse, et altre cose, che possono accadere.' Tarr 1987.
58. 'bisogna che il Flauto, sia di trè pezzi; come oggi di usano . . .'.
59. 'Occorendo slongare il Flauto; in occasione di calarlo di uoce, per farlo chorista; bisogna, che il Flauto, sia di trè pezzi; come oggi di usano; e poi bisogna prima slongarlo in cima, e poi anco slongarlo un tantino in fondo, con le Giunte; acciò le uoci tutte uenghino giuste.'
60. Haynes 2002, lii, 64–66.
61. 'Trillo alla Francese; per questo passo quà di sotto; nel Flauto all'Italiana; e sè il Flauto, non facesse, ò non cavasse detto Trillo; non sarà Flauto giusto.' Castellani 1977, 78.
62. Dickey et al. 1978, 158.
63. d'Avena Braga 2015, 32–34.
64. Castellani 1977, 79.
65. Ibid., 79.
66. Voice 2014, 184–87. Other possible makers are shakily documented: the IMILIA mark on a crumhorn, possibly seventeenth century; the mark Ia. Ne. (Jacopo Neri?), probably sixteenth or seventeenth century; the mark Pietracenus on cornamuses in Manfred Settala's collection (catalogued 1664); Grassi, perhaps not the sixteenth-century maker C. Raffi as previously thought, in the Settala collection; P. Grece, who made a set of Renaissance recorders now at the Accademia Filarmonica di Bologna, perhaps copied from Raffi's; and Stefano Iacomelli, mentioned by Langwill. Ibid., 258–59, 405.
67. Biblioteca Nazionale Marciana, Mss. Ital. Cl. IV. No. 486.
68. Van Heyghen 1995, 27; d'Avena Braga 2015, 15–17.
69. Nickel 1971, 187; Grassi Museum für Musikinstrumente der Universität Leipzig, Inv. No. 1112.
70. See also Lerch 1996, 231.
71. Brown 2018, 248.
72. Email message to DL, 19 September 2021. Larger sizes of recorder by Gahn have survived, but information about these instruments is lacking at the present time.
73. Nickel 1971, 278, 469.
74. Bachhaus, Eisenach, Inv. No. 115.
75. Germanisches Nationalmuseum, Nuremberg, Inv. No. MIR 213; Münchner Stadtmuseum, Inv. No. Mu 175.
76. Warner 1967.
77. The song sheet for 'If Sorrow the Tyrant' (1687), 'Set for the Voice, Violin, and Recorder. And for the Flute and Flagelet the Dot way.' https://library.chethams.com/blog/musical-monday/. Curiously, the 'Recorder' part requires an instrument in C; the 'Flute' part, one in F.
78. Mezger 1995, 423.
79. Ibid..
80. British Library, Add. 35043; Dart 1959; Davies 1993.
81. Paris, Bibliothèque Nationale, fonds fr. n. a. 6355, xix–xx.
82. Ranum 1991.

83. 'la Flute Traversiere, est un Instrument des plus agréables, & des plus à la mode'. Hotteterre 1707, Preface.

84. 'La flute a bec ayant son merite & ses Partisans, ainsi que la Flute Traversiere'. Ibid., 55.

85. 'les sons peu en usage sur la flute, c'est-à-dire ceux qui montent au dessus de son etendue ordinaire, et ceux dont on ne se sert que dans les transpositions'. Loulié 1680s, f. 203r.

86. 'en sorte que ce premier son ne sois point changé, battre du doigt lentement'. Ibid., f. 202r.

87. 'On observera qu'il faut faire des flattements presque sur toutes les notes longues, et qu'il les faut faire, aussi-bien que les tremblements et battements, plus lents ou plus précipités, selon le mouvement et le caractere des Pièces.'

88. 'il seroit difficile d'enseigner à connoître précisement tous les endroits où l'on doit les placer en joûant. . . . On ne peut guere donner de Regles plus certaines de la distribution de ces agréments, c'est le goût & la pratique, qui peuvent apprendre à s'en servit à propos, plutôt que la Theorie.'

89. Ranum 1995, 241.

90. Ibid.

91. 'Tous ceux qui enseignent a jouer de la flute se servent de tu et de ru, et l'on trouve que le melange de ces deux syllabes, pronouncees tour a tour dans de certains endroits, rend les coups de langue moins rudes, et le jeu plus coulant; Mais la manière de les placer n'est plas bien constante, Car ils ont chacun leur manière particulière. . . . Toustes ces manières peuvent etre bonnes, mais il faut que l'Ecolier qui a un bon maitre en prenne les manières.' Loulié 1680s, f. 200r.

92. Ranum 1995, 235.

93. Johann Joachim Quantz, letter published by Marpurg: 'Buffardin und Blavet machten vom Zungenwerke wenig. Den Gebrauch mit dem *ti* und *tiri* und dem *di* und *diri* haben sie eben so gut als ich.' Marpurg 1970, IV, 173.

94. 'Autre-fois on se servoit des deux syllabes tu, ru, pour exprimer les coups de langues: Mais les Virtuoses d'aprésent ne les montrent plus par tu, ru; et regardent cela comme une chose absurde qui ne sert qu'a embarasser l'Ecolier.' Corrette ca. 1739, 20.

95. 'Come anco avertire, che nel suonare qual si voglia Strumento da Fiato; suonarlo con maniera Cantabile, e non altrimenti; et anco, con Imitatione, di chi Canterà.'

96. 'Altre due Lingue; non usate; mà alle volte fanno un bel sentire; in accompagnare in Stile cantabile.'

97. For another explanation, see Dickey et al. 1978, 153, n. 14.

98. 'Bisogna poi far il Trillo, ad ogni nota; pur che siano di meza Battuta; ò d'una intiera; ò d'un quarto; et anco à tutte quelle, che havranno il punto.'

99. Dickey et al. 1978, 155, n. 19.

100. 'e nel pigliar Fiato; avertire di pigliarlo in modo, che, niuno sè nè possi accorgere; e questo sarà, nè Sospiri, ò Pause di Battuta, ò Note con il punto, come non si può far di meno'.

101. Salas Machuca 1999.

102. *Diary* 1970, passim.

103. *London Stage* 1965, 95.

104. Sir Robert Stapylton, *The Slighted Maid*, III (Duke's Company, Lincoln's Inn Fields, 23 February 1663; attended by Pepys; *London Stage* 1965, 62); Edward Howard, *The Chorus of Crowns*, II.i (King's Company, Bridges, 15 April 1667; attended by Pepys; ibid., 106); John Dover, *The Roman Generals* (licensed 7 November 1667 but apparently never performed; ibid., 116); anon., *The Woman Turn'd Bully*, II.iii (Duke's Company, Dorset Garden, 24 March 1675; ibid., 231).

105. *London Stage* 1965, 24–25.

106. *Diary* 1970, IX, 94; *London Stage* 1965, 131.

107. *Diary* 1970, IX, 100; *London Stage* 1965, 131.

108. Ibid., 135.

109. *Diary* 1970, IX, 157.

110. Ibid., IX, 164.

111. Godman 1956, 21.

112. Hunt 1962, 58.

113. Lasocki 2012a, 79.
114. Oldham 1956, 97.
115. Rawson 2002, 13, 326; unpublished.
116. Ibid.
117. Lasocki 2019.
118. Rowland-Jones 2009.
119. Buttrey 1995.
120. 'prenant un extreme plaisir a entendre chanter Gillet, La forest et Godonesche; il veut encore les faire repéter demain pour la quatrieme fois, le recit du sommeil; Cambert accompagne les voix avec son clavessin et on y joindra les flustes; il y a ici deux francois qui en joüent parfaittement bien; le Roy dela g^de Bretagne bat toujours la mesure, il admire aussi bien que toutte sa Cour la beautée des voix, et la justesse de vos Musiciens.' Ibid., 200.
121. 'le Roy de la g^de Bretagne a entendu souvent chez elle les Srs Gillet, La forest et Godonesche qui lui ont chanté plusiers fois la scène du sommeil, et beaucoup d'autres scènes d'Alceste, de Cadmus, de Thésée et d'Atis; le Sr Camberg les accompagnoit avec son clavessin; ily avoit cinq ou six hommes qui jouent fort bien de la fluste; les Musiciens de V[ostre] M[ajes] ont acquis ici une grande réputation, et touttes les Dames se sont fait un honneur de les attirer chez elle.' Ibid., 205.
122. Lasocki 2020, 214–16.
123. Section based on Lasocki 2018c.
124. Cessac 1995, 376–77.
125. Holman 2001.
126. Ibid., 259.
127. Bergmann 1965; Levin 1981; Davis 1996.
128. Hell 2017.
129. Heidecker 1996.
130. Levin 1981, 375–78.
131. Rampe 2009.
132. Rampe 2010.
133. Cameron and Talbot 2013, 105–8.
134. Laurent 2021, 72.
135. Sardelli 2007, 166, 170.
136. Ibid., 89.
137. Ibid., 283–85.
138. Ibid., 129–30.
139. Ibid., 130.
140. Ibid., 73–83.
141. Ibid., 246–47.
142. d'Avena Braga 2015, 256.
143. Ibid., 135.
144. Carpena 2007.
145. *Flauto e voce* III.
146. *Flauto e voce* I. More Keiser arias in vols X and 17.
147. Marissen 1991; 1995.
148. Lasocki 2020, 223–27.
149. A pair of small recorders of different tonal and dynamic characteristics, marked I and II on the middle pieces, and joined together at the head piece by a brass flange (anonymous, probably Saxon, late eighteenth century; Grassi-Museum, Leipzig).
150. Rampe and Zapf 1997.
151. Marissen 1985; Bach 2022.
152. Section based on the summaries in Lasocki 2020.
153. Collection of H. Iino, Tokyo, Japan.
154. Mu 151 (sopranino), Mu 156 (tenor), Mu 160 (alto), and Mu 164 (sopranino) have survived; Mu 156 or 158 (tenor), Mu 157 (bass), and Mu 161 (alto) were destroyed.

155. Robinson 2003, 115.
156. 'Beim Trio . . . wo zwo Flöten sind, dieselben zum Basse lieber einen sanft geblasenen Fagott haben wollen, als ein Violoncello, dessen Töne doch nicht so viel Aehnlichkeit mit den Flötentönen haben. Im vorigen Jahrhunderte gab man hierauf besser Achtung, da man die schwachen *Flutes douces* mit den Flötenbässen oder Baßflöten begleitete, welche aber nun aus der Mode gekommen sind, weil sie so sehr viel Athem erfordern.' p. 185.
157. 'Bas-Fluyten die al haer toonen geven als op een gemeene Fluyt'.
158. Bouterse 2005, 306–7.
159. 'alderhande soorten van uitstreekende goede Fluyten, die niet stoppen, en 't speelen nooit afvallen, als mede Hautbois, bassons, Dwars en Bas-Fluyten, op een nieuwe manier door hem zelf uytgevonden, en nooit voor dezen van niemand so gemaekt'.
160. Young 1993, 60; Waterhouse 1993, 291.
161. 'Une Flute douce longue de Basse.'
162. Lasocki 2018a, 232.
163. Rowland-Jones 2002.
164. Lasocki 2019, 63.
165. Quagliozzi 2021, who shows that the first name Charles, which first appears in Hawkins 1776 and is often cited in modern sources, is incorrect.
166. *Mises en Concert par Monsieur Dieupart Pour un Violon & flûte avec une Basse de Viole & un Archilut.*
167. 'Cette Suite se doit jouer en C sol ut sur une flute de voix.'
168. *Daily Post*, 3–5 March 1702.
169. *Flauto e voce* II, XII.
170. Holman 2012, 480, 483; Haynes 2002, 116–17, 175–78.
171. 'Il commença par le Basson, le Violon, la Flute Allemande, la Flute Douce, la Flute à voix, en faisant deux parties, & le Haut-bois.' *Mercure de France*, August 1727, cols 1905–6.
172. Sardelli 2007, 87.
173. 'Da ich nicht weis, was für gattung flauto piccolo hier ist, so hab ich es in den *Natürlichen Ton* gesetzt; man kann es allzeit übersetzen.' *Kritischer* 1995, b/25.
174. Lasocki and Neate 1988.
175. Section based on Lasocki 1983; 1999.
176. Tilmouth 1957. *Collection for Improvement of Husbandry and Trade*, 22 February, 19 April 1695.
177. Bellhouse 2011.
178. Wilson 1959, 160.
179. Quarrell and Mare 1934, 17–18.
180. 'Herr Gramm, ein Luneburgischer von Adel, der in unserer Compagnie und ein Liebhaber von der Flote war, wollte bey ihm lernen; er forderte aber vor achtzehn Stunden drey Guineen, welches ihn abschreckte. . . .' Preussner 1949, 15; Quarrell and Mare 1934, 66–67.
181. Lasocki 1983, 805.
182. All the newspaper advertisements cited in the remainder of this section may be found in Lasocki 2018a.
183. Byrne 1984, 102.
184. Lasocki 1997.
185. Section based on Lasocki 1987.
186. Lasocki 2020, 121–22.
187. Holman 2012.
188. The first seems to have been Schickhardt's Op. 20, No. 1 (Amsterdam: Roger, 1715 and advertised by his London agent; Walsh, 1718).
189. Section based on Johnstone 2007; 2008.
190. Johnstone 2007, 30.
191. Lasocki 1983; 1984b.
192. Hawkins 1963, II, 823.
193. *Daily Journal*, 11 May 1731.
194. Lasocki 2019, 24–27.

195. Lasocki 1983, passim.
196. Ginger 1998.
197. January 1729. Ibid., 163.
198. April 1729. Ibid., 239.
199. November 1728. Ibid., 141.
200. *Daily Journal*, 11 June 1730.
201. October 1728. Ginger 1998, 115.
202. May 1729. Ibid., 243.
203. 26 and 29 August 1728. Ibid., 75, 77.
204. Hawkins 1963, I, 482–83.
205. Bodleian Library, Oxford, Ms.Mus.Sch.g.239 and g.40; MacMillan 2017, 239.

4 DUCT FLUTES IN THE NINETEENTH CENTURY

1. Nicholson 1809, IV, unpaginated.
2. See Tarasov 2023 for details. On the flageolet in the United States, see Lasocki 2010.
3. 'Nebendem wird sich Herr Heberle, aus Freundschaft für den Unternehmer, auf einem hier unbekannten Blasinstrumente von besonderer Form, und sehr angenehmen Ton, hören lassen. Die Benennung des Instrumentes behält man sich der Ueberraschung wegen bevor.' Strebel 2016, 648.
4. Reproduction of the concert placard of one of the csakan's earliest public appearances. Heberle used the following instruments: 'Flöte; Trauer-Flöte, ein Instrument, das vor 300 Jahren bekannt war, und gebraucht wurde; Knottenstock, dessen Aeste die Klappen sind; Ungarischer Tsákány, ein Instrument, welches wegen seinem liebevollen Tone besondere Aufmerksamkeit verdient.' Betz 1992a, 14–15.
5. 'Flauto doulce: Der allzu leise Ton, und der geringe Umfang des Instruments, hat es heut zu Tage beynahe aus der Mode gebracht: man hört es weder in der Kirche, noch bey Concerten mehr.' Schubart 1806, 209.
6. 'Der Csakan ist zu Folge seines Ursprunges und der Art wie er geschrieben und ausgesprochen wird, ein ungarisches Instrument. Ein lustwandelnder Musiker fand ihn zu Anfange des 19. Jahrhunderts in einer verfallenen Erimitage in Ungarn.' Krähmer 1830, Preface.
7. 'Haiduckenczakan: . . . Beil . . . zum Werfen und Hauen nach dem Kopfe.' Pierer 1859, 855.
8. 'XXIII. Der Streithammer: Mit dem Zigeunerworte *Czakan* bezeichnet man im Slavischen (ungarisch *Czakany*) eine Art Streithammer oder Bergstock. Auf kurzem Knüttelstiel ist hier der Hammer, welcher einen beilartigen oder spitzen Ansatz auf der entgegengesetzten Seite hat, mit Zwingen befestigt. Beim kaiserlichen Heiduckenkorps war derselbe Ende des 17. und Anfang des 18. Jahrhunderts in Gebrauch. *Teutscher Czakan* hieß dieser Bergstock, wenn er mit einer Schießvorrichtung versehen war. Solche im Ungarischen auch Puzikan, und Pusdogean, im Russischen *Tschekan* genannte kurze Hammerstöcke wurden ferner, früher sowohl in Ungarn wie in Polen, von den höheren Offizieren als Zeichen ihres Standes geführt.' Demmin 1893, 809.
9. Betz 1992a, 28.
10. 'XXII. Die Kriegstonwerkzeuge. – Das Feldspiel: Czakan heißt die slavische Stockpfeife.' Demmin 1893, 699.
11. 'Eine Charakt[er] Sonate für Csakan in welcher ausgedrückt wie die neue Schiffbrücke in Presburg gebaut wird.' Beethoven's conversation books, vol. 8, booklet 93, September 1825; Tarasov 2000, 6.
12. Betz 1992a, 188.
13. 'Stockflöte oder Czakan, wie in Böhmen besonders das Instrument genannt wird, ist ein Flöteninstrument oder eigentlich nur ein Flötenstock (und daher der Name), um im Freien satt auf der Flöte zum Vergnügen blasen zu können. Es ist besonders im Oesterreichischen sehr gebräuchlich, eine neuere Erfindung, und der Plock- oder Schnabelpfeife sehr ähnlich.' Schilling 1835, 505.
14. 'Stockflöte, czechisch; Czakan. . . . Jetzt wird es immer seltener gefunden.' Mendel 1878, 458.

15. Köhler 1886; Barth ca. 1900.
16. 'Die Stockflöte, dieses gegenwärtig, des angenehmen Tones, und der geringen Anstrengung wegen sehr beliebte Instrument, welches auch den passenden Nahmen 'Flute douce' führt. . . .' Klingenbrunner 1816, preface. Dating of this tutor from a large advertisement in the *Wiener-Zeitung* from 6 June 1816, where it is described as 'ganz neu erschienen und zu haben' (newly published and available).
17. 'Sein Spiel auf der Flûte douce oder Czakan hat aber einen noch größeren Enthusiasmus geweckt. . . .' *Der Sammler* 14 (1822): 560; Betz 1992b, 131.
18. 'Bei der Flöte: Ernst Krähmer (Flûte douce; tot).' First published 1861–63 in the Viennese journal *Rezensionen und Mitteilungen über Theater und Musik*; Deutsch 1957, 298.
19. Third verse: 'Von seinem Wanderstabe / schraubt jener Stift und Habe / und mischt mit Flötentönen / sich in des Hornes Dröhnen. . . .' Fröschle and Scheffler 1980, 146.
20. *Vereinigte Ofener und Pester Zeitung*, 13 August 1807, Supplement No. 65; Betz 1992a, 16.
21. 'Oft bin ich gefragt worden, warum der Csakan in As steht. Ich könnte antworten, weil der erste diese Stimmung hatte, oder, ist As dur nicht eine der schönsten Tonarten, allein besser beweisst uns Folgendes. Ein jedes Stoppel oder Kerninstrument, wenn es höher als in As steht, wird zu schreiend, und hauptsächlich in der Höhe zu unangenehm, steht es tiefer so ist die Höhe wohl schöner, aber die Tiefe wird zu schwach, und versagt wohl gar manchmal den Ton. Nur die Stimmung G will ich noch gelten lassen, da aber alle für den Csakan im Stich erschienenen Musikalien rücksichtlich des Accompagnements für die Stimmung As berechnet sind, so finde ich auch für rathsamer bei dem As Csakan zu verbleiben, ausgenommen jemand spielt ohne Begleitung oder will dieselbe einen halben Ton tiefer transponieren lassen.' Krähmer 1830. The second and third parts of the tutor date from 1833.
22. Fingering charts in Krähmer 1830.
23. 'Dieses damals noch sehr unvollkommene Instrument kam in die Hände des in Pressburg wohnenden Instrumentenmachers Franz Schöllnast, welcher dieses zuerst imitierte und dann bald mehrere gelungenere unter das Publikum brachte. . . . Allein bald fand man, dass am Csakan selbst, noch viele Vervollkomnungen angebracht werden könnten, und so weit sind die Versuche jetzt gelungen, dass er sowohl an äusserer Form, als auch an Complication überhaupt ausserordentlich gewonnen hat.' Krähmer 1830, preface.
24. 'hat sich hauptsächlich in Hinsicht der Form verdienstlich gemacht, auf Verlangen verfertigt er Csakans in der gefälligen Form einer Oboe, nur das Mundstück abgerechnet.' Ibid., 4.
25. Evident from Schöllnast's surviving account books; Betz 1992a, 72–86. This fitting belonged to the basic equipment for which there was an extra charge.
26. 'folglich fällt hier eine nicht unbedeutende Schwierigkeit von selbst weg, und man kann im nöthigen Falle den Daumen ganz wegrücken.' Klingenbrunner 1816, 3.
27. Krähmer 1822.
28. Krähmer 1833, 21, second footnote.
29. Betz 1992a, 72–86.
30. Clarified and illustrated by a production timetable in Betz 1992a, 76.
31. Stifter 1840.
32. 'Sendet mir doch einen Chakan, er soll mir dienen: um mich bey der Überfarth zu amüsieren und meine Finger in Bewegung zu halten.' Letter of 5 March 1828; Betz 1992a, 95.
33. 'Ref. freuet es, von diesem bescheidenen Künstler mit gerechtem Lobe sprechen zu können; den sein Spiel, sowol auf diesem Instrumente, als auch auf der Flöte, zeugte von vielem Gefühl, und einem seltenen, ausdrucksvollen Vortrage.' 'Nachrichten', *AMZ* 12, no. 38 (20 June 1810), 607.
34. Evident from Schöllnast's business books, 42; Betz 1992b, 128.
35. 'und befriedigte die Wünsche – des Concertgebers. Denn man kann sagen, es war gedrängt voll. Sey es nun, dass die grosse Menge an Czakan-Spielern und Liebhabern den Saal so gefüllt, oder dass Hr. Krähmer bey Veranstaltung seines Concertes mit mehr Umsicht zu Werke gegangen war, als manche Concertgeber thun. . . .' 'Novellistik' 1821.
36. 'vor einem zahlreichen Publicum gegeben. . . . Herr Krähmer blies sehr schwierige Variationen auf dem Czákan. Er machte damit vieles Vergnügen, zumal durch Nachahmung *Drouetischer Passagen*. Nicht leicht wird man Ähnliches auf diesem Instrumente hören.' 'M' 1822.

37. Poster of a concert with Anton Heberle from 28 May 1816 in Vészprém: 'Variationen für den ungarischen Csákány mit Begleitung des ganzen Orchesters'; anonymous review in *AMZO* 5, no. 24 (24 March 1821), 189, of a Krähmer concert in Vienna: 'Variationen auf dem ungrischen Csakan mit Orchesterbegleitung'.

38. 'Die brillantesten Concertstücke werden für den csakan geschrieben, und sobald sie von ausgebildeten Spielern gut vorgetragen werden, sowohl vom grösseren Publikum, als auch in kleineren Zirkeln mit entscheidenden Beifalle aufgenommen.' Krähmer 1830, preface.

39. 'In der Sexta, Quinta, Quarta haben wir auf diesen Czakanflöten ohne Daumenloch gespielt, wo man die Oktaven durch stärkeres Pusten erzeugen musste. Wenn da so 60 oder 70 Schüler einstimmig Choräle gespielt haben, können Sie sich vorstellen, daß es einem die Schuhe auszog, so wie es sich angehört hat.' Schmidt 1987, 518.

40. Paetzold, personal communication, 2007.

41. Betz 1992a, 98.

42. 'Allgemeine Regeln für den Fingersatz'. Krähmer 1830, 26.

43. 'obwohl die Klappen zur reinen Stimmung des Instrumentes, und zur grösseren Erleichterung des Spieles erfunden wurden, so hat man doch oft Fälle, dass Stellen von einem und mehreren Takten ohne Hülfe der Gabelgriffe äusserst schwierig und unvollkommen auszuführen seyn werden'. Ibid.

44. 'Diese sind jedoch nur für Jene geschrieben, welche sich gerade dafür capricieren, und deren Instrumente diese Töne gut und rein geben sollten.' Marginal note in etude no. 86, Krähmer 1833.

45. Tromlitz 1791; Quantz 1752.

46. 'Der Csakan ganz vorzüglich eignet sich dazu, da sie auf demselben nicht so schwer ausführbar ist als Viele glauben, ja selbst leichter, runder und schneller ausgeübt werden kann, als auf jedem andern sich dazu eignenden Instrumente.' Krähmer 1833, 20.

47. 'Die Leichtigkeit der Embouchure gestattet natürlich den Vortrag der schnellsten Passagen, und wenn jemand so auf der Oboe blasen könnte, er wäre ein Zauberer zu nennen.' 'Novellistik' 1821.

48. Suggested by a sentence such as: 'Zur grösseren Erleichterung für Schüler und Meister rathet der Verfasser dieser Schule, (und zwar aus langjähriger Erfahrung) dem Schüler anfänglich nicht die Tonleiter durchgehen zu lassen.' (For greater facilitation for student and teacher, the author of this method [from long-standing experience] recommends not allowing the student initially to skip over scales.) Krähmer 1830, 5.

49. 'sein Anschwellen und Abnehmen der Töne, bis in das kaum hörbar Laute anstaunen und bewundern'. 'M' 1823.

50. 'viele Piecen, Rondeaux, Variationen, Polonaisen, Potpourri's u.s.f'. Albrechtsberger 1837, 171.

51. 'N.B. Il suono di questo strumento è molto esile, e sembra adattato per uso di Camera, ma è noto che in Germania si usa con successo ance nell'Orchestra.' Tosoroni 1850, 47.

52. 'Allein gegenwärtig würde es unter den übrigen Blasinstrumenten keiner großen Erwähnung verdienen, wenn nicht die Nachahmung desselben bei gewissen Virtuosen auf der Violine als ein Kunststück betrachtet würde.' *Conversations-Lexikon* (Amsterdam), II (1809), 29.

53. 'Das größere [Flageolet] braucht man an schicklichen Orten, z. B. in Opern, wo diese Flöten ungemein gut klingen.' Schubart 1806, 210.

54. 'Julien Clarchies, qui eut longtemps de la célébrité pour son talent de directeur d'orchestre de contredanses, engagea Collinet à appliquer son instrument à ce genre de musique; celui-ci goûta ses conseils, et bientôt la vogue dont il jouit fut telle qu'on ne voulut plus danser à Paris qu'au son du flageolet de Collinet.' Fétis 1866, I, 337.

55. Gardeton 1822, 570.

56. Planque 1836, 'Artistes pour bals et soirées', 190–206; 'Professeurs de musique, instrumens à vent', 248–57.

57. Gardeton 1819, 570: 'Roy (C. Eugène) professeur de flageolet, flageoletiste-solo des fêtes de Tivoli et de Prado. . . .' Ibid., 48: 'Roy (C. E.), flageolet solo des fêtes de Tivoli et du Prado. . . .'

58. Planque 1836, 56.

59. Ibid., 103.

60. Collinet ca. 1851–67, 1.

61. 'Jullien in Glasgow', *Musical World* 25, no. 3 (19 January 1850): 41–42.

62. Advertisement, *New York Daily Times*, 26 September 1853.

63. 'Ici nous pouvons citer les noms de quelques artistes bien connus par leur talent exceptionnel sur le Flageolet: Collinet, Bousquet, Bonnisseau, Carnaud, Saint-Jacome, Ribeault, Baton, etc.' Catalogue (Paris: Millerau, 1890), 24.

64. 'French Flageolets', *List & Catalogue* (London: J. R. Lafleur & Son, ca. 1891–99), 109.

65. 'Ich habe von einem sehr jungen Franzosen, dem Begleiter des Erfinders, mit einer Annehmlichkeit, Präcision in den Doppelläufen, überhaupt mit einer solchen künstlerischen Vollendung auf demselben phantasiren hören, dass die Wirkung davon auf mich überaus reizend, ja wirklich eingreifend gewesen ist. Besonders wusste der junge Mann kleine fugenartige Sätze mit einer wirklichen Meisterschaft zu executiren. . . .' Sievers 1818.

66. Tarasov 2010.

5 THE RECORDER IN THE TWENTIETH CENTURY

1. Musée des Instruments de Musique (MIM), Brussels, accession nos 1023-01–1023-08.

2. Germanisches Nationalmuseum, Nuremberg, accession nos MI98–MI104.

3. Accession no. MI642; Mahillon 1909, 283–85.

4. 'Historic Concerts', 1885 (italics and punctuation original).

5. Moore 2020.

6. Shaw 1981, 322.

7. Boston Museum of Fine Arts, accession nos 17.1805–17.1806. Williams 2005, 57–61, 331–36.

8. Grosvenor Museum, Chester, accession nos O.S.25a–O.S.25d. Williams 2005, 47–51.

9. Kinsell 1976, 157.

10. Ibid., 158–59 (score).

11. Hunt 1962, 131; Williams 2005, 51–52.

12. Welch 1911.

13. https://www.loc.gov/item/dcmphot.a0169/; accessed August 2021.

14. *English Music* 1906, 121–63.

15. Kirnbauer 1992, 59–67.

16. Ibid., 54–58.

17. Ibid., 38, 45.

18. Ibid., 50–52, 63–64.

19. Ibid., 43–46, 51–52; Grill 2007, 58–62.

20. Campbell 1975, 12.

21. Ibid., 164–65; Meadows 1995, 87–88; O'Kelly 1990, 3, 7.

22. A. Dolmetsch 1915.

23. Campbell 1975, 166; Williams 2005, 74–75, 349–54.

24. *The New Age*, 7 January 1915, 246–47; Schafer 1978, 35–36.

25. Thomson 1995a, 145–46; Williams 2005, 339–47.

26. Campbell 1975, 208–9; O'Kelly 1990, 5–6; Thomson 1995a, 145.

27. www.dolmetsch.com/handmaderecorders.htm; accessed August 2021.

28. Hunt 1977a, 130; Williams 2005, 85, 365.

29. Ibid., 85–88, 366–68.

30. Haskell 1988, 29–35.

31. *Saturday Review*, 2 April 1898, 461–62; Haskell 1988, 34.

32. Haskell 1988, 52, 55–56.

33. Gudewill 1952; Potter 1994, 100–1; Platen and Fenlon 2001.

34. Williams 1994, 138–42.

35. Degen 1939, 106; Gudewill 1952, col. 1560.

36. Haskell 1988, 57; Williams 2005, 142–51.

37. Moeck 1978, 19–20; Haskell 1988, 56; Thalheimer 2010, 47–48.

38. Accession no. N 26–N 29. Thalheimer 2010, 203–4.

39. Rummel 1977, 17; Thalheimer 2010, 49–50.
40. Denner: Germanisches Nationalmuseum, Nuremberg, accession no. MI 139 or 140; Heitz: Bachhaus Eisenach, accession no. I99.
41. Moeck 1978, 20; Katz and Potter 2001.
42. https://web.archive.org/web/20050209181801/http://www.ruach.net/Grospapa.html; accessed August 2021.
43. Thalheimer 2006 and 2010 make helpful contributions.
44. Klampfenamt der Wandervogelkanzlei GmbH, Peter Harlan & Karl Ernst, Markneukirchen, founded 6 March 1920. Weller 2001, 17.
45. See www.moneypedia.de/index.php/Wechselkurs_zum_Dollar#1919-1923 and https://www.measuringworth.com/dollarvaluetoday; accessed August 2021.
46. 'einerseits braucht man für eine Laien-"Gemeinschaftsmusikkultur", an der sehr viele beteiligt werden sollen, einfache, leicht spielbare, möglichst billige Instrumente, andererseits sucht man Alternativen zu den Instrumenten des bürgerlichen Konzertbetriebs . . .' Kolland 1979, 84.
47. Böhle 1982, 104–61; Puffer 2001, 29; Antholz 2016.
48. *RMM* 2 (1966): 94; Scholz 1980, 1012; Jordan 2001, 12; Weller 2001.
49. Harlan 1931, 17–23. In Harlan 1951, 158, he states incorrectly that they visited the second festival in 1926 and implies that he was already manufacturing recorders before his visit to Haslemere, so the development of his instruments occurred in parallel to, or even preceding, Dolmetsch's work. For this to appear plausible, it was necessary for him to claim to have travelled to England one year later than he did. Furthermore, Harlan's claim that Dolmetsch was making only soprano and alto recorders in 1926 is false, as the Haslemere Festival that year featured performances on five different sizes of recorder.
50. Harlan 1951, 158 ('Die ersten Freiburger Instrumente waren unbrauchbar'). The assertion that Harlan 'bought a set of . . . instruments from Dolmetsch with the intention of copying them' on the occasion of his 1925 trip (Hunt 1977a, 130) is probably incorrect, as only alto recorders in F at A 415 were available from Dolmetsch at the time. See also Rummel 1977, 20–21 and Thalheimer 2010, 52–55.
51. On the controversies regarding the Berlin alto, see Thalheimer 2010, 54–60.
52. Letter from Jacob's daughter, I. Spranger, to Rudolph Michael (1946), cited in Rummel 1977, 19; Moeck 1978, 81; Thalheimer 2010, 52–53.
53. Thalheimer 2013, 14, 86; Rummel 1977, 21–24.
54. 'Meine Mutter sagt, daß diese Besprechungen oft schrecklich waren und die beiden oft fast verzweifelten. Man müßte die Flöte aufschneiden und wieder zusammensetzen können, wurde gesagt'. Letter from Klaus Harlan to Luise Rummel dated 15 January 1977; Michel 1995, 80.
55. Zuckermann 1970, 108–12; Haskell 1988, 31.
56. Dolmetsch 1960, 5 (italics original); Dolmetsch 1996, 55–56.
57. Moeck 1978, 81; Thalheimer 2010, 218–19.
58. Harlan 1931.
59. 'Klangidee, Mensur und Griffweise unterscheiden sich so sehr von den historischen Vorlagen, daß man aus heutiger Sicht von einer Neuschöpfung sprechen muß'. Thalheimer 1998, 270.
60. Hunt 1977a, 130–31.
61. 'Sie ist leicht mit Hilfe von Gabelgriffen beinahe vollständig chromatisch zu blasen. (Eine historische Grifftabelle liefere ich bei den Flöten mit.)' Transcription of leaflet enclosed with recorders sold by Harlan in 1926, in Rummel 1977, 59; Brauer 1928, 40; Thalheimer 2010, 522.
62. 'Man wollte den Gabelgriff nicht, obgleich ich wirklich schon ganz von Anfang an immer auf seine Richtigkeit aufmerksam gemacht habe'. Harlan 1951, 157–58; Thalheimer 2010, 74–77.
63. 'Da nun die Chromatik der Blockflöte nicht angemessen ist, sollte man . . . auch nicht unbedingt das Gegenteil beweisen wollen, sondern hierin nur den erfreulichen Anlaß zu einer schlichten Diatonik erblicken, die heute allgemein eine überspitzte Chromatik abzulösen beginnt.' Twittenhoff 1936a, 37.
64. Gofferje 1937, 818; Moeck 1994, 183.
65. *NRD* 1932–34, passim.
66. *NRD* nos 7 and 9 (ca. summer 1933 and winter 1933/34): n.p.

67. Thalheimer 2010, 154–61; 2013, 20–21, 70–71, 116–17.
68. 'Gofferje dagegen hielt sich bei Konstruktion seines Modells nicht sklavisch an alte Vorlagen, sondern beschritt aus vorwiegend pädagogischen Erwägungen heraus neue Wege, um ein einwandfreies und trotzdem billiges Instrument zu erhalten. Material (Ahorn), äußere Form, Bohrung, Aufschnitt, Labium und Kernspalte – und damit last not least der Toncharakter – zeigen das bewußte Abweichen von den Museumsexemplaren'. // 'Die Dolmetschflöten sind allerdings für uns in Deutschland . . . fast unerschwinglich; doch ist der Preis gerechtfertigt angesichts der bis ins letzte gehende Präzision ihrer Ausführung. Die Reinheit der Stimmung jedes einzelnen Instrumentes ebenso wie das vollkommene Zusammenstimmen eines Chores, die leichte Ansprache bis in die höchsten Lagen bei ganz ausgeglichener Tonstärke und schließlich die saubere handwerkliche Arbeit befriedigen alle berechtigten Ansprüche. Es ist klar, daß solche Präzisionsarbeit nicht um ein Butterbrot geboten werden kann.' Ruëtz 1933, n.p.
69. Thalheimer 2010, 145–46.
70. 'die Dolmetschflöten haben Charakter: sie verlangen, um gut zu klingen, große Meisterschaft vom Spieler, aber sie bieten ihm auch die notwendigen Voraussetzungen dazu. Diese werden jedoch nie gegeben sein, wenn der Instrumentenbauer nicht auch gleichzeitig Handwerker und ein ausgezeichneter Spieler ist; das ist das Geheimnis der Dolmetschs und aller großen Instrumentenbauer und neben dem Zwang zu niedrigen Preisen der Grund für die bisher so wenig befriedigenden Ergebnisse im deutschen Blockflötenbau'. Ruëtz 1934b, n.p. Carl Dolmetsch (1941, 73) later wrote that his instruments had been 'obtained quite openly' by German manufacturers for the purpose of copying.
71. Ruëtz 1934a, n.p.
72. Thalheimer 2010, 123–34; 2013, 96–97.
73. Moeck 1940, 38–39.
74. Thalheimer 2010, 158–59.
75. '*Die MOECK-Schulflöte bietet den ernsthaften Einstieg in die Welt der Musik*.' Moeck 2003, 13; www.moeck.com/en/recorders/recorders-for-beginners/series/schulfloete; accessed August 2021.
76. Hunt 1998, 12–14.
77. Thalheimer 2010, 59.
78. Thalheimer 2013, 17.
79. 'was er damit begründete, daß ja diese Stimmung günstige Zusammenspielmöglichkeiten mit Lauten und Gamben zuließ'. Schumann 1957, 110.
80. Woehl 1930, 23; Thalheimer 2013, 18–19.
81. Dolmetsch 1941, 68–69; Hunt 1998, 12; Williams 2005, 88–89.
82. Advertisements in periodicals, notably in *CM* 1932/4, n.p.; Moeck 1978, 85.
83. Moeck 1932, n.p.
84. 'Es wäre Not, sich in einem Köcher, ähnlich wie ein Golfspieler, die verschiedenen 'notwendigen' Flöten nachtragen zu lassen!' Gofferje 1931.
85. Woehl 1930.
86. Blankenburg 1932, 41–48.
87. Moeck 1978, 85.
88. 'Trotz alledem ist ohne Zweifel, daß ein Quartett aus a- und d-Flöten viel geschlossener, abgerundeter klingt als ein c–f-Quartett. Abwechselndes Spielen des gleichen Stückes . . . auf d–a- und auf f–c-Blockflöten vor einem größeren Zuhörerkreis hat stets zur einstimmigen Bevorzugung des d–a-Quartetts geführt.' Ruëtz 1936, 248.
89. '*Blockflötenstimmung* Reichseinheitlich wird für die *volks*musikalische Arbeit (Liedbegleitung, kleine Instrumentalsätze usw.) in Zukunft die f–c-Stimmung vorgesehen, nachdem fast überall im Reich und auch in der Schularbeit diese Stimmung sich durchgesetzt hat. Es werden die Sopran–c-Flöten und Alt–f-Flöten in der Arbeit verwendet. Die d–a-Stimmung ist, wenn überhaupt, nur bei kammermusikalischen Aufgaben neben f–c zu verwenden.' *Reichsbefehl* 1937 (emphases original).
90. Hindemith 1952; Thalheimer 1995, 586–93.

91. 'Ich kann mich noch deutlich an den Eindruck erinnern, den die Blockflötenmusik bei uns und unseren Schülern hinterließ. Blockflöten wurden angeschafft und in kleinen Gruppen ausprobiert . . .' Schumann 1957, 110.
92. Degen 1939, 7.
93. 'Blockflöten brachen gleich epidemisch aus'. Hermann Reichenbach, *Der Kreis* (1929), cited in Schumann 1957, 133.
94. 'in so vielen Kreisen, Schulklassen, ja Familien Blockflöten auftauchen, so, als wären sie auf einen geheimnisvollen Ruf hin mit einem Male von ihrem jahrhundertelangen Schlaf aufgewacht'. Reusch 1929, 73.
95. 'Es hat nicht den Anschein, als ob eine Welle abebbte, man fühlt sich im Gegenteil beklommen, da die Flut noch steigt. // . . . irregeleitet durch unwahre Angaben, glauben, die Blockflöte sei eine Art Spielzeug und in einer Woche zu erlernen. // . . . wissen aber nicht, wie das Instrument gespielt wird, wie es klingen muß. // Die Blockflöte müßte das Glück haben, die Instrumentenmacher zu finden, die sie nicht bauen, weil Konjunktur zu wittern ist, weil sie 'gefragt' wird.' Gofferje 1931, 372–73.
96. 'Blockflötenrummel' // 'Die Blockflötenmode hat ein Ausmaß angenommen, wie es sich A. Dolmetsch, der zuerst in England die alten Instrumente für die Aufführung alter Originalmusik verwendete, bestimmt nicht träumen ließ.' Neeman 1932, 378.
97. Adolf Hitler was referred to within the Nazi movement as the *Führer*, an association that would have been clear to any reader in 1932.
98. 'Beinahe monopolisierte Händler liefern die Instrumente, staatliche Behörden geben die Unterstützung, und nun erscheinen Schulen und Ausgaben von meist ungeeigneter Musik für Blockflöte. . . . Eine Blockflötenzeitschrift (!) darf nicht fehlen, und auch geistesverwandte andere Zeitschriften richten Blockflötenecken, Instrumentenverkaufs- und Beratungsstellen ein. Kurse und Vorträge bei Schulungs- und Singwochen, Tagungen und Treffen . . . werden eingerichtet, damit die gläubige Schar auch ihren falschen Propheten folgt. Reklamekonzerte und Rundfunkdarbietungen mit Blockflöten tun ein übriges. // Keineswegs werden etwa diese alten Originalwerke bevorzugt und entsprechend vollkommen dargeboten, sondern man "bearbeitet" irgendwie Mögliches und Unmögliches. Die urteilslose Gefolgschaft merkt gewöhnlich zu spät, daß sich um eine künstlich propagierte Mode handelt und daß die *ernsthafte* Beherrschung der klappenlosen Blockflöte, die doch "so leicht" und "nach wenigen Minuten" spielbar sein soll, schwieriger ist als etwa die der modernen Querflöte.' Neeman 1932, 378 (italics original).
99. 'Treibhausatmosphäre'. Gofferje 1931, 372.
100. Böhle 1982, 63–70; Gruhn 1993, 233–47. See Williams 2005, 108–26 on contemporaneous developments in Britain.
101. Rummel 1977, 6–7. On the desperate situation of the Vogtland musical instrument-making industry during this period, see the journal *Das Musik-Instrument* (Cologne, 1912–34).
102. *NRD* no. 7 (ca. summer 1933): n.p.: 'Peter Harlan bringt gleich drei neue Dinge auf einmal heraus. Zunächst eine billige Volks-Blockflöte. . . .' A correction in *NRD* no. 9 (ca. winter 1933/34): n.p. suggests that the term was rapidly adopted by other recorder makers: '*Die Volksblockflöte von Harlan*, die im Nachrichtendienst Nr. 7 angezeigt worden ist, kostet leider nicht RM 4.–, sondern RM 4.80. Es ist eine bedauerliche Verwechselung mit dem Preis der Volksblockflöte von Nagel unterlaufen' (emphasis original). Harlan's advertisement in *Neues Musikblatt* 15, no. 17 (1936): 10 refers to 'Die Harlan-Volksflöte', perhaps to assert his claim to the term.
103. For a brief introduction to contemporary associations of the word *Volk*, see https://en. wikipedia.org/wiki/Volk; accessed August 2021.
104. *NRD* 4 and 8 (ca. autumn 1932 and autumn 1933). The fluctuations are accounted for by the exchange rate to the British pound, which was not fixed at the time. Wages and prices for consumer goods in Germany remained remarkably stable from 1925 until 1945, so we can make meaningful comparisons of the cost of recorders in Germany without having to allow for inflation.
105. Rummel 1977, 59; advertisement, *Musikantengilde* 5, nos 6–7 (1927): n.p.

106. *NRD* 4 (ca. autumn 1932).
107. Advertisement, *NM* 15, no. 17 (1936): 10.
108. *NRD* 12 (ca. autumn 1934). Around 1940, some manufacturers offered more expensive models, e.g. Herwiga's Dea alto with 'English' fingering and double holes, which cost RM 76. See Thalheimer 2013, 114–15.
109. Advertisement, *NM* 15, no. 17 (1936): 10.
110. Advertisement for a 'Volksschulblockflöte', *ZfH* 4, no. 2 (March–April 1935): n.p.
111. Advertisement, *ZfH* 3, no. 4 (July–August 1934): inner back cover.
112. Advertisement, *ZfH* 4, no. 4 (July–August 1935): n.p.
113. 'Strahlende Kinderaugen werden es Ihnen danken!!' Advertisement, *CM* 1932, no. 4: n.p.
114. www.dolmetsch.com/handmaderecorders.htm; accessed August 2021. Small quantities of instruments were also made by Oskar Dawson, Robert Goble, and the flute manufacturers Rudall Carte (Williams 2005, 134–35, 143).
115. 'Wem, wie mir, etwa 150 000 Blockflöten durch die Hände gegangen sind, der darf sich wohl ein Urteil über die Brauchbarkeit einer Blockflöte erlauben.' *Der Celler Spielmann* 1941, no. 1: n.p.
116. 'innerhalb weniger Monate mehrere Tausend Stück'. Advertisement, *ZfH* 4, no. 4 (July–August 1935): n.p.
117. Ruëtz 1934c, 110–15.
118. E.g. advertisement for E. Hess Nachfolger in *Die H-J, das Kampfblatt der Hitler-Jugend* 3, no. 7 (1937): outer back cover.
119. 'In zwei Jahren 11 000 Stück verkauft! *Die* einfachste und klarste, auch pädagogisch Wertvollste, mit reichem Notenmaterial ausgestattete, auch zum Selbstunterricht geeignet und daher die *beste* Blockflötenschule / ist von Waldemar Wöhl. . . . RMk. 3.00 / Für Kinder genügt schon Sprengers [sic] Anleitung zur Schulblockflöte RMk. 0.60' (emphases original). Advertisement for Verlag Adolph Nagel, Hannover, *BS* 2, no. 3 (March 1932): n.p.
120. *ZfS*, primarily a series of sheet-music publications, included editorial material and general essays on music until the end of the Second World War.
121. BArch, R 9361-V/147996.
122. *RN* 4 (1940–41): 1–2; *Consort*, no. 30 (1974): 83; Hunt 1977a, 136; Ferguson 1982, 13. Williams 2005, 134, quotes an unpublished essay by Hunt in which he recorded the following prices in 1928–30, soprano 5 guineas; alto 7 guineas; tenor 10 guineas; bass 15 guineas. Five guineas was the equivalent of 105 shillings, or two weeks' wages for Hunt in the mid-1930s, working for the music printing factory of Novello.
123. *RN* 2 (1938–39): 20.
124. Hunt 1967, 157; Ehrlich 1993a, 532.
125. Quotation from Hunt 1977a, 133–34; Bate Collection, Oxford GB, accession no. 112. This instrument can be seen at https://www.heinz-ammann.ch/inhalt_e/historik/galerie/08.html; accessed August 2021.
126. *GSJ* 51 (1998): 12.
127. Hunt 1977a, 135–36.
128. Ferguson 1982, 12.
129. Hunt 1977a, 135.
130. Ibid., 135.
131. Ibid., 136; Ehrlich 1993a, 533; Williams 2005, 137; Thalheimer 2010, 145–47.
132. Priestley and Fowler 1937; *RN* 1 (1937–38): 3; Hunt 1977a, 136; Ferguson 1982, 13. Williams 2005, 129–33, probably erroneously, states that the Bradford course was held in 1938 and *The School Recorder Book* was published in 1939.
133. Successful candidate Rosa Laundra. Ehrlich 1993a, 535; Williams 2005, 232–47.
134. Hunt 1997, 131; *GSJ* 51 (1998): 13. Hunt 1977a, 139–40, gives the date of his appointment at Schott's as 1937.
135. Handel, HWV 369, Dolmetsch 1933. USA tours, *RN* 1 (1937–38): 12; Bixler and Wollitz 1988, 138; Williams 2005, 365–404.
136. Mayes 2003.

137. Dolmetsch 1941, 68–69.
138. *RN* 1 (1937–38): 5.
139. *RN* 2 (1938–39): 2–3; *RN* 3 (1939–40), 3; Thomson 1972, 37; Ferguson 1982, 13.
140. *RN* 1 (1937–38): 19–20.
141. *Musical Times and Singing-Class Circular* 79: 655–56.
142. Mayes 2003, 5–18.
143. Levi 1994, 267–80; Kater 1997, 14–21; Potter 1998, 1–30.
144. 'In Germany To–day [sic] / Young Musicians wanted', *The Times*, 10 February 1940, 5.
145. BArch, R 9361-V/143978.
146. Gärtner 1984, 119.
147. Scheck 1938.
148. BArch, R 9361-V/82791; Thalheimer 2001, 460–67.
149. Ruëtz 1939, 74–75. In a letter to the Kreismusikerschaft Berlin dated 12 May 1938, Ruëtz states that he had just returned from a foreign tour lasting several months. BArch, R 9361-V/90197.
150. Marx 1978, 30–32.
151. Partial bibliography in Puffer 2001, 155.
152. Quotation from letter dated 11 November 1944 from Dr Siegfried Göslich to the Propaganda Ministry: 'Ruëtz ... darf wohl als der führende virtuose Blockflötist der letzten Jahre bezeichnet werden und hatte in Konzerten große Erfolge.' BArch, R 9361-V/96103.
153. 'Arbeitsgemeinschaft Berliner Blockflötenlehrer in der Reichsmusikkammer.' Thirty-five active members attended weekly meetings in summer 1939.
154. BArch, R 9361-V/85625.
155. Heister 2001, 444–45.
156. Equivalent to the grade of *Feldwebel* (Staff Sergeant) in the regular army.
157. BArch, R 9361-II/305819; BArch, R 9361-III/56340; BArch, NS 21/1356.
158. Degen 1939.
159. 'Seine politische Zuverlässigkeit steht ausser Zweifel.' Confidential character reference from the 'Führer' of the Nazi university teachers' association, dated 5 August 1938: BArch, R 9361-II/153898.
160. De Vries 1998, 198.
161. 'Eine gotische Madonna mit Blockflöte. . . .' Heister and Klein 1984, 253–64; BArch, R 9361-V/88409; BArch, R 9361-V/88409; Brückner and Rock 1938; Stengel and Gerigk 1941.
162. John 1994, 333–35; Davenport 1995, 7–15, 34–39.
163. Bohlmann 1992, back cover illustration (capitals original).
164. Thomson 1972, 13; Martin 2002, 8–27.
165. Applegate 2003, 144–46.
166. Photograph of orchestra's general rehearsal in *NM* 15, no. 19 (August/September 1936): 1, and of its performance in *Carl Orff* 1976, 205.
167. Ibid., 204–5.
168. 'kindliche Reigenspiele führen zu den Tänzen und freudigen Ballspielen der Mädchen; die Knaben tummeln sich in härteren und ungebändigten Spielen und Wettkämpfen, – sie stählen sich darin zum höchsten Dienst am Volke, dem Einsatz von Leib und Leben im Kriege – hier symbolisch in einem "Waffentanz" dargestellt. Eine getanzte "Totenklage" der Frauen beweint die Gefallenen.' Twittenhoff 1936b, 214–15.
169. 'Die gesamte deutsche Jugend ist außer in Elternhaus und Schule in der Hitlerjugend körperlich, geistig und sittlich im Geiste des Nationalsozialismus . . . zu erziehen.' Gesetz über die Hitlerjugend vom 01.12.1936, *Reichsgesetzblatt* 1936 I, 993.
170. 'die Blockflöte . . . hat heute eine feste Heimat auch in der HJ'. Messerschmidt 1936, 232. Munich, Bayerische Staatsgemäldesammlungen – Pinakothek der Moderne, 14568: https://www.sammlung.pinakothek.de/de/artwork/anxgkNKxEq; accessed August 2021.
171. Böhle 1982, 237–39, 275–79.
172. 'Es ist nicht vorstellbar, daß Hitlerjugend oder Jungvolk Blockflöten mit auf den Marsch nimmt, wohl aber ist es denkbar, dass sie gelegentlich am Heimabend Verwendung finden. Einen größeren Aufgabenkreis haben sie im Bund Deutscher Mädel bei Volksliedsingstunden.' Kurka 1936, 291.

173. 'Ich glaube, daß wir aufgrund all dieser Tatsachen zur Blockflöte "ja" sagen müssen'. 'jegliche Hilfsmittel fehlen, Halbtöne zu erzeugen. Auch die 2. Oktave sauber zu spielen, erfordert . . . intensive Arbeit. . . .' *Das Deutsche Mädel* (December 1937): 30.

174. 'Blockflötenmusik ist besonders bei den Mädeln beliebt' and 'Die beliebte Blockflöte', *ZfM* 105, no. 10 (1938): between 1116 and 1117.

175. 'Deutsche Reichspost Bildtelegramm . . . zum 50. Geburtstag des Fuehrers', reprinted in Wulf 1963, plate 14.

176. 'notwendig, daß der z. Zt. aufkommenden "Knüppel" musik die stille Hausmusik entgegengesetzt wird . . . // Täglich erhalte ich Nachricht von kleinen Gruppen, die nicht mehr arbeiten können, weil ihre Mitglieder durch die politische Umwälzung für andere Dinge in Anspruch genommen werden und keine Zeit für Musik haben.' *BS* 3, no. 8 (August 1933): 110.

177. 'Sechs Nationale Lieder'. 'Ich habe Lust im weiten Feld zu streiten mit dem Feind . . .'; 'Wach auf, wach auf, du deutsches Land, du hast genug geschlafen. . . .' *ZfS*, no. 12 (September 1933): n.p.

178. *BS* 3, no. 9 (September 1933): 5.

179. E.g. Krieck 1934.

180. '*Neue Bayerische Tänze*'. // '*2. vollständig erneuerte Auflage*'. // '*Unser Kamerad Alfred von Bekerath schickte mir aus dem Felde. . . .*' *ZfS*, no. 26 (originally published November 1934; 2nd edn, August 1940) and no. 57 (originally published June 1937; 2nd edn, March 1941).

181. 'Ein Vorgang, wie der Siegeszug der Blockflöte, hat in unserer Zeit nur eine Parallele, nämlich in dem Werden des neuen Staates selbst.' Moeck 1940, 10. In *Tibia* 10 (1985): 373 Hermann Moeck Jr implied that he, not his father, wrote this text in his final school year ('*Abiturjahr*'). It is, however, inconceivable that this 47-page promotional book was published without the close supervision, approval, or indeed co-authorship of Hermann Moeck Sr.

182. 'Seine Einstellung zum nat. Soz. Staat war anfangs ablehnend, jetzt nach aussen hin bejahend, ob innerlich zustimmend, bleibt zweifelhaft. // . . . seine lange Jahre hindurch gezeigte offen[e Ab]lehnung des Nationalsozialismus (z.B. Verweigerun[g des] Deutschen Grusses) ist erst seit einiger Zeit – m[öglicher]weise unter dem Einfluss seiner Kinder – einer H[altung ge]wichen, die äusserlich keine Gegensätze zum Nati[onalsozi]alismus erkennen lässt'. Letter from the *Kreisleiter* (director) of the Nazi Party in Celle, Packebusch, to the Reich Propaganda Office in Lüneburg, dated 4 April 1940: BArch, R 9361-V/147996.

183. Letter from the *Bereichsleiter* (head of department) of the Nazi Party in Celle, Milewski, to the Gestapo office in Celle, dated 11 January 1944: BArch, R 9361-V/147996.

184. Internal Nazi Party memorandum dated 22 June 1944, 'Vaterlandsverräter und Lumpen'; undated letter to the *Arbeitsamt* (Labour Exchange) in Celle: BArch, R 9361-V/147996. Pratt 1973, 4.

185. Williams 2005, 143–45.

186. Dolmetsch 1941, 72–73.

187. www.capriccio-kulturforum.de/index.php?thread/291-der-nominierungsthread-zu-verfolgt-emigriert-ermordet/&postID=42398&highlight=Erich%2BKatz#post42398; accessed August 2021.

188. Martin 2002, 40–58.

189. *RN* 4 (1940–41): 2–3; Hunt 1977a, 142.

190. *RN* 4 (1940–41): 15–16; Hunt 1977a, 156. Overview of Dushkin family papers at http://asteria.fivecolleges.edu/findaids/sophiasmith/mnsss14_bioghist.html; accessed August 2021.

191. Dayton C. Miller Flute Collection, Library of Congress, Washington, DC. Accession no. DCM 1386.

192. *Etude* 59 (November 1941): 732–33.

193. Bixler and Wollitz 1988, 139–40.

194. *RN* 5 (1947): 16.

195. Mann 1952.

196. Von Huene 1999, 443–44.

197. Bixler and Wollitz 1988, 139.

198. Contribution by Martha Bixler to 'Erich Katz' 1973, 123.

199. Davenport 1995, 5.
200. https://www.mollenhauer.com/wissenswert#acc9; accessed August 2021.
201. https://www.blockfloeten-museum.de/blockfloeten/veb/; accessed August 2021.
202. http://www.schneider-blockfloeten.de/; accessed August 2021; Thalheimer 2010, 283–84.
203. Heister 2001, 444–45; Kolland 1979, 1011; de Vries 1998, 8.
204. Könecke 1977, 223–26; Eicken 2001, 203–4.
205. Ruëtz 1956; Höffer-von Winterfeld 1965; Behrmann 1994, 53–54.
206. Peter 1953, 66–68.
207. Barthel 1955; Moeck 1997, 595.
208. 'die 1939 geschaffene Staatsprüfung in Blockflöte . . . unter den Tisch schob'. // 'die Blockflöte künftig durchaus in den Hintergrund zu rücken sei, da sie das "Lieblingsinstrument des Führers" gewesen'. Staeps 1975, 13–14.
209. M. Dolmetsch 1953, n.p.
210. Hunt 1939, 2–3.
211. BArch, R 9361-V/147996 (underlining original).
212. Martin 2002, 61–78.
213. Mayes 2003, 307–13, 323–25.
214. www.dolmetsch.com/handmaderecorders.htm; accessed August 2021; Ball 1975, 14.
215. Farleigh 1950, 182–83.
216. *SRN* 1 (Christmas 1950): 5–6.
217. *SRN* 2 (Midsummer 1951): 7–10.
218. *RN*, n.s. 4 (September 1951): n.p.; n.s. 11 (September 1954): 4–5; Van der Klis 1991, 101–2; *SAJMZ* 26, no. 5 (September 1998): 10.
219. 'Ik heb de hele oorlog blokfluitend doorgebracht.' *VN*, 5 June 1982, 19; 'Frans Brüggen' 1982, 193; Moeck 1984, 191.
220. Kenyon 1983, 150.
221. Thomson 1972, 52–54; www.antenna.nl/kees.otten/biografie.html; accessed August 2021.
222. *NRCH*, 6 October 1978, CS3; *VN*, 5 June 1982, 19.
223. Van der Klis 1991, 106: the first recorder diploma was awarded to Truus ten Cate-de Marée. Year of Brüggen's graduation quoted variously as 1952 (*M&M* 37, no. 7 [March 1989]: 29); 1953 (Thomson 1972, 16; *VN*, 5 June 1982, 19; Loretto 2001, 3); and 1954 (Van der Klis 1991, 106).
224. Luxemberger 1997, 127–32.
225. Van der Klis 1991, 105; *SAJMZ* 26, no. 5 (September 1998): 11; www.antenna.nl/kees.otten/biografie.html; accessed August 2021.
226. *SAJMZ* 26, no. 5 (September 1998): 11.
227. *AR* 2, no. 3 (fall [*recte* summer] 1961): 14.
228. Robert Ehrlich gratefully acknowledges having benefited from a postgraduate scholarship from the Dutch government in the academic year 1987–88.
229. See Rubinoff 2009.
230. Luxemberger 1997, 218–19.
231. Brüggen 1961, 6.
232. Brüggen 1962a LP.
233. Brüggen 1962b LP.
234. Dolmetsch 1960 single; Conrad 1962 LP; Linde 1962 LP.
235. Hunt 1977a, 84–85.
236. Wigmore Hall recital, London, 11 April 1970; Conrad 1966 LP.
237. Dolmetsch 1960 single.
238. 'die Blockflöte als "objektives" Musikinstrument. . .'. Conrad 1950, 9; 'der empfindungsreichen und ausdrucksbetonten Querflöte gegenüber der objektiv klaren Blockflöte', Conrad 1953, 6; 'den indifferenten Blockflötenklang gegen den modulationsfähigen eines anderen Instrumentes . . . die "affektarme" Blockflöte. . . .' Conrad 1956, 80.
239. Reusch 1938, 17.
240. 'die ausgegrabenen Farben werden goutiert um ihrer Unfarbigkeit, Unsinnlichkeit, Sprödigkeit willen. Man braucht nur den zugleich nüchternen und läppischen Klang einer Blockflöte zu

hören und dann den einer wirklichen: die Blockflöte ist der schmählichste Tod des erneut stets sterbenden großen Pan.' Adorno 1956, 81.

241. Review by Hunt, *Consort* 21 (1964): 345–46.
242. Morgan 1982, 21, 18, 16.
243. Hunt 1965, 346; 1977a, 154–55.
244. Hunt 1962, 159–60.
245. Dolmetsch 1968, replying to Haynes 1968, 240; Silverstein 1968, 329–30.
246. Brüggen 1972 LP.
247. 'Die Faszination, die zu gleichen Teilen von seinem ungemein subtil differenzierten Spiel (von seiner stupenden Virtuosität gar nicht zu reden) wie von den ungeahnten Klangschattierungen der verwendeten Originalinstrumente ausgeht, ist einfach nicht mit Worten zu beschreiben . . . . diese Platten . . . sind imstande, selbst den hartnäckigsten Skeptiker zu bekehren und seine Vorurteile gegen die angeblich begrenzten Ausdrucksmöglichkeiten der Blockflöte in helle Begeisterung zu verwandeln.' Jacques Delalande, *HiFi Stereophonie* 12, no. 3 (1973): 286.
248. Copy after Denner: Brüggen 1971 LP.
249. Copy after Bressan: Brüggen 1981 LP.
250. Kliphuis 1968.
251. Moeck 1982, 12.
252. Moeck 1979; Burgess 2015, 119–22.
253. Moeck 1979.
254. *R&M* 5, no. 10 (June 1977): 340.
255. Hunt 1977b.
256. Burgess 2015, 159–60.
257. Selection republished as Brüggen 1995, CD.
258. 'Zo'n serie van die keiharde, prachtige Italiaanse canzonas. . . .' *VN*, 5 June 1982, 19.
259. *M&M* 37, no. 7 (March 1989): 31.
260. 'Je ne peux pas emplir ma vie avec Dieupart, Couperin, Bach, Telemann et les autres. Mais je peux emplir ma vie en les *jouant*.' *Flûte à bec*, no. 3 (June 1982): 5 (italics original).
261. 'Record Artistry', *The Times*, 8 December 1966, 18.
262. Bach 1973.
263. Brüggen 1974.
264. 'De Kunst van de seventiende en de achttiende eeuw is ook de kunst van het simuleren. . . . // Je had de kritieken in Duitsland moeten lezen. . . . // Dat kan helemaal niet, een cello op een blokfluit imiteren. Alsof ik dat zelf niet wist. De bedoeling was: namaakimitatie. Kunstivoor.' *VN*, 5 June 1982, 19.
265. 'Frans Brüggen' 1982.
266. *AR* 2, no. 3 (summer 1961): 14.
267. Brüggen 1982. In a conversation with David Lasocki, Utrecht, August 2003, Brüggen stated that Stravinsky had said not clarinet but 'flute.'
268. O'Kelly 1990.
269. Through his own compositions, his tutor *Il flauto dolce e acerbo* (Celle: Moeck, 1969), his performing editions of works by composers such as Rob du Bois and Sylvano Bussotti, and his collaboration with Karlheinz Stockhausen on performances of *Spiral* (1969), notably at the Expo '70 World Fair in Osaka, Japan. See also *GMO*, s.v. 'Vetter, Michael', by David Lasocki (2001); accessed 22 December 2020.
270. 'een ander walgelijk, zogenaamd modern stuk . . .'. *VN*, 5 June 1982, 19.
271. See Rubinoff 2009.
272. 'International Competition' 1973.
273. *AR* 14 (1973): 89.
274. Cohen 1985, 64; Burgess 2015, 58.
275. 'das in den Ohren schmerzte und sich bis zur Unerträglichkeit steigerte, so daß viele Zuhörer den Saal verließen. Diejenigen, die ausharrten, waren größtenteils schockiert, deprimiert oder ärgerlich'. Hechler 1978, 182.
276. Brüggen 1968 LP.

277. 'Frans Brueggen' 1974, 103.
278. Kottick 1974; Rowland-Jones 1986; Van Hauwe 1984–92; Fischer 1990.
279. 'Record Artistry', *The Times*, 8 December 1966, 18; 'Enterprising Recital for Recorder Enthusiasts', ibid., 7 March 1966, 9.
280. 'Frans Brueggen' 1971; Hedlund 1973.
281. Potts 1975.
282. Duncan 1982.
283. E.g. Mozart 1975 LP.
284. E.g. Mozart 1988 CD.
285. Robinson 1971, 456–57.
286. *RMM* 3 (1971): 399.
287. Brüggen 1971 LP.
288. Robert Ehrlich: My ability to hear and interpret the recording in this way may be determined by my own conditioning as a recorder player trained partly in the Netherlands.
289. Thomson 1972, 17.
290. Back cover picture from Brüggen 1970 LP.
291. *R&M* 4, no. 8 (December 1973): cover picture, 269.
292. Cf. Van Hauwe 1984–92, vol. 1, 10.
293. Vitz 1969, 12; *NRCH*, 6 October 1978, CS3.
294. https://www.youtube.com/watch?v=_fPxbmpBm-A, from 25′36″; accessed August 2021.
295. 'C. G.', *The Times*, 20 January 1969, 5.
296. G. W. 1969.
297. *R&M* 4: 291.
298. *R&M* 4: 385.
299. Brüggen 1972 LP; see also Cohen 1985, 61.
300. Conversation with the author, London, 13 April 1989. For Brüggen's own opinion of Telefunken's marketing strategy, see Van der Klis 1991, 170.
301. Brüggen 1970 LP, inside front cover.
302. E.g. in Bruggen 1979 LP.
303. 'Ik bespeurde twee dingen. Ten eerste een achteruitgang in mijn speel. Weet u, lesgeven in een instrument is sprookjes vertellen en verleiden. Daar word je moe en oncreativ van.' *NRCH*, 6 October 1978, CS3.
304. 'Ik werd er gek van. Ne hoor, niet omdat ze me nadeden. Ik had genoeg van gewone leerlingen, ik wilde alleen nog maar met meesters omgaan. Ik vermijd ook alle gesprekken met oudleerlingen, met uitzondering van Walter [van Hauwe] en Kees [Boeke].' (Square brackets original.) *VN*, 5 June 1982, 19.
305. *NRCH*, 6 October 1978, CS3; *M&M* 37, no. 7 (March 1989): 31.
306. Brüggen 1985 video.
307. Ehrlich, interviews in Amsterdam, The Hague, and Rotterdam, March 1989; Ehrlich 1993a.
308. Griscom and Lasocki 1994, [v].
309. Ehrlich, interview with Thera de Clerck, Rotterdam, 21 March 1989.
310. G. W. 1969.
311. Monk 1973, 34.
312. Ehrlich, interview with Michael Barker, The Hague, 10 March 1989.
313. Van Hauwe 1984–92.
314. Related to RE by Marion Verbruggen during a lesson, Amsterdam, 6 May 1988.
315. *De Ijsbreker* Amsterdam, 18 October 1988.
316. Thomson 1969.
317. 'had ik genoeg van de genus leerling . . .' // 'veel te veel vragen, vragen, alsof ik dat allemaal moest weten'. // 'Die vroegen niks en studeerden veel'. *NRCH*, 6 October 1978, CS3.
318. Ehrlich, interview with Van Hauwe, Amsterdam, 15 March 1989.
319. 'Dat is de fysieke binding met het instrument.' *VN*, 5 June 1982, 19.
320. 'Zoals en baby niet zonder zijn fles kan, zo zou ik geen dag zonder mijn blokfluit kunnen.' *NRCH*, 6 October 1978, CS3.

321. From Our Correspondent 1973, 39.
322. Ehrlich, interview with Barker.
323. Pohl 1948.
324. Amis 1954.
325. Updike 1963, n.p.
326. Updike 1988.
327. Eco 1992.
328. Borutzki 2020.
329. 'Conversation' 1966.
330. Hunt 1962, 143; *RM* 13 (1993): 17.
331. www.erta-international.eu/PORTAL.3.0.html; accessed August 2021.
332. Haenggli 2002; Richter and Bernhard n.d.; Suter-Krüger 2001.
333. Schweizer Arbeitsgemeinschaft für Jugendmusik und Musikerziehung (Swiss Working Group for Youth Music and Music Education).
334. To Marie Sumpf-Refardt, a student of Ina Lohr (1903–83).
335. For more information on the hamburger as an international measure of economic prosperity and relative expense, see www.economist.com/markets/Bigmac/Index.cfm; accessed August 2021.
336. Email message from Brian Blood to Robert Ehrlich, 12 January 2005; advertisement, *R&M* 3 (1970): 288.
337. See https://www.measuringworth.com/dollarvaluetoday; accessed August 2021.
338. British Standards Institution B.S. 3499 Part 2A, Recorders (1964). See 'Kite Mark' 1967 and Hunt 1977a, 162.
339. *Test 12/84* (Berlin: Stiftung Warentest, 1984), 1142–48; *Neue Musikzeitung* 34 (1985): 60–61.
340. Van Hauwe 1984–92, vol. 1, 7; Bowman 1993.
341. Scheuer 1988.
342. *Der Tagesspiegel*, 21 December 2020; available from https://plus.tagesspiegel.de/die-blockfloete-als-folterinstrument-verpfeift-euch-83144.html; accessed August 2021.
343. 'Kalaschnikow' 2009; available from https://blogs.faz.net/stuetzen/2009/07/04/die-vergeblichkeit-musikalischer-zwangsmassnahmen-518/; accessed August 2021.
344. 'Ohne Gnade' 2015; available from https://www.tz.de/muenchen/stadt/tag-blockfloete-kommentar-4612873.html; accessed August 2021.
345. 'Mit brutaler Energie ziehen sie ihre löchrigen Fiepwerkzeuge heraus und beginnen die Tortur.' *Die Tageszeitung*, 23 December 2020; available from https://taz.de/Vom-Stamme-Floete/!5735367/; accessed August 2021.
346. 'Quiiiiiiiiiiieeeeeeeeetsch!!!' *Nordwest-Zeitung*, 10 January 2020; available from https://www.nwzonline.de/plus/friesoythe-tag-der-blockfloete-in-friesoythe-quiiiiiiiiiiieeeeeeeeetsch_a_50,6,3870800217.html; accessed August 2021.
347. 'Man leidet still vor sich hin und fragt sich, wo Amnesty International ist, wenn man die Hilfe der Organisation dringend braucht. Kurzum: Die Blockflöte ist bekannt als das Instrument des Grauens.' *Die Welt*, 2 March 2013; available from https://www.welt.de/regionales/koeln/article114001257/Koelner-Quartett-will-mit-Blockfloeten-China-erobern.html; accessed August 2021.
348. https://www.musikschulen.de/musikschulen/fakten/die-beliebtesten-instrumente/index.html; accessed August 2021.
349. 'Abgesang auf die Blockflöte: Fiep, Fuuup, Pffft.' *Süddeutsche Zeitung*, 19 December 2013, available from www.sueddeutsche.de/leben/abgesang-auf-ein-musikinstrument-geliebte-gehasste-blockfloete-1.1847512; accessed August 2021.
350. 'Kinder lassen Blockflöte liegen – Alternativen sind hipper.' *Nordwest-Zeitung*, 10 January 2020; available from https://www.nwzonline.de/familie/kinder-lassen-blockfloete-liegen-alternativen-sind-hipper_a_11,5,91789072.html; accessed August 2021.
351. Sloboda 2005, 418.
352. 'Recorder strikes dull note', *The Guardian*, 4 July 2002; available from http://arts.guardian.co.uk/news/story/0,,749036,00.html; accessed August 2021.

353. Ehrlich 1993c.
354. Ehrlich 1989, 8.
355. Anderson 1994, 8–10.
356. Holtslag 1994 and replies.
357. Joint third prize with Shigeharu Hirao-Yamaoka (Japan, b. 1950).
358. E.g. Telemann 1984.
359. Sørensen 2020; Petri 1977 LP.

BIBLIOGRAPHY

WRITINGS

Adorno, Theodor W. 1956. 'Kritik des Musikanten.' *Dissonanzen.* Göttingen: Vandenhoeck & Ruprecht.

Agricola, Martin. 1529, ²1545. *Musica instrumentalis deudsch.* Wittenberg: Georg Rhau. Trans. and ed. William E. Hettrick. *The 'Musica instrumentalis deudsch' of Martin Agricola: A Treatise on Musical Instruments, 1529 and 1545.* Cambridge: Cambridge University Press, 1994.

Albrechtsberger, Johann Georg. 1837. *Sämtliche Schriften über Generalbass, Harmonielehre und Tonsatzkunst.* Herausgegeben von I. Ritter von Seyfried. 2., sorgfältig rev. Aufl. Vienna: Haslinger.

Aleo Nero, Carla. 2013. 'Un flauto di età islamica recentemente rinvenuto a Palermo (metà X–metà XI secolo).' In *Strumenti musicali in Sicilia.* A cura di Giovanni Paolo di Stefano, Selima Giorgia Giuliano, Sandra Proto, 228. Palermo: CRicd.

Amis, Kingsley. 1954. *Lucky Jim.* London: Gollancz; New York: Viking Press.

The Ancient Cornish Drama. 1859. Ed. and trans. Edwin Norris. Oxford: Oxford University Press. Reprint, New York: Benjamin Blom, 1968.

Anderson, Natasha. 1994. 'Streamlining for the Future.' *Australia's Journal of Recorder and Early Music,* no. 18 (November): 8–10.

Anglès, Higini. 1936. 'El músic Jacomí al servei de Joan I i Martí I durant els anys 1372–1404.' In *Homenatge a Antoni Rubió i Lluch,* 613–25. Barcelona: s.n.

Antholz, Heinz. 2016. *MGG Online,* s.v. 'Jugendmusikbewegung. Organik.'

Applegate, Celia. 2003. 'Past and Present of Hausmusik in the Third Reich.' In Michael H. Kater and Albrecht Riethmüller, ed. *Music and Nazism,* 137–47. Laaber: Laaber-Verlag.

Ashbee, Andrew, and David Lasocki assisted by Peter Holman and Fiona Kisby. 1998. *A Biographical Dictionary of English Court Musicians, 1485–1714.* Aldershot, Hampshire: Ashgate.

Bacon, Francis. 1627. *Sylva Sylvarum; or, a Naturall history in ten centuries.* London.

Baines, Anthony. 1967. *Woodwind Instruments and Their History.* 3rd edn. London: Faber & Faber.

Baker, Geoffrey. 2003. 'Music in the Convents and Monasteries of Colonial Cuzco.' *Latin American Music Review* 24: 1–41.

———. 2008. *Imposing Harmony: Music and Society in Colonial Cuzco.* Durham, NC: Duke University Press, 2008.

Bali, János. 2007a. *A furulya.* Budapest: Editio Musica.

———. 2007b. 'Vier kaum beachtete Renaissanceblockflöten.' *Tibia* 32: 419–25.

Ball, Christopher. 1975. 'Renaissance and Baroque Recorders.' *EM* 3: 11–19.

Ballester i Gibert, Jordi. 1990. 'Retablos marianos tardomedievales con ángeles músicos procedentes del antiguo reino de Aragón. Catálogo.' *Revista de musicología* 13: 123–201.

———. 2000. 'La flauta dulce en la antigua corona de Aragón a finales del siglo XIV.' *Revista de flauta de pico,* no. 15: 9–12.

Baret, John. 1574. *An Alvearie or Triple Dictionarie.* London.

Baroncini, Rodolfo. 2002. 'Zorzi Trombetta e il complesso di piffari e tromboni della Serenissima.' *Studi musicali* 31: 57–87.

———. 2018. '*Ridotti* and Salons.' In *A Companion to Music in Sixteenth-century Venice*. Ed. Katelijne Schiltz, 149–202. Leiden: Brill.

———. 2022. Lecture, conference *Cultural Exchange, Interaction and Innovation in Early Sixteenth-Century Venice: The Interdisciplinary Artistic Milieu of Silvestro Ganassi*, organized by the Royal Netherlands Institute in Rome, 5 May.

Barth, L. ca. 1900. *Schule für Czakan oder Flageolet (auch für Stock- und Blechflöte)*. Berlin.

Barthel, Rudolf. 1955. *Aus der Arbeit eines Blockflöten-Chores*. Celle: Moeck.

Barwick, Steven. 1993. 'Mexico.' In *The Early Baroque Era: from the Late 16th Century to the 1660s*. Ed. Curtis Price, 349–60. Houndmills, Hampshire: Macmillan.

Behrmann, Karsten. 1994. 'Linde Höffer-van Winterfeld.' *Tibia* 19: 53–54.

Bellhouse, David R. 2011. *Abraham de Moivre*. Boca Raton, LA: CRC Press.

Benoit, Marcelle. 1971. *Musiques de Cour*. Paris: A. & J. Picard.

Bergmann, Walter. 1965. 'Henry Purcell's Use of the Recorder.' *RMM* 1: 333–35.

Bergstrøm, Ture. 2020. 'A Late Medieval Recorder from Copenhagen.' *GSJ* 73: 220–22.

Bermúdez, Egberto. 2020. 'Church Music in Colombia, 1550–1950.' In *Chiesa, musica e interpreti, un dialogo necessario*. A cura di Carlos Alberto Moreira Azevedo, Richard Rouse, 207–81. Canterano: Aracne.

Betscher, Gloria J. 1995–96. 'A Reassessment of the Date and Provenance of the Cornish *Ordinalia*.' *Comparative Drama* 29: 447–49.

Betz, Marianne. 1992a. *Der Csakan und seine Musik*. Tutzing: Hans Schneider.

———. 1992b. 'Ernest Krähmer (1795–1837).' In *Travers & Controvers: Festschrift Nikolaus Delius: eine Sammlung von Beiträgen mit und über Musik*, herausgegeben von Mirjam Nastasi, 127–35. Celle: Moeck.

Bismantova, Bartolomeo. 1677/94. 'Compendio musicale.' Ferrara.

Bixler, Martha, and Ken Wollitz. 1988. 'An Interview with Suzanne Bloch.' *AR* 29: 136–40.

Blankenburg, Walter. 1932. 'Der gegenwärtige Stand der Auseinandersetzung über die Frage der Blockflötenstimmung.' *Collegium Musicum* 3/1932: 41–48.

Bluteau, Rafael. 1713. *Vocabulario portuguez e latino*. Coimbra.

Boetticher, Wolfgang. 1963. *Aus Orlando di Lassos Wirkungkreis*. Kassel: Bärenreiter.

Böhle, Ingrid. 1982. 'Musikinstrumente im Zeichen der Reformpädagogischen Bewegungen.' Doctoral diss., Dortmund.

Bohlmann, Philip. 1992. *The World Centre for Jewish Music in Palestine 1936–1940*. Oxford: Oxford University Press.

Boragno, Pierre. 1998. 'Flûtes du Moyen Age.' *Les cahiers de musique médiévale* 2: 6–20.

Borgerding, Todd Michael. 1997. 'The Motet and Spanish Religiosity ca. 1550–1610.' PhD diss., University of Michigan.

Borjon de Scellery, Pierre. 1672. *Traité de la musette*. Lyons.

Borutzki, Simon. 2020. https://www.berliner-blockfloeten-orchester.de. Accessed October 2021.

Bottrigari, Hercole. 1962. *Il desiderio or Concerning the Playing Together of Various Musical Instruments*. Trans. Carol MacClintock. n.p. Rome: American Institute of Musicology.

Bouckaert, Bruce, and Eugeen Schreurs. 2005. 'Hans Nagel, Performer and Spy in England and Flanders (c.1490–1531).' In *Tielman Susato and the Music of His Time*, ed. Keith Polk, 101–15. Hillsdale, NY: Pendragon Press.

Bougenot, M. S. 1891. '*Psyché* au Théâtre des Tuileries.' *Bulletin historique et philologique du Comité des travaux historiques et scientifiques*: 71–82.

Bouterse, Jan. 2005. *Dutch Woodwind Instruments and their Makers, 1660–1760*. Utrecht: Koninklijke Vereniging voor Nederlandse Muziekgeschiedenis.

Bowman, Peter. 1993. 'The Teacher's Lot.' *RM* 13: 19–20.

Boyd, Morrison Comegys. 1973. *Elizabethan Music and Musical Criticism*. 2nd edn. Westport, CT: Greenwood Press.

Brade, Christine. 1975. *Die mittelalterlichen Kernspaltflöten Mittel- und Nordeuropas*. Neumünster: Karl Wachholtz.

Bradley, Robert John. 1992. 'Musical Life and Culture at Savoy, 1420–1450.' PhD diss., City University of New York.

Brásio, António. 1954. *Monumenta Missionaria Africana*, vol. IV. Lisbon: Agência Geral do Ultramar.

Brauer, Emil. 1928. 'Blockflöten.' *Der Kreis* 6, no. 4 (May): 40.

Brewer, Charles E. 2000. 'French Ars Nova.' In *A Performer's Guide to Medieval Music*. Ed. Ross W. Duffin, 190–207. Bloomington: Indiana University Press.

Brown, Adrian. 2006. 'The Ganassi Recorder.' *AR* 47: 11–18.

———. 2018. 'The Recorders "SAM 130, 140 and 148".' In *Sammlung* 2018, 237–49.

———, and David Lasocki. 2006. 'Renaissance Recorders and their Makers.' *AR* 47: 19–31.

Brown, Adrian, with David Lasocki. 2023. 'Sets or Consorts of Recorders c1500–1670, with an appendix, Confirmation of the Bassanos' Maker's Mark.' *GSJ* 75.

Brown, Howard Mayer. 1973. *Sixteenth-century Instrumentation*, n.p. Rome: American Institute of Musicology.

———. 1975. 'A Cook's Tour of Ferrara in 1529.' *Rivista italiana di musicologia* 10: 216–41.

———. 1995. 'The Recorder in the Middle Ages and the Renaissance.' In Thomson 1995b, 1–25.

———, and Keith Polk. 2001. 'Instrumental Music, c.1300–c.1520.' In *Music as Concept and Practice in the Late Middle Ages*. Ed. Reinhard Strohm and Bonnie J. Blackburn. Oxford: Oxford University Press.

Brückner, Hans, and C. M. Rock. 1938. *Judentum und Musik mit dem ABC jüdischer und nichtarischer Musikbeflissener*. 3rd edn. Munich: H. Brückner.

Brüggen, Frans. 1961. 'The Recorder in Holland.' *AR* 2, no. 4 (fall): 6.

———. 1982. Editorial, *EM* 10: 5.

Burgers, Jan W. J. 2016. 'Johann Thysius and His Music.' *Tijdschrift van de Koninklijke Vereniging voor Nederlandse Muziekgeschiedenis* 66: 105–22.

Burgess, Geoffrey. 2015. *Well-tempered Woodwinds*. Bloomington: Indiana University Press.

Buttrey, John. 1995. 'New Light on Robert Cambert in London, and his *Ballet et Musique*.' *EM* 23: 198–222.

Byrne, Maurice. 1984. 'More on Bressan.' *GSJ* 27: 102–11.

Cabral de Vasconcellos, Paulino. 1787. *Poesias*. Porto.

Calahorra Martínez, Pedro. 1978. *La música en Zaragoza en los siglos XVI y XVII*. Zaragoza: Institución 'Fernando El Católico'.

Cameron, Jasmin, and Michael Talbot. 2013. 'A Many-sided Musician: The Life of Francesco Barsanti (c. 1690–1775) Revisited.' *Recercare* 25: 95–154.

Campbell, Margaret. 1975. *Dolmetsch, the Man and his Work*. London: Hamish Hamilton.

Canova-Green, Marie-Claude, ed. 1997. *Benserade: Ballets pour Louis XIV*. Toulouse: Société de Littératures Classiques.

Carbonell, Pere Miquel. 1546. *Chroniques de Espãya*. Barcelona.

Cardan, Jerome. 1663. *De Musica*, ca. 1546. First published in *Hieronymi Cardani Mediolensis opera omnia*. Lyons.

———. 1930. *The Books of My Life (De Vita Propria Liber)*. Trans. Jean Stoner. London: E. P. Dutton.

Carl Orff und sein Werk: Dokumentation. 1976. Tutzing: Hans Schneider.

Carpena, Lucia Becker. 2007. 'Caracterização e uso da flauta doce nas óperas de Reinhard Keiser (1674–1739).' Doctoral diss., Universidade Estadual de Campinas, Brazil.

Castellani, Marcello. 1977. 'The *Regola per suonare il flauto italiano* by Bartolomeo Bismantova (1677).' *GSJ* 30: 76–85.

Castiglione, Baldassare. 1968. *La seconda redaxione del 'Coregiano' di Baldassare Castiglione*. Edizione critica per cura di Ghino Ghinassi. Florence: G. C. Sansoni.

Cerone, Pietro. 1613. *El melopeo y maestro*. Naples.

Cessac, Catherine. 1995. *Marc-Antoine Charpentier*. Trans. E. Thomas Glasow. Portland, OR: Amadeus Press.

Chaucer, Geoffrey. 1961. *The Works of Geoffrey Chaucer*. 2nd edn, ed. F. N. Robinson. Boston, MA: Houghton Mifflin.

Coelho, Victor, and Keith Polk. 2016. *Instrumentalists and Renaissance Culture, 1420–1600*. Cambridge: Cambridge University Press.

Cohen, Joel. 1985. *Reprise*. Boston, MA: Little, Brown.

Collinet, Hubert. ca. 1851–67. *Collinet's Handbook for the Flageolet*. London.

The Compleat Flute-Master, or, The Whole Art of Playing on ye Rechorder. 1695. London: Walsh & Hare.

Conrad, Ferdinand. 1950. 'Die Blockflöte im Klangbild der alten Musik.' *Hausmusik* 14, no. 1: 8–15.

———. 1953. 'Brief an einen Blockflöten-Liebhaber.' *Hausmusik* 17, no. 1: 6–11.

———. 1956. 'Die Blockflöte als künstlerisches Instrument.' *Musik im Unterricht* 47: 78–82.

'Conversation at Saratoga.' 1966. *AR* 7: 7–11.

Conversations-Lexikon. 1809. Amsterdam.

The Cornish Ordinalia. 1969. Trans. Markham Harris. Washington, DC: Catholic University of America Press.

Corrette, Michel. ca. 1739. *Methode pour apprendre aisément à joüer de la flute traversière*. Paris.

Costa, Claudio Manoel da. 1768. *Obras*. Coimbra.

Couto Soares, Pedro. 2021. ' "Da uno labro a laltro": An Interpretation of Ganassi's "Lingua laquale non proferisse sillaba niuna".' Paper.

Crane, Frederick. 1972. *Extant Medieval Musical Instruments*. Iowa City: University of Iowa Press.

D'Accone, Frank A. 1997. *The Civic Muse*. Chicago: University of Chicago Press.

d'Alvarenga, João Pedro. 2002. *Estudos de Musicologia*. Lisbon: Edições Colibri; Centro de História da Arte, Universidade de Évora.

———. 2015. 'On Performing Practices in Mid- to Late 16th-century Portuguese Church Music.' *EM* 43: 3–21.

Dart, Thurston. 1959. 'Recorder "Gracings" in 1700.' *GSJ* 12: 93–94.

Davenport, Mark. 1995. 'Carl Orff, the Katz Connection.' *AR* 36, no. 3 (September): 7–15, 34–39.

d'Avena Braga, Inês. 2015. 'Dolce Napoli: Approach for Performance.' Doctoral diss., Universiteit Leiden.

Davis, Alan. 1996. 'Purcell and the Recorder.' *RM* 16: 9–15.

Davies, Malcolm. 1993. 'The Marks and Rules for Gracing.' *RM* 13: 39–41, 69–71.

De Vries, Willem. 1998. *Sonderstab Musik: Organisierte Plünderungen in Westeuropa 1940–1945*. Cologne: Dittrich.

Degen, Dietz. 1939. *Zur Geschichte der Blockflöte in den germanischen Ländern*. Kassel: Bärenreiter.

Deguileville, Guillaume de. *Le pèlerinage de la vie humaine*. Ed. J. J. Stürzinger. London: printed for the Roxburghe Club by Nichols & Sons, 1893.

Demmin, August. 1893. *Die Kriegswaffen in ihren geschichtlichen Entwickelungen von den ältesten Zeiten bis auf die Gegenwart*. 4th edn. Leipzig: P. Friesenhahn.

Deutsch, Otto Erich. 1957. *Schubert: die Erinnerungen seiner Freunde*. Leipzig: Breitkopf & Härtel.

The Diary of Samuel Pepys. 1970–76. Ed. Robert Latham and William Matthews. Berkeley and Los Angeles: University of California Press.

Dickey, Bruce, Petra Leonards, and Edward H. Tarr. 1978. 'The Discussion of Wind Instruments in Bartolomeo Bismantova's *Compendio musicale* (1677).' *BJhM* 2: 143–87.

Dit is een seer schoon boecxken. 1568. Antwerp.

Doht, Julia. 2006. 'Die Göttinger Blockflöte.' *Tibia* 31: 105–7.

Dolmetsch, Arnold. 1915. *The Interpretation of the Music of the Seventeenth and Eighteenth Centuries Revealed by Contemporary Evidence*. London: Novello.

Dolmetsch, Carl. 1941. 'The Recorder or English Flute.' *Music & Letters* 22: 67–74.

———. 1960. 'Accessories for the Modern Recorder.' *RN*, n.s., no. 31 (November–December): 3–5.

———. 1968. 'Which Way to Turn the Clock?' *RMM* 2: 283–84.

———. 1996. 'The Recorder in Evolution.' *RM* 16: 55–56.

Dolmetsch, Marie. 1953. 'Israel.' *RN*, n.s., 3 (June): n.p.

Drayton, Michael. 1595. *Endimion and Phœbe*. London.

Du Val, J. B. 1607. *Les remarques triennales*. Paris, Bibliothèque nationale, Ms. fr. 13977.

Duncan, Angela. 1982. 'Walter van Hauwe and Peter Holtslag Master-classes.' *R&M* 7: 147.

Dupont-Danican Philidor, Nicolas. 1997. *Les Philidor*. Paris: Aug. Zurfluh.

Dyche, Thomas, and William Pardon. 1737. *A New General English Dictionary*. London.

Earp, Lawrence. 1995. *Guillaume de Machaut*. New York: Garland.

———. 2011. 'Reception.' In *The Cambridge Companion to Medieval Music*. Ed. Mark Everist, 335–70. Cambridge: Cambridge University Press.

Eco, Umberto. 1992. *Il secondo Diario Minimo*. Milan: Bompiani 1992. English trans. William Weaver. *How to Travel with a Salmon and Other Essays*, 39–42. New York: Harcourt Brace 1994.

Edwards, Warwick. 1974. 'The Sources of Elizabethan Consort Music.' PhD diss., Cambridge University.

Ehlich, Liane, and Jörg Fiedler. 2003. 'Introductio geschriben uf Piffen.' *Glareana* 52, no. 2: 44–63.

Ehrlich, Robert. 1989. 'Recorder Tuition in Dutch Conservatories.' MPhil. thesis, Cambridge University.

———. 1993a. 'Edgar Hunt.' *Tibia* 18: 532–36.

———. 1993b. 'Frans Brüggen oder die Vermarktung eines Star–Musikers.' *Tibia* 18: 449–53.

———. 1993c. 'Our Recorder Culture: A Pyramid Built on Sand?' *AR* 34, no. 3: 7–11.

———. 2021. *The Great German Recorder Epidemic, 1925–1950*. Portland, OR: Instant Harmony.

Eicken, Alexa. 2001. 'Hört doch! Der sanften Flöten Chor.' *Tibia* 27: 203–4.

English Music 1604–1904. 1906. London and New York: Walter Scott and Charles Scribner's Sons.

'Erich Katz: Teacher–Composer, 1900–1973.' 1973. *AR* 14: 115–34.

Estudante Moreira, Pedro. 2007. 'Les pratiques instrumentales de la musique sacrée portugaise dans son contexte ibérique. XVIe–XVIIe siècles.' Doctoral diss., Université de Paris IV–Sorbonne; Universidade de Évora.

États de la France (1644–1789): La musique. 2003. Paris: Picard.

Farleigh, John. 1950. *The Creative Craftsmen*. London: G. Bell & Sons.

Favà, Cèsar. 2011. 'La *Mare de Déu dels Àngels* de Tortosa i el seu pas per l'àmbit privat.' *Porticvm: Revista d'Estudis Medievals*, no. 2: 68–89.

Ferguson, Suzanne. 1982. 'An Interview with Edgar Hunt.' *AR* 23: 11–16.

Fernández de Oviedo, Gonzalo. 1535. *Libro de la cámara real del príncipe don Juan*. http://parnaseo.uv.es/Editorial/CamaraReal/Edicion.pdf

Fernández Sanz, Alejandra. 2018. 'Evidencias iconográficas de la flauta de pico en el arte europeo del siglo XVI.' Bachelor's thesis, Conservatorio Superior de Música Manuel Castillo, Seville.

Ferrari, Pierluigi. 1993. 'Una collezione di strumenti musicali verso la fine del Cinquecento: Lo *studio di musica* di Luigi Balbi.' *Liuteria, Musica e Cultura*: 15–21.

Fétis, François-Joseph. 1866. *Biographie universelle des musiciens et bibliographie générale de la musique*. 2nd edn. Paris.

Fiala, David. 2002. 'Les musiciens italiens dans la documentation de la cour de Bourgogne entre 1467 et 1506.' In *Regards croisés*. Ed. Nicoletta Guidobaldi. Paris: Minerve.

Fischer, Johannes. 1990. *Die dynamische Blockflöte*. Celle: Moeck.

Foster, Charles. 1992. 'The Bassanelli Reconstructed.' *EM* 20: 417–25.

Fowler, David C. 1961. 'The Date of the Cornish "Ordinalia".' *Mediaeval Studies* 23: 91–125.

'Frans Brueggen and the New Mannerism.' 1971. *RMM* 3: 399–403.

'Frans Brueggen on the Baroque Recorder.' 1974. *EM* 2: 101–3.

'Frans Brüggen im Gespräch mit Mirjam Nastasi.' 1982. *Tibia* 7: 193–96.

Freitas da Silva, André Luis. 2011. 'Reduções Jesuítico-Guarani: espaço de diversidade étnica.' Doctoral diss., Universidade da Grande Dourados, Brazil.

From Our Correspondent. 1973. 'International Recorder and Early Music Competition.' *EM* 1: 37–39.

Fröschle, Walter, and Walter Scheffler. 1980. *Ludwig Uhland, 'Das Schifflein'*. In his *Werke*, vol. 1: *Sämtliche Gedichte*. Munich: Winkler.

Frutuoso, Gaspar. 1998. *Saudades da Terra*. Revisão de texto e reformulação de índices de Jerónimo Cabral. Ponta Delgada: Instituto Cultural.

'G. W.' 'Stylish Dutch Recital.' 1969. *The Times*, 27 March, 7.

Ganassi, Silvestro. 1535. *Opera intitulata Fontegara*. Venice.

García Herrero, María del Carmen. 1984. 'La aduana de Calatayud en el comercio entre Castilla y Aragón a mediados del siglo XV.' In *Estudios dedicados al profesor D. Angel Ferrari Núñez*, I, 363–90. Madrid: Universidad Computense.

Gardeton, César. 1819. *Annales de la Musique pour l'an 1819, contenant le Répertoire de la Musique publiée en 1817 et 1818*. Paris: Au Bureau des Annales de la Musique. In *Annales de la musique ou Almanach musical pour l'an 1819 et 1820*. Geneva: Minkoff, 1978.

———. 1822. *Bibliographie musicale de la France et de l'étranger*. Paris: Niogret. Reprint, Geneva: Minkoff, 1978.

Gärtner, Jochen. 1984. 'Abschied von Gustav Scheck.' *Tibia* 9: 118–19.

Giannini, Tula. 1993. 'Jacques Hotteterre le Romain and His Father, Martin.' *EM* 21: 377–95.

Gilliodts-Van Severen, L. 1904–06. *Cartulaire de l'ancien estaple de Bruges*. Bruges.

———. 1912. *Les ménestrels de Bruges*. Bruges.

Ginger, John, ed. 1998. *Handel's Trumpeter*. Stuyvesant, NY: Pendragon Press.

Glixon, Jonathan. 1979. 'Music at the Venetian "Scuole Grandi": 1400–1540.' PhD diss., Princeton University.

———. 2003. *Honoring God and the City*. Oxford: Oxford University Press.

Godman, Stanley. 1956. 'Greeting's "Pleasant Companion for the Flagelet".' *Monthly Musical Record*, no. 86: 20–26.

Gofferje, Karl. 1931. 'Blockflöten, die große Mode.' *Singgemeinde* 5.

———. 1937. 'Zum gegenwärtigen Stand des Blockflötenspiels.' *Die Musik* 29: 818.

Gómez Muntané, María del Carmen. 1979. *La música en la casa real catalano-aragonesa durante los años 1336–1442*. Barcelona: Antoni Bosch.

———. 1984. 'Musique et musiciens dans les chapelles de la maison royale d'Aragon (1336–1413).' *Musica disciplina* 38: 67–86.

———. 1990. 'Minstrel Schools in the Late Middle Ages.' *EM* 18: 212–16.

Green, Richard Firth. 1978. 'Lydgate and Deguileville Once More.' *Notes and Queries* 223: 105–6.

Griffioen, Ruth van Baak. 1991. *Jacob van Eyck's Der Fluyten Lust-hof (1644–c1655)*. Utrecht: Vereniging voor Nederlandse Muziekgeschiedenis.

Griffiths, George. 1894. *A History of Tong, Shropshire*. 2nd edn. Newport: Horne & Bennion.

Grill, Tobias. 2007. 'Die Rezeption der Alten Musik in München zwischen ca. 1880 und 1930.' Magisterarbeit, Ludwig-Maximilians-Universität München.

Griscom, Richard, and David Lasocki. 2012. *The Recorder: A Research and Information Guide*. 3rd edn. New York: Routledge. 1st edn 1994.

Grodecki, Louis. 1968. 'Les vitraux de la cathédrale d'Evreux.' *Bulletin monumental* 126: 55–73.

Gruhn, Wilfried. 1993. *Geschichte der Musikerziehung*. Hofheim: Wolke.

Gudewill, Kurt. 1952. *MGG Online*, s.v. 'Collegium Musicum'.

Guzmán-Bravo, Jose Antonio. 1978. 'Mexico, Home of the First Musical Instrument Workshops in America.' *EM* 6: 350–55.

Haenggli, Urs. 2002. 'Blockflötenszene Schweiz' (Report on a survey of 24 Swiss recorder teachers and players in 2002). https://web.archive.org/web/20050409003047/http://www.erta-schweiz.ch:80/Umfrage.htm. Accessed 24 June 2022.

Hakelberg, Dietrich. 1994. 'Eine mittelalterliche Blockflöte aus Göttingen.' *Göttinger Jahrbuch* 42: 95–102.

———. 1995. 'Some Recent Archaeo-organological Finds in Germany.' *GSJ* 48: 3–12.

———. 2002. 'Was von einer "Klangschaft" blieb?' *Archäologie in Deutschland – Das Magazin* 4: 30–31.

Hall, Edward. 1809. *Hall's Chronicle*. London.

Harlan, Peter. 1931. 'Wie kam die Blockflöte wieder in unser Leben?' *Der Blockflötenspiegel* 1: 17–23

———. 1951. 'Die Entstehung der neuen Griffweise.' *Hausmusik* 15, no. 6: 158

Haskell, Harry. 1988. *The Early Music Revival*. London: Thames & Hudson.

Hawkins, Sir John. 1976. *A General History of the Science and Practice of Music*. London. Ed. Charles Cudworth. New York: Dover, 1963.

Haynes, Bruce. 1968. 'The Decline . . . A Further Scrutiny.' *RMM* 2: 240–42.

———. 2001. *The Eloquent Oboe*. Oxford: Oxford University Press.

———. 2002. *A History of Performing Pitch*. Lanham, MD: Scarecrow Press.

Hechler, Ilse. 1978. 'Musica-Antiqua-Woche 1978 in Brügge.' *Tibia* 3: 182.

Hedlund, H. Jean. 1973. 'An Untenable Esthetic Posture.' *AR* 14: 12–14.

Heidecker, Martin. 1996. 'Block- und Querflöten in den Opern Georg Friedrich Händels.' *Tibia* 21: 2–10.

Heister, Hans-Werner, ed. 2001. *Entartete Musik 1938*. Saarbrücken: Pfau.

———, and Hans-Günter Klein, ed. 1984. *Musik und Musikpolitik im faschistischen Deutschland*. Frankfurt: Fischer.

Hell, Michael. 2017. 'Der seinesgleichen nie gehabt – Der Blockflötenvirtuose Jacques Paisible und seine Blockflötensonaten.' *Tibia* 4: 563–73.

Hettrick, William E. 1980. 'Martin Agricola's Poetic Discussion of the Recorder and Other Woodwind Instruments (Part I: 1529).' *AR* 21: 103–13.

'Historic Concerts at the Inventions Exhibition.' 1885. *Musical Times* 26: 478.

Höffer-von Winterfeld, Linde. 1965. *Der neue Weg. Blockflötentechnik*. Hamburg: Sikorski.

Holland, Hugh. 1613. *Parthenia*. 2nd edn. London.

Holler, Marcos Tadeus. 2006. 'Uma história de cantares de Sion na terra dos brasis: a música na atuação dos jesuítas na América Portuguesa (1549–1759).' Doctoral thesis, Universidade Estadual de Campinas.

Holman, Peter. 2001. 'Compositional Choices in Henry Purcell's *Three Parts upon a Ground*.' *EM* 29: 251–61.

———. 2012. 'A Purcell Manuscript Lost and Found.' *EM* 40: 469–87.

Holtslag, Peter. 1994. 'The Present State of the Recorder in England.' *RM* 14: 79; replies by Roy Brewer, 14: 143, and Evelyn Nallen, 15: 9.

Homan, Frederic W. 1964. 'Final and Internal Cadential Patterns in Gregorian Chant.' *JAMS* 17: 66–77.

Homo-Lechner, Catherine. 1993. 'Les instruments de musique.' In *Les habitats du lac de Paladru (Isère) dans leur environnement: La formation d'un terroir au XIe siècle*. Sous la direction de Michel Colardelle et Eric Verdel. Paris: Editions de la Maison des Sciences de l'Homme.

———. 1996. *Sons et instruments de musique au moyen âge: Archéologie musicale dans l'Europe du VIIe au XIVe siècle*. Paris: Editions Errance.

Hornbostel, Erich M. von, and Curt Sachs. 1961. 'Classification of Musical Instruments.' *GSJ* 14: 3–29.

Hotteterre, Jacques. 1707. *Principes de la flûte*. Paris.

———. 1715. *Pièces pour la flûte traversière . . .* Op. 2. 2nd edn. Paris.

———. 1719. *L'art de préluder*. Paris.

———. 1738. *Méthode pour la musette*. Paris.

Hunt, Edgar. 1939. 'Editorial.' *RN* 3: 2–3.

———. 1962. *The Recorder and its Music*. London: Herbert Jenkins. 2nd rev. and enlarged edn. London: Eulenburg, 1977a.

———. 1965. 'True Baroque Fingering.' *RMM* 1: 346.

———. 1967. 'Life of a Bressan.' *RMM* 2: 157.

———. 1977b. 'Recorders Based on Eighteenth-century Models.' *RMM* 5: 340.

———. 1997. 'Obituary: Carl Frederic Dolmetsch CBE . . . .' *RM* 17: 131.

———. 1998. 'Carl Frédéric Dolmetsch.' *GSJ* 51: 12–14.

Hunter, Hilda. 1966. 'Recorders Rampant.' *RMM* 2: 18.

Jambe de Fer, Philibert. 1556. *Epitome musical*. Lyons.

Jambou, Louis. 1983. 'La capilla de música de la catedral de Sigüenza en el siglo XVI.' *Revista de musicología* 6: 271–98.

Jiménez Caballé, Pedro. 1998. *Documentario musical de la Catedral de Jaén I*. Granada: Centro de Documentación Musical de Andalucía.

John, Eckhard. 1994. *Musikbolschewismus*. Stuttgart and Weimar: Metzler.

Johnstone, H. Diack. 2007. 'Instruments, Strings, Wire and Other Musical Miscellanea in the Account Books of Claver Morris (1659–1727).' *GSJ* 60: 29–35.

————. 2008. 'Claver Morris, an Early Eighteenth-century English Physician and Amateur Musician *Extraordinaire*.' *Journal of the Royal Musical Association* 133: 93–127.

Jordan, Hanna. 2001. 'Peter Harlan und seine Werkstätten für historische Musikinstrumente.' *Neikirnger Heimatbote* 9, no. 2: 12.

Kater, Michael. 1997. *The Twisted Muse*. New York: Oxford University Press.

Katz, Israel J., and Pamela M. Potter. 2001. *Grove Music Online*, s.v. 'Danckert, Werner'; accessed 22 December 2020.

Kenyon, Nicholas. 1983. 'An Interview with Frans Brüggen.' *AR* 24: 150–53.

Kenyon de Pascual, Beryl. 1982. 'Ventas de instrumentos musicales en Madrid durante la segunda mitad del siglo XVIII.' *Revista de Musicología* 5: 309–23.

————. 1995. 'The Recorder Revival in Late Seventeenth-century Spain.' In Lasocki 1995b, 65–74.

Kilbey, Maggie. 2002. *Curtal, Dulcian, Bajón*. St Albans: Author.

Kinkeldey, Otto. 1910. *Orgel und Klavier in der Musik des 16. Jahrhunderts*. Leipzig: Breitkopf & Härtel.

Kinsell, David. 1976. 'J. C. Bridge and the Recorder.' *R&M* 5: 157–60.

Kirk, Douglas Karl. 1993. 'Churching the Shawms in Renaissance Spain.' PhD diss., McGill University.

Kirnbauer, Martin. 1992. ' "Das war Pioneerarbeit" – Die Bogenhauser Künstlerkapelle, ein frühes Ensemble alter Musik.' In *Alte Musik – Konzert und Rezeption*, 43–46. Winterthur: Amadeus.

————. 2002. 'Musikzeugnisse des Mittelalters.' *Archaeologie in Deutschland* 6/2002: 54–55.

————, and Crawford Young. 2001. 'Musikinstrumente aus einer mittelalterlichen Latrine.' *Institutsbeilage der Schola Cantorum Basiliensis* 1/2001.

'Kite Mark Recorder.' 1967. *RMM* 2: 107.

Klingenbrunner, Wilhelm. 1816. *Neue theoretische und praktische Csakan-Schule*, Op. 40. Vienna.

Kliphuis, Harry. 1968. 'First "Coolsma Bressan" Presented to Edgar Hunt, Owner of Original.' *RMM* 2: 334–35.

Knighton, Tess. 2016. 'Instruments, Instrumental Music and Instrumentalists.' In *Companion to Music in the Age of Catholic Monarchs*. Ed. Knighton, 97–144. Leiden: Brill.

Köhler, Ernesto. 1886. *Self Instructor for Flageolet, Czakan and Stickflute*. Leipzig.

Köhler, Wolfgang. 1987. 'Die Blütezeit der Blockflöte.' *Tibia* 12: 421–26.

Koldeweij, Jos. 1993. ' "Van eens esels been de beste fleuyten comen": De blokfluit in de Nederlandse kunst van de 17e eeuw = ' "The Best Flutes Come from a Donkey's Bone": The Recorder in 17th-century Dutch Art.' In *Programma: Holland Festival Oude Muziek, 27 Augustus–5 September 1993*. Utrecht: STIMU.

Kolland, Dorothea. 1979. *Die Jugendmusikbewegung*. Stuttgart: Metzler.

Könecke, Hans W. 1977. 'Ferdinand Conrad zum 65. Geburtstag.' *Tibia* 22: 223–26.

Kottick, Edward L. 1974. *Tone and Intonation on the Recorder*. New York: McGinnis & Marx.

Krähmer, Ernest. 1822. *Neueste theoretisch-praktische Csakan-Schule nebst 30 fortschreitenden Übungsstücken und einer Triller Tabelle für alle Töne*, Op. 1. Vienna: Diabelli.

————. 1830. *Neueste theoretisch-practische Csakan-Schule*, Op. 1. 2nd edn. Vienna: Anton Diabelli. 1st edn. 1822.

————. 1833. *100 Übungsstücke in allen Dur- und Moll-Tonarten mit deren Scalen . . . als zweyter und dritter Theil der Csakan-Schule*, Op. 31. Vienna: Diabelli.

Krautwurst, Franz. 1977. 'Konrad Paumann.' *Fränkische Lebensbilder*, Series VI A, 7, 33–48.

Kreitner, Kenneth. 1995. 'Music in the Corpus Christi Procession of Fifteenth-century Barcelona.' *EMH* 41: 153–204.

————. 2003. 'The Cathedral Band of León in 1548, and When it Played.' *EM* 31: 41–62.

Krieck, Ernst. 1934. 'Kulturpleite?' *Der Blockflötenspiegel* 4, no. 6: 79–80.

Kritischer Bericht, Serie IV: Orchesterwerke, Werkgruppe 13: Tänze und Märsche, Abteilung 1: Tänze, Band 2. 1995. Neue Mozart-Ausgabe, herausgegeben von Marius Flothuis. Kassel: Bärenreiter.

Kunkel, Otto. 1953. 'Ein mittelalterlicher Brunnenschacht zwischen Dom und Neumünster in Würzburg.' *Mainfränkisches Jahrbuch für Geschichte und Kunst* 5: 293–309.

Kurka, Walter. 1936. 'Musikliteratur der Hitlerjugend.' *Völkische Musikerziehung* 2, no. 6: 291.

La Chesnaye, Nicolas de. 1991. *La Condamnation de banquet*. Édition critique par Jelle Koopmans et Paul Verhuyck. Geneva: Librairie Droz.

La Gorce, Jérôme de la. 2002. *Jean-Baptiste Lully*. Paris: Fayard.

Lacroix, Paul. 1868–70. *Ballets et mascarades de cour de Henri III à Louis XIV (1581–1652)*. Geneva.

Lairesse, Gerard de. 1712. *Grot schilderboek*. Amsterdam.

Lander, Nicholas. 2021. 'A Memento: The Medieval Recorder.' Recorder Home Page.

Lasocki, David. 1983. 'Professional Recorder Players in England, 1540–1740.' PhD diss., University of Iowa.

———. 1984a. 'The Recorder in the Elizabethan, Jacobean and Caroline Theater.' *AR* 25: 3–10.

———. 1984b. 'A New Look at the Life of John Loeillet (1680–1730).' *RMM* 8: 42–46.

———. 1987. 'Dudley Ryder, an Amateur Musician and Dancer in England (1715–16).' *AR* 28: 4–13.

———. 1995a. 'Instruction Books and Methods for the Recorder from around 1550 to the Present Day.' In Thomson 1995b, 119–35.

———, ed. 1995b. *The Recorder in the Seventeenth Century: Proceedings of the International Recorder Symposium Utrecht 1993*. Utrecht: STIMU Foundation for Historical Performance Practice.

———. 1997. 'The London Publisher John Walsh (1665 or 1666–1736) and the Recorder.' *Sine musica nulla vita*. Herausgegeben von Nikolaus Delius, 343–74. Celle: Moeck.

———. 1999. 'Amateur Recorder Players in Renaissance and Baroque England.' *AR* 40: 15–19.

———. 2004. 'Renaissance Recorder Players.' *AR* 45: 8–23.

———, ed. 2005a. *Musicque de joye: Proceedings of the International Symposium on the Renaissance Flute and Recorder Consort Utrecht 2003*. Utrecht: STIMU Foundation for Historical Performance Practice.

———. 2005b. 'Tracing the Lives of Players and Makers of the Flute and Recorder in the Renaissance.' In Lasocki 2005a, 363–405.

———. 2010. 'New Light on the Recorder and Flageolet in Colonial North America and the United States, 1700–1840, from Newspaper Advertisements.' *JAMIS* 36: 5–80.

———. 2012a. 'Woodwind Makers in the Turners Company of London, 1604–1750.' *GSJ* 64: 61–91.

———. 2012b. 'The Recorder in English Newspapers, 1730–1800.' *AR* 53/2: 29–37.

———. 2018a. *Flutes, Recorders, and Flageolets in Inventories, Purchases, Sales, and Advertisements, 1349–1800*. Portland, OR: Instant Harmony.

———. 2018b. *The Recorder and Other Members of the Flute Family in Writings from 1100 to 1500*. 2nd edn. Portland, OR: Instant Harmony.

———. 2018c. *Marc-Antoine Charpentier and the* Flûte*: Recorder or Traverso?* Portland, OR: Instant Harmony.

———. 2019. *Jean-Baptiste Lully and the* Flûte*: Recorder, Voice Flute, and Traverso*. Portland, OR: Instant Harmony.

———. 2020. *Not Just the Alto*: Sizes and Types of Recorder in the Baroque and Classical Periods. Portland, OR: Instant Harmony.

———. 2021. 'Confirmation of the Bassanos' Maker's Mark.' *FoMRHI Quarterly*, no. 153 (April), Communication 2149.

———. 2022. *Recorder Players of the Renaissance*. Cerquilho, SP, Brazil: Instant Harmony.

———. 2023. *The Creation and Dissemination of the Baroque Recorder and Traverso, with Looks at the Cromorne, Oboe, Flageolet, and Bassoon*. Cerquilho, SP, Brazil: Instant Harmony.

Lasocki, David, and Helen Neate. 1988. 'The Life and Works of Robert Woodcock, 1690–1728.' *AR* 29: 92–104.

Lasocki, David, with Roger Prior. 1995. *The Bassanos: Venetian Musicians and Instrument Makers in England, 1531–1665*. Aldershot: Scolar Press, 1995. E-book, Portland, OR: Instant Harmony, 2013, together with Lasocki, *Research on the Bassano Family, 1995–2012*.

Lasocki, David, Giulia Tettamanti, and Patricia Michelini Aguilar. 2022. *The Recorder in Spain, Portugal, and Their Colonies in the Sixteenth and Seventeenth Centuries*. Cerquilho, SP, Brazil: Instant Harmony. Also Portuguese and Spanish translations.

Laurent, Benoît. 2021. ' "So Sweet Martini Claims Attention Here": Nouveaux regards sur le hautboïste et compositeur Giuseppe Sammartini, son répertoire et l'interprétation de sa musique (en particulier ses sonates solos).' Doctoral diss., Université libre de Bruxelles.

Legêne, Eva. 1995. 'The Early Baroque Recorder: "Whose Lovely, Magically Sweet, Soulful Sound Can Move Hearts of Stone".' In Lasocki 1995b, 105–24.

————. 2005. 'Music in the Studiolo and Kunstkammer of the Renaissance, with Passing Glances at Flutes and Recorders.' In Lasocki 2005a, 323–61.

Lerch, Thomas. 1996. *Vergleichende Untersuchung von Bohrungsprofilen historischer Blockflöten des Barock*. Berlin: Staatliches Institut für Musikforschung, Preußischer Kulturbesitz, Musikinstrumenten-Museum.

Lesure, François. 1956. 'Le recueil de ballets de Michel Henry (vers 1620).' *Les fêtes de la Renaissance* 1: 205–19.

Levi, Erik. 1994. *Music in the Third Reich*. New York: St Martin's Press.

Levin, Lia Starer. 1981. 'The Recorder in the Music of Purcell and Handel.' PhD diss., International College, Los Angeles.

'Il "libro dell'arte del danzare" di Antonio Cornazano.' 1915. *La Bibliofilía* 17, no. 1: 1–30.

Lingbeek-Schalekamp, C. 1984. *Overheid en muziek in Holland tot 1672*. Rotterdam: Blok & Flohr.

Li Rois, Adenès. 1865. *Li roumans de Cléomadès*. Ed. André van Hasselt. Brussels.

Livre plaisant et tres utile. 1529. Antwerp.

Lizárraga, Reginaldo de. 2015. *Descripción colonial (libro primero)*. Fundación Biblioteca Virtual Miguel de Cervantes, www.cervantesvirtual.com.

LMR (Lexique musicale de la Renaissance). http://www.ums3323.paris-sorbonne.fr/LMR

The London Stage, 1660–1800, Part I: *1660–1700*. 1965. Ed. William Van Lennep, with a critical introduction by Emmett L. Avery & Arthur H. Scouten. Carbondale: Southern Illinois University Press.

Lopes Monteiro, Maria Isabel. 2010. 'Instrumentos e instrumentistas de sopro no século XVI português.' Master's diss., Universidade Nova de Lisboa.

López Suero, Ana. 2016. '*Flautas, pífanos*, and *çabevas* in the Inventories of the House of Mendoza.' Lecture, International Congress, Tomar, Portugal, 30 October. https://uvadoc.uva.es/handle/10324/25944.

————. 2021a. 'The Network of Musicians in Valladolid, 1550–1650: Training, Companies, Livelihoods, and Related Crafts and Trades.' Doctoral thesis, Universidad de Valladolid.

————. 2021b. 'Flautas, albogues, zampoñas, jabebas y pífanos en los textos castellanos del Renacimiento.' In *Musique et lexique à la Renaissance*. Ed. Cristina Diego Pacheco and Amaya García Pérez, 247–69. Paris: Classiques Garnier.

López-Calo, José. 1963. *La Música en la Catedral de Granada en el siglo XVI*. Granada: Fundación Rodríguez-Acosta.

————. 1981. *La música en la Catedral de Palencia*. Palencia: Diputación Provincial de Palencia.

————. 1996. *La música en la Catedral de Burgos, III*. Burgos: Caja de Ahorros del Círculo Católico.

Loretto, Alec V. 1995. 'Don't Judge a Book by its Cover and Don't Judge Recorder Bores by Outside Shapes!' *RM* 15: 11–12.

————. 2001. 'Kees Otten, born November 28, 1924.' *RM* 21a: 3–5.

Loulié, Étienne. 1680s. 'Méthode.' Paris, Bibliothèque Nationale, fonds fr. n. a. 6355, xix–xx.

Luscinius, Othmar. 1536. *Musurgia, seu praxis musicae*. Strasbourg.

Luxemberger, Carol K. 1997. 'The Developing Role of the Recorder in the Conservatories and Music Schools of the Netherlands from Post-World War II to 1980.' EdD diss., University of Houston.

Lydgate's Fall of Princes. 1923. Ed. Henry Bergen. Washington, DC: Carnegie Institution of Washington.

Lydgate's Reson and Sensuallyte. 1901. Ed. Ernst Sieper. London: Oxford University Press.

Lydgate's Temple of Glas. 1891. Ed. J. Schick. London: Kegan Paul, Trench, Trübner.

Lyndon-Jones, Maggie. 1998. 'A Case for the "Ganassi Recorder" in Vienna.' *FoMRHI Quarterly*, no. 92 (July): 20 (Communication no. 1584).

————. 1999. 'A Checklist of Woodwind Instruments Marked !!' *GSJ* 52: 243–80.

'M'. 1822. *AMZO* 6, no. 89: 705–6.

————. 1823. 'Concert.' *AMZO* 7, no. 12: 95.

Maaler, Josua. 1971. *Die Teütsch spraach* (Zurich, 1561). Facsimile, ed. Gilbert De Smet. Hildesheim: Georg Olms.

Machaut, Guillaume de. 1877. *La Prise d'Alexandrie ou Chronique du Roi Pierre 1er de Lusignan*. Ed. M. L. De Mas Latrie. Geneva.

————. 1911. *Œuvres*. Ed. Ernest Hœpffner. Paris: Didot.

————. 1998. *Le Livre dou Voit Dit (The Book of the True Poem)*. Ed. Daniel Leech-Wilkinson, trans. R. Barton Palmer. New York: Garland.

MacMillan, Douglas. 2017. 'The Octave Flute in England, 1660–1800.' DPhil thesis, University of Oxford.

Mahillon, Victor-Charles. 1909. *Catalogue descriptif et analytique du Musée Instrumental du Conservatoire Royal de Musique de Bruxelles II*. 2nd edn. Ghent: A. Hoste.

Mancinus, Dominicus. 1518. *De quatuor virtutibus* as *Myrrour of Good Maners*. Trans. Alexander Barclay.

Marissen, Michael. 1985. 'A Trio in C major for Recorder, Violin and Continuo by J. S. Bach?' *EM* 13: 384–90.

————. 1991. 'Organological Questions and Their Significance in J. S. Bach's Fourth Brandenburg Concerto.' *JAMIS* 17: 5–52.

————. 1995. *The Social and Religious Designs of J. S. Bach's Brandenburg Concertos*. Princeton, NJ: Princeton University Press.

Marix, Jeanne. 1939. *Histoire de la musique et des musiciens de la cour de Bourgogne sous le règne de Philippe le Bon (1420–1467)*. Strasbourg: Heitz.

Marjanović, Petar. 1995. 'The Theatre.' In *The History of Serbian Culture*. Ed. Pavle Ivi, trans. Randall A. Major. Edgware, Middlesex: Porthill.

Marolles, Michel de. 1657. *Suitte des memoires*. Paris.

Marpurg, Friedrich Wilhelm. 1970. *Historisch-kritische Beyträge zur Aufnahme der Musik*. Berlin, 1759. Reprint, Hildesheim & New York: Georg Olms.

Martin, Anne. 2002. *Musician for a While: A Biography of Walter Bergmann*. Hebden Bridge, Yorkshire: Peacock Press.

Martín, Mariano. 1985. 'La flauta de pico y la flauta travesera en el siglo XVIII en España.' *Revista de musicología* 8: 115–18.

Marvin, Bob. 1978. 'A Ganassi flauto.' *FoMRHI Quarterly*, no. 11 (April): 40–46 (Communication no. 118).

Marx, Karl. 1978. 'Begegnungen mit der Blockflöte.' *Tibia* 3: 30–32.

Mayes, Andrew. 2003. *Carl Dolmetsch and the Recorder Repertoire of the 20th Century*. Aldershot: Ashgate.

McCabe, William H. 1938. 'Music and Dance on a 17th Century College Stage.' *MQ* 24: 313–22.

McGee, Timothy J. 1989. *Medieval Instrumental Dances*. Bloomington: Indiana University Press.

————. 1998. *The Sound of Medieval Song*. Oxford: Clarendon Press.

————. 2009. *The Ceremonial Musicians of Late Medieval Florence*. Bloomington: Indiana University Press.

McGowan, Margaret M. 1994. 'The Arts Conjoined: A Context for the Study of Music.' *EMH* 13: 171–98.

Meadows, Hilary. 1995. ' "Happy Birthday, Whenever That May Be": Further Thoughts on Mr Loretto's Article.' *RM* 15: 87–88.

Mendel, Hermann. 1878. *Musikalisches Conversations-Lexikon*. Continued by August Reissmann. Berlin.

Mersenne, Marin. 1635. *Harmonicorum libri*. Paris.

————. 1636. *Harmonie universelle*. Paris.

Messerschmidt, Felix. 1936. 'Ein Volksinstrument.' *Völkische Musikerziehung* 2: 232.

Meyer, G. M. de, ed. 1971. *De Stadsrekeningen van Deventer, II: 1401–1410*. Groningen: Wolters-Noordhoff.

Mezger, Marianne. 1995. 'Vom *Pleasant Companion* zum *Compleat Flute Master*.' *Tibia* 20: 417–31.

Michel, Winfried, ed. 1995. *Der Noten und des Glückes Lauf*. Münster: Mieroprint.

Michelini Aguilar, Patricia. 2017. 'A flauta doce no Brasil: da chegada dos jesuitas à década de 1970.' Doctoral diss., Universidade de São Paulo.

Miller, Clement A. 1971. 'Jerome Cardan on the Recorder.' *AR* 12: 123–25.

Miller, Julia. 2018. 'Recorder Use in Spanish Churches and Cathedrals in the Sixteenth and Early Seventeenth Centuries.' *Revista portuguesa de musicologia*, n.s. 5, no. 2: 341–56.

'Mittelalter-Blockflöte in Tartu/Estland gefunden.' 2006. *Windkanal* /2: 7.

'*Die MOECK-Schulflöte bietet den ernsthaften Einstieg in die Welt der Musik.*' 2003. Celle: Moeck.

Moeck, Hermann. 1967. *Typen europäischer Blockflöten in Vorzeit, Geschichte und Volksüberlieferung.* Celle: Moeck.

———. 1978. 'Zur "Nachgeschichte" und Renaissance der Blockflöte' (first part). *Tibia* 3: 19–20.

———. 1979. 'Friedrich der Große Fünfzig (20.2.1979).' *Tibia* 4: 327.

———. 1982. 'Recorders: Hand-made and Machine-made.' *EM* 10: 10–13.

———. 1984. 'Frans Brüggen 50.' *Tibia* 9: 191.

———. 1994. 'Con flauti dolci.' *Tibia* 19: 179–85.

———. 1997. '50 Jahre Blockflötenorchester Berlin Neukölln.' *Tibia* 22: 595.

Moeck, Hermann, Sr. 1932. *TUJU Blockflöte*. Celle: Moeck.

———. ca. 1940. *Das Blockflötenbüchlein*. Celle: Moeck.

Monk, Christopher. 1973. 'Where the Wind Blows.' *EM* 1: 34.

Montagu, Jeremy. 1997. 'Was the Tabor Pipe Always as We Know it?' *GSJ* 50: 22–28.

Moore, Tom. 2020. 'Jean Dumon, flutist.' www.academia.edu/35536158/Jean_Dumon_flutist_article_docx.

Morgan, Fred. 1982. 'Making Recorders Based on Historical Models.' *EM* 10: 14–21.

Moroney, Davitt. 2007. 'Alessandro Striggio's Mass in Forty and Sixty Parts.' *JAMS* 60: 1–69.

Moser, Hans Joachim. 1918. 'Zur Mittelalterlichen Musikgeschichte der Stadt Köln.' *Archiv für Musikwissenschaft* 1: 135–44.

———. 1966. *Paul Hofhaimer*. 2nd edn. Hildesheim: Georg Olms.

'Motolinía' (Fray Toribio de Benavente). 2014. *Historia de los índios de la Nueva España*. Ed. Mercedes Serna Arnaiz y Bernat Castany Prado. Madrid: Real Academia Española, Centro para la Edición de los Clásicos españoles.

Müller, Mette, ed. 1972. *From Bone Pipe and Cattle Horn to Fiddle and Psaltery*. Copenhagen: Musikhistorisk Museum.

Müller-Blattau, Joseph. 1968. *Geschichte der Musik in Ost- und Westpreussen*. 2nd edn. Wolfenbüttel: Möseler.

Muratori, Lodovico Antonio, ed. 1900–75. *Rerum italicarum scriptores ab anno aerae Christianae quingentesimo ad millesimumquingentesimum*. [Milan], 1723–51; nuova ed. riv., ampliata e corr. Città di Castello: S. Lapi.

Myers, Herbert W. 2001. 'Flutes.' In *A Performer's Guide to Medieval Music*. Ed. Ross W. Duffin, 376–83. Bloomington: Indiana University Press.

———, with Boaz Berney and Adrian Brown. 2005. 'An Important Case Study: The Augsburg *Futteral*.' In Lasocki 2005a, 513–21.

Nádas, John. 1998. 'A Cautious Reading of Simone Prodenzani's *Il Saporetto*.' *Recercare* 10: 23–38.

Naumann, Norbert. 1999. 'Der Schatz aus der Latrine.' *GEO Epoche*, no. 2: 116–23.

Neeman, Hans. 1932. 'Blockflötenrummel.' *Allgemeine Musikzeitung* 59: 378.

New and Complete Instructions for the Common Flute. ca. 1794. London: Goulding.

Nicholson, William. 1809. *The British Encyclopedia*. London.

Nickel, Ekkehart. 1971. *Der Holzblasinstrumentenbau in der Freien Reichsstadt Nürnberg*. Munich: Kaltzbichler.

'Novellistik.' 1821. *AMZO* 5: 188–90.

'Ohne Gnade, ohne Rücksicht auf Verluste.' 2015. *Tageszeitung* [Munich], 15 January.

O'Kelly, Eve. 1990. *The Recorder Today*. Cambridge: Cambridge University Press.

Oldham, Guy F. 1956. 'Import and Export Duties on Musical Instruments in 1660.' *GSJ* 9: 97.

Olson, Greta J. 2002. 'Angel Musicians, Instruments and Late-sixteenth-century Valencia (Spain).' *Music in Art* 27: 46–67.

Ongaro, Giulio. 1985. '16th-century Venetian Wind Instrument Makers and Their Clients.' *EM* 13: 391–97.

———. 1992. 'New Documents on the Bassano Family.' *EM* 20: 409–13.

Paganuzzi, Enrico. 1970. 'Mario Bevilacqua, amico della musica.' In *Per una storia del collezionismo. Verona: la galleria Bevilacqua*. Ed. Lanfranco Franzoni, 145–58. Milan: Edizioni di Comunitá.

Paganuzzi, E., C. Bologna, L. Rognini, G. M. Cambié, and M. Conati. 1976. *La musica a Verona*. Verona: Banca Mutua Popolare di Verona.

Page, Christopher. 1982. 'German Musicians and Their Instruments.' *EM* 10: 192–200.

———. 1992a. 'Going Beyond the Limits.' *EM* 20: 446–59.

———. 1992b. 'The English *a cappella* Heresy.' In *Companion to Medieval and Renaissance Music.* Ed. Tess Knighton and David Fallows, 23–29. New York: Schirmer Books.

Palsgrave, Jean. 1530. *Lesclarcissement de la langue francoyse.* London.

Partridge, Eric. 1983. *Origins.* New York: Greenwich House.

Pasquale, Marco di. 2019. 'Silvestro Ganassi: A Documented Biography.' *Recercare* 31: 29–102.

Pearsall, Eileen Sharpe. 1986. 'Tudor Court Musicians, 1485–1547.' PhD diss., New York University.

Peter, Hildemarie. 1953. *The Recorder, its Traditions and its Tasks.* Berlin: Robert Lienau.

Peters, Gretchen. 2012. *The Musical Sounds of Medieval French Cities.* Cambridge: Cambridge University Press.

Pierer's Universal-Lexikon der Vergangenheit und Gegenwart. 1859. 4. umgearbeitete Ausgabe. Altenburg.

Pietzsch, Gerhard. 1960. 'Beschreibungen deutscher Fürtenhochzeiten von der Mitte des 15. bis zum Beginn des 17. Jahrhunderts als musikgeschichtliche Quellen.' *Anuario musical* 15: 21–62.

Planchart, Alejandro Enrique. 2001. 'Polyphonic Mass Ordinary.' In *A Performer's Guide to Medieval Music.* Ed. Ross W. Duffin, 83–104. Bloomington: Indiana University Press.

Planque. 1836. *Agenda musical.* Paris.

Platen, Emil, and Iain Fenlon. 2011. *GMO*, s.v. 'Collegium Musicum.'

Pohl, Gerhart. 1948. *Die Blockflöte.* Stuttgart: Deutscher Verlags-Anstalt.

Polk, Keith. 1987. 'Instrumental Music in the Urban Centres of Renaissance Germany.' *EMH* 7: 167–74.

———. 1992. *German Instrumental Music of the Late Middle Ages: Players, Patrons and Performance Practice.* Cambridge: Cambridge University Press.

———. 2005. 'The Recorder in Fifteenth-century Consorts.' In Lasocki 2005a, 17–29.

Popławska, Dorota. 2004. 'Flet prosty i fujarka: nowe odkrycia archeomuzykoligii Elgbąga.' In *Archaeologica et historia urbana*, 483–88. Elbląg: Muzeum w Elblągu.

———, with additions by Martin Kirnbauer and Nik Tarasov. 2008. 'Blockflöte und Pfeife.' *Windkanal* / 2: 14–17.

Popławska, Dorota, and Hubert Lachowicz. 2014. 'Drewniane flety proste z wykopalisk archeologicznych na terenie Europy = Wooden Recorders from Archaeological Sites in Europe.' *Sylwan* 158: 72–80.

Post, Chandler Rathfon. 1958. *A History of Spanish Painting*, XII, pt II: *The Catalan School in the Early Renaissance.* Cambridge, MA: Harvard University Press.

Potter, Pamela M. 1994. 'German Musicology and Early Music Performance, 1918–1933.' In *Music and Performance during the Weimar Republic.* Ed. Bryan R. Gilliam, 94–106, 195–99. Cambridge: Cambridge University Press.

———. 1998. *Most German of the Arts.* New Haven, CT: Yale University Press.

Potts, J. C. 1975. 'Frans Bruggen and Walter Bergmann: Royal Northern College of Music, Manchester, 16 November 1974.' *R&M* 5: 27.

Praetorius, Michael. 1619. *Syntagma musicum.* Wolfenbüttel.

———. 1986. *Syntagma musicum II: De Organographia, Parts I and II.* Trans. and ed. David Z. Crookes. Oxford: Clarendon Press.

Pratt, Bill. 1973. 'Dr. Hermann Moeck Talks about His Firm.' *AR* 14: 3–8.

Preussner, Eberhard. 1949. *Die musikalischen Reisen des Herrn von Uffenbach.* Kassel: Bärenreiter.

Priestley, Edmund, and Frederick Fowler. 1937. *The School Recorder Book Part One.* Leeds: E. J. Arnold.

Prinz, Ulrich. 2005. *Johann Sebastian Bachs Instrumentarium.* Stuttgart: Internationale Bachakademie; Kassel: Bärenreiter.

Prizer, William. 1981. 'Bernardino Piffaro e i pifferi e tromboni di Mantova.' *Rivista italiana di musicologia* 16: 151–84.

———. 1986. 'The Frottola and the Unwritten Tradition.' *Studi musicali* 15: 3–37.

Prochno, Renate. 2002. *Die Kartause von Champmol: Grablege der burgundischen Herʒöge 1364–1477.* Berlin: Akademie Verlag.

Puffer, Gabriele. 2001. *Blockflötenunterricht in der ersten Hälfte des 20. Jahrhunderts*. Frankfurt: Lang.

Quagliozzi, Michel. 2021. ' "Mʳ Dieupar de Londres": nouveaux documents.' Academia.edu.

Quantz, Johann Joachim. 1752. *Versuch einer Anweisung die Flöte traversiere ʒu spielen*. Berlin.

Quarrell, W. H., and Margaret Mare, ed. 1934. *London in 1710 from the Travels of Zacharias Conrad von Uffenbach*. London: Faber & Faber.

Rampe, Siegbert, ed. 2009. *Händels Instrumentalmusik*. Laaber: Laaber Verlag.

————. 2010. 'Neues und Altes zu Händels Sonaten für und mit Blockflöte(n).' *Tibia* 35: 187–89.

————, and Michael Zapf. 1997. 'Neues zu Besetzung und Instrumentarium in Joh. Seb. Bachs Brandenburgischen Konzerten Nr. 4 und 5.' *Concerto: Das Magaʒin für alte Musik*, no. 129 (December): 30–38.

Ranum, Patricia M. 1991. 'Étienne Loulié.' *AR* 32: 7–11.

————. 1995. '*Tu-Ru-Tu* and *Tu-Ru-Tu-Tu:* Toward an Understanding of Hotteterre's Tonguing Syllables.' In Lasocki 1995b: 217–54.

Rawson, Robert. 2002. 'From Olomouc to London: The Early Music of Gottfried Finger (c1655–1730).' PhD diss., University of London.

Records of English Court Music, vol. VII (1485–1558). 1993. Calendared and Ed. Andrew Ashbee. Aldershot: Scolar Press.

Reichenthal, Eugene. 1976. 'Partial Venting.' *R&M* 5: 193–35.

Reichsbefehl der Reichsjugendführung der NSDAP, Befehle und Mitteilungen für die Führer und Führerinnen der Hitler-Jugend 30/II (13 August 1937). Summary in *Musik in Jugend und Volk* 1 (1937–38): 64.

Reiners, Hans. 1997. 'Reflections on a Reconstruction of the 14th-century Göttingen Recorder.' *GSJ* 50: 31–42.

Reusch, Fritz. 1929. 'Von unseren Blockflöten.' *Der Kreis* 7, no. 7: 73.

————. 1938. *Musik und Musikerʒiehung im Dienste der Volksgemeinschaft*. Osterwieck and Berlin: Zickfeldt.

Reynaud, François. 1996. *La polyphonie tolédane et son milieu des premiers témoignages aux environs de 1600*. Turnhout: CNRS Éditions, Brepols.

Richter, Elisabeth, and Andrea Bernhard. n.d. 'Blockflötenunterricht im Spannungsfeld von Musikschule und Volksschule.' www.erta-schweiz.ch/Bibliothek/Blfl%20-%20Forschungsbericht.pdf

Roa Alonso, Francisco Javier. 2015. 'Alonso Mudarra, vihuelista en la Casa del Infantado y canónigo en la Catedral de Sevilla.' Doctoral diss., Universidad Complutense de Madrid.

Robin, Vincent. 2004. 'Hautbois et cromorne en France aux XVIIe et XVIIIe siècles.' *BJhM* 28: 23–36.

Robinson, Andrew. 2003. 'Families of Recorders in the Late Seventeenth and Eighteenth Centuries.' *RM* 23: 113–17; 24: 5–9.

Robinson, M. B. 1971. Letter. *RMM* 3: 456–57.

Rowland-Jones, Anthony. 1986. *Recorder Technique: Intermediate to Advanced*. 2nd edn. Oxford: Oxford University Press.

————. 1996. 'La flauta de pico en el arte catalán.' *Revista de flauta de pico*, no. 6: 15–20; no. 7 (1997): 9–15; no. 8 (1997): 9–13.

————. 1997a. 'The Iconography of Two (or Three) Recorders.' *RM* 17: 12–17, 48–52.

————. 1997b. 'Recorders and Angels: First Sightings in Catalan Art.' *AR* 38, no. 5 (November): 7–13.

————. 1999. 'The First Recorder: How? Why? When? . . . and Where?' *AR* 40, no. 5 (November): 10–14, 33.

————. 2000a. 'Einige Überlegungen zum Begriff *Recorder*.' *Tibia* 25: 89–97.

————. 2000b. 'Quantz dediddled.' *RM* 20: 54–55.

————. 2001. 'Some Thoughts on the Word "Recorder" and How it was First Used in England.' *EMP*, no. 8: 7–12.

————. 2002. 'The Coalman Reveal'd.' *RM* 22: 142–44.

————. 2005. 'Iconography in the History of the Recorder up to c.1430, Part 1.' *EM* 33: 557–74.

————. 2006a. 'The First Recorder . . .? Some New Contenders.' *AR* 47, no. 2: 14–20.

———. 2006b. 'Iconography in the History of the Recorder up to c.1430, Part 2.' *EM* 34: 3–27.

———. 2009. 'Lully's Use of Recorder Symbolism.' *EM* 37: 217–49.

Rubinoff, Kailan R. 2009. 'Cracking the Dutch Early Music Movement: The Repercussions of the 1969 Notenkrakersactie.' *Twentieth-Century Music* 6: 3–22.

Ruëtz, Manfred. 1933. 'Dolmetsch- und Gofferje/Merzdorf-Blockflöten.' *NRD* no. 8, undated (ca. autumn): n.p.

———. 1934a. 'Dolmetsch- und "Harlan-Barock"-Blockflöten.' *NRD* no. 10 (ca. spring), n.p.

———. 1934b. '"Herwiga/Rex"- und Dolmetsch-Blockflöten.' *NRD* no. 12 (ca. autumn): n.p.

———. 1934c. 'Schulblockflöten in d″ und c″.' *ZfH* 2: 110–15.

———. 1936. 'Klang- und Spielmöglichkeiten der Blockflöte.' *Musik und Volk*, 1936–37: 288.

———. 1939. 'Das Berliner Blockflötenquartett.' *ZfH* 7: 74–75.

———. 1956. *Hohe Schule des Blockflötenspiels*. Ed. Linde Höffer-von Winterfeld. Kassel: Bärenreiter.

Ruffatti, Alessio. 1998. 'La famiglia Piva-Bassano nei documenti degli archivi di Bassano del Grappa.' *Musica e storia* 6: 349–67.

Ruiz Jiménez, Juan. 2020a. 'Flautas y chirimías para la evangelización agustina en Nueva España (1551).' *PSH*. http://www.historicalsoundscapes.com/evento/1196/mexico/es

———. 2020b. 'Enseñanza de la música en colegio franciscano de San Juan Evangelista y de San Andrés (c.1551–1581).' *PSH*. http://www.historicalsoundscapes.com/evento/1206/quito/es

———. 2020c. 'Música sacra e instrumental en la evangelización agustina del obispado de Nueva Segovia (1581–1596).' *PSH*. http://www.historicalsoundscapes.com/evento/1148/nueva-segovia/es

———. 2021. 'Instrumentos para el convento de Porta Coeli en Valladolid (1618).' *PSH*. http://www.historicalsoundscapes.com/evento/1276/valladolid/es

Ruiz y Quesada, Francesc. 2005. 'Pere Serra.' In *L'Art gòtic a Catalunya. Pintura* I. Ed. Rosa Alcoy i Pedrós, 284–96. Barcelona: Enciclopèdia Catalana.

Rummel, Luise. 1977. 'Zur Wiederbelebung der Blockflöte im 20. Jahrhundert.' Diplomarbeit, Karl-Marx-Universität, Leipzig.

Russell, Craig H. 2009. *From Serra to Sancho: Music and Pageantry in the California Missions*. New York: Oxford University Press.

Russell, Eleanor. 2002. 'Music in the House of the Third Duke of Béjar, *ca*. 1520–1544.' In *Encomium musicae: Essays in Memory of Robert J. Snow*. Ed. David Crawford and George Grayson Wagstaff, 285–304. Hillsdale, NY: Pendragon Press.

Rusu, Doina Cristina, and Christoph Lüthy. 2017. 'Extracts from a Paper Laboratory: The Nature of Francis Bacon's *Sylva sylvarum*.' *Intellectual History Review* 27: 171–202.

Saint-Évremond, Charles de. 1709. *Oeuvres meslées*. London.

Salas Machuca, Alonso. 1999. 'Consideraciones sobre la aportación de la flauta dulce al establecimiento de la justa entonación.' *Revista de flauta de pico*, no. 13: 22–31.

Sansovino, Francesco. 1581. *Venetia citta nobilissima et singolare*. Venice.

Sardelli, Federico Maria. 2007. *Vivaldi's Music for Flute and Recorder*. Trans. Michael Talbot. Aldershot: Ashgate.

Sauval, Henri. 1724. *Histoire et recherches des antiquités de la ville de Paris*. Paris.

Schafer, R. Murray, ed. 1978. *Ezra Pound and Music*. London: Faber & Faber.

Scheck, Gustav. 1938. *Der Weg zu den Holzblasinstrumenten*. Hohe Schule der Musik: Handbuch der gesamten Musikpraxis, IV. Potsdam: Athenaion.

Scheuer, Wolfgang. 1988. *Zwischen Tradition und Trend*. Mainz: Schott.

Schilling, Gustav. 1835. *Encyclopädie der gesammten musikalischen Wissenschaften oder Universal-Lexikon der Tonkunst*. Stuttgart.

Schmidt, Susanne. 1987. '"Primitives Instrument voller Rätsel" – Ein Gespräch mit dem Tübinger Flötenbaumeister Joachim Paetzold.' *Tibia* 12: 518–19.

Scholz, Wilhelm, Waltraut Jonas-Corrieri, and Archiv der Jugendmusikbewegung, ed. 1980. *Die deutsche Jugendmusikbewegung in Dokumenten ihrer Zeit von den Anfängen bis 1933*. Wolfenbüttel: Möseler.

Schrifistücke von der Hand Johann Sebastian Bachs: Kritische Gesamtausgabe. 1963. Volgelegt und erläutert von Werner Neumann und Hans-Joachim Schulze. Kassel: Bärenreiter.

Schubart, Christian Daniel Friedrich. 1806. *Ideen zu einer Ästhetik der Tonkunst.* Vienna.

Schumann, Heinrich. 1957. 'Jugendmusik und Blockflöte.' In *Fritz Jöde, Leben und Werk.* Herausgegeben von Reinhold Stapelberg. Trossingen: Edito Intermusica.

Sela, Sarig. 2020. 'Division Ornamentation Practice – Guidelines, Theory, and Statistical Evidence. A Case Study Based on Giovanni Bassano's Transcriptions Using a Computational Approach.' PhD thesis, Hebrew University of Jerusalem.

Shaw, George Bernard. 1981. *Shaw's Music.* Ed. Dan H. Lawrence. London: Bodley Head.

Siekiera, Anna. 2000. *Tradurre per musica: Lessico musicale e teatrale nel cinquecento.* Prato: Cav. Alfredo Rindi.

Sievers, [Georg Ludwig Peter]. 1818. 'Musikalisches Allerley aus Paris, vom Monate August, 1818.' *AMZ* 20: 694–95.

Silva Rego, António da, coligida e anotada por. 1952. *Documentação para a história das missões do Padroado Português do Oriente.* Lisbon: Agéncia Geral do Ultramar, Divisão de Publicações de Biblioteca.

Silverstein, Steven. 1968. 'Dr Dolmetsch under Fire.' *RMM* 2: 329–30.

Sloboda, John. 2005. *Exploring the Musical Mind.* Oxford: Oxford University Press.

Smith, Anne. 1978. 'Die Renaissancequerflöte und ihre Musik.' *BJhM* 2: 9–76.

———. 2005. 'A Newly Found Fingering Chart for the Renaissance Flute.' *Glareana* 54: 62–65.

Sørensen, Lilo. 2020. 'Michala Petri.' *Dansk Kvindebiografisk Leksikon.* www.kvinfo.dk/side/597/bio/1748/origin/170/.

Sousa Silva, Pedro. 2018. 'Gammaut and *le sette voce di piu.*' Symposium paper. Academia.edu.

Staeps, Hans Ulrich. 1975. 'Die Blockflöte in der Parteien Hass und Gunst.' *Resonanzen*, no. 12 (December): 13–14.

Stengel, Theo, and Herbert Gerigk. 1941. *Lexikon der Juden in der Musik.* Berlin: B. Hahnefeld.

Stevenson, Robert. 1952. *Music in Mexico.* New York: Thomas Y. Crowell.

———. 1964. 'Music in 16th-century Guatemala.' *MQ* 50: 341–52.

———. 1985. *La música en la Catedral de Sevilla, 1478–1606.* Madrid: Sociedad Española de Musicología.

Stewart. Alison G. 1989. 'Sebald Beham's Fountain of Youth – Bathhouse Woodcut.' Faculty Publications and Creative Activity, School of Art, Art History and Design, 15. https://digitalcommons.unl.edu/artfacpub/15

Stifter, Adalbert. 1840. 'Liebfrauenschuh,' from *Feldblumen.* http://gutenberg.spiegel.de/?id=5&xid=2741&kapitel=25&cHash=a790d780802#gb_found

Strebel, Harald. 2016. *Anton Stadler.* Vienna: Hollitzer.

Strohm, Reinhard. 1990. *Music in Late Medieval Bruges.* Rev. edn. Oxford: Clarendon Press.

Suter-Krüger, Babette. 2001. 'Die Wiederentdeckung der Blockflöte im 20. Jahrhundert und ihr Weg in die Schweiz' (essay). https://web.archive.org/web/20150525023344/http://www.erta-schweiz.ch/downloads/Diplomarbeiten/Blfl_im_20_Jahrhundert.pdf

Tarasov, Nikolaj. 2000. 'Neues von Beethoven – Teil 1.' *Windkanal* /3: 6–10.

———. 2010. 'Barockblockflöten 2.0. Indizien für die Verwendung von Barockblockflöten um 1800.' *Windkanal* /1: 12–15.

———. 2014. 'Interview mit Jewgenij Ilarionow.' *Windkanal* /1: 8–13.

———. 2023. *Csakan, Flageolets, and Recorder: Duct Flutes in the Nineteenth Century.* Cerquilho, SP, Brazil: Instant Harmony.

Tarr, Edward H. 1987. 'Bartolomeo Bismantova und die früheste bekannte Grifftabelle für Oboe.' *Tibia* 12: 413–21.

Tettamanti, Giulia da Rocha. 2010. 'Silvestro Ganassi: *Obra Intitulada Fontegara.* Um estudo sistemático do tratado abordando aspectos da técnica da flauta doce e da música instrumental do século XVI.' Master's diss., Universidade Estadual de Campinas.

———. 2016. 'Pronuntiatio na obra de Silvestro Ganassi (1492–c.1557).' *Revista música* 16: 205–16.

———. 2020. 'Silvestro Ganassi and Pietro Aretino's Talking Cards: A New Reference on the *Fontegara's* Author.' *Revista 4'33"* 9: 116–26.

———. 2023. *Silvestro Ganassi on the Abilities and Virtues of the Valente Instrumental Master.* Cerquilho, SP, Brazil: Instant Harmony.

Thalheimer, Peter. 1995. 'Hindemith heute.' *Tibia* 20: 586–93.

———. 1998. '"Fünf kleine Suiten für eine Blockflöte" von Helmut Bornefeld.' *Tibia* 23: 268–73.

———. 2001. 'Kammermusik mit Blockflöte von Johann Nepomuk David.' *Tibia* 26: 460–67.

———. 2006. 'Peter Harlan und die Wiederentdeckung der Blockflöte.' *Tibia* 31: 183–91.

———. 2010. *Die Blockflöte in Deutschland, 1920–1945: Instrumentenbau und Aspekte zur Spielpraxis.* Tutzing: Hans Schneider.

———. 2013. *Vergessen und wieder entdeckt: Die Blockflöte.* Markneukirchen: Verein der Freunde und Förderer des Musikinstrumenten-Museums Markneukirchen.

Thomson, J. M. 1969. 'Brüggen Masterclass.' *RMM* 3: 32.

———. 1972. *Recorder Profiles.* London: Schott.

———. 1995a. 'The Recorder Revival I: The Friendship of Bernard Shaw and Arnold Dolmetsch.' In Thomson 1995b, 137–49.

———, with Anthony Rowland-Jones, ed. 1995b. *The Cambridge Companion to the Recorder.* Cambridge: Cambridge University Press.

Tilmouth, Michael. 1957. 'The Royal Academies of 1695.' *Music & Letters* 38: 327–34.

Titan, Dina Maria de Oliveira. 2019. 'The Origins of Instrumental Diminution in Renaissance Venice: Ganassi's *Fontegara*.' Doctoral diss., Universiteit Utrecht.

Tobler–Lommatzsch Altfranzösisches Wörterbuch. 1954. Wiesbaden: Franz Steiner.

Tomich, Pere. 1970. *Historias e conquestas dels excellentissims e Catholics Reys de Aragón* e *de lurs antecessors los Comtes de Barcelona* (edition of 1534). Facsimile with index by Juan Saez Rico. Valencia: Anubar.

Torralba, Antonio. 1997. 'Reflexiones (casi en forma de pregunta) sobre las flautas en la Edad Media. Capitulo primero: ¿Qué era la ajabeba?' *Revista de flauta de pico*, no. 7: 27–30.

Tosoroni, Antonio. 1850. *Trattato pratico di strumentazione.* Florence.

Troiano, Massimo. 1980. *Die Münchner Fürstenhochzeit von 1568. Massimo Troiano: Dialoge, italienisch/deutsch.* Herausgegeben von Horst Leuchtmann. Munich: Emil Katzbichler.

Tromlitz, Johann George. 1791. *Ausführlicher und gründlicher Unterricht die Flöte zu spielen.* Leipzig.

Trottein, Gwendolyn. 1993. *Les enfants de Vénus.* Paris: Lagune.

Trowell, Brian. 1957. 'King Henry IV, Recorder-Player.' *GSJ* 10: 83–84.

Tvauri, Andres, and Taavi-Mats Utt. 2007. 'Medieval Recorder from Tartu, Estonia.' *Estonian Journal of Archaeology* 11: 141–54.

Twittenhoff, Wilhelm. 1936a. 'Von den Grenzen des Blockflötenspiels.' *Musik und Volk* 4 (1936–37): 37.

———. 1936b. 'Musik bei den Olympischen Spielen.' *ZfH* 5–6: 214–15.

Updike, John. 1963. *Midpoint and Other Poems.* New York: Knopf.

———. 1988. 'The Man Who Became a Soprano.' *New Yorker*, 26 December, 28–35.

Upton, Elizabeth Randell. 2013. *Music and Performance in the Later Middle Ages.* New York: Palgrave Macmillan.

Van Hauwe, Walter. 1984–92. *The Modern Recorder Player*, 3 vols. London: Schott.

Van Heyghen, Peter, 1995. 'The Recorder in Italian Music, 1600–1670.' In Lasocki 1995b: 3–63.

———. 2005. 'The Recorder Consort in the Sixteenth Century.' In Lasocki 2005a: 227–321.

———. 2009. Programme notes to *Recorders Greate and Smale*. Performed by Mezzaluna. CD, Ramée.

Van der Klis, Jolande. 1991. *Oude Muziek in Nederland.* Utrecht: Stichting Organisatie Oude Muziek.

Vander Straeten, Edmond. 1885. *La musique aux Pays-bas avant le XIXe siècle.* Brussels: Van Trigt.

Vieira, Ernesto. 1900. *Diccionario Biographico de Músicos Portuguezes.* Lisbon: Mattos Moreira e Pinheiro.

Vieyra, Antonio. 1773. *A Dictionary of the Portuguese and English Languages.* London.

Vio, Gastone, and Stefano Toffolo. 1987. 'La diffusione degli strumenti musicali nelle case dei nobili, cittadini e popolani nel XVI secolo a Venezia.' *Il flauto dolce*, no. 17–18 (October 1987–April 1988): 33–40.

Virdung, Sebastian. 1511. *Musica getutscht und ausʒgeʒogen.* Basel. *Musica getutscht: A Treatise on Musical Instruments (1511) by Sebastian Virdung.* Trans. and ed. Beth Bullard. Cambridge: Cambridge University Press, 1993.

Virgil. 1882. *The Works of P. Virgilius Maro, including the Æneid, Bucolics and Georgics.* Ed. Levi Hart and V. R. Osborn. Philadelphia, PA: Charles De Silver.

Virgiliano, Aurelio. ca. 1600. 'Il dolcimelo d'Aurelio Virgiliano dove si contengono variati passaggi, e diminutioni cosi per voci, come per tutte sorte d'instrumenti musicale; con loro accordi, e modi di sonare.' Bologna, Civico Museo Bibliografico Musicale, Ms. C. 33.

Vitz, Carol. 1969. 'Frans Brueggen: A Personal Portrait of the Dutch Recorder Virtuoso.' *AR* 10: 12–14.

Voice, Nichola J. 2014. 'Turners' Guilds of Northern Italy: Their Role in Enabling Woodwind Instrument Manufacture from 1680–1844.' PhD diss., University of Otago.

Von Huene, Friedrich. 1999. 'The Charles Darwin of Early Music: Friedrich von Huene im Gespräch mit Ralf Ehlert und Sabine Haase-Moeck.' *Tibia* 24: 443–44.

Wackernagel, Bettina. 2003. *Musikinstrumentenverʒeichnis der Bayerischen Hofkapelle von 1655.* Tutzing: Hans Schneider.

Warner, Thomas E. 1967. *An Annotated Bibliography of Woodwind Instruction Books, 1600–1830.* Detroit: Information Coordinators.

Waterhouse, William. 1993. *The New Langwill Index.* London: Tony Bingham.

Watkins. Timothy D. 2009. 'Performance Issues in Early Colonial Mexican Polyphony: A Critical Examination of Some Colonial Accounts.' In Watkins, ed., *Performance Practice: Issues and Approaches.* Ann Arbor: Steglein, 45–58.

Weaver, Robert W. 1961. 'Sixteenth-century Instrumentation.' *MQ* 47: 363–78.

Weber, Rainer. 1976. 'Recorder Finds from the Middle Ages, and Results of Their Reconstruction.' *GSJ* 29: 35–41.

Wegman, Rob C. 2002. 'The Minstrel School in the Late Middle Ages.' *HBSJ* 14: 11–30.

Weinmann, Karl. 1917. *Johannes Tinctoris (1445–1511) und sein unbekannter Traktat 'De inventione et usu musicae.'* Regensburg: Friedrich Pustel.

Welch, Christopher. 1911. *Six Lectures on the Recorder and Other Flutes in Relation to Literature.* London: Henry Frowde, Oxford University Press.

Weller, Enrico. 2001. 'Das Klampfenamt.' *Neikirnger Heimatbote* 9, no. 2: 17.

Wessely, Othmar. 1956. 'Archivalische Beiträge zur Musikgeschichte des Maximilianischen Hofes.' *Studien ʒur Musikwissenschaft* 23: 79–134.

Wicki, Joseph. 1962. *Documenta Indica VII (1566–1569).* Rome: Apud 'Monumenta Historica Soc. Iesu.'

Wienpahl, Robert W. 1979. *Music at the Inns of Court During the Reigns of Eliʒabeth, James, and Charles.* Ann Arbor: University Microfilms International.

Williams, Alexandra Mary. 2005. 'The Dodo was Really a Phoenix.' PhD diss., Melbourne University.

Williams, Peter. 1994. 'The Idea of *Bewegung* in the German Organ Reform Movement of the 1920s.' In *Music and Performance during the Weimar Republic.* Ed. Bryan R. Gilliam, 138–42. Cambridge: Cambridge University Press.

Williamson, Magnus. 1997. 'The Early Tudor Court, the Provinces and the Eton Choirbook.' *EM* 25: 229–43.

Wilson, John, ed. 1959. *Roger North on Music.* London: Novello.

Wind, Thiemo. 2006. 'Jacob van Eyck en de anderen: Nederlands solorepertoire voor blokfluit in de Gouden Eeuw.' Doctoral diss., University of Utrecht.

———. 2011. *Jacob van Eyck and the Others: Dutch Solo Repertoire for Recorder in the Golden Age.* Utrecht: Koninklijke Vereniging voor Nederlandse Muziekgeschiedenis.

———. 2021. *Adriana vanden Bergh (Berch): The* Euterpe *of Jacob Backer and of Paulus Matthijsʒ.* Portland, OR: Instant Harmony.

———. 2024. 'Nuremberg Woodwinds as Bulk Goods in Amsterdam Stores during the Seventeenth Century.' To be published.

Woehl, Waldemar. 1930. *Die Blockflöte.* Kassel: Bärenreiter.

Woodley, Ronald. 1985. 'The Printing and Scope of Tinctoris's Fragmentary Treatise "De inventione et vsv mvsice" ('De inuentione et usu musice').' *EMH* 5: 239–68.

Wright, Craig. 1979. *Music at the Court of Burgundy, 1364–1419.* Henryville: Institute of Mediaeval Music.

Wulf, Joseph. 1963. *Musik im dritten Reich.* Gütersloh: Mohn.

Wylie, James Hamilton. 1898. *History of England under Henry the Fourth.* London: Longmans.

Young, Phillip T. 1993. *4900 Historical Woodwind Instruments: An Inventory of 200 Makers in International Collections.* London: Tony Bingham.

Zacconi, Lodovico. 1596. *Prattica de musica.* Venice.

Zuccollo da Cologna, Simeon. 1549. *La pazzia del ballo.* Padua.

Zuckermann, Wolfgang Joachim. 1970. *The Modern Harpsichord.* London: Peter Owen.

Zuluaga, David Puerta. 1988. *Los caminos del tiple.* Bogotá, Colombia: AMP damel.

EDITIONS OF MUSIC

Bach, Johann Sebastian. 1973. Arranged by Frans Brüggen. *Suites I–III for Violoncello solo, Arranged for Alto Recorder Solo.* Tokyo: Zen-On.

———. 2022. *Trio Sonata in C major for Alto Recorder, Violin, and Basso Continuo (Reconstruction of the Source for the Sonata in A major for Flute and Obbligato Harpsichord, BWV 1032).* Ed. Michael Marissen. Cerquilho, SP, Brazil: Instant Harmony.

Flauto e voce I: Geistliche und weltliche Arien von Georg Philipp Telemann, Johann Peter Guzinger und Reinhard Keiser; Originalkompositionen für hohe Stimme (S oder T), Blockflötenensemble, Cembalo (Nr. 4) und Basso continuo. Herausgegeben von Peter Thalheimer and Klaus Hofmann-Herbipol. 1995. Stuttgart: Carus-Verlag.

Flauto e voce II: Geistliche und weltliche Arien von Bach, Telemann, Capricornus, von Wilderer, Rohde und Theile. Herausgegeben von Peter Thalheimer and Klaus Hofmann-Herbipol. 1998. Stuttgart: Carus-Verlag.

Flauto e voce III: Arien von Vivaldi, Telemann, Keiser und Torri; Originalkompositionen für Sopran, Blockflöte und Basso continuo. Herausgegeben von Peter Thalheimer and Klaus Hofmann-Herbipol. 2000. Stuttgart: Carus-Verlag.

Flauto e voce X: Arien von Ariosti, Bach, Fedeli, Gaparini, Keiser und Telemann; Originalkompositionen für hohe Stimme (Sopran oder Tenor), Blockflöte und Basso continuo. Herausgegeben von Peter Thalheimer and Klaus Hofmann-Herbipol. 2011. Stuttgart: Carus-Verlag.

Flauto e voce, Heft 17: Originalkompositionen für Sopran oder Tenor, Blockflöte und Basso continuo, von Badia, Campra, Dubourg, Fischietti, Keiser, Scarlatti und Telemann. Herausgegeben von Klaus Hofmann and Peter Thalheimer. 2021. Magdeburg: Edition Walhall.

Hindemith, Paul. 1952. *Trio for Recorders from the Plöner Musiktag.* Edition for recorders in C and F. London: Schott.

DISCOGRAPHY

Brüggen, Frans. 1962a. *The Virtuoso Recorder.* Brüggen, recorder; Janny van Wering, harpsichord. London: Brunswick SXA 4506; New York: Decca DL 710049, LP.

———. 1962b. Georg Friedrich Händel, *Sechs Sonaten für Blockflöte und Basso continuo.* Brüggen, recorder; Anner Bylsma, violoncello; Gustav Leonhardt, harpsichord. Hamburg: Telefunken SAWT 9421–B, LP.

———. 1968. *Italienische Blockflötensonaten um 1700.* Brüggen, recorder; Anner Bylsma, violoncello; Gustav Leonhardt, harpsichord. Hamburg: Telefunken SAWT 9518, LP.

———. 1970. *Blockflötenwerke des Barock, 2.* Hamburg: Telefunken SAW 9622–M, LP.

———. 1971. *Französische Blockflötenmusik.* Brüggen, Kees Boeke, Walter van Hauwe, recorders; Anner Bylsma, violoncello; Gustav Leonhardt, harpsichord. Hamburg: Telefunken SAWT 9570–B, LP.

———. 1972. *Frans Brüggen spielt 17 Blockflöten.* Hamburg: Telefunken SMA 25 073–T/1–3, LP.

————. 1974. Johann Sebastian Bach, *Suiten Nr. 1–3 für Violoncello solo*. Brüggen, alto recorder. Cologne: EMI C 06581833, LP.

————. 1979. Georg Philipp Telemann, *Trios für Block- oder Traversflöte*. Brüggen, recorder and flute, et al. Hamburg: RCA Red Seal RL 30343, LP.

————. 1981. Arcangelo Corelli, *Sonaten op. 5, no. 7–12*. Brüggen, recorder; Anner Bylsma, violoncello; Gustav Leonhardt, harpsichord. Hamburg: RCA SEON Red Seal RL 30393, LP.

————. 1985. Johann Sebastian Bach, arr. Brüggen, *Concerto in D major BWV 1053*. Brüggen, recorder; Orchestra of the Eighteenth Century. www.youtube.com/watch?v=WjMeXlfRfl8. Accessed September 2021.

————. 1995. *Frans Brüggen Edition*. Hamburg: Teldec 4509–97475–2, CDs.

Conrad, Ferdinand. 1962. *George Frederick Handel: 4 Sonatas from 'Solos for a German Flute' etc., Op. 1*. Conrad, recorder; Johannes Koch, viola da gamba; Hugo Ruf, harpsichord. Hamburg: Deutsche Grammophon Archiv 14163 APM, LP.

————. 1966. *Georg Philipp Telemann: Die Kleine Kammermusik*. Conrad, recorder; Johannes Koch, viola da gamba; Hugo Ruf, harpsichord. Kassel: Bärenreiter Musicaphon BM 30 SL 1540, LP.

Dolmetsch, Carl. 1933. Dolmetsch, recorder; Rudolph Dolmetsch, harpsichord; Millicent Dolmetsch, viola da gamba. London: Columbia History of Music by Eye and Ear DB 1115.

————. 1960. *Music for Recorder and Harpsichord*. Dolmetsch, recorder; Joseph Saxby, harpsichord. Haselmere: Arnold Dolmetsch, SLE 43, 45 rpm single.

Linde, Hans-Martin. 1962. *Georg Friedrich Händel, Sonaten für Blockflöte und Generalbass*. Linde, recorder; August Wenzinger, viola da gamba; Gustav Leonhardt, harpsichord. Freiburg im Breisgau: Harmonia Mundi 1C 065-99 720, LP.

Mann, Alfred. 1952. *Handel, Recorder Sonatas*. Mann, alto recorder; Helmut Reimann, cello; Helma Elsner, harpsichord. New York: Vox PL7910, LP. https://youtu.be/cBfBk81bgyU. Accessed 27 February 2022.

Mozart, Wolfgang Amadeus. 1975. *Concertos for Piano and Orchestra*. Friedrich Gulda, piano; Vienna Philharmonic Orchestra cond. Claudio Abbado. Hamburg: Deutsche Grammophon 453 079–2, LP.

————. 1988. *Concertos for Piano and Orchestra*. Malcolm Bilson, piano; English Baroque Soloists cond. John Eliot Gardiner. Hamburg: Archiv 423 595–2, CD.

Petri, Michala. 1977. *Michala Petri Recorder Recital*. Michala Petri, recorder; David Petri, cello; Hanne Petri, harpsichord. London: BBC REC 298, LP.

Telemann, Georg Philipp. 1984. *Wassermusik*, Three Concertos. Musica Antiqua Köln, dir. Reinhard Goebel. Hamburg: Archiv 413 788–2, LP.

INDEX